KU-257-293

EuroDiversity
A Business Guide to
Managing Difference

George F. Simons, D.Min.

With Contributions by
Arjen Bos
Marie-Thérèse Claes, Ph.D.
Elena A. A. Garcea, Ph.D.
Nigel Holden, Ph.D.
Michael Stuber, Diplom Wirtschafts-Ingenieur

BUTTERWORTH
HEINEMANN

An imprint of Elsevier Science
Amsterdam   Boston   London   New York   Oxford   Paris
San Diego   San Francisco   Singapore   Sydney   Tokyo

Butterworth–Heinemann is an imprint of Elsevier Science.

Copyright © 2002, Elsevier Science (USA).

All rights reserved.

No part of this publication may be reproduced, stored in a retrieval system, or transmitted in any form or by any means, electronic, mechanical, photocopying, recording, or otherwise, without the prior written permission of the publisher.

∞ Recognizing the importance of preserving what has been written, Elsevier Science prints its books on acid-free paper whenever possible.

Library of Congress Cataloging-in-Publication Data

Simons, George F.
    EuroDiversity : a business guide to managing difference / George F. Simons.
        p. cm.—(Managing cultural differences series)
    Includes bibliographic references and index.
    ISBN 0-877-19381-9 (alk. paper)
    1. Corporate culture—European Union countries—Cross-cultural studies.
    2. Management—European Union countries—Cross-cultural studies.
    3. Pluralism (Social sciences)—European Union countries—Cross-cultural studies.
    I. Title. II. Managing cultural differences series (Boston, Mass.)

    HD58.7 .S582 2002
    658.3′008′094—dc21

                                                        2002023024

British Library Cataloguing-in-Publication Data
A catalogue record for this book is available from the British Library.

The publisher offers special discounts on bulk orders of this book.
For information, please contact:

Manager of Special Sales
Elsevier Science
225 Wildwood Avenue
Woburn, MA 01801-2041
Tel: 781-904-2500
Fax: 781-904-2620

For information on all Butterworth–Heinemann publications available, contact our World Wide Web home page at: http://www.bh.com

10 9 8 7 6 5 4 3 2 1

Printed in the United States of America

QUEEN MARY
UNIVERSITY OF LONDON
LIBRARY

HF5549.5. M5
SIM

QM Library

23 1272326 0

EuroDiversity

EuroDiversity: A Business Guide to Managing Difference
George F. Simons

Global Strategic Planning: Cultural Perspectives for Profit and
Nonprofit Organizations
Marios I. Katsioloudes

Succeeding in Business in Central and Eastern Europe: A Guide to Cultures,
Markets, and Practices
Woodrow H. Sears and Audrone Tamulionyte-Lentz

Competing Globally: Mastering Multicultural Management and Negotiations
Farid Elashmawi

Intercultural Services: A Worldwide Buyer's Guide and Sourcebook
Gary Wederspahn

Managing Cultural Differences, Fifth Edition
Philip R. Harris and Robert T. Moran

Multicultural Management 2000: Essential Cultural Insights for
Global Business Success
Farid Elashmawi and Philip R. Harris

International Directory of Multicultural Resources
Robert T. Moran and David O. Braaten

International Business Case Studies for the Multicultural Marketplace
Robert T. Moran, David O. Braaten, and John E. Walsh

Developing the Global Organization:
Strategies for Human Resource Professionals
Robert T. Moran, Philip R. Harris, and William G. Stripp

Transcultural Leadership: Empowering the Diverse Workforce
George F. Simons, Carmen Vazquez, and Philip R. Harris

Dynamics of Successful International Business Negotiations
William G. Stripp and Robert T. Moran

FORTHCOMING TITLES

Uniting North American Business: NAFTA Best Practices
Jeffrey Abbott and Robert T. Moran

Managing Cultural Diversity in Technical Professions
Lionel Laroche

RELATED TITLES

Diversity Success Strategies
Norma Carr-Rufino

Mentoring and Diversity
Belle Rose Ragins and David Clutterbuck

Contents

1

Patchwork: The Diversities of Europeans and
Their Business Impact 1
George F. Simons
The Challenge of Cultural Diversity 3. A History of Assimilation 4. The
Nature of European Diversity and the Challenge of Managing It 11.
Stakeholder Diversity 22. The ABCDs of Managing Diversity for Adding
Value 27. Localizing a Global Diversity Effort 32. A Richer Definition of
Culture 33. Onward to the Challenges of EuroDiversity 34.

2

The Legacy of the Past: How National and Regional
Differences Continue to Effect Trade, Cooperation,
Politics, and Relationships 35
Elena A. A. Garcea
Uncovering Bias in Attitudes and Behavior 35. The Cultural Undertow
of Crisis Management 41. Dealing with the Needs and Ambitions of
Powerful Regional Cultures 44. Managing the In-Country Challenges of
Diversity 51. Adjusting to New Roles for Women 52.

6

7

8

9

Equal Opportunities for Women and Men in the European
Union: The Case of E-Quality in Belgium 217
Marie-Thérèse Claes

Gender Mainstreaming 218. Gender Imbalance in the Labor Market 219.
Gender Balance in Decision-Making 225. Women in Management 227.
The Wage Gap 230. Putting the "E" into Quality 232. The E-Quality
Award 235. The Case of Belgium 238. Conclusion 249.

10

Who Is the European? Prognosis and Recommendations 251
George F. Simons

E.U. Abstainers: Switzerland and Norway—The Rich and the Nouveau
Riche 255. Cultural Boundaries: Do Good Fences Make Good
Neighbors? 257. Why We Must Learn to Construct Culture 259. Can
Only Europeans Be Europeans? 261. Fictitious Bloodlines and Faith—
Healing the Hurts of History 262. Preserving and Accommodating
European Regional Culture 267. Diversity Strategies at the Demographic
Crossroads 271. Capitalism and Democracy: The Unbridled Team 272.

About the Authors

George F. Simons, D.Min., George Simons International, Santa Cruz, California, and Mandelieu la Napoule, France, is president of George Simons International, a virtual consulting group (http://www. diversophy.com) specializing in intercultural communication and global management. Serving clients worldwide, he is on the faculty of Management Centre Europe (MCE), where he delivers courses in virtual global teamwork and sits on its e-Commerce and General Management Advisory Boards. Currently he is participating in a project to assist MCE faculty and clients to create digital instruction. He is a member of the advisory Board of the *European Business Review*. Simons is the creator of the award-winning *DIVERSOPHY®* training tools for which he is now developing online learning components. A part-time resident of Mandelieu la Napoule, France, he is author of another book in this series, *Transcultural Leadership*, as well as numerous other books and articles on diversity and intercultural management. He may be reached at gsimons@diversophy.com.

Arjen Bos is an owner and training manager of Engage! InterAct, a training and consultancy organization in Utrecht, the Netherlands (http://www.engage.nu/interact/). He has an educational background in theater and organizational anthropology. Since the start of his professional career he has been focusing on the promotion and stimulation of ethics and integrity through pedagogical principles, as well as on training and consulting for organizations. Engage! InterAct is an interactive and creative organization that encourages people to look at the benefits of difference and diversity, and helps them work together to promote and celebrate the values of respect, cooperation, and creativity.

Engage! InterAct is committed to a way of learning, at all levels and all stages of life, in which the learner takes responsibility, supported in that process by his or her facilitators or trainers and peers. It is the belief of Engage! InterAct that learning to reflect critically, being open-minded, and acting decisively in relation to a set of clear moral values is essential if the world is to realize a successful multicultural society, an active and democratic citizenship, and a dynamic self-empowering knowledge-society. Bos also serves as the Director of Training on the board of the European Federation for Intercultural Learning (EFIL). He may be reached at arjen@engage.nu.

Marie-Thérèse Claes, Ph.D., is professor of Intercultural Communication and Intercultural Management at the Institut Catholique des Hautes Etudes Commerciales (ICHEC) Brussels Business School and at the Université Catholique de Louvain in Belgium. She trains business students and managers in many countries around the world, and is the author of numerous publications. Her research focuses on the intercultural aspects of different areas of management, such as business communication, human resources management and diversity, and marketing. She is past president of EWMD (European Women Management Development network) and of SIETAR Europa (Society for Intercultural Education, Training, and Research). She may be reached at Claes@ilv.ucl.ac.be.

Elena A. A. Garcea, Ph.D., Università di Cassino, Italy, and European Federation for Intercultural Learning, Brussels, Belgium, is research professor in the Department of Philology and History at the University of Cassino, Italy. She teaches undergraduate and graduate courses in different fields comprising the origin of language and communication, cultural dynamics in prehistoric Africa, and ancient Near- and Middle-Eastern history. She is also coordinator of the European Master's program on Conservation and Management of Cultural Resources in the same university. She carries out field research in Sudan and Libya and has been a visiting scholar in Mali, the United States, Germany, France, Switzerland, and Turkey. Her research interests focus on the relations among the cultural dynamics, human behavior, and material culture of past and present populations from Western and non-Western countries.

As an interculturalist, Garcea has worked as a trainer for E.U. programs funded by the European Social Fund in the fields of intercultural communication, intercultural awareness, and intercultural negotiation. She provides intercultural services in guidance and career counseling for E.U.-funded programs (Rainbow and Leonardo for vocational training) to professional counselors with foreign clients and graduate university students seeking training opportunities abroad. She is a trainer and consultant in intercultural relations management for Eni Group and Iri Management in Italy. She also serves as deputy chair on the board of directors of the European Federation for Intercultural Learning in Belgium. She sits on the editorial board of the journal *Intercultural Education* and has published five books, including *La comunicazione interculturale: Teoria e pratica* (Rome, 1993), and over 80 articles in major international journals.

Nigel Holden, Ph.D., takes up the post of professor of Cross-Cultural Management at the newly established Kassel International Management School in May 2002 and holds visiting professorships at the Vienna School of Economics and Business Administration and the Leiden University School of Management. He was professor of Cross-Cultural Management at Copenhagen Business School from 1997 to 2001, and was previously senior lecturer in International Marketing at the Manchester School of Management, University of Manchester Institute of Science and Technology.

Holden obtained his Ph.D. from Manchester Business School (1986) and his M.A. from the School of Slavonic and East European Studies of the University of London (1981). He has wide international experience as a management educator, researcher, and consultant and has been a keynote speaker at academic and business conferences in the United Kingdom, in various countries in the European Union, and in the United States. His academic and research fields embrace cross-cultural knowledge management, management and business development in Russia and East/Central Europe, Japanese management, and international business communication. Holden was an associate editor of the *International Handbook of Organizational Culture and Climate* (Wiley, 2001), responsible for the international section. His latest book is *Cross-Cultural Management: A Knowledge Management Perspective* (Financial Times/Prentice Hall, 2002) and he wrote the foreword to a companion book in the Managing Cultural Differences Series, *Succeeding in Business in Central and Eastern Europe* (Butterworth–Heinemann, 2001).

Michael Stuber, Diplom Wirtschafts-Ingenieur, is the founder and principal of mi·st [Consulting, Cologne, Germany, which specializes in Diversity Management and Marketing Services. He holds a master's degree in industrial engineering and management and has conducted pan-European projects since 1989. After working as a consultant with two leading consulting firms in the field of human resources, he became self-employed in 1997. Most of his clients are European subsidiaries of U.S.-owned global corporations. He specializes in helping his clients pursue a strongly business-related, strategic approach to implementing diversity on a European level. This includes research and analysis work around the business case for diversity in Europe, on internal and external communication issues, and the development of success measurement systems. In addition to consulting support, he has been involved in a number of "diversity mainstreaming" activities in the fields of marketing, public affairs, and recruitment.

Stuber is a diversity pioneer in Europe and Germany. His involvement includes a great deal of networking with the academic world, with NGOs (non-governmental organizations), and in the public sector. He is a frequent author on diversity-related issues and accepts speaking engagements in a variety of contexts. His clients include Hewlett-Packard, Ford Motor Co., and Motorola, as well as global European corporations such as Deutsche Bank or nonprofit organizations such as the Heinrich Böll Foundation. He has conducted the first comprehensive corporate practice survey on diversity in Europe, the results of which provided the basis for his chapter in this book. He may be reached at www.european-diversity.com and www.ungleich-besser.de.

Series Preface

Culture is a fascinating concept. It has so many applications, whether between nations, organizations, or peoples. Communicating effectively across cultures, negotiating on a global scale, and conducting international business are always challenging. To thrive, and in many cases to survive, in the twenty-first century, individuals and institutions must incorporate cultural sensitivity and skills into their relations, strategies, and structures. Inability to deal with differences or diversity in human cultures is a sign of weakness and obsolescence in persons and groups. The new millennium has no tolerance for "ethnic cleansing," anti-Semitism, or any other form of religious, racial, or gender discrimination.

As originally conceived, our book, *Managing Cultural Differences*, was intended to increase human effectiveness with people who differ in cultural backgrounds. With the new century, our "flagship" text sails into her fifth edition. We are particularly gratified that business organizations have not only found the book useful, but in academia, more than 200 universities worldwide have adopted our work as a textbook. But this pioneering publication has also spawned many "offspring," so the *Managing Cultural Differences Series* was launched and has subsequently grown into more than a dozen titles.

As series editors, we are pleased with these outstanding products. We trust that you will continue to find our literary efforts helpful as you seek to address transcultural challenges in our rapidly changing, highly interdependent communities!

We hope you will visit the website of our publisher, Butterworth–Heinemann, for continuing updates on the MCD Series (www.bh.com). To make inquiries about the availability of our Authors' Network for consulting or training, contact by electronic mail, Karen.Maloney@bhusa.com.

Philip R. Harris, Ph.D.
LaJolla, California
Robert T. Moran, Ph.D.
Scottsdale, Arizona

Acknowledgments

The survey of diversity challenges survey in Chapters 2, 3, and 4 was thoroughly carried out in Italy thanks to the cooperation of the Iafe training center of the Eni Group, a largely national but partly multinational group of business organizations based in Italy. Thirty-two young graduate employees from the following organizations responded: Agip Petroli, Ambiente, Aquater, Eni divisione Agip, Enichem, Enidata, Saipem, Snam, Snamprogetti, Sofid Sim, and Temars (Garcea, 2001). We would like to thank Dr. Annino Tudini of the Iafe-Formazione Manageriale e Ricerca of the Eni Group for his kind cooperation.

In addition, the following professionals participated in our survey: Myrtha B. Casanova, President, The European Institute for Managing Diversity; Barcelona, Spain; Ernst Bruckmüller, Professor of Economic and Social History, Institut für Wirtschafts und Sozialgeschichte, Universität Wien, Austria; Robin M. Mills, Shell E&P Technology, London, United Kingdom; Veera M. Laitalainen, Project Coordinator, The Helsinki Institute, Helsinki, Finland; Fabrizio Maimone, Consultant, Assistant of Economy and Technique of Enterprise Communication, and Sociology of Cultural Processes, Università Libera Universita Maria SS. Assunta, Rome, Italy; Petra K. Schruth, Technology Strategy and Planning and Business Interface Management, Rijswijk, the Netherlands; Gary Nerdrum, Offshore Controller, Britvic International, London, United Kingdom; Fredrik Fogelberg, Nomadic Life Consultants, Voorschoten, the Netherlands; Richard Hill, Consultant, Europublic SA/NV, Bruxelles, Belgium; Dagmar Bauer, Hamburg, Germany; Margaret Oertig, Riehen, Switzerland; Anthony Norman, Psychologie für Organisationen Beratungsgesellschaft mbH, Ginsiheim, Germany; Mike Mattner, Project Manager, Degussa, Grasse, France; Dr. Roberto Ruffino, Secretary General, Intercultura, Rome, Italy; Kerstin Sturm, GSM Product Manager, Lucent Technologies, Germany.

We wish to thank Regine Mehl, president of the Arbeitsstelle Friedensforschung Bonn (AFB) for providing information and data on German "Ossies" and "Wessies" and for her insights on a larger Europe.

Thanks go to Herman Coquel and Laurence Wilson of the Management Centre Europe eLearning Team for their contribution to our review of the Management Centre Europe eTrain project in Chapter 5.

Thanks also go to Pippa Goldfinger for her advice on England-Britain-U.K. and for everything associated with the "kingdom," and to Ainger Scanlon of Barcelona, Spain, for providing us with feedback and information about events in Spain.

Gratitude goes to Marleen Janssen Groesbeek whose Dutch book on sustainable entrepreneurship was a major source of ideas and inspiration for Chapter 8, along with the insights and knowledge that derived from the advisory report from the Dutch Social-Economic Advisory Board (SER) on sustainable entrepreneurship.

The book was put into its final form for submission by Kate Berardo, who also provided us with invaluable assistance in the process of getting the needed permissions for quotes and illustrations. Kate is looking forward to a career in the intercultural field. We are deeply grateful for her efforts and wish her godspeed.

Thanks to Philip Harris, coeditor of the Managing Cultural Differences Series, whose prods, tips, and virtual presence helped us get and stick to a deadline.

Finally, we would like to thank the editorial and marketing professionals at Butterworth–Heinemann for their ongoing concern, support, and assistance with this book. Particular thanks go to Karen Maloney, Jennifer Pursley, Jodie Allen, and Katie Hennessy.

Prologue

We expect that you are reading this book because you are a business or management professional in the public or private sector, or on the road to becoming one. You are looking for a deeper understanding of the impact of culture on your present or future efforts and for better tools to manage it. Whether you are part of a large organization or a sole entrepreneur, a teacher or student of business, whether you come from abroad or from the European Union itself, this book is addressed to you. It defines the distinctive nature and challenges of diversity in Europe. It surveys what businesses are doing to manage intercultural issues and to add bottom-line value from doing so. It opens a portal to the resources and practice of managing diversity in the E.U. region that can benefit those entering the European Union from without as well as current business ventures within the Union and its sphere of influence.

A Practical Context

In this prologue, we will preview the questions to be raised in this collection of essays, give you an overall picture of what to expect in these pages, and provide some directions on how to make best use of this book.

Our present diversity challenges are being determined by the forces shaping the economy and the business world generally and cannot be discussed in isolation from them. Diversity is about globalization, organizational learning, and the growing importance of knowledge management just as much as it is about recruitment, equal opportunity, workforce demographics, and social integration. It concerns the information technology that is almost daily revolutionizing communication. It affects interactive networking and transport. It is perhaps the critical issue in many mergers and acquisitions—and often the least attended to. It is at the root of how organizations transform themselves. The spectacular transformation of the automobile industry in recent years is only one outstanding example of the depth and breadth of organizational change that is loose in the world.

Social Concern and Beyond

Though we continue to speak in terms of discrimination, injustice, and inequality between men and women, and are deeply involved in such movements as gender mainstreaming, the notion of diversity has been steadily moving toward the inclusion and empowerment of all people and the incorporation of good business sense. Because of the interface of globalism and communications technology, today's management professionals must be concerned about not only compliance with the law and the external appearances of the company, but must learn to align internally the wide diversity of individuals and cultures found in the organization, including its shareholders and other stakeholders. This diversity promises to bring innovative ideas to market and more effective responses to culturally diverse and global markets and customers—if we know how to mobilize it to do so.

North American Influences

We should not go forward without taking note of the powerful influence that the terminology and practice of diversity in North America has had in shaping diversity discourse and practice worldwide. It is beyond the scope of this book to discuss either the history or nature of this influence in detail. Part of this phenomenon is no doubt due to the vast literature that has been developed in the English language. It would be extremely interesting to discuss the role that British colonialism and the dominance of Anglo-Saxon culture and the English language have had in shaping both the problems and solutions found in the United States, Canada, South Africa, Australia, and Britain itself. However enlightening this enterprise would be, we fear it must be left to more patient researchers.

Nonetheless, the reader may expect comparisons and critiques of North American diversity initiatives and thinking to appear in the pages that follow. This is in part due to the fact that the book itself will be first published in the United States and that many of our readers will be coming from this perspective. However, this is incidental to the more telling fact that North American efforts have so shaped the field that discussing them is unavoidable. In addition, many U.S. diversity professionals see Europe as a market for their wares and are aggressively promoting them with culturally insensitive U.S. marketing attitudes. Some U.S. professionals, such as Cornelius Grove and Willa Hallowell, have recognized the need for diversity in the practice of diversity. Studying diversity in Japan, Germany, the United Kingdom, and Mexico, they concluded:

> Americans deeply value equal opportunity and fairness, individualism and personal achievement, objectivity and quantification. It is this constellation of quintessentially American values that gives urgency to our diversity concerns. Yet this very constellation of values sets us apart from most of the world's cultures. People in other cultures rarely emphasize these values as much as we do.
>
> More precisely, what we found is that outside the United States, one or more of the following might be true
>
> - People do not put nearly as much effort into categorizing one another as Americans do.
> - People assume that human differences are a *proper* basis for assigning certain types of people to economic or social roles.
> - People are comfortable organizing their lives around the notion that some types of people have more intrinsic worth than others.
> - People view "discrimination," in the sense of sorting human beings, as a *desirable* personal skill and socially useful activity.
>
> We found that people abroad aren't preoccupied with "level playing fields." Most don't recognize our meaning of "diversity." (Grove and Hallowell, 1994)

The best of U.S. diversity practice can serve as an inspiration and an idea bank for approaching European problems, but because of this the authors of this book will, as needed, point out that assumptions and approaches drawn from U.S. and Canadian sources (and often impelled or even imposed by North American businesses and business people overseas) may not necessarily be the appropriate ones for the European business environment. Quite the contrary, they may disrupt relationships, create confusion and result in lost productivity, and leave a bad taste in the mouth when the next diversity initiative is served up.

There is, of course, much that is useful, but the choice to use it must rest on careful analysis of the local diversity challenges, indigenous interpretations and reactions to them, as well as the local resources and cultural and historical context in which they arise. Europe already has a strong tradition of diversity initiatives, characterized by generous volunteerism supported by governmental resources and advocacy, rather than being mandated by law. In Europe's more socially supportive environment, there is clearly a focus on quality of life for all. Because of this, Canada's similar social models are often more attractive than U.S. ones to the European mentality.

How to Use This Book

Our methodology will be to examine the challenges and threats to the management of European diversity to discover where the resistance is, not in order to suppress or resolve it, but to tap its energy for higher levels of cultural synergy and competence, and, above all, to provide some thinking, tools, and resources for doing this. As a colleague once remarked about participants' resistance to training, "Resistance is a bag of goodies, if you know how to open it." Diversity management requires precisely this skill. This book will provide you with considerable information and a number of useful perspectives for speaking about and working with diversity in Europe. Here is an overview of what you can expect:

Chapter 1 looks at diversity and diversity management from a European perspective: its objectives, philosophy, tools, and methodologies, and how these may differ from North American and other diversity models.

Chapters 2, 3, and 4 all address the challenges that are peculiar to, but often not exclusive to, diversity in Europe. They look at these challenges, respectively, in terms of their past, present, and future influences on business in society. The information and insights found in these chapters is organized around the structure and results of a questionnaire that was submitted to a select group of managers and professionals throughout Europe. The aims of the survey were to identify the principal challenges that diversity in Europe faces. It also sought to recognize how these challenges affect business and organizations in the region, and to help them report the best practices that have been developed in response to these challenges.

Chapter 5 focuses on a particular challenge, the future of European diversity in a wired world, and addresses the changing nature of commerce, organizational learning, and expatriation with examples of some leading efforts and technologies.

Chapter 6 is based on a survey of best practices in European-based global corporations conducted by its author's organization. It provides a good picture of how diversity is conceived of and acted upon as well as identifies gaps in the corporate response to being and working in diverse environments.

Chapter 7 examines the knowledge management practices of three European-based corporations, paying particular attention to how these firms address the complex cross-cultural challenge of transferring knowledge, experience, and values throughout their organization worldwide.

Chapter 8 provides us with an intriguing look at the growing sense of corporate citizenship that is essential to providing a framework for diversity and social responsibility within our globalization efforts.

Chapter 9 deals primarily with gender relations in the European workplace and provides an excellent case study of the Belgian efforts in this regard.

Finally, Chapter 10 looks at the troubling question of European identity, not as a psychological phenomenon but as an agenda for determining both the social and economic future of the expanding E.U. and of the diversity initiatives that the coming years will require.

As the title of Chapter 10 suggests, we had trouble settling on *EuroDiversity* as the title for this book. The "European Union" is not all of "Western Europe." "Western Europeans" are only perceived as such by non-Western Europeans. Western Europeans will not tell you that they are "from Western Europe." They will tell you the country they are from and, immediately after that, will specify the region. You are even less likely to hear someone say, "I am from the European Union." People (and peoples), apart from a limited number of visionaries, do not belong to the European Union or see themselves as European citizens. A person might speak of being "European," but usually in the context of saying what he or she is not, for example, not Middle-Eastern, or not Latin American.

On an everyday basis, people in Europe see the European Union as a common project and service to which their national governments subscribe. It is perceived in those terms by most people and betimes cynically as "just another tax collector!" North Americans and some other non-Europeans tend to lose sight of the current state of the European Union and project their own understanding of "federal" governance onto it; and in a sense, by speaking of it this way, attempt to push it in this direction. Thus, when we speak in these pages of "EuroDiversity," it is a shortcut for speaking of diversity in the E.U. Member States and the region itself, as well as including the efforts undertaken in common via the European Union's many governmental functions and by NGOs in the area.

EuroDiversity makes no pretense at being an exhaustive resource about diversity in the E.U. From the buffet of possibilities, we have filled our plate with things that we the authors are familiar with as well as tasting a variety of unfamiliar areas through our research. We have tried to be incisive rather than extensive, hoping that our efforts will stimulate interest in our readers. We see you as future contributors, making many trips to the groaning board of knowledge about European diversity, sharing what you discover with others, and above all making sound decisions and taking decisive action for the future well being of all the peoples who make up this hard-to-define continent called Europe.

As this book was being finalized, the world was shaken by the most accomplished acts of terrorism in history, the hijacking attacks on New York and Washington. These events sorely test our sincerity and skill at dealing with diversity both in domestic situations and in policy decisions abroad. It showed both that our thinking about human solidarity had progressed, and at the same time that there were both great gaps in our knowledge of each other and our political will and consensus to bring it about. It is the authors' hope that this volume will make some small contribution to that end. In the long run it will be the little acts of everyday commerce and personal cooperation that will weave the best safety net for humankind.

George F. Simons

EuroDiversity

Patchwork: The Diversities of Europeans and Their Business Impact

George F. Simons

Historically, Europe, or "the Old World," is different from the lands in which European emigrants settled and made their own. Europe has always been very diverse, and Europeans are fully conscious of their diversity. They differ from North Americans in what to do about it. In the best of times, Europeans believe that "good fences make good neighbors." In the worst of times, those who attempt to create or reshape these boundaries discover that they have been painted in blood.

At the outset, particularly for non-Europeans, it is important to keep telling ourselves that "Europe is a continent not a country!" As U.K. diversity specialist Graham Shaw reminds us, Europe contains many different models of social and political organization—including the European Union, to which not all states adhere. Each differs in its commitment to the social support of its population, and legal systems differ both in style and content when it comes to if and how they regulate what we may identify as diversity issues (Shaw, 2000, p. 12).

Diverse by nature, the European Union got its start in the search for peace and prosperity after history's most devastating war (World War II, 1938–1945). While Canada and the United States may have discovered the bottom line challenge of diversity in the unused potential of their disadvantaged people, Europe started with the commercial bottom line as a reason for managing its differences. North American diversity started with social and government initiatives that extended into the private sector; in Europe, economic cooperation among

Exhibit 1.1

Piet Mondrian, "Composition with Red, Yellow, and Blue" 1921, oil on canvas, cm 39.5 × 35

Patchwork. An image, a metaphor is needed to grasp the complexity of European history, culture, and the contemporary challenge of creating value from the enormous diversity of this place called Europe.

Patchwork. Something cobbled together of bits and pieces, respecting the nature and possibilities of each, and creating fresh value and utility. A patchwork quilt that keeps us safe and warm.

Patchwork. Something that can be added to; pieces that can be rearranged if necessary. The look and feel of Europe; the Mondrian perspective (Exhibit 1.1) one gets while flying over much of it; and the clear boundaries of the E.U. Member States with the now abandoned customs houses one sees when driving across borders.

Patchwork. The result of imagination and compromise, today more often hastily sewn together by corporate expansion, mergers, and acquisitions than by politics and policies.

Source: The Haag's Gemeentemuseum.

diverse peoples was the starting point. Only later did this cooperative enterprise begin to take responsibility for a social and cultural European integration whose necessity, utility, and desirability continue to be questioned every step of the way.

This does not mean that Europe has lacked or lacks either humanitarian motivation or social concern for its diversity. There are countless local, regional, national, and supranational governmental efforts as well as abundant NGOs (nongovernmental organizations) and private initiatives for assisting the continent's disadvantaged, its asylum seekers, and those targeted by bias and racist violence. We shall be paying attention to how these affect and support related business policies and activities.

The Challenge of Cultural Diversity

In what ways is cultural diversity a bottom-line challenge for European businesses and those doing business in Europe, and what does managing diversity involve? In European businesses these questions are being asked more and more often. Charles Black, Medical Director of NovoNordisk Europe, points out that the cultural challenge facing modern business managers is in many ways new (Black, 2001, Introduction, p. 1). He sees this fresh challenge as one brought about by globalization and the technological revolution in communications and travel. According to Black, global managers should be asking themselves,

> How can I . . .
> 1. maintain strong corporate strategic alignment in the face of increasing cultural and personal diversity in the company workforce?
> 2. find opportunities in cultural diversity to better meet my need to be responsive to my global and culturally diverse customers?
> 3. learn to deal with cultural diversity in other stakeholder groups, notably my shareholders?
> 4. harness and manage cultural diversity to enhance innovation? (Black, 2001, p. 2–3)

For organizations that would operate in a global environment, managing culture is also an essential part of the inevitable and constant change process. Black likens this to a child growing into adulthood:

> Most companies have an organization that is derived in part from the national "parent" culture from which they originate. . . . [T]he *globalizing* company must free itself of its own home country cultural heritage with all its inherent limitations to manage a global business. In the process, it must keep the beneficial aspects of that culture while ridding itself of the negative ones. (Black, 2001, p. 3)

Our U.S. and Canadian colleagues who have been engaged in national debates on diversity for years now look at the incredible diversity on the continent of Europe and scratch their heads in amazement that the word "diversity" itself has been, until recently, so rarely mentioned here. Equivalent terms like *kulturelle Vielfalt* (cultural diversity) and *gerer diversité* (managing diversity) have been used in Germany and France, respectively, but almost always to discuss North American diversity. Why then has diversity not been the "hot topic" in Europe that it is in North America? The answer is that the issues have been very important ones, but they have been conceived of and dealt with in a different form of discourse. We are not questioning whether diversity exists or diversity initiatives make sense for European businesses, but we are asking how and when do they do so. What are the differences? How have they been dealt with, and how should they be dealt with? To answer these questions we need to look for insights in the history and culture of Europe.

A History of Assimilation

While the E.U. as a whole is extremely multicultural, its *Member States* and regions are traditionally far more monocultural than are the United States and Canada, for example. This requires some qualification, as within each country there is a highly diverse mixture of assimilated ethnicity over the centuries. Wars, treaties, dislocations, and intermarriage make Europeans a very mixed bag in terms of bloodlines, but not in their sense of national and ethnic identity. It sheds little light on the subject to learn that, for example, Greeks and Turks are virtually identical at the genetic level, or that 80% of all Europeans are descended from a common ancestor. In other words, assimilation has been occurring and continues to occur as a managing diversity strategy. Even in a country with such a liberal reputation as the Netherlands, the pressure on today's immigrants to the Netherlands and other European countries to learn the national language and culture is much stronger than would be politically possible in the United States or even Canada. Businesses, of course, benefit from these policies by getting entry-level workers who are easier to communicate with and instruct.

Assimilation strategies are part of a monocultural mentality resulting from long-defended boundaries and can even be a conscious strategy in countries with plural language cultures like that of Switzerland. Where assimilation has been unsuccessful, usually as a result of forced political settlements, regional cultures assert themselves, and resentment and even open hostility are always possible. Northern Ireland and the former Yugoslavia are the most current examples of this, but smoldering resentments still exist in Belgium and Spain and wherever historical ethnicity and regional autonomy are still at odds with national unity.

Assimilation strategies have also been taking place in businesses as well, with English as the corporate language of many large organizations despite their country of origin or the location of their headquarters. Meeting each other on the common ground of English is often an important strategy for not only overcoming the Babel of languages, but for sidestepping otherwise incompatible histories and cultures. Homogenization of language and assimilation to the organizational culture, however, notes Black, may have already reached its limits, as the truly savvy global manager needs both cultural knowledge and agility to apply it both internally and externally (Black, 2001).

Paradoxically, Europeans in U.S. owned or affiliated companies often resist the arrival of diversity initiatives, seeing them as assimilationism on the part of Americans and another attempt on their part to make the world over in their own image. Indeed, U.S. missionary zeal and free market ideology may accompany such efforts, as many Americans have long been convinced that it is their role to "make the world free for (their version of) democracy," and have thus ethnocentrically evangelized the world with it. As Juan Moriera-Delgado of the Spanish Ministry of Education points out, "The American performance in the international arena casts the image of a solid political nationalism. From the outside there is unity and American nationalism. From the inside the discussion is about multiculturalism, any reference to nationalism pointing at a foreign affair" (Delgado-Moreira, 1997, electronic document at http://www.sociology.org/content/vol002.003/delgado.html). U.S. sponsored initiatives often run aground because U.S. diversity specialists lack cultural knowledge and experience in Europe, and many Europeans have a simplistic cultural understanding of the United States.

Defense of Boundaries and Frontiers

The use of the word "frontier" provides a good illustration of how the European and North American sense of boundaries differ. Michael Berry, Docent in Intercultural Relations at the Turku School of Economics in Finland, has highlighted that when a European speaks of the "frontier," he or she refers to the nation's borders, usually in the sense of boundaries that need to be defended (1994). Traditionally, when a soldier was assigned to a country's "frontier," it meant literally that. Such a sense of boundaries has resulted in a stricter sense of nationality and of personal national identity than North Americans are used to. In the world of business, new forms of openness, transparency, and open-door policies can be at first bewildering to Europeans. One of the diversity challenges to the European Union and European businesses has been to create the necessary openness for cooperation across traditional boundaries and to decompartmentalize business procedures.

On the other hand, when a North American speaks of "the frontier" or even "a frontier," it usually points to a border that is meant to be crossed or an achievement that is intended to be surpassed. Indeed, the metaphorical use of the word is more common today in such expressions as "the frontiers of cyberspace." Labeling something a "frontier" challenges the listener to make a "breakthrough." Of course, "frontier" in North America may not roll so pleasantly from the tongues of Latinos and Native Americans or First Nations. They experienced quite differently the belief in Manifest Destiny that led European adventurers and immigrants to possess and dominate the New World "from sea to shining sea" as if it were their own or theirs for the taking.

Exhibit 1.2A is an early eighteenth-century matrix showing the cultural characteristics of representative peoples found in Europe. It is interesting to note that this antique "snapshot" of Europe includes Central Europe as well as Turks and Greeks who are lumped together. German-speaking peoples are treated as a single category. Political boundaries have changed since then and, if anything, became more fiercely delineated in the twentieth century. We have attempted to translate this chart in Exhibit 1.2B, to illustrate how distinctly Europeans saw each other at that time and also to show how many of the characteristics and stereotypes mentioned then are still quite common almost two centuries later.

In June of 2000, the University of Central Lancashire held an international, interdisciplinary conference about current tensions in the representation of "Britishness" (Relocating Britishness, June 22–24, 2000). The themes were wide ranging, but it was clear that despite changing roles, the devolution of government in Scotland and Wales, and ambivalence about participation in the European Union, Britain contained a variety of regional and class identities that have been heightened by the need to accommodate immigration and diversity. Traditional stereotypes of Britain as the colonial power, the agent of the industrial revolution, the home of courtly society, and the tourist destination often obfuscate these real identities (see Lorbiecki and Hutchings, 2000). Simply put, a sense of identity is a contemporary hotspot in the discussion and practice of diversity, and not only for Brits, as we will show toward the end of this book. Contrary to, and perhaps as a result of the U.S. experience, in which diversity practice belatedly and grudgingly admitted white men as potential partners in and subjects of diversity initiatives, diversity work in Europe will be, and needs to be, an inclusive discussion from the beginning.

Languages as Boundaries

I recently spent over four years living and working in the Netherlands. Driving 200 kilometers from home in any direction, I was not able to speak my newly acquired Dutch with much likelihood of being understood. I grew up in Cleveland, Ohio in the United States. From my native town, I could drive a thousand or more miles in any direction with the almost sure expectation of being understood. These odds were pretty good even if I happened to temporarily find myself in rural Quebec or passing through an ethnic or immigrant enclave. A Belgian colleague told me quite a different story:

> We use over a dozen languages in the European Union. Most of us in business speak one or more second languages. The meaning of words and phrases can differ very much. We have used this linguistic diversity to protect local markets, products, and economies. Most young Europeans, in fact, do not speak another language well until they are about 14 to 16 years old, well beyond the critical age where they still influence each other at a fundamental cultural level. The dominant language groups do not subtitle films and television broadcasts but synchronize the speech. We have had wars and economic disputes to reinforce linguistic divisions and stereotypes. Religious segregation can complicate matters further.

Language reinforces boundaries in Europe. While English has, paradoxically, become the *lingua franca* of international business, most of Europe consists of smaller cultural areas that have to live together and must speak their own languages and dialects to do business together, despite the fact that their economies are increasingly dependent on each other. Language preserves identity and, as the French strongly insist, cultural heritage. In much of Europe, however, it is national identity and unity that have long dominated the political geography, and language initiatives have largely supported a national language, despite the resistance of regionalists and separatists. In France, as we note in Chapter 10, language and culture have been treated as if they have a common identity, yet efforts to impose French as the common language began at the time of the French Revolution:

> [I]n the 1850s, one in five Frenchmen still could not speak French. How tongues change. In 1914, for example, some 1.3 m people in

Exhibit 1.2

(A) Early Eighteenth-Century Description of European Peoples from the Austrian Museum of Folk Life and Folk Art, Vienna; (B) Early Eighteenth-Century Description of European Peoples (this is an English translation of Exhibit 1.2A)

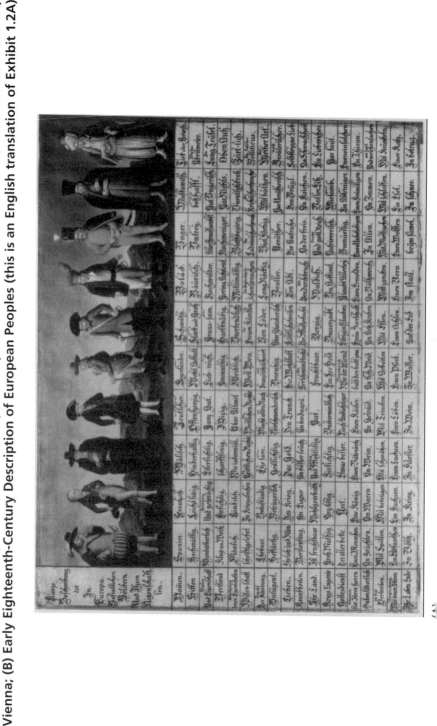

A Short Description of the Peoples Found in Europe and Their Characteristics

	Spaniard	Frenchman	Italian	German	Briton	Swede	Pole	Hungarian	Russian	Turk or Greek
Names	Arrogant	Frivolous	Reserved	Openhearted	Good appearance	Big and strong	Coarse	Faithless	Malicious	Like April weather
Behaviors	Marvelous	Good spirited & talkative	Jealous	Very good	Charming	Cruel	Very wild	The cruelest	Quite Hungarian	A quick devil
Nature and characteristics	Smart and wise	Farsighted	Astute	Witty	Annoying	Stubborn	Poorly attentive	Even less	None at all	Superficially open
Intellect	manly	Childish	However you please	Well balanced	Feminine	Unknowable	Mediocre	Bloodthirsty	Infinitely coarse	Tender
Expression of the characteristics	Learned in letters	In the affairs of war	In spiritual authority	In worldly authority	Worldly wise	In liberal arts	In different languages	In the Latin language	In the Greek language	In political falsehood
Sciences	Respectable	Inconsistent	Crazy	Imitate everything	French fashions	Leather	Long coats	Colorful	In fun	After the fashion of women
How they dress	Arrogance	Cheating	Lecherous	Wasteful	Restless	Superstitious	Loudmouth	Treacherous	Quite treacherous	Even more treacherous
Vices	Praise and fame	War	Gold	Drink	Sensuality	Rich food	Titles	Turmoil	Brawling	Their own body
What they love	Constipation	Genetic	Plague	Gout	Consumption	~Y	Hernia	Fright	Coughing	From. weakness
Diseases	Is Fruitful	Well worked	Pleasing and sensual	Good	Fruitful	Mountainous	Forested	Rich in produce and gold	Full of ice	Charming
Their land	Very courageous	Deceitful	Foresight	Unconquerable	Heroic at sea	Without failure	Immovable	In formation	Wearing	Quite lazy
Virtues in war	The very best	Good	Somewhat better	Even more pious	Changeable as the moon	Zealous Faith	Believes all kinds of things	Not boring	A schismatic	Also one
Worship	A monarch	A king	A Patriarch	An Emperor	Now this, now that	Liberal rule	An elected one	An unconquerable one	A freebooter	A tyrant
Recognize as their ruler	Fruit	Goods	Wine	Grain	Bogs	Mines	Fur pieces	Everything	Swarms of bees	In things that are tender and soft
Have a surplus of	With games	In deception	Discussing the latest news	By drinking	With work	By drinking	Quarreling	Criticizing and complaining	By sleeping	From wounds
How they pass the time	An elephant	A fox	A fox	A lion	A horse	An ox	A bear	A wolf	A donkey	A cat
Compared with the animals	In bed	In war	In the cloister	In wine	In water	On the earth	In the stable	By the saber	In snow	Through deceit
Their life's end										

(B)

France spoke Breton; in 1945 the figure was still 1 m. And now?
To the dismay of the separatists, the answer is fewer than 300,000,
of whom barely 3% use Breton more than French. ("How
Multilingual Is France?" 2000, p. 26)

In North America, diversity of language is debated hotly in several
areas. Most notable is the insistence on the part of many in Quebec
that strict language laws are needed, not primarily to protect the
French language itself, but to protect Quebecois culture itself from the
depredations of the media that occur through the internationalization
of English. While the situation of Quebec is historically different
from that of France itself, the rationale for linguistic protectionism
is expressed along similar lines in both places and may help North
Americans to understand the situation they will encounter living and
working in France. Even many French who possess relatively strong
English skills may not reveal their ability, but proceed in French even
in multilingual business situations.

Although the United States has never insisted on a single language,
"nativist" pressure has often built up against speakers of languages
other than English. Controversy over bilingual education of immigrant
children in schools and movements insisting that English be declared
the official state and national language continue into the present
as fresh waves of immigrants arrive. Such debates can be extremely
polarized and emotional and often reveal assimilationist tendencies,
fear of immigrant groups, uncertainty about the future of a multicultural society, even fears about the disintegration of the educational
system itself.

USA Today Snapshots® Tuesday, April 11, 2000
by Anne R. Carey and Quin Tian, *USA Today*

Bilingual business

Senior executives speak an average of two languages. Average number
spoken by executives in:

Netherlands 3.9
Sweden 3.4
Germany 2.7
Japan 2.6
Hong Kong 2.3
United Kingdom 1.5
United States 1.5

Source: Global Literacies: Lessons on Business Leadership and National
Cultures.

The Nature of European Diversity and the Challenge of Managing It

Despite steps taken by the European Union to reduce economic barriers and create uniform policies and regulations for free trade and the free movement of people, Europe cannot be considered as integrated as North America, politically, economically, or socially, even when the issues surrounding Quebec are included in the discussion. Not every European country or region has the same numbers of different cultures, colors, language, backgrounds, and so on. Although the dominant cultural streams are Latin, Anglo-Saxon, and Germanic, each is historically influenced by religion, its record of aggression or being aggressed upon, its centralized or decentralized structure, and the presence or absence of colonialism resulting in minorities in its present population. The colonial history of France, for example, has led to a large population of Maghreb people (North Africa), while Dutch society contains larger numbers of people from Indonesia, Surinam, and the Antilles. Belgium hosts large numbers of Congolese, while countless Commonwealth people have come to roost in Britain.

Euro Disney's disastrous early efforts to impose the Disney home culture in its training of workers for its Paris theme park have been discussed ad infinitum from the perspective of how the company misread French working culture. What most commentaries miss, however, is that only two-thirds of the Euro Disney employee base was French. The other third—close to 5,000 people—were rooted in over 90 other nations and cultures (Jarvis, 1997). Diversity in the service and hospitality sectors of European business yields quite a different and far more diverse picture than what one expects when dealing with European corporate decision-makers.

In Europe there are several sorts of minority individuals. There are managers transferred from other E.U. countries and abroad, and people coming from other E.U. countries for low- as well as high-paid jobs. Added to this are the economic immigrants and asylum seekers from many backgrounds who have flooded into various European countries in recent years. In some countries a newcomer can acquire citizenship, in others not. Though stricter protection in the form of labor laws may prevent certain inequalities, these different groups can occupy quite different social places in each country and pose a variety of problems for potential employers. As a result of this diversity of diversities, we are likely to find several different emerging patterns for managing diversity in Europe today, as our discussion and search for best practices will illustrate later in this book. But first, let's round out the picture of how diversity is seen in Europe.

The Dangers of North American Diversity as Seen by Europeans

Accentuating differences within and between European nations, particularly in tense times, is fraught with danger. Within living European memory, emphasis on difference has created pogroms, mass dislocations of peoples, and the Holocaust. Hatreds lie beneath the surface and can fester for a thousand years and renew themselves in fresh bloodbaths, as the recent story of the former Yugoslavia illustrates. Prominent and successful nationalistic movements, usually far to the right, as those led by Le Pen in France and Haider in Austria, on the one hand appeal to the desire for security in changing times, and on the other provide an alarming connection to their past for many Europeans. Unemployment deploys skinheads to the streets where, more than likely, their targets are people who are different, people who are seen as bleeding the welfare systems if not actively stealing jobs from natives in the workplace.

With dreaded old memories and equally frightening current events, the average European may try to avoid thinking about such events, even when they are occurring in what North Americans, with their less bounded sense of space, would consider "their backyard." Diversity, North American style, with its desire to celebrate certain differences, may feel dangerous or even provocative—as Protestant marches in Ulster would, for example. Other things Americans do in the name of celebrating diversity seem silly or incongruous (like Oktoberfest in October), or even oppressive (such as minute insistence on "politically correct" words and behaviors).

We all have our forms of avoidance. Many North Americans would claim that they escaped from Europe's history of ethnic and religious conflict and oppression by emigrating, either themselves or their recent ancestors, to the "New World." To a degree this is true, but North America has to face a tarnished history of its own. Racism, the virulent residue of black slavery, dominates North American consciousness. Anti-immigrant bias and exclusion have continued from colonial times to the present. It has often been observed, for example, that in many ways Britain uses "class" to avoid having to deal directly with "race," while in the United States racial issues have made it almost impossible to deal with or even speak about "class." Racism, a primary challenge to multicultural success in the United States, affects the Canadian way of life as well, more strongly than many Canadians would like to believe. (See Margaret Cannon's 1995 book, *The Invisible Empire: Racism in Canada.*) Many immigrants to the New World brought with them the attitudes and practices they thought they had left behind.

Political Correctness

Diversity in the United States, like so many other societal and even personal issues, is worked out to a great deal in lawmaking and the courts, in the form of conflicts within democratic boundaries of debate. In its legal framework, the United States also enjoys a wider range of freedom of speech than is allowed in the E.U. Member States. U.S. courts punish neither rightist diatribe or fanatical political correctness. When faced with North American models of immigration and diversity management, Europeans rightly fear beliefs and behaviors that might get out of hand in a European context.

Nothing raises European resistance to North American diversity ideas quite so readily as the phenomenon known as *political correctness (pc)*. Many who lived through National Socialism and ideological Communism in the last century very easily identify the fascistic tendencies of *pc* as it is often practiced in universities, government, and even businesses in the United States and Canada. When it comes to U.S. organizational life, in fact, John Wayne is dead and the Lone Ranger has ridden off into the sunset. Rugged individualism is gone for the most part, though it persists as a mythic ideal for many Americans.

The current functional myth of U.S. diversity that often finds its way into workplaces, both public and private, is that the world is divided into victims and oppressors. Victims belong to specific target classes (blacks, women, Latinos, etc.) and by definition cannot be aggressors. If I am an angry victim, the howling beast in me is the oppressor's fault. I occupy the moral high ground. Oppressors are likewise defined by their group identity, usually white men, not because they have individually chosen to behave oppressively but simply because they belong to this specific class of people and thus automatically behave oppressively and as a group benefit from oppressing others. It is de facto bad faith not to acknowledge one's status as an oppressor, and many U.S. diversity-training programs are not complete without a white person confessing to being an oppressor. To European sensibilities, these extremes of U.S. diversity practice, echoed in news reports, sound familiarly like fascism and are a direct affront to individual liberty and social responsibility; they want no part of them in the workplace.

Despite constitutional guarantees of freedom of speech in the United States, outsiders can see that the country seems to go through a kind of moralistic paranoia on a regular basis. Movements emerge that create forms of social control, often curbing self-expression and defining acceptable language and images. Following the patriotism of World War II there were the anti-Communist crusades of Senator Joseph McCarthy, which playwright Arthur Miller carefully identified as a reincarnation of the New England "witch hunt," an old American psychological tendency reborn in the 1950s. It is not surprising that quite a few Europeans see *pc* as the logical extension of that tendency, particularly as it carries over into the evaluation of new hires and promotions. Despite its paradoxical emergence in the U.S. New Left in the 1970s, *pc* is seen as a rightist phenomenon that has co-opted the liberal left in such a way as to actually serve as an effective tool for homogenization and globalization. Aidan Rankin, observing the rise of *pc* in the United Kingdom, where it is abetted by the affinity of the language and dominant culture with North America, argues that *pc* has co-opted the liberal left there as well where it likewise encourages culturally insensitive globalization (2001).

Dealing with European Stereotypes

Rejection of North American *pc* does not mean that Europeans are not concerned with language from a social perspective. Hate speech and other forms of verbal or written attacks on the continent do not enjoy the same legal protection as they do in the United States. Groups arguing extremist positions may be outlawed in some places. Germans have undertaken a revision of their language itself, and one of its effects is to reduce structural sexual bias in grammar and orthography. No German candy manufacturer labels a chocolate cream bonbon or "kiss" as a *"Negerkuss"* any more, though one is unlikely to be called down for doing so in everyday speech. Note that the word *"Neger"* in German never approached the degree of offensiveness that the term "nigger" has in the United States. There is a discernible tendency in European advertising, journalism and business life to replace questionable terms with more appropriate ones.

Generally speaking, however, in the less litigious atmosphere of Europe, inappropriate terms, biased or off-color humor, and even intentional slights in the workplace tend to be taken care of by being ignored, recognized as déclassé, or otherwise dealt with on a personal basis rather than becoming the subject of explicit policies and procedures. The French easily distinguish between the humorous, careless, and harmless use of certain material and its use with the intention to harm. Britain may be somewhat the exception in this respect in that stereotypical humor and wit are seen somewhat as a sport and readily indulged in by many. Currently, some pressure is mounting to tone down the language used in the House of Commons. Though recognizing the outdated and stereotypical nature of, for example, having monocled Germans in lederhosen, and bereted and mustachioed Frenchmen in turtleneck sweaters, hardly anyone in Europe would be seriously offended by such depictions. And indeed, some intercultural trainers of high stature such as John Mole (*Mind Your Manners: Managing Business Cultures in Europe*) and Richard Hill (*Sharks and Custard: The Things that Make Europeans Laugh*) use stereotypes in jokes and cartoons as starting points for intercultural understanding.

There is, however, growing sensitivity to the misuse of minority images in advertising, though the ads themselves tend to be seen more as tasteless than aggressive, as in an Uncle Ben's rice ad which showed a black child with the legend, in French, "The baby in Uncle Ben's family likes it when you pull her ears," advertising a new product package with easy-to-open "ear" tabs. One senses a gradual elimination of these kinds of images in responsible marketing and promotion, though kitch statues and representations still abound as restaurant and shop decorations.

Cultural icons are more resistant. On December 6 in the Low Countries, Sinterklaas, the stylized St. Nicholas, makes his rounds of parties, children's events, shops, factories, and offices. He is accompanied by Zwart Piet (Black Peter), a Moorish boy (usually played now by young women in blackface) dressed in a Moroccan costume of the sixteenth century. Zwart Piet records the names of all the naughty children in order to deliver punishment or carry them off in his sack to Spain; the good children (and adults) receive gifts, usually candies. Zwart Piet comes from the time when the Low Countries were part of the Empire of Spain during the first 75 years of the sixteenth century ("The Helpers"). Of course, most of today's office workers would relish the trip to Spain in the "dark days before Christmas." There is some reaction to this tradition, including the occasional Zwart Sinterklaas with a Witte Piet, the equivalent of a black Santa with a white slave, but certainly no one would seriously try to eliminate this yearly visit from their office or factory. There is also a great commercial investment and retail profit to be made in this seasonal event, which raises the question of how to respect rich cultural heritage and diminish less savory elements that it may contain. In the United States, Christmas parties have been largely banned from businesses. Europeans would prefer something less culturally destructive. They often think that Americans fail to realize that deliberately taking offense is as destructive as deliberately giving offense.

In much of Europe there is significantly less obsession with modesty and human bodily processes in general than in North America. Art and advertising rarely provide impetus to censorship, and again, cleverness and good taste are primary. A recent advertisement for a perfume in the Netherlands clearly inferred that a nude male model was getting an erection as the young woman wearing the product entered the drawing class late. She sniggered and so did the rest of the class. One hears occasional objection to making sex objects of women, but it appears that the contemporary European solution is not to cease doing so but to give men an equal share and perhaps do so with a good sense of humor, as in an ad for Eram shoes (Exhibit 1.3).

Diversity, Economics, and Power

Diversity, particularly in the United States, has been less cultural than sociopolitical and commercial. On the sociopolitical level, righting the wrongs of the past through the redistribution of power and opportunity has given rise to and shaped the diversity agenda and produced legislation and policies of equal employment. This has resulted in the identification of excluded or targeted populations, efforts to include them, and strict penalties for not doing so. Blacks in the United States, as with many other Americans, can be very mixed in terms of nationality and race, but it is hardly safe to discuss this. Rarely does one hear of U.S. blacks finding an environment where it is acceptable to own and value a mixed heritage.

U.S. constitutional guarantees of equality of opportunity for individuals drive the nation's social legislation. Europeans must remember that this equality is equality of opportunity not equality of distribution. North Americans feel that the playing field should be level, but even if fairly played, the game remains very competitive and there will inevitably be winners and losers in this system, as the wide disparity of incomes and the dwindling of the middle class in the United States demonstrate. What one does with opportunity is believed to have everything to do with what the person becomes and earns. It is connected to identity. North Americans are what they do. As a result, the economic disparities found in the United States, for example, bother many U.S. Americans far less than they do many Europeans. Social legislation, though increasingly threatened in Europe, continues to do a more equitable job of distribution of salaries and human services than it has in North America. Many Europeans are torn between the Scylla of social deregulation and the Charybdis of marginalization of the disadvantaged.

Exhibit 1.3

"No woman's body was exploited in the making of this ad"

Source: Ad for the French shoe manufacturer Eram S.A., by the DeVarrieux Villaret Agency.

Corporate Diversity Assets

On a commercial level, diversity has become a corporate must in large North American organizations, forced on them by an increasingly diverse marketplace and the need to make the growing multicultural workforce creative, productive, and competitive. Diversity in a working organization can be seen as the sum total of potential found in a group of people because of their differences, a resource to be exploited for marketplace success, both domestically and globally. Getting added value (generally used in Europe to indicate how the handling of a product or service adds value to it) from an organization's diversity, or a nation's for that matter, is common ground on which European and North American diversity concerns may meet as they inevitably do in global organizations. Suffice it to say that this is a vision and a goal rather than something that can be taken for granted or easily accomplished.

Diversity in the United States has a way of bringing the ghosts of the past to life in very unsettling ways. In the United States, histories of discrimination and harassment are disinterred and prosecuted. Running for a minor political office or being nominated for a political appointment will send the opposition scurrying for enough scandalous sound bites to sway voters or decision-makers. Youthful peccadilloes can have character damning consequences in business and public life, to say nothing of diversity gaffes on the job. To put things in perspective, however, accusations of individual, governmental, and corporate wrongdoing, however high the judgments and settlements, affect very few U.S. citizens directly. The Enron disaster may be the exception that proves this rule in this regard, but at this writing all Europeans can do is shake their heads in amazement at the lack of integrity they sense lying beneath the attempts to deny and sanitize the affair. There have been numerous instances in Europe where business or governmental officials' past dealings have become a source of scandal and a career liability. Outside of Britain, however, this is more likely to be for shady financial dealings, abuse of public monies, and in some cases, collaboration with the Nazi regime, than it is on accusations of moral turpitude.

Diversity and Privacy

Diversity U.S. style threatens to open historical wounds, a reality that many Europeans, remembering old injuries and the ongoing infliction of new ones in the Balkans, rightly fear and resist. This has a personal dimension as well. In 1998 and 1999, fear for invasion of privacy nearly brought e-commerce to a halt because the compilation of private dossiers on the Internet was not welcomed in a part of the world where "the secret policeman's knock on the door is still a live memory, and privacy has a fragility that few U.S. people understand." When American industry executives like Scott McNealy of Sun Microsystems say, "You already have zero privacy; get over it," they only confirm Europeans' worst fears about American indifference to history" (McGrath, 1999, p. 90).

Being open about one's private life, feelings, and sentiments, modeled on the talk shows, is shunned by many Europeans, and at the height of the Clinton scandals, many Europeans were more shocked by the invasion of personal privacy than they were by the President's lascivious behavior. When the Lewinsky affair broke into the news, it was greeted with incredulity on the part of many Europeans, not because it occurred, but because of the breach of personal privacy that it entailed and the international damage that such reckless meandering into the lives of highly placed officials would have on confidence in the international arena (Simons and de Raaff, 1998). Prurient interest runs highest in the British tabloids, followed perhaps by late-night German television, but in general these are not media with which most businesses wish to associate.

Freedom to Be Different

There are subtle but striking differences between European approaches to personal freedom on the cultural, legal, and practical levels and those found in North America. U.S. and other visitors to Europe often have romantic, stereotypical, and often quite false images of Europe, its cities, and its people. These images are often fueled by travel writers like Peter Mayle, in books such as *A Year in Provence* and *French Lessons: Adventures with Knife, Fork, and Corkscrew*, and Bill Bryson, in *Notes from a Small Island* and *Neither Here Nor There: Travels in Europe*. These books can be terribly entertaining to those who share their ethnocentricity, but they rarely penetrate the real culture of their surroundings, and, when they do, have little practical advice to offer.

The ways, areas, and means in which social control is exercised in European countries differ greatly. There is a different balance between law, ethics and morals, social norms, and the ways in which the rules can be questioned. The United Kingdom, for example, has no bill of rights guaranteeing freedom of speech, but it does have Hyde Park Corner, where norms governing freedom of speech are relaxed. Privacy laws in France severely limit what may be said about others in public or printed in the news media. Extremist speech, demonstrations, and organizations may be and frequently are banned in Germany. In many places the law forbids mentioning a competitor or a competitor's products or comparing them with your own in advertising.

"Moral" Constraints

A Dutch visitor to Santa Cruz, California, compared the city to a police state because of its legal and socially enforced restrictions on smoking, perfume, food ingredients, and even the choice and use of "politically correct" words in everyday speech. Much behavior in any culture is regulated by informal social pressure. Europeans would tend to foster "social climates" rather than create and enforce laws. The spirit of this underlies the confusion over the recent attempt of other E.U. countries to use pressure internationally by creating sanctions against Austria when it allowed a coalition including Jörg Haider's FPÖ (Austrian Freedom Party) with its anti-immigrant agenda to come to power.

But what happens when limits, borders, and frontiers do not exist any more? The development of the European Union and the advance of globalization inevitably challenge social norms and practices. Although film and broadcast media have been and can be controlled in many ways, the Internet is much harder to steer. Americans are moralistic about pornography and child abuse, while Europeans are much more concerned with controlling racism and violence.

Freedom of Conscience and Religious Separation

How issues of religious freedom are conceived of and handled differ significantly between European Nations and the United States. Although the United States considers freedom of conscience and separation of church and state as absolutes, generally European governments see it as their duty to the commonwealth to support religion, usually with a goal of disinterested and equitable distribution of benefits. Thus churches as well as social and charitable enterprises may receive subsidies from tax monies.

France serves as a good example, not only of this difference but also of the differing sociopolitical thinking that surrounds government behavior concerning religion. Dominique Dechert highlights how acute some of these differences can be:

> Despite different religious histories, France and the United States have both long embraced religious freedom in their constitutional documents.

But from a common starting point, U.S. courts have erected a higher and more impenetrable "wall of separation," as Justice Hugo Black called it . . . , than have their French counterparts. Controversies that are still divisive today within American society, such as religious discussion in public schools after teaching hours and government subsidies to faith-based organizations, have never been weighty political issues in France.

Since 1959, the French government pays the salaries of teachers in private schools, most of which are religious, and gives subsidies directly to those schools. Churches, temples, and synagogues built in France before 1905 are the property of the state. National and municipal governments maintain these buildings, which are used free-of-charge by the clergy. Religious feasts are official holidays in France.

The four other main religions in France have, like the Catholic Church, been organized at the national level, and the French government is currently discussing with several Islamic groups to achieve a similar national representative body for Islam.

In the United States, the International Religious Freedom Act of 1998 (IRFA) imposed sanctions on countries around the world that were convicted of violating religious freedom. The new law created a U.S. Commission for International Religious Freedom and appointed an Ambassador-at-large to head an office on international religious freedom at the State Department. In France (on the very next day, by coincidence), the National Assembly recommended the creation of a governmental taskforce, the Inter-Ministerial Mission against Sects (MILS), to monitor so-called dangerous cults. In each case, the legislation was approved unanimously.

In general, religious freedom is regarded in France as a human right, but never in isolation from other universal human rights. France therefore objects to a special status for religious freedom over freedom of conscience. (Dechert, Dominique 2001, at The Brookings Institute Website, http://www.brook.edu/dybdocroot/fp/cusf/analysis/relfreedom.htm)

Generally speaking, in Europe, as in the United States, religion is not much considered a part of the practice of diversity in corporate efforts, despite its being at the major fault lines of many cultural differences, such as those separating Northern and Southern Europe. Fresh issues, such as those currently arising from the growing number of Islamic groups, seem to be more a part of public and social policy-making in Europe and do not directly address the private sector. Businesses in Europe, however, are asking whether or how they should react when large numbers of people of different beliefs and customs join their payroll.

Stakeholder Diversity

Both the strength and the weakness of the culture of corporate Europe and the European economy are entangled in complicated forms of ownership and vested interest. Mapping the relationships between government, banking, and industry yields a picture of traditional power blocs and a stifling network of cross-holdings. Marco Becht, of the European Centre for Advanced Research in Economics and Statistics (ECARES), specializes in issues of corporate governance and ownership. In a 1999 study, Becht and Ailsa Roëll, of the Economics Department of Princeton, analyzed these power blocks and their influence on corporate governance and performance. Generally speaking, the insiders are mighty and the smaller stakeholders powerless. Ownership by small clans of major stakeholders, protected by special voting rights, results in strong direction from owners and weak management. It protects from takeovers but stagnates productivity and profitability, making these organizations undervalued in the world market because they are in fact underperforming.

The *Economist* recently detailed some of the more startling cultural configurations uncovered by Becht and Roëll's study in various European countries:

- In Italy, Germany, Belgium, and Austria, more than half of the listed companies studied had a single shareholder, or known group of allies, with more than 50% of the voting rights.

- In France and Germany, the vast majority of tradable companies are protected by a majority voting block or a blocking minority. In France, it comes down to a combination of the state's wish to see big business in friendly hands and the lack of institutional investors.

- In Italy, banks and holding companies often, with minimal capital layout, control networks of firms through pyramidal cross-shareholding schemes, known as "Chinese boxes."

- Swedish companies can issue shares with up to 1,000 times the voting power of ordinary shares.

- In the Netherlands, an independent Shell Oil shareholder with a 40% stake would have less than 0.0003% of the vote on some important issues, while "priority shareholders" owning less than one five-millionth of the group's capital have huge blocking power. ("Cross about Holdings," 2000, p. 14–18)

Change is in the air. More transparency is needed to create cross-border mergers and acquisitions and to fund expansion, as well as growing pressure from employees and smaller stakeholders for reforming ownership and governance principles. Inevitably this is a slow process, and it goes a long way to explaining a number of phenomena that relate to the focus of this book, for example:

- The lack of shareholder diversity and hence the lack of pressure from shareholders to address diversity issues.
- Weighty disincentives to entrepreneurship and the creation and expansion of new businesses on the part of younger people, women in particular, and the diverse population.
- Hierarchical structures favoring seniority and disempowering younger employees.
- Slowness of adaptation to diverse customers and markets.

Mergers, Acquisitions, Diversification, and Diversity

It is far beyond the scope of this chapter and this book to document the full cultural impact of investment, mergers, and acquisitions. Despite every evidence to the contrary, when M&As occur there is usually the tendency to ignore or underplay cultural factors or assume that they will take care of themselves in time. From an intercultural perspective, all too many of these M&As play themselves out like romantic love affairs. The passion and haste to be together, or to possess the other, blinds the parties to their differences. They are rife with expectations about the future that they do not share with each other. The marriage is celebrated and the honeymoon is short. Everyday reality sets in. The masks are dropped and differences of behavior, attitude, and personality take their toll. Organizational and professional cultures clash, to say nothing of ethnic, linguistic, and regional values and preferences. Someone may recognize the need for neglected intercultural services. But often this "marriage counselor" faces fortified resentments, intractable demands, broken trust, and levels of stress that are almost impossible to penetrate because the demand for the organization to become productive leaves little time for reflection on what is not working. Divorce becomes inevitable, though in most cases it is not a separation of the organizations that occurs, but dismissal by those in power of the talent that, as they see it, is incapable of integrating into a workable whole.

In those M&As where culture is actually seen as an element in a potential corporate investment or relationship, it is rarely viewed from the perspective of the value it can add but as cautionary grounds for avoiding engagement, as the *Economist* recently illustrated:

> "British firms are run by accountants, German firms by engineers, and Italian firms by designers. We don't always share the same vision," says one European manager. Giovanni Agnelli, Fiat's chairman, put the point more bluntly when he explained why the Italian carmaker recently formed an alliance with America's General Motors. He said he simply trusted the Americans more than the Germans. ("Mariage à la mode," 2000, p. 12)

The years 1999 and 2000 saw record numbers of M&As. European deals doubled their cross-border deals, tripled their stakes in other European firms, and invested heavily abroad, in the United States and elsewhere. Many of these mergers cross national borders and enter related or even new sectors of activity as technologies where TV, the Internet, and telecommunications interconnect and merge with each other. This means not only managing the national and linguistic cultures of the people involved but the cultures of diverse sectors as well.

Cultural compromises are not easy to make, as DaimlerChrysler and others have discovered to their ruin. When one reads reports such as the following, it is still legitimate to wonder, when all the political and symbolic compromises have been carried out, what is there or who is there to extend cultural adjustments and competence into the everyday activities of these organizations and their people?

> The problems of straddling borders are exemplified by Aventis, a life-sciences group formed last December by France's Rhône-Poulenc and Germany's Hoechst—the first merger as equals of two large companies from Europe's core economies. Because the deal was politically sensitive, top jobs as well as research and production sites had to be carved up evenly between France and Germany. The merged company has moved to Strasbourg, in France but nestling against the German border. It has a German-style two-tier board structure, but without the union representation on the supervisory board it would have had in Germany. ("Mariage à la mode," 2000, p. 10–14)

Different Diversity Strategies and the Search for Common Ground

In sum, Europeans need to and are developing different strategies for their diversity and different forms of cultural competence that are based on their own populations, social structures, historical boundaries, and value systems. This is not to say that Europe and North America do not have much to learn from each other in the development of cultural competence and that Europeans should not borrow approaches and ideas. It does mean that models and practices cannot be indiscriminately imported and exported, as many North American corporations have discovered when trying to take their diversity programs to European affiliates and when European organizations have attempted to manage North American employees. Not too long ago I had the occasion to help a European affiliate of a U.S. company address its diversity issues from scratch. When I did focus-group interviews with European employees from six different nations who worked there, and asked them about cultural differences that cause conflict, their unanimous response was "U.S. management style."

Interculturalist Barbara Pirie provides additional cultural insight into this "transfer of technology":

> Given that part of the U.S. culture is "free-market capitalism" (a.k.a. globalization), it is only logical that U.S.A.-based diversity professionals would look to "international markets" for their business growth in parallel with the U.S.A.-based corporations. As with any other product, how the market in each target area responds will determine whether they can expand into it—or have to adjust—or retrench back to the United States. (Pirie, 2001)

Americans fail to recognize that they also see diversity as a product—in fact, a big business—and one that U.S. practitioners are not loath to commercialize and export. This unconscious American cultural imperative is quite apparent to Europeans.

The Changing Social Context of Business

In the heating up of the European economy in the last years of the 1990s, shifts began to occur in the socioeconomic cultures of E.U. countries and the business models they produce. As the *Economist* reports,

> In large parts of continental Europe, especially the north, companies have been used to a softer, more "caring" business model than their adversarial American and British cousins. This emphasizes continuity, consensus, and social justice, and is framed by tough job-protection laws. Although many criticize this model as a drag on business, it is not without its defenders. Many European managers, and even a few in America, see the fuzzier European way as a more acceptable alternative to the financial and social brutality

(or flexibility, depending on your particular perspective) of corporate America, arguing that it provides better training for workers and better long-term prospects for the firms. American-style restructuring, they say, can cause a loss of morale that may damage long-term profitability. ("Lean, mean European," 2000, p. 3–9)

These shifts all impact on how diversity initiatives will be seen and used in European businesses and what expenditure of time, money, and personnel will be made to carry them out. The *Economist* report goes on to delineate more of the cultural effects of these economic shifts on the traditional strengths of the business communities in each country:

Europe is no homogeneous lump. Just as different countries occupy different industrial niches—Italy its sprawling financial-industrial groups and clusters of family firms, Germany its engineering companies, Scandinavia its high-tech multinationals—so their versions of the social-market vary. Like Britain, the Netherlands has a large stock market dominated by pension funds; unlike Britain, it shares the principles of its corporate law with France and its two-tier board system with Germany. Unlike France, Germany has a tradition for collective leadership, hence the prevalence of "speakers of the board" rather than chairmen. Unlike their German peers, Spanish unions have no representation on boards. The maturing of financial markets following the introduction of the euro is also giving Europe's companies a more Anglo-Saxon hue. Across the continent, an equity culture is developing. In Germany, the Neuer Markt, a new high-tech stock market, has aroused interest among ordinary savers; the number of shareholders recently passed the number of trade-union members for the first time. Companies have had to seek investors elsewhere, often among Britain's and America's liquid mutual and pension funds, which has meant adopting Anglo-Saxon accounting and disclosure norms. ("Lean, Mean European," 2000)

How Shall Europe Measure Its Diversity Initiatives?

Much effort has gone into the challenge of defining and quantifying the bottom line benefits of diversity initiatives and education in corporate and public life in North America and elsewhere. "Value-added," like "customer satisfaction," is subjective in its definition, but once defined can usually be turned into some kind of measurement, such as retention or turnover of personnel or sales in a particular market segment. Useful attitudes, competencies, individual behaviors, and organizational best practices can be distinguished and fostered.

Assessing benefit continues to be a useful exercise in that it often points up the costs of not attending to these matters. As in many educational and social initiatives, though, it may prove impossible to draw a clear connection between each specific activity and a precise number on the annual balance sheet. Diversity is not a manufacturing process. In the matter of diversity, it is very important what people feel, experience, want, resist, walk away from, or try to change. It must not only be profitable but also intuitive, personal, and consisting of matters to be negotiated between people if it is to be a full success.

Moreover, as the European Union has been traditionally less addicted to short-term bottom line definitions of benefit and more willing than North America to make coherent social policy a part of corporate responsibility and mission, there is perhaps more room for good business and good corporate citizenship to develop, and to share with each other both a clear definition of diversity and creative ways to manage it. It is one of the aims of this book to stimulate such sharing.

The obvious utility of managing diversity begins to appear in the day-to-day operations of organizations that are becoming globally competent. The organization that learns how to incorporate and manage diversity and benefit from the value that it adds will become:

- less susceptible to disintegration from within,
- better equipped to meet challenges from without, and
- more fully adapted to cooperate, survive, and succeed in a global environment.

This diversity is no longer limited to the differing backgrounds of managers and employees of an organization, but extends itself to the organization's "business context." This includes its suppliers, partners, competitive alliances, customers, and the social structures in place wherever it does what it does, whether in analog or virtual space.

The ABCDs of Managing Diversity for Adding Value

Several years ago I led a team of international management consultants in attempting to develop a high-level model for managing diversity well both domestically and across international borders (Simons et al., 1996). Despite rapid changes in the nature of work and the economy, the four areas of challenge that they identified still provide an

Exhibit 1.4

The ABCDs of Diversity

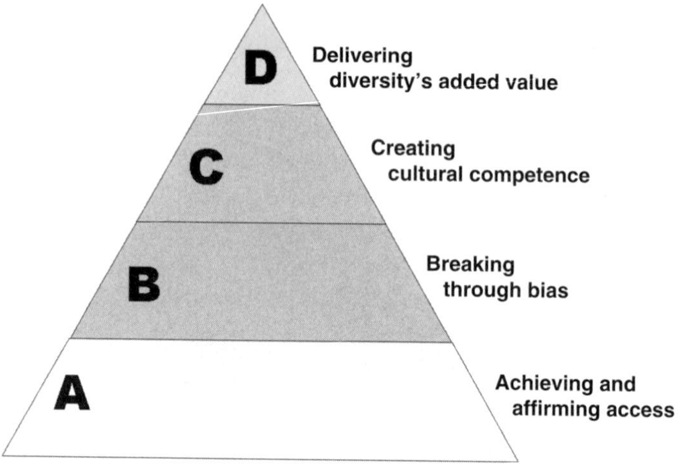

- **D** Delivering diversity's added value
- **C** Creating cultural competence
- **B** Breaking through bias
- **A** Achieving and affirming access

excellent framework for understanding what it means to manage diversity in the global and increasingly wired economy. These four areas are labeled mnemonically as A, B, C, and D in Exhibit 1.4.

The following table provides a fuller description of each of these four challenges. These four challenges are distinct from each other because each requires a different set of methods and activities for it to be met successfully. The technologies of one level cannot do the tasks of the other levels. The matrix lists some of the specific methods needed to meet the goals of each level, as well as some of the outcomes that can be expected as progress is made. Individual and "grassroots" efforts can be powerful in raising awareness, highlighting critical issues, and in carrying out all of the stages below. It has been almost universally reported, however, that diversity initiatives are most likely to succeed when leadership makes them an essential part of the company's mission and culture. Leaders must say, however they express it, that "valuing diversity is the way we do business around here," and then embody their words in a campaign that shows both problems and solutions and explores concrete steps to move from one to another. Corporate electronic communications and Intranets are proving to be more and more powerful tools for both doing and supporting this work.

Although initiatives on levels A, B, C, and D can contribute to and support the work done on other levels, there is little possibility and

CHALLENGE	DESCRIPTION	METHODOLOGY	OUTCOMES AND BENCHMARKS
A Assuring and Affirming Access	Uses society's legal system, institutions and resources, and the organization's mission, policies, and procedures to assure that all members of the group contribute to and participate fully and fairly in the common good, e.g., protection, safety, economic and job opportunity, life-work balance, etc. Restructures groups and organizations to create and preserve fairness of access. Ensures that justice and fairness are not only real and available but are seen as such by all stakeholders.	Investigate and learn to use economic, legislative, cultural, and institutional processes; political action, e.g., through campaigning, lobbying, and social initiatives. Use OD strategies to create or modify structures needed to achieve justice and fairness. Review of policies, e.g., hiring, firing, promotion, and pay equity for class and other disparities. Create public relations efforts to help all stakeholders understand these efforts and to raise the general expectations of fair access. These methodologies lead to fair structures and systems.	Fair laws, policies, and procedures, e.g., recruiting, hiring, promotion, mentoring, benefits, etc., that increase and support diversity, show up in reduced turnover, and identification and resolution of harassment and other disempowering working conditions. People create or participate in interest, support, and affinity groups or task forces as needed formally or informally. The organization supports or constructively responds to these groups. The organization is capable of mainstreaming and is seen from within and without as equitable, "a good place to work," a good group to do business with, and a socially responsible corporate citizen.
B Breaking Bias Barriers	Helps individuals and, through them, groups to recognize and deal with their personal prejudice mechanisms so that these do not lead to biased or prejudicial behavior against or toward other individuals or groups. Recognizes and deals with historical animosities between peoples and groups. Encourages social contacts and transactions among differing groups.	Cultural, psychological, and even spiritual interventions that change inappropriate stereotypes, values, and beliefs and the internal mechanisms that perpetuate them. Training seminars, video documentaries, simulation games, peer counseling skills, promoting intercultural contact, etc. These methodologies produce self-aware, other-aware, and tolerant individuals.	Members of the organization are and are perceived by their fellows as fair, sensitive, and unbiased. Reduced cost from polarization in and between groups, less waste from interpersonal and intergroup conflict and fear or avoidance of others. Increased understanding of each other's ethnic, racial, gender, professional, and other cultural issues, and more cooperation for resolving them. Fewer incidents of mobbing harassment. A safer, more comfortable and productive workplace.

(continues)

CHALLENGE	DESCRIPTION	METHODOLOGY	OUTCOMES AND BENCHMARKS
C Cultural Competence	Gain a multicultural and transcultural view of the world. Become aware of one's own culture and cultural "blind spots," and hence of the limitations one brings to interactions with others. Learn specific information about other cultures' beliefs, values, behaviors, and preferences, and learn how to put this information into practice to function successfully in other cultures or with persons from them.	Cross- and transcultural living, learning, and skill development, and global management skills, applied to communicating, negotiating, teamwork, and etiquette through training. Specific tools may involve culture-specific videos, workbooks, learning games, online programs and work enhancements, etc. These methodologies produce culturally knowledgeable and effective individuals and groups.	Ability to recognize, understand, manage, and work effectively with differences in values, beliefs, behaviors, communication styles, etc. Cultural skill in dealing with customers, with marketing and selling, and with advertising and promotion. Fewer false starts, mistakes, etc. Individuals (and hence the organization) become locally and globally competent and effective.
D Delivering Diversity's Added Value	Learn how to habitually and creatively look at differences as social or organizational strengths, using and managing them as resources that contribute to the survival and success of the group or organization. Learn how to leverage this competence in the workplace and the marketplace or to achieve the objectives of the organization.	Assessment tools, benchmarking, best practices, appreciative inquiry, and other whole-system and open-space technologies. Technologies for creative visioning, thinking, and marketing. These methodologies enable diverse resources to become known and used well in the core business and in one's network of vendors and customers.	The diverse range of the skills, perceptions, ideas, etc., in the organization's system and environment are generated and profitably employed. Diversity is part of the organization's competitive edge. Quality products and services succeed in its diverse environments and markets because of their attention to diversity. The organization is seen from within as a fine place to exercise one's talents and from without as excellent to do business with.

therefore little point in attempting to meet the higher-level needs if the lower-level needs on which they are based are not being addressed. Much as in Maslow's hierarchy of the stages of human ethical development, there is little substance to advanced behaviors if they are not grounded in a successful passage from the earlier stages to the later ones. In the case of diversity, people need to see themselves making satisfactory progress at these levels, as managing diversity is not a one-time event but an ongoing process.

Without losing sight of the necessity of building "a solid pyramid" for the diversity edifice, it is also helpful to view the dynamics of the challenges from another perspective in order to decide which efforts from diversity management will add most value. One can also view the first three levels as overlapping to produce the environment and readiness for businesses critical task of delivering diversity's added value (Exhibit 1.5). The letters A, B, C, and D represent the same challenges as before: Achieving and Affirming Access; Breaking Bias Barriers; Creating Cultural Competence; and Delivering Diversity's added value. Once again A, B, and C each support and contribute to the fullness of each other; and when these three challenges are being met, D becomes possible.

Besides providing an overall picture of what managing diversity is all about, the model in Exhibit 1.5 can be used on a micro level as an analytic tool to assist organizations to prioritize their diversity efforts.

Exhibit 1.5

How the Challenges Interact to Deliver Diversity's Value-Added

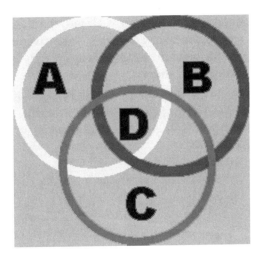

Although all parts of an organization may not be at the same level, it is ineffective to invest resources in a division or department where more basic groundwork does not yet exist, or where basic diversity challenges are not being identified or managed. In some situations, for example, A may be well handled, but C is the primary challenge to be addressed if D (value-added) is to be realized.

Localizing a Global Diversity Effort

To overcome their own ethnocentrism, sponsors of diversity efforts in multinational organizations and those they are working with in the new context must ask and answer certain critical questions about each challenge:

- How do the various groups or cultures see the diversity effort if it has originated in the parent country of the organization? What obstacles or challenges does this create? Using this model can diffuse concerns that headquarters are being "imperialistic" in promoting diversity initiatives and encourage on-target discussion of the real issues as seen by the diverse people represented in the organization.

- How are these challenges perceived and prioritized locally in comparison with how they are seen in the parent or headquarters culture; in other words, what must each wheel contain to be on target for local conditions?

- Which challenges are already addressed or given emphasis in the group culture? Which are not? For example, a number of quality of life issues that are labeled and tackled as diversity objectives in the United States and Canada are already handled as a matter of course in certain European countries. Initiatives about family life and work balance tend to be separate initiatives in Europe and not a primary focus of diversity.

- Which challenges are easiest or most difficult to do? Why? The model can be used to chart these. What does the local group need to do, or what resources do they need to meet the challenges that are difficult for them?

- What values, attitudes, and best practices already exist locally in each "wheel" that can be utilized to deliver diversity as value-added? This validates local efforts, rather than imposing outside approaches.

- How can the diversity effort become a locally owned initiative? How will its sponsors contribute to but not dominate these efforts?
- How are the organization's diverse cultures, groups, teams, and others stronger or weaker in meeting these challenges?
- Using the parent or headquarters' experiences not as norms but as examples, what do these suggest about possible cultural blind spots of initiatives in the new environment?

A Richer Definition of Culture

The question "What is culture?" can be answered in many ways, from the standard organizational nostrum, "Culture is the way we do things around here," to the listing of the variety of forms of creative expression such as music, dance, cuisine, and the like. Europeans, when speaking of culture and diversity, tend to see these two definitions as more intimately linked than do North Americans, and frequently Europeans will perceive North American discussions of cultural diversity as being culturally empty and as a result even culturally destructive. Europeans see what a culture makes and does as the vehicle of culture in the sense of attitudes and behaviors, and as a key to understanding, accepting, and enriching each other. This connection can be seen very clearly in the Culture 2000 program of the European Commission. This five-year program (2000–2004) aims to help build up a common cultural space for the peoples of Europe, characterized both by a common heritage and by cultural and artistic diversity. It encourages transnational cooperation between artists, cultural players, and cultural institutions in the Member States, to encourage:

- dialogue and mutual knowledge of culture and history;
- transnational dissemination of culture and the movement of artists, creators, and other cultural operators, with a strong emphasis on young and socially disadvantaged people;
- the highlighting of creativity and the development of new forms of cultural expression;
- highlighting, at the European level, the common cultural heritage of European significance;
- taking into account the role of culture in socioeconomic development;

- the fostering of intercultural dialogue and the explicit recognition of culture as an economic factor and as a factor in social integration and citizenship. ("Culture 2000 Programme," 2000)

Onward to the Challenges of EuroDiversity

With this background in place, and some caveats about the practice of diversity itself, we can now go further in seeing the challenges of diversity as Europeans themselves see them and are reacting to them. Subsequent chapters will help us to see through European eyes what has been done, what needs to be done, and some of the ways in which we may effectively go about doing it.

The Legacy of the Past: How National and Regional Differences Continue to Effect Trade, Cooperation, Politics, and Relationships

Elena A. A. Garcea

Uncovering Bias in Attitudes and Behavior

Subtle Historical Bias

At the start of the new millennium, it is possible to identify a number of diversity challenges to Western Europe that will continue to affect society and require action on the part of both public and private sectors (Simons, 2000). Often these cultural issues lie beneath ongoing E.U. issues. For example, many Europeans agree that the Anglo-French fight over British beef was an example of a situation where more smoke than light was generated. The more recent mad cow disaster started as a local U.K. problem and became a global European issue with ongoing cultural undertones.

There are more strictly bilateral fights, such as the Italian-French fight over wine, or the Italian-Austrian fight over connecting routes across the Alps. The question regarding the ingredients of chocolate (only cocoa versus the inclusion of vegetable fats) is another case; it split Europeans into two groups, along the lines of their economic arrangements with third countries (Africa and the United States). These culturally rooted issues have enormous business and political implications involving the selection of the countries for raw material procurement, production lines, marketing, and distribution.

Economic interests can also be hidden behind national issues. The German laws on purity of beer, or those on cocoa's content in chocolate defended by Belgium and Italy, are other examples of national protectionism. They were originally based on economic interests, but became political and cultural issues. As a consequence, each country's advertising and marketing reflect both the different economic and cultural interests.

Current economic conflicts and national adversities tend to revive the historical biases Europeans hold against each other. If it seems impossible to count the number of cultures living in the United States, it is even more complicated to number European cultures. In the United States, cultures are countless because they are mixed; in Europe, cultures are innumerable because they are overly separated. More than 100,000 local and regional authorities have representatives in the European Union.

Linguistic and Unconscious Bias

Many European biases are rooted in over a thousand years of history whose highlights are largely wars fought amongst Europe's very diverse peoples. Today, for the first time in history, the Single European Space has been free of war for over half a century. Nevertheless, European peoples remain very diverse, and even more focused on grassroots than ever.

Historical conflicts are often reflected in proverbs, idiomatic expressions, and words found in everyday speech and local dialects. For instance, in northern Italy there are words that refer to the Germans as barbarians, and in southern Italy the Turks are identified with evil. There, for example, the local exclamation, "Oh, mother, the Turks!" is used to indicate an impending catastrophe. The underlying assumptions of such ways of speaking are rarely brought into the open, and it would not be socially acceptable to take them seriously today. However, they inevitably play a role in shaping people's unconscious attitudes and expectations. Such local expressions show up in the workplace as well. They may sound unusual, unexpected, or even highly inappropriate to those accustomed to the strict controls of language and humor common in the U.S. workplace.

The Single Market opened European companies to cross-border competition. Now they are required to address cultural diversity and take into account historical biases in managing diverse clients through sophisticated marketing techniques like database marketing. Likewise, politicians have to compete for the support of their local and national grassroots voters and demonstrate how marketing to this diversity may pay off.

Some people believe that the integration of new countries into the European Union, at the rate that some politicians have planned, may reduce or delay the possibilities of a macro socioeconomic policy convergence. They also believe that the role of politicians in Europe will have to be redefined in order to create structures that permit further development at the European level. In this process, the cultural difference between styles of government is likely to become a serious issue. Even before the European Union embraces the Slavic cultures and other cultures of Central and Eastern Europe, the transparent approach to governing, business decision-making, and political influence practiced by the Nordic countries already differs from and is sometimes in conflict with the "behind the scenes" maneuvering common in Mediterranean lands. New and unfamiliar biases are likely to show up after the enlargement planned for 2004 takes place.

Other observers reckon that historical biases can be overcome by means of education and changes in attitude. Finland, for example, had a much stronger bias against Russians until a generation ago. The younger generation generally does not have strong anti-Russian sentiments. Russian-Finnish relations have changed considerably at a political, diplomatic, and economic level. In Finland, though, a language controversy between the Finnish majority and the Swedish minority continues unabated, an inheritance of over 500 years of Swedish dominance.

Language issues affect other cultural entities as well. French and Flemish speakers in Belgium as well as Dutch and Flemish speakers have tensions that go back to historical and religious factors. Language issues are frequently ways of expressing—unconsciously, but openly—historical and cultural prejudices.

Most European companies are good at labeling products and providing instructions for their use in the various languages of their markets and regions, but newcomers to this market must pay attention to this issue. This often means dealing with not one but as many as three or more foreign languages. In addition, in most areas of Europe there is a considerable number of people of non-European origin, working in English as an international language, who are challenged daily by the lack of English instructions and labeling on products that they buy that were not created for the U.K. market.

Increasingly, Europeans who belong to historically conflicting cultures are working successfully on multinational teams to reach clearly defined and committed goals, with the result that their historical differences fall into the background. Mixing people does not improve relations per se, but well-managed cooperative efforts often do. In more international companies, humor may just be humor and not the sign of deeply held prejudice. Focusing on business and paying less attention to historical or political matters tends to dominate the culture of these companies and favors cultural integration over time. However, in stressful circumstances, unconscious biases easily resurface and may play a critical role.

Personal initiatives can make a difference as well. For example, when a Spanish employee who had recently been transferred to Germany was having trouble finding someone to let him a flat, his boss simply decided to go with him on the search for living space. By doing this she both enhanced his credibility and modeled open-minded behavior for the hesitant landlords.

The Unification of Germany

Europe's severest historical biases go back to World War II. In some international companies there seems to be a strong bias against Germans, possibly even more than against women. Or, at least, this is what Germans often report. One German manager said, "Some of our English managers seem to imagine us Germans marching around in jack boots, saying '*Heil Hitler!*'" Even Austrians and German-speaking Swiss can be biased against Germans.

On the other hand, Germans of the younger generations are often reluctant to talk about the war. Before the collapse of the wall, they knew only from their parents' accounts that parts of their families were on the other side of the wall. Some reacted with curiosity and made trips to what they considered the "wild East," while others simply ignored the fact that there was a wall in the middle of their families and their lands.

An Englishman once explained differing attitudes between English and Germans in that Germany has historically been surrounded by threatening states, whereas the United Kingdom is surrounded by water. In addition, Germany's center of gravity has been swinging back and forth from west to east every hundred years or so. The swing is going eastward at the moment. This makes Germans stiff competitors in Central Europe and in many of the potential new entry states to the European Union. Non-German competitors for business in this region may find that success depends on their ability to transact business in German as well as or in preference to English.

The recent unification of Germany brought to light real diversity as well as cultural biases that had long existed but had remained hidden for two generations because of the wall. When the wall collapsed, these differences and biases were once again in evidence. The unification that occurred on October 3, 1990 might be looked on as one of the first mergers in the new E.U. era. It was not companies but people who did the merging. Some argue that it was a hostile takeover, a new *Anschluss*, reminiscent of annexation of Austria by Germany in 1938 instead of a merger, as often happens in the business world. Sixteen million East Germans were united, or rather assimilated into, a population of 62 million West Germans. European, national, and local institutions as well as NGOs, private organizations, and enterprises have since been making enormous efforts to reduce economic, social, and cultural discrepancies, encourage mobility, and promote cross-cultural exchanges. The Arbeitsstelle Friedensforschung Bonn (AFB) or Peace Research Information Unit Bonn (PRIUB), an independent body mostly financed by the federal government, lists over a hundred organizations and individuals active in the field of peace research and conflict resolution in Germany. This is the largest number of peace organizations in a single country in the whole of Europe.

This expensive undertaking for both European and German citizens is destined to continue for quite some time. At the end of 2000, economic growth in the eastern part of Germany was stuck at 1.2 to 2% and unemployment was over 17%. Average net wages were 15% lower than in western Germany, productivity was 35% lower, and the GDP was less than two-thirds of that in the west; and since 1997, the GDP increased at an even slower pace than in the west. It has been calculated that 200 to 280 billion euros in public money is still needed to create an infrastructure equal to that in the west. East Germany was erased from the maps of Europe, and East Germany has been westernized more quickly and more radically than any other nation in the history of the West.

West German models entirely replaced the East German system that had been in power since 1948, a system that had produced the habits, norms, rules, traditions, and attitudes that made up East German culture. East Germany was torn down to be rebuilt, erased from the geography and the ethnography of Europe. The political structures, educational system, laws, health and welfare services, police, currency, industrial fabric, institutions, and managerial and political elites changed. Nothing was saved. Even the *Economist* declared, "Unification was not the fruit of mature reflection by political leaders" ("German Unification: Togetherness: A Balance Sheet," 2000, p. 27). Easterners still feel that they are treated like second-class citizens. As their salaries are lower, they try to move to the west to obtain better wages for the same jobs. At the same time, westerners move to the east to take on top jobs. Westerners control the management of business, banking, public administration, universities, law, and the media.

French social philosopher Alain Finkielkraut is one of the few voices that have been raised about this disdain for the former Soviet Bloc nations by their western counterparts. In his book *Ingratitude: Conversation sur notre temps* (1999), Finkielkraut speaks accusingly about western Europeans ingratitude and forgetfulness about their own history. Central Europe played a critical role in the development of European culture and economic and political life, and it has a potential to continue to do so. Yet today most westerners tend to look on Eastern Europe with the same eyes that they use to discount "underdeveloped" countries in other parts of the world.

In the new Germany, behaviors differ and remain divisive. Easterners perceive westerners' self-assurance, assertiveness, and the ability to sell themselves as arrogance. Easterners' more direct, unsophisticated attitudes can be taken as naïveté and lack of political strategy. Foreigners perceive West Germans as more reliable, harder working, and more open to novelty ("German Unification: Togetherness: A balance sheet"). We must ask if such positive stereotypes, like negative ones, do not get in the way of seeing and profiting from the human resources we actually have at hand.

Cultural factors easily remain transparent when economies are doing well, but they tend to come to the forefront when crises occur. Witness the furor in recent years as practices of animal husbandry became sources of political, economic, and cultural friction between European nationalities. We will examine two examples of this in some detail.

The Cultural Undertow of Crisis Management

Mad Cows and Angry People

The first cases of the latest burst of BSE (Bovine Spongiform Encephalopathy) appeared in 1986 in Britain. They were brought to public attention in the British Parliament 10 years later with the appearance of a new variant called VCJD (Variant Creutzfeldt-Jakob disease). The British Ministry of Agriculture, Fisheries, and Food (MAFF) admitted that it did not act when it found out that sheep were fed BSE contaminated cattle bits until 1988, when the practice was at last banned ("The BSE Inquiry: Wait for It," 2000). This tragedy cost Britain over 27 million pounds (39.4 million U.S. dollars) and more than 85 human lives.

A report of a British public enquiry was released on October 26, 2000. It denounced the shortcomings of the MAAF, its inertia in dealing with scientific advice, and its lack of rigor in imposing regulations ("Britain: Of Secrecy and Madness," 2000). The government apparently did not want to scare its citizens and penalize its farmers. However, the resultant paranoia and costs turned out to be higher in the end than they would have been had they been addressed from the beginning. In the United Kingdom farmers became so desperate that some were driven to suicide. But the matter did not end there. It served to resurrect national and cultural animosities toward Britain and, conversely, in Britain toward other E.U. members.

BSE in the United Kingdom decreased rapidly between 1993 and 1995, from over 350,000 to around 178,000 cases, with over 1,000 in the year 2000. However, as cases went down in the United Kingdom, they went up in other European countries, particularly France, Ireland, Portugal, and Switzerland.

Figures in these countries were much lower than in Britain, not exceeding 200 cases in each country. France was one of the first countries where the virus spread. During the first four months of 2001, 42 new cases of mad cow and 3 cases of VCJD were declared in France. Spain had their first cases at the end of 2000. In Italy, the first case appeared at the beginning of 2001. In Germany, two members of the government resigned because of BSE, even if there were only 14 cases at the beginning of 2001. Repeatedly, Britain was blamed.

There is more animosity toward the French in rural Britain, where farmers are struggling. In the metropolitan areas, to the contrary, cultural diversity is greater and people feel more open to the influences of

Europe. Differences between the French and British are eroding, but there still can be a negative feeling amongst the British that the French are citizens and the British are sometimes considered subjects or less sophisticated citizens.

Italians first perceived the Anglo-French fight over beef as an Anglo-European fight, where the British were the "enemies" of the Europeans. Then, when they found cases of mad cow in their country, Italian farmers acted as victims of a universal plague. The first case was signaled in northern Italy at the beginning of 2001, and 190 heads of cattle were killed until March 2001, even though only 5 clear cases were detected.

The results are that the prices of beef on average fell by 27% in the European Union between the end of 2000 and the beginning of 2001. The highest devaluation of beef occurred in Germany, where it collapsed by almost 40%, in spite of only 25 cases of BSE in that country. Alarming losses also occurred in the Netherlands, where prices went down by 35%.

The European Parliament tried to find a common European solution to the BSE case and proposed that all cattle more than 30 months old had to be tested for infection. As a consequence, veterinary laboratories were overwhelmed with requests of tests that had to be delivered in a very short time. Slaughterhouses and incinerators were also overburdened by massive quantities of infected and healthy animals. Even if one animal was found with the infection, the entire herd had to be eliminated. France favored massive slaughtering; Germany and the Netherlands opposed it, partly for ethical reasons.

Following the recommendations of the European Union, some countries are spending enormous amounts of money to reimburse their farmers. The Italian Ministry of Health gave cattle breeders over 15,000 euros per head of cattle that had to be killed to indemnify their losses. Other countries remained more hesitant. Austria, Finland, Sweden, Denmark, and the Netherlands refused to compensate farmers who killed cattle over 30 months old. Furthermore, some countries took unilateral actions against individual states. Austria, Germany, and Italy banned French meat and France banned British meat.

Germany reacted to the panic over infected meat by encouraging alternative models of farming, which were already partially practiced in several European countries even before the outburst of mad cow and foot and mouth diseases. The government supported environment-friendly farming and rural development by investing $5 billion in converting intensively into organic farming.

As a matter of fact, some European politicians have used the mad cow issue as a negotiating tool with their local voters and supporters.

This shows that Europe is still not completely ready for cultural and political integration.

Foot and Mouth Disease

Nationalist feelings and cultural differences were again highlighted by the outbreak of foot and mouth disease (FMD). FMD is a viral condition affecting cloven-hoofed young animals. It is rarely fatal to adult stock. Though several persons have been afflicted in Britain, FMD is usually not harmful to humans unless they incautiously handle infected animals with bare hands. The disease, known for at least 400 years both inside and outside Europe, reappeared at the start of 2001 in Britain. The United Kingdom counted 1,438 confirmed cases as of April 2001, a number far fewer than that of BSE (Ministry of Agriculture, Fisheries, and Food). The Netherlands reported 7 cases, France 2, and Ireland 1. The virus was spread in Europe by importing infected live animals from one country to another ("Foot-and-Mouth Disease: The Costs and the Cures," 2001, p. 81–83).

From a scientific point of view, the plague of foot and mouth disease (FMD) appears less serious than BSE, but unfortunately it broke out just when social hysteria over meat consumption had reached a peak. Therefore, it stoked the cultural fires that had already been lit around BSE. The foot and mouth disease, even more than BSE, raised the cultural questions related to perceptions and values around ecology, health, economy, and mobility among Europeans. Culture as always lurks in the background, and while it is rather easy to address the traditional issues of intercultural communication, expatriation, and marketing, it is at these moments of crisis that the cultural components are usually overlooked.

This time the British government took very drastic action. In three weeks 116,000 animals were killed and every farm was safeguarded within disinfected enclosures. To stroll in the English countryside, you had to walk through disinfected straw and meet angry farmers. Crossing borders in Europe became a new adventure. Some airports had wet disinfecting mats at strategic locations in the landing control areas. After disinfecting their shoes, passengers continued on with sticky soles, probably grateful that the cold European spring of 2001 meant that they were not wearing sandals! This raised cultural hackles about freedom and control, mobility and health.

FMD severely damaged the agricultural sector and, in turn, affected other sectors. Tourism was hit hard. Hotels and national parks had to close down. British Airways and Virgin Atlantic offered to reschedule trips that had been canceled ("Foot-and-Mouth Disease: The Costs and the Cures"). Horse races and rugby matches were canceled. Compensation offered by the British government went to farmers but not to other businesses indirectly affected. The United Kingdom itself had to regain its disease-free status before being allowed to export meat. In 2000, the British export of sheep products accounted for £250 million. In 2001, compensations to farmers for slaughtered live-stock exceeded £600 million, over twice the lost revenue for exports ("Time to Save the Sacrificial Lambs," 2001, p. 26). Meat continues to be a main staple food in most European diets. The paranoia over beef extended to lamb and pork, with a consequent fall of prices. The European Union lost 73% of third-country pork meat exports.

Some British farmers called for vaccination to control FMD; others favored slaughter, particularly as slaughtered animals were compensated, whereas vaccinating reduced market value. But it was not just an economic concern. Ethicists and animal rights proponents in the European Union differed widely on what and whose values should be respected. Despite Britain's strong animal rights sentiments, the U.K. government chose a slaughter policy as their only disease control. The slaughter policy spread from Britain to the rest of Europe. Soon, confusion, suspicion of others and their motives, and fear became more serious than the disease itself. Slaughtering probably seemed to be the safest guarantee for meat consumers.

Dealing with the Needs and Ambitions of Powerful Regional Cultures

The Deliberate Suppression of Diversity

Europe's historical attempts to suppress its identities, be they real or fictitious, in the effort to establish powerful nation states (whether led by Napoleon, Bismarck, Mussolini, or Stalin and his successors) has not been entirely able to stamp out regional and linguistic diversity. Regions of Europe continue to demand recognition, cultural protection, and, in some cases, independence. There is a specific Directorate General within the European Union (DG XVI)* with the following two websites: (1) www.cor.eu.int, where the Committee of the Regions offers a bridge between cities and regions and European citizens at

---

* The Regional Policy Directorate-General is the department in the European Commission responsible for European measures to assist the economic and social development of the less-favored regions of the European Union.

large; and (2) www.inforegio.org/dg16_en.htm, providing informat
on the activities of the European Regional Development Fund.

Scotland, Flanders, Bourgogne, Catalonia, and many other regions
insist more and more on recognition and improved treatment. Popular
sentiment about regions can affect how business is done. Sending
the "wrong" person to manage, sell, or train (e.g., a Neapolitan
in the heart of the Northern League (where education and economic
development is looking for independence from the poorer south
of Italy), whatever the person's competence, may turn out to be
counterproductive.

At worst, suppressing diversity has also left behind animosities, lust
for revenge, hatred, and distrust. These emotions are often latent in
popular memory, but are very much alive in extremist groups.
Diversity is, in fact, the norm of European history, and should not be
ignored, given the emphasis on history in all levels of European education. Europe's best days have been when diversity has been respected, managed, and enjoyed. As John Coleman points out,

> Europe's main periods of trouble and violent discord occurred
> when some state or nation tried to impose uniformity on that
> great diversity that runs through Greek and Roman culture, the
> Renaissance and even the Enlightenment. Europe's deep but inter-
> national culture cannot be expressed in a single concept but in a
> multiplicity of concepts which form a great social organism.
> (Coleman, 1999)

The phrase "managing diversity" may have been coined in North
America, but the truth for Europe is that managing diversity has not
been and is not just one solution to conflict, economic stability, and
sustainability. It is the only ethically acceptable solution. As many
businesses have already discovered, it is the only practical solution if
they wish to succeed within the Member States, across their boundaries, and beyond the European Union. Diversity management is a
characteristic behavior of world-class companies.

Integration versus Diversity

Europe is living in the crossfire of geopolitical integration on the one
hand and information integration on the other hand. As one European
said: "What do we turn to when we don't know what we'll become,
and so quickly change where we are coming from?"

Many Europeans feel that grassroots, nationalistic feelings will
grow. The more global and integrated Europe becomes, the stronger is

s peoples to hold on to their own history and culture. are usually at ease being both local and European in and behavior. Most accept being part of a European as their regional cultures and identities are respected. For egional culture and development deserve fostering. As new identities and loyalties are being forged at the European level, and as national powers are weakened, people find security in their "small homelands" or *petites patries*.

Weaker regional identities worry about being assimilated by stronger ones. For some people, regional diversity is simply a matter of enjoying one's own historical and cultural heritage, but for others it could result in extreme tension if not addressed at an international level. This makes diversity initiatives both necessary and fraught with peril. North American models of integration often seem like reckless assimilation to Europeans.

Regional cultures and cultural enclaves exist in every European country. The Council of European Municipalities and Regions (CEMR) represents more than 100,000 local and regional authorities in Europe. Some are larger and more powerful than others. Not only individual states recognize regional entities, but also the European Union supports the regions with a number of programs. At the European level, regions are highly respected and protected. They pose both an opportunity and a threat to the European Union and its people.

Some regional representatives see membership in the European Union as a way to autonomy or independence while avoiding the disadvantages of becoming a small country. The Scottish National Party (SNP) in Scotland is an example. This of course leads to fresh debates. For example, to whom do the oil revenues accrue to in the event of Scottish independence? Similar attitudes are strong in many other parts of Europe, the best known being Brittany in France, Wallonia in Belgium, and the Basque countries in Spain.

In the United Kingdom and Ireland

The United Kingdom is probably the European country with the longest tradition of coexisting cultural diversities. Even before it became a land of immigration, its peoples had different languages and cultures. This is probably why many Brits say they feel unencumbered by a sense of national identity and are suspicious of it.

Many also say they have mixed feelings about regionalization, pointing to cultural and ethnic diversity as one of Britain's strengths. England seems to be facing a major cultural identity crisis: not in thriving cities, like London, as much as in the countryside. Together, Scotland, Wales, and England are the largest British island. With Northern Ireland they form the United Kingdom, which is a kingdom, not a country. Both the English and other Europeans often use these terms in a very casual manner. When asked for their country of birth, they put England, Scotland, Britain, or United Kingdom. They enter the Olympics as the United Kingdom, but in other sporting events, they can be registered as separate countries. The Republic of Ireland has a completely separate football team from Northern Ireland, but the rugby union team is cross-border, representing the island of Ireland.

Every part of the military is under the British army, and it includes the Irish guards, who are mainly Northern Irish Protestants, with but a few Irish Catholics in the highest ranks. In the past, in the north of Ireland, there was a great antagonism between Welsh soldiers in the British army and the Republicans.

Wales is full of English people, and it struggles to establish its identity. At present, there is a strong new Welsh cultural movement based in Cardiff. Pop music, which is well known and appreciated in England, is sometimes in Welsh. A referendum on independence produced weak results and made it unlikely that the Welsh would seek to become an independent nation.

Scotland has long had its own legal and educational systems and seems more of a country in its own right. There are also many Italians in Scotland. Many of them are ex-Prisoners of War who married local women. Edoardo Paolozzi, for example, was Scotland's most famous modern artist. However, ethnic pride is strong in Scotland, even though the Scottish are less a real ethnic group than they are a cultural group. When first the Scottish financial industry opened to the outside market, many Scots feared losing their independence and anticipated a loss in corporate power and jobs in their region. In fact, when outsiders moved in and Scottish bankers started to look outward, Edinburgh became the sixth biggest fund-management center in Europe, just after London, Paris, Zurich, Amsterdam, and Frankfurt, and before Milan and Geneva ("Scottish Finance: Raising the Standard," 2000).

Ethnicity can be used by politicians to manipulate strongly felt differences that in fact have cultural origins, but are confused as ethnic or racial diversities. Wales has a large cultural identity problem, but it only narrowly voted for a National Assembly, as people did not feel they could solve cultural problems at a political level. In Northern Ireland, the problems start even with its name. Northern Ireland is the neutral term for the region. Republicans call it North Ireland;

Unionists call it Ulster, which is an ancient name for the Northwest of Ireland, including Donegal. The challenge includes what seems to be a rather patronizingly simplistic reference to the "lessening of the grip of Westminster on Ulster." However, many Brits would be happy to let go of Northern Ireland, as they do not feel part of it, it is expensive, and its problems are seemingly unsolvable.

Cultural and political conflicts that are regional can have profound consequences on business. Some U.K. companies, for example, have bought out Irish grocery stores and have faced a trading backlash from the media. As a consequence, local products are identified on the shelves and imported products receive inferior shelf space.

In Italy

Regional institutions have become very ambitious and very powerful in Italy. This did not develop simply because of weak national boundaries, but was also a reaction to a loss of authority and credibility in the central political system. The already existing strong regional cultures reacted by demanding more power and independence.

The Northern League is the Italian political party that proposes implementation of the federalist idea as a solution to the cultural and economic crisis. It sees the centralized government in Rome as "the big thief," even though there are Northern League ministers in the present Berlusconi government. Members wear a uniform (green shirts); claim hypothetical Celtic origins; celebrate formalized rituals and para-religious ceremonials, like meeting with flags at the outlet of the Po River to take an ampoule of water from the the river that brings water to the Paduan Plain. Raising common generic interests, like paying less taxes and greater independence from the central authority, have become powerful tools for the Northern League to develop a populist consensus.

Rather than a political entity, the Northern League can be described as a subculture based on individualism, xenophobia, and lack of historical, economic, and political perspectives. This movement, existing in the rich northern Italian regions, challenges the values of the European Union. Northeastern Italy is one of the most highly industrialized areas of Europe, but at the same time it suffers from one of the lowest levels of education in the industrialized West. Business in this area, and particularly advertising, is not affected by the low education level as long as it is at a local or regional level where local means of communication can be used. However, communication difficulties arise when the market extends beyond regional borders, where local language uses are unknown or even rejected.

In Spain

Regional issues vary from country to country and even cross national borders, not just because regional issues differ, but also because government policies are based on different cultural values and take different approaches to managing issues. Nation states discourage the formation of a federal "Europe of the regions," despite a continuing trend in this direction. In this respect, the Spanish have exercised a different kind of foresight, though Basque separatism in particular seems resistant to its efforts.

Five languages are spoken in the 17 Spanish autonomous regions of Spain. Catalan is spoken in Catalonia, Valencia, the Balearic Islands, Andorra, southern France, and in some Mediterranean islands. In many schools in these regions, lessons are taught in Catalan. In Galicia, they speak Gallego, a language that is very similar to Portuguese. Euskera is the national language in the Basque countries. Bable, a dialect, is spoken in the region of Santander, but as it has no literature and no formal grammar, it is not compulsory in schools.

Spanish is spoken in the rest of Spain, but it is called "Castellano" (Castilian) in order not to offend the nationalist sensitivities in other regions. The Castilian language is the bone of contention for movements of political nationalism and independence from the central government in Madrid and has social, economic, and political implications.

In Germany

With the opening of the borders within Germany, as we already mentioned, the identity of the people from the German Democratic Republic (GDR) was simply erased. Nevertheless, the new federal territories that were formerly a part of the GDR have strongly regionalized themselves. Moreover, while the western economic system first attracted East Germans, their previous social organization provided securities and protections that vanished before they could enjoy the benefits of the new system. As a consequence, some people reconsidered their opening to the west and defended their earlier local culture even more strongly.

Differences among "wessies" as the former West Germans are called and "ossies," those coming from the former GDR, are gradually disappearing, especially amongst youngsters. A traveler to Berlin who tries to recognize who is from the west and who is from the east by looks and outfits—an easy task 10 years ago—will probably fail today. However, there is a considerable language education gap. If you speak English to a German who attended a western school, he or she will often answer fluently, while too often someone who went to an eastern school may stare at you helplessly.

Political as well as social actions have been taken to eradicate gaps between East and West Germans. In the former GDR, the ex-communist Party of Democratic Socialism (PDS) has regained power for several reasons. Some easterners believe that this party takes the problems in former East Germany more seriously than other parties and can manage them. Others vote for it out of disappointment with other parties, or because they feel discriminated against after the unification, or because they want to support the reconstruction of a socialist society (Mehl, 1999).

As mentioned above, there are over a hundred organizations working with economic, social, and cultural diversity within Germany. In addition, there are corporate initiatives aimed at bridging regional differences. Sharing business customs and rituals is a neutral and interesting way to create contact between different cultures. Lucent Technologies, for example, promoted multicultural get-togethers to explore customs from about 10 different regions of Germany, under the motto of *Brauchtum zum Reichtum für alle!* ("Turning customs into riches for everybody!").

In the European Union

Though there are strongly differing opinions, some suggest that a federal Europe with a strong principle of subsidiarity would be a good way to manage regionalism. The challenge would be to create a twofold identity: a "Europe of the markets" and a "Europe of the peoples." The former would express unity, the latter diversity.

The European Union earmarks specific funds to support investment in infrastructure and training in less well-off regions (the European Union Structural Funds). It aims to provide concentrated help for business in regions that are lagging behind, to move them out of crisis and into growth, and to support the regions needing education, training, and employment (*Europe's Agenda 2000*, 1999). It is also a priority of the European Investment Bank to foster investment in under-developed regions. Its aims are to close the gap in living standards, create efficient communications and power transmission infrastructure networks, promote new economic activity, and protect the environment. However, the funds are allocated to the programs proposed by the Member States, not by the regions. Therefore, the individual states select the regions where they want European investments and, unfortunately, their selection may be influenced by the lobbying skills of the regional officers or politicians, rather than based on an objective analysis of the actual area needs. Thus the Nice summit, held in December 2000, decided that national authorities can have vetoes on E.U. decisions on particular matters like tax, social security policy, subsidies to poorer countries, and defense ("The Nice Summit: So That's All Agreed, Then," 2000).

Managing the In-Country Challenges of Diversity

Balancing Cultural Preservation, Public Order, and Economic Stability

The presence of native residents, expatriates, traditional enclaves, immigrants, asylum seekers, ex-colonials, and economic migrants in societies and workforces provide new diversity challenges that need management. Europeans have always taken for granted the fact that they have different cultures, languages, and so on, but now the economy and information technology are bringing together more people who have to interact in the workplace, in business, and in social life. Not all Europeans are fully aware of such economic and social changes yet. Even European companies who might be concerned about sending their employees overseas pay very little attention to the issues of expats living and working in their home offices and branches throughout Europe. This applies to both European citizens moving to other European countries and to non-European arrivals. Challenges do exist for both groups, even though the former experience softer but still very real culture shocks.

Different languages and cultures put immigrants at a disadvantage. At work, their different culture may affect or be seen to affect their skills and commitment. Many African immigrants to Europe find unfriendly and unhelpful officials, even when they come to work as highly skilled professionals.

How shall we establish an appropriate balance between the preservation of languages, values, and habits, and the necessary common principles, policies, and practices required for the success of the European Union? As one European remarked "I believe that in the end we shall not be able to preserve everything—we are not building the Museum of European Cultures." One part of the solution is certainly fostering local independence and subsidiarity as part of national policy.

Having well-integrated social and working communities is a desirable goal, but businesses tend to see immediate costs in terms of time and money for efforts at culture change, which would make them less competitive in the face of the pressures coming from abroad. European law was created for a Christian society, and though the practice of religion is rarely at issue, the bias remains. People with different religious beliefs or different lifestyles may not be protected and indeed may be threatened by the legal system. A Muslim man who is by Muslim law married to two wives may encounter difficulties in the recognition of his legal rights, to say nothing of heavy moralistic judgment.

Adjusting to New Roles for Women

In Chapter 9 we will take a more extensive look at equal opportunities for women and men in the European Union and examine in particular the case of E-quality initiative for workplace parity in Belgium. We need, however, to take a quick overview of changing roles and new challenges here.

The Economic Role

Postmodern European society is promoting skill competence, entrepreneurship, creativity, innovation, quality, and adaptability—elements that cannot be measured in terms of hours spent in an office. Therefore, women may often be better prepared than men to take on the changes imposed by the new working conditions, as we shall see in the following discussion. Conversely, men are beginning to realize that they need to think about how to adjust to new roles, as the traditional paradigm of "man as breadwinner" declines.

In the European Union more women than men complete their university studies, so that women are beginning to display higher levels of competence both in and beyond the educational system. In Britain, for example, boys now score significantly lower marks in school than girls, which will, in a few years, inevitably impact both university education and employment. This occurs despite the fact that hierarchical structures of both companies and academic administrations have historically failed to provide equal opportunities to women.

Despite the relatively higher obstacles to self-employment in Europe than in North America, many women set up their own companies and are driving the trend toward new ways of working (distance work, self-employment, etc.). Although these new working environments offer women more opportunities than before, they also benefit men. Location and time can be important issues when selecting or retaining human resources in companies. Thus, distributed workplaces and remote teams appeal to employers of both women and men.

Nonetheless, women are being integrated into the workforce increasingly but unevenly. Technical companies recruit relatively few women. Even those who have higher percentages of women than other companies in the same sector may be poor at retaining and promoting women. The culture and career paths of these companies are rarely favorable or attractive to women. Maternity leave is regarded as a nuisance by some managers, and paternity leave is often discouraged for men. Arriving at a senior management position usually requires a term of expatriation, often more difficult for a woman with a family or a working spouse than for a man in the same situation.

It is probably a fact that women's perspectives commonly differ from men's. Women prefer to harmonize their personal and professional life. A study of the French Employment Ministry statistics bureau, Direction de l'animation, de la recherche, des études et des statistiques (DARES) identified the evolution of several different models along which women's professional and familial roles are developing. Younger women see both employers and the European Union as responsible for pursuing initiatives in order to give them the opportunity to choose children, work, or a combination of both. Women expect that reliable childcare, which was common in the Eastern bloc before the fall of the Wall, should, instead of disappearing, be made broadly available throughout Europe.

The Social Role

Women today often have to face the fact that their economic role may conflict with their expected social role. Popular culture still often conceives their professional life as a side activity carried out in parallel with their primary engagement as wives and mothers.

In some countries such as Italy, for example, the percentage of women with management positions is particularly low because executive positions tend to be given to people in their 50s or even 60s. Very few women in that age bracket have the requisite professional background, as their generation experienced far more gender separation than occurs in today's workplace. Nevertheless, changes are occurring even in traditionally male-oriented countries. In Italy, occupations that were previously reserved for men, such as engineers, taxi drivers, and police officers, are becoming available to women. Women were introduced into the Italian army in the year 2000. However, the prevailing social model is still the so-called "3Ms": *Moglie, Manager, Madre*, or wife, manager, mother. Clearly no new model for women has replaced the older ones of wife and mother. It has simply incorporated a new role. Women continue to be expected to be wives and mothers. The novelty lies in their occasionally being allowed to be executives as well. This ambivalence is expressed in Germany with the "3Ks": these no longer mean the traditional *Kinder, Küche, und Kirche* (children, cooking, and church) but now mean *Kinder, Küche, und Karriere* (children, cooking, and career).

In reality, the need to harmonize professional and private life is not only a women's matter. Women, however, seem to have created some of the conditions for possible solutions. Equal opportunity does not need to be conceived of as sharing men's opportunities with women, but more broadly as creating new opportunities to which both women and men have equal access. This requires mechanisms that allow or even encourage women and men to have and raise a family and share housekeeping in harmony with working life. Men, too, are recognizing that it can be hard to change work and social patterns that require frequent traveling and excessive working hours. Lifestyle, as we will later see, is less and less a diversity issue, particularly in northern Europe, and more simply one of normal work expectations.

Particularly in countries where women do not have independent jobs, new opportunities offered to them can be seen as threatening men's employment opportunities. Italy offers no formal support to working women. It is up to them to adjust between their job and family duties. Therefore, new roles may look possible but remain unattainable. As caring for the family is considered an entirely female responsibility, business organizations often view a woman's career as one that is in conflict with her desires to have a family. On the other hand, men have to adjust to mixed working environments and change certain behaviors developed earlier in all-male environments.

In the United Kingdom and many other European countries, women choose to marry and have children after they have put a career track record in place that allows them to go back to work after their children are born. Women can occupy many positions throughout the organization, though they rarely become members of the board. Some companies are even operating a positive discrimination policy for women at director level to bring more women into those top positions.

Women without children in Britain seem to have experienced fewer major obstacles in the workplace, particularly in the last 20 to 30 years. The problems arise when addressing the role of mothers. The British system expects women to work, but it provides no state child-care for children until they are school age (5 years). Single mothers are chastised for appearing irresponsible and not looking after their children properly and at the same time they are forced to go out to work. Some English families have actually moved to France because the childcare infrastructure is better and the state recognizes that looking after children is work.

Scandinavians tend to be very pragmatic in addressing women's issues with a distinct absence of political hysteria or pseudopolitical correctness. A female lecturer in an international British university outlawed the use of the term "master copy." The Swedish students were vaguely amused, whereas their female U.K. colleagues lapped it up.

It is also important to look at the role of women, especially young, European-born women, within minority ethnic communities. They can often find themselves as minorities within a minority, particularly if their ethnic background offers them little social status. For instance, a British manager working in the Netherlands observed that young minority ethnic women in Britain seem to have a much higher profile in employment, higher status jobs, and higher levels of education than they would in the Netherlands. Such differences may be related to both differences between British and Dutch cultures, as well as to the cultures of South Asia (in Britain) versus Turkey, Surinam, and North Africa (in the Netherlands).

E.U. Regulations and Initiatives

The Treaty of Amsterdam created a solid legal basis for women's rights. By its terms, the European Union is committed to enforce equal treatment and pay, training and education, recruitment conditions and employment, new forms of work organization, health protection, fighting unemployment, parental leave, better access to positions of responsibility, and establishing more compatibility between working and home life. However, in practice there is much to be done to surmount the many differences in the treatment of men and women as workers.

Sometimes, compliance to European regulations can even erase social gains that had resulted from long-lasting negotiations and conflicts in some countries. In France, for example, the Parliament was asked to remove the prohibition against overnight work for women in order to "harmonize" their national legislation with the European one.

The strategy of gender mainstreaming is seen as a comprehensive recipe for creating an egalitarian future for both women and men. As the Provincial government of Lower Saxony put it simply, gender mainstreaming demands that "(re)organizing, improving, developing, and evaluating the decision-making process in establishing policy be done from the point of view of establishing equality between women and men in all areas" (cited in Rösgen, 2001).

Sexual Orientation—The Pink Euro

Gay and lesbian groups in Europe are becoming more outspoken in terms of recognition of their human rights, particularly in Northern European countries like Denmark, the Netherlands, and the United Kingdom, where at times they constitute a serious political bloc. This visibility has caused businesses to begin to recognize the importance of a "pink pound" or a "pink euro" to be gained by respectful and attractive marketing targeted to this segment of the population.

Discrimination based on sexual orientation is not yet illegal in several European countries. Even those countries that declared it illegal did so later than the United States, where several states, cities, and counties banned discrimination in the early 1990s (Zuckerman and Simons, 1994). Official legal protection from the European Union to European gay men, lesbians, bisexuals, and transsexuals only came in 1997. Article 13 of the Treaty of Amsterdam was the first legal act that stated that the European Union can establish provisions to fight discriminations based on sex, race or ethnic origin, religion or personal beliefs, handicaps, age, or sexual tendencies.

In March 2000, the European Parliament passed a resolution asking all countries in the Union to recognize the cohabitation of people of the same sex and to give them the same rights and duties as heterosexual couples. It made it the duty of each E.U. member to abolish discrimination in fiscal legislation, patrimonial estate, social rights, and access to the army. It also lamented that criminal codes in some countries contain discriminatory norms on the age of consent in homosexual relationships.

Ages of consent vary from country to country in the European Union. It extends from the earliest, which is 12 years old in Spain, to the latest, which is 18 for British males. In fact, some countries even practice gender discrimination. The age of consent comes two years earlier for British and Irish females than for males.

The northern European countries, that is, Sweden, Norway, Island, Denmark, and the Netherlands, are the only ones to have recognized registered homosexual unions for a number of years. France just approved a civil solidarity pact that includes gay couples. The debate on legal recognition of partnership is currently underway in Spain, Italy, and Portugal. Countries that delay the recognition of gay couples may incur a censure by the European Union. The European Union also admonished Italy for failing to defend gays' human rights. In that country homosexuality may be still legally considered egodistrophic (an ego disturbance, from a psychiatric point of view) and be treated as a crime.

The 2000 celebration of World Gay Pride in Rome, Italy, forced the Vatican-influenced Italian government to take a position on gay issues. Laura Balbo, who was then Minister of Equal Opportunities, presented a law favoring de facto couples, which includes homosexual cohabiting couples. The law will have a long way to run through the gauntlets of boycotts by conservative Catholics and right-wing politicians in the Italian Parliament before being approved. Nevertheless, after the 2000 gay pride celebrations, Italy gave some recognition to its gay citizens. Until that time, gay Italians had no right even to donate their blood or organs. Actions were also taken to grant political asylum to citizens persecuted for their homosexuality in their home countries.

On November 9, 1999, after lengthy debate, France passed "Le pacte civil de solidarité" (PACS—The Civil Solidarity Pact) which, although not exclusively aimed at gay relationships, defined and established the legality of a nonmarital relationship, endowed this relationship, and amended the general code to recognize certain rights in regard to taxation, inheritance, and social services as well as residency in the case of partners who are not citizens of France or the European Union. (The full text of this legislation may be found at http://www. legifrance.gouv.fr/citoyen/jorf_nor.ow?numjo=JUSX9803236L.)

In Germany, the government recently proposed to grant gay couples rights similar to those of heterosexual couples. It discussed a bill to allow gay couples to register their partnership with the state. The purposes were to entitle gay couples to enjoy the same rights as straight ones with regards to income tax, inheritance, welfare benefits, change of name, landlord-tenant relations, immigration, and civil-service privileges. The issue created serious ideological and political tensions in the Parliament. The Second Chamber of the Parliament, where the Christian Democrats have the majority, rejected all issues related to the tax system. Therefore, the government divided the law into two parts. The first part included the more simple benefits to which the Second Chamber did not have to agree. It became effective on August 1, 2001.

The second part is still under discussion and does not seem to have much chance of being approved by the present coalition in the Second Chamber.

The Treaty of Nice may be considered a memorable milestone in the history of the present European Union, with its 15 members, and the future Union, with another prospective 12 or 13 members, but it was much less successful with regards to human rights. A Chart of Rights was proclaimed, but no agreement came about with regards to its legal action.

Current Cultural Crises, Fears, Fantasies, and Foreseeable Futures

Elena A. A. Garcea

The British diversity specialist Graham Shaw has noted that, "Raising the awareness of social, political, demographic, and business trends is key to building the business case for diversity in Europe" (2000). This chapter will focus on a number of those elements, not only providing indications of the points at which successful organizations must understand and manage diversity, but also yielding a near-future picture of a diverse Europe. The next 30 years of European decision-making are likely to change the face of Europe as much as it changed after the European shifts of population and power that occurred with the discovery and colonization of the Americas.

Managing Shifts in Demographics

Fly from one European city to another and you will often see a number of other aircraft crossing the sky as you look out your window. Like all spaces in Europe, even airspace is small and crowded. Space limitations make demographics in Europe a critical concern at cultural, social, economic, and political levels.

Demographics constantly shift both within individual European countries and in Europe as a whole. When it comes to the mobility of people, Europe is far less isolated and far more permeable than North America. It shares its geographic boundaries with other continents. The Mediterranean Sea washes the coasts of Europe, Asia, and Africa.

The Danube River flows through Germany and Austria and continues across Central Europe until emptying into the Black Sea. From a cultural standpoint, Europe is surrounded by many different entities with varying levels of political stability. Southeastern Europe, now in its second decade of turmoil, is a scant few hundred kilometers from Vienna, Milan, and Athens.

Culture travels with demographics. The future Europe will be very different from the North American melting pot. There, assimilation prevailed over integration, and minorities were and continue to be pressured by the culture itself to adapt to largely homogeneous standards throughout the country. This homogenization goes on inexorably despite efforts to sustain ethnic communities in the past and to respect and manage diversity in more recent years. Europe, even without recent migrants and traditional minorities, is not homogeneous and is unlikely to easily become so. Therefore, a different pattern of social integration is settling into place. Ongoing diversity is actually Europe's most distinctive feature. Nowhere else in the world do so many distinct cultural identities coexist in such a relatively small place. Future Europe could actually face demographic, physical, and geographic limits. It is already heavily populated. Many areas, not just cities, seem to be reaching critical levels of congestion. Nevertheless, the biggest European cities are smaller than many other megalopolises in the Americas, Africa, or Asia and are bound to grow further.

Moving the Population

The mobility of Europeans within Europe is common nowadays, and it is even encouraged by E.U. institutions at all levels: in secondary schools and universities, and among workers and young professionals. The European Union has even created a European employment agency, called Eures, which is available online at http://europa.eu.int/comm/employment_social/elm/eures/index.htm. It offers information on employment, the labor market, and working conditions in the different E.U. countries. It also offers an open invitation to job mobility.

Although there are several types of "immigration," mobility within the European Union itself should not normally be thought of as immigration. Many companies send their employees wherever they have operations in Europe, and these employees have clearly established contractual agreements. Those who move understand that they will operate in a different cultural environment. Considering the relatively small size of European states, Europeans are used to crossing borders.

They are aware of the difficulties of being in a foreign country with another language and different habits. The Europeans who move from one country to another within the Union tend to be highly competent and therefore occupy staff and managerial positions in companies.

Nevertheless, culturally biased protectionist policies hinder the mobility of Europeans. According to the law, it is now illegal to restrict job offers to citizens of a single nation, even for government, public, or educational positions. Every tender must be open to all European citizens. However, the simplest way to overcome such regulation is to require a perfect knowledge of the national language, which obviously favors mother-tongue nationals.

Mobility has increased even in countries like Italy, which has high employment rates in the public sector, but mobility remains largely an opportunity for men who have more freedom to move than women. Italy's birth rate is particularly low as there are few socially secure opportunities for working women. Maternity threatens to slow down or hinder career promotions. Women with children have little professional support from either their employers or the welfare system. Reasonably priced public childcare is rare and not always efficient. Housekeeping remains a female task also for working women. Raising a child increases the workload for mothers much more than it does for fathers.

Mobility is considered a transitory condition of younger employees. Professionals tend to accept mobility early in their career, while those over 50 prefer to avoid it (Garcea, 2001). This situation feeds the generation gap.

Older employees see younger ones as threatening, and this causes tensions that undermine cooperation among colleagues of different ages. Job opportunities in Italy do not yet offer much career flexibility, and strong regional cultures do not encourage mobility even within the same country.

Paradoxically, England, although among the most populated regions of the world, has the lowest urban housing density in the European Union. Other European cities, such as Barcelona, are between 10 to 50 times more populated than British cities. The British government developed a new urban policy in 2000 to reduce urban anxieties by discouraging crime, vandalism, hooliganism, garbage, graffiti, and noise. Over the past 40 years, many people left old industrial centers. Manchester and Liverpool, for example, lost 40% of their populations. The government is planning to create new housing opportunities in these areas. Some politicians argue that such a policy should be accompanied by tax incentives, while others disagree. At the moment, professionals are leaving poor inner-city areas, rendering those areas even poorer and more run-down ("Waiting for Lord Rogers's Urban Renaissance," 2000).

Growing immigrant populations also cause demographic shifts amongst the existing national population. High rates of immigration to certain areas lead to an exodus of the younger and more mobile locals and result in an aging population being left behind. Creating working opportunities for immigrants in the less developed areas has also been attempted, although this has the attendant risk of producing new ghettos.

Enlarging the Population

In the past, only a few European countries hosted foreign labor forces that came from the less well-off countries in Europe. Switzerland was one of the most desirable destinations, a "dreamland" for many Europeans in search of work. However, many E.U. countries blamed Switzerland for admitting economic migrants into their country during boom periods and ejecting them later, or denying them rights and social security when the economy entered a recession. Still, a majority of Swiss favor having foreign workers. In September 2000, they rejected a referendum that proposed to force some foreign residents in Switzerland to leave, limiting foreigners to a maximum of 18% of the population. It has been estimated that the foreign labor force will thus increase from the present 19.2% to about 23% by the year 2020. Disagreements arose regarding the different linguistic cantons of the Swiss population while the referendum was being debated. German-speakers supported an immigrant population cap, while French-speakers had already given rights to foreigners to take part in local elections ("Switzerland: Foreign Relief," 2000).

Immigrants are needed for high-tech positions, not just entry-level ones. Romano Prodi, as president of the European Commission, was well aware of the lack of skilled labor in Europe. He has even criticized the strict restrictions recently applied in some E.U. countries to discourage labor mobility in Europe. TMP Worldwide, a recruitment agency, has the same criticism. European managers have declared that skill shortages have serious negative effects on their businesses. A group of industrialists even tried to attract the interest of European ministers on the matter ("Bridging Europe's Skills Gap," 2001). Jobs are available not only for computer engineers, but also for skilled bricklayers and masons, hoteliers, and farmers.

English, Spanish, German, Belgian, and Irish farms are increasingly in need of foreign workers to fill jobs that the local population cannot. At the same time, legal immigration in the whole of Europe has been declining since the early 1990s ("Europe's Immigrants: A Continent on the Move," 2000).

Ireland and the Netherlands are facing particularly serious shortages of labor due to their strong economies. In order to keep its booming economy, Ireland needs about 200,000 foreign workers by 2005, a number equal to more than a tenth of the workforce in 2000 ("Ireland: Come Back!" 2000). The Irish state training agency used to send its citizens abroad to find jobs. Now, it is trying to recruit workers from abroad. It created a specific agency called Jobs Ireland that operates in Canada, England, and South Africa.

Spain, with a declining native population of 10 million people, will grow through massive immigration from South America and Africa. This country needs 1.25 million information technology workers in the next two years, just to narrow their present technology gap with the rest of the European Union. These new realities will require new types of strategic management and will create a social environment with cultural implications that many local citizens are still not prepared for.

Integrating the Population

In countries with little historical tradition of immigration, accepting immigrants often depends on the socioeconomic condition of the European citizens. Those who live in the suburbs and in poor urban areas feel more threatened, as they often share the same living spaces with the newcomers; those in the upper-class neighborhoods have the liberty of pretending to tolerate them. The welfare state in Europe is quite different from that of the United States. In Europe, there is a recognized difference between employment and work. Employment means a permanent position in a company. Work does not require one to be hired as an employee. Employment guarantees benefits and protections that often remain more valuable than any independent job. Work in the United States is not considered as much of a right as it is in Europe. The European welfare state confers social and civil rights to citizens with a job, along with rights of health services and education. Therefore, European citizens' identity is dependent on employment. For this reason, Europeans fear that immigrants may reduce their employment opportunities or diminish the benefits that employment brings.

Immigration problems are complex and extend beyond simple economics. All European countries are sufficiently well off to appear desirable to the many jobless outsiders who often live below poverty levels. It is expected that Europe's declining demographics will force the European Union to integrate 1.6 million outsiders each year for the next 50 years, a total of between 50 and 75 million immigrants. This minimum will be necessary just to keep the working-age population stable ("Go for It," 2000). Considerable increases in populations from developing countries, greater disparities of wealth, cheaper travel, and encouragement given by those who have already migrated to their families and others in their home countries are among the main external causes of migration to Europe ("Europe's Migrants: Riding the Tide," 2000).

The flood of asylum seekers to Europe has now reached about half a million a year and is bound to increase. Cheaper air flights, growing poverty, demands for cheaper labor, as well as increased illegal trafficking in people will further swell the tide. Harried European countries have reacted by tightening the procedures for obtaining refugee status. They grant temporary asylum to those fleeing wars and deny permits to stay to those who lost their asylum application. Once the status of asylum seekers expires, people either go back to their home countries or move to Eastern Europe ("Displaced People: When Is a Refugee Not a Refugee?" 2001).

Many European business organizations still believe that immigration issues do not concern them directly. They expect governments to create effective policies to regulate, manage, and plan immigration, as well as establish clear working and residency policies. This is not realistic, as already the majority of factories in many industrialized areas, like northern Italy for example, directly recruit immigrant workers, in numbers often reaching 20 to 30% of the labor force. Behavior toward immigrants has changed in countries that have had foreign workers for a longer time. Some German citizens now identify their values and constitutional rules in the *Leitkultur*, which can be translated as "the leading culture among Germans" or "the German culture that leads." These people expect immigrants to abide by these values and concepts. A range of politicians, not all rightists, recently introduced the term. In Hitler's time, the *Leitkultur* concept was associated with the *Dominanzkultur* ideal. Remembering their overly nationalist past, many other Germans feel uneasy even with the concept of nationalism, and prefer to identify themselves either with the region they come from or live in, such as "Bavarians," or simply as "Europeans."

Institutions, such as the French Chamber of Commerce admit that the confusion between legal and illegal foreign workers produces alarmist reactions. Foreign workers are desperately needed on the one hand and vigorously rejected on the other. The social conditions of national protectionism are still more influential than the economic ones of workforce sustainment and international development.

Countries with Longer-Standing Immigrant Groups

A number of European countries have enjoyed the benefits of immigrant workers for several decades. As a result, their institutions and their citizens are more accustomed to and equipped for living in multicultural societies.

In the Netherlands, foreigners and ex-colonials from places like Indonesia have been established for a long time and their status is therefore well recognized. The Dutch are now discussing to what degree they should further assimilate immigrants, and if and how Dutch culture should let itself be influenced by immigrant cultures.

The question of assimilation is clearly evident in the United Kingdom as well. In the past, Britain has had numerous political and economic immigrants. Due to relatively high degrees of tolerance and acceptance, often based on the high value that many Brits give to the concept of "fairness," there is more integration now. Britain today has more mixed race children per capita than does the United States. Entrants to Britain in the past legally became citizens and were entitled to all the rights of citizens. However, mixed-nationality couples and families still often face special challenges. A British person married to an Indonesian will face much more official questioning when obtaining British nationality for his or her spouse.

In Germany, there is increasing tolerance toward Turks, who form up to 20% of the population in some parts of the largest cities. Turkish workers have played an important role in German industry since the 1980s. Now, since opening to the east, Berlin and Hamburg need to settle asylum seekers and police criminality among Poles and Russians. Berlin has been rebuilt to host Germany's government institutions and officers. Along with them came NGOs and lobbies, business executives and peacekeepers. In the last few years, the city has changed as much as its citizenry.

Many former Berliners, who first looked on radical change in their city with fear and suspicion and planned to escape, eventually stayed on and continued their lively cultural existence. Huge social, cultural, and commercial events take place in Berlin. For example, in 1989, Berlin DJ, Dr. Motte rallied together with other groovers and the Love Parade was born. His idea to promote house music evolved into a demonstration *for* tolerance, respect, and understanding among people. Instead of speeches and pamphlets there was music. This Love

Parade has become a yearly occurrence, gathering millions from all over Europe, East as well as West. Those who support this event and participate in it are attracted by the sense of freedom, the booming techno music, the carefree crowds made up of all types of people. Those who criticize it do so for just about the same reasons. They are skeptical about the apparent lack of ideals and resent the heavy commercialization, though commercial sponsors are needed to organize such massive events. The music business has always sponsored social and cultural events, and techno seems to work well for long-lasting dance sessions with huge groups of people. "Lack of ideals" may be in the perception of a different generation with cultural values that differ from the contemporary set. More serious critics attack the widespread use of the drugs in the late 1990s that went hand in hand with the music and ideals of the period.

Foreigners born in Switzerland often behave "more Swiss than the Swiss." These people, some Italians for example, see their original culture as "wrong" and are closed to anything but the Swiss way of life. Like many second-generation immigrants in the United States, they overadapt and feel threatened by diversity. In fact, in Swiss society (and in others as well), diversity of lifestyle is discouraged, except when it is relegated to being an art form. It is art to see Turkish women dancing a traditional dance at an international *Fest*, but it is not acceptable for them to cover their heads at work.

Countries with New Immigrants

Some European lands, such as Ireland and Italy, have traditionally been emigrant countries, sending their citizens abroad for work and settlement. This has changed. Italy is facing large waves of immigration from North Africa and Southeastern Europe. The country and its peoples were scarcely prepared and organized for this new turn of events. Voluntary organizations that receive economic support from national and European funds are often at the forefront of assisting immigrants. On the one hand, this is an admirable expression of humanitarian concern. On the other hand, it shows that governmental institutions lack power, strategy, and initiative—in short, the capability to manage such challenges. The high-tech and service industry boom in Ireland brought home such large numbers of former emigrants and invited so many new immigrants that the population has shown a net gain from immigration for the first time in its recent history.

In countries such as Finland, most citizens see immigrants as a threat to their national culture. Finnish society, including its long-standing Swedish minority, had remained essentially monocultural until the 1990s. Due to the geographic position of the country, people were more isolated from the waves of migration and trade that criss-crossed Europe for centuries.

The Enduring Migrants

The Roma are a very special enclave in Europe. They provided an important contribution to the history of Europe and their numbers are considerable. The Roma population is larger than that of many European countries, estimated at between 4 and 15 million. In consideration of their population density, they would like to be recognized as a nation without a territory, and see the enlargement of the European Union to Central Europe as a chance for them to be recognized and heard by E.U. institutions.

The Roma land of origin is unclear. Early it was asserted that they came from Egypt. This hypothesis proved wrong, but left them with the name "Gypsies," still commonly used. Even though there are no written documents, their ancestors were most probably metal workers and entertainers who moved westward from India during the seventh century.

The International Romany Union gathers Roma from 30 countries. Its purposes are to develop a standard oral and written language and to lobby the United Nations and the European Union. It has an office in Brussels, and its members include educated lawyers, members of parliament, and mayors ("Europe's Gypsies: Are They a Nation?" 2000).

In spite of all this, the Roma are frequently a persecuted minority that easily becomes the focus of racial hatred. With the inclusion of Central European countries in the European Union, where they are even more poorly thought of and ill-treated than in other regions of Europe, they will pose an extremely grave international diversity challenge. Age-old biases against them and their poverty level may cause them to be seen as a threat to the welfare system and to public order. Their painful situation is centuries old and seems like it could take centuries more to be resolved. It involves the stubborn dilemma of either changing and destroying a very distinctive culture, or finding a global solution that respects identity but addresses issues of social exclusion, bias, and economic disadvantage.

Ultimately, seen as an E.U. governance issue, the Roma could require a focused effort with a specific framework program and initiatives over a long period of time. Some countries, like Ireland for example, have nongovernmental organizations attending to the situation and needs of the Roma and other nomadic groups.

Skeptical versus Enthusiastic Euro Partners

Certain countries in Europe refused to adopt the euro as their common currency and did not join the European Monetary Union (EMU). In Denmark, a referendum on joining the monetary union in September 2000 was turned down by 53% of the voters. The Danes preferred to defend their independence and their welfare state, which operates above E.U. standards. Their financial link to Europe is maintained by pegging the krone first to the German mark and now to the euro. Whether this choice for financial independence will imply isolation from the other important European affairs remains to be seen.

The other E.U. countries that are not part of the EMU are Sweden, which joined the European Union in 1994, and the United Kingdom, which is certainly influenced by the Danish decision. The British, in particular, seem to prefer to stay out of the Euro zone, while attempting to influence its decisions and policies.

The completion of a motor and railway bridge between Denmark and Sweden in 2000 was one response to the economic stresses of European competition. In addition, it represented the political desire to physically unite two cousin countries that tend to dislike each other as individuals, but are prone to defend each other in front of other nations. This investment of over 2 billion U.S. dollars was expected to enhance the fastest-growing and richest part of Europe. However, the cost of crossing the bridge ($26.40) was so much higher than what the ferries charged that many companies, like Novo Nordisk and Ikea, limited or forbade their employees the use of it. Only the increase of tourism via the bridge has had a positive impact on business, which is largely reflected in the success of the cafés and art galleries in Copenhagen and Malmo. Local newspapers in Copenhagen (*Berlinske Tidende*) and in Malmo (*Sydsvenska Dagbladet*) publish a daily supplement about cross-border ventures in health, education, and information technology ("A Not-So-Popular Nordic Bridge," 2000).

Switzerland is the only fairly large country in Europe that firmly refuses to join the European Union. It joined the International Monetary Fund, the World Bank, and the International Trade Organization only during the past decade. The Swiss turned down their most recent chance to join the European Union in a referendum held in March 2001, and limited themselves to approving a few economic agreements with the E.U. countries in another more recent referendum. The Swiss majority still resists participating in the European Union. Younger Swiss are apparently even less motivated to belong to either the European Union or the United Nations than the older generation. One-fifth of the Swiss population comes from outside the country, but these too have embraced the well-protected Swiss identity. The majority of the population fears they will lose their traditionally independent and neutral position in the world if they join the European Union. They also feel that their trade is not affected by this choice as 70% of it is already with E.U. countries.

On the other hand, Luxembourg, the other major financial investment center in Europe, is one of the 15 countries of the Union. It is the smallest, but one of the most powerful. It is telling that Luxembourg has twice held the presidency of the European Commission. Currently, several European institutions are located in Luxembourg, providing significant benefit for its citizens, who are amongst the most convinced supporters of the European Union.

Mediation is Luxembourg's major contribution to the European Union, and it seems likely that these skills will be even more needed as the Union grows. Luxembourg's role is followed with interest for the new opportunities it offers to other E.U. citizens, particularly the Danes, who are much more skeptical about the Union (Hall, 1995, p. 20).

Growing the European Union

With few exceptions, a number of countries from Central and Eastern Europe strongly desire to belong to the European Union. The European Union is currently negotiating its expansion to include those 12 or 13 (if one includes Turkey) countries that have applied to join the Union by 2004 (Exhibit 3.1). There are a variety of issues related to enlargement. The European Union's main concerns about the applicant countries can be divided into two areas. Economic conditions, such as control over inflation, deficits, and unemployment are one area of concern. Secondly, social conditions, such as fraud and corruption, the treatment of women and children, and the handling of minorities such as the Roma are also of concern to current E.U. members.

The first applicant group includes the six countries (the Czech Republic, Cyprus, Estonia, Hungary, Poland, and Slovenia) that started their negotiations in 1998. The second group comprises another six countries (Bulgaria, Latvia, Lithuania, Malta, Romania, and Slovakia) that started their negotiations in 2000. Turkey formally started negotiating at the end of 2000. Every new country will have to be accepted by every member of the Union, and ratification is expected to take at least 18 months. Therefore, it is more likely that any new Member State will not enter the E.U. before 2004 or even 2005. For economic interests, some present E.U. Member States favor particular countries. Germany, for example, wants Poland to be among the first to have

Exhibit 3.1

The European Union and Applicant Countries

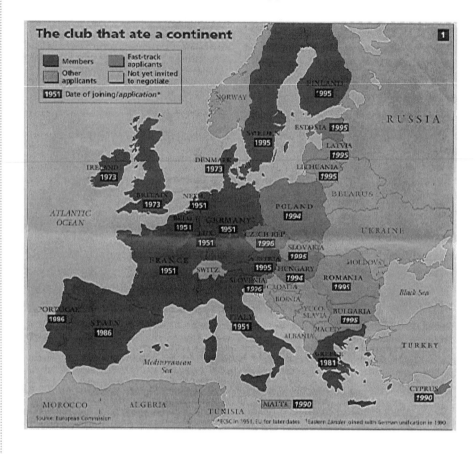

access to the Union, even though other countries, like the Czech Republic, Malta, and Cyprus are economically more advanced ("The European Union: Bigger When?," 2000).

When new countries are admitted, demographic shifts are likely to increase, particularly among bordering countries. Current Member States fear that a large influx of workers would threaten their social systems. In Germany, for example, workers are afraid of losing their jobs and giving up their salaries, since their eastern rivals are accustomed to earning about a tenth of a West German worker's salary. Companies in Eastern Europe have lower labor costs and less stringent safety and environmental standards that could competitively threaten small businesses. Farmers in the west are worried about competition from cheaper food. Taxpayers fear they will have to pay for the integration of eastern citizens. Some worry about an increase in criminality and a decrease in living standards. Others feel the threat of losing their identity.

On the other hand, both real and potential gains are numerous. Germany holds a privileged position on the eastern border. Since the fall of the Iron Curtain, Germany's trade has doubled, and Central Europe has replaced the United States as its largest trade partner outside the European Union, absorbing about a tenth of Germany's exports. The enlargement of the Union is also expected to bring more work to Germany, pushing both economic growth and improving living standards. Estimates on immigration rates predict that a westward flow will mostly take place during the first year after the enlargement, then will slow considerably afterwards. The estimated number of immigrants will roughly maintain labor force at its present level. As for taxes, an agreement has already been made in Brussels that Germany will not spend more than 4% of the GDP on the incoming easterners ("Germany: A Row about a Bigger E.U.," 2000).

Large numbers of Eastern and Central Europeans, in fact, already live and work in Western Europe. Numerous Western European companies have long been hiring Eastern European professionals, who possess excellent educational standards and who are economically less demanding than their Western European colleagues. Some western countries are particularly keen on the enlargement to the east. Austria sees the opportunity to regain its position as the center of a new *Mitteleuropa*. Hungary, Slovenia, Croatia, the Czech Republic, and parts of Poland actually play an important role in its economy and culture. Austria's chancellor Wolfgang Schuessel expressed the hope that Austria's enhanced role in the European Union would reduce the effects of the seven-month diplomatic sanctions against his country that were imposed in 2000 in response to the admission of the far-right Freedom Party into the ruling coalition. Many European citizens did not favor this boycott against Austria, and some E.U. ruling politicians did not support this international decision. Regardless of the political beliefs of the Freedom Party, for E.U. institutions to take such an official stance risks setting an undesirable precedent. Boycotting future governments undercuts the union and interferes in the internal democratic processes of the individual Member States.

Facilitating Enlargement

There are economic, social, and political risks related to opening the European Union to the other 12 or 13 new members with their differing languages, economies, political systems, historical traditions, and cultures. These need to be dealt with in advance as much as possible by both governments and businesses. In order to reduce these risks, the European Union has developed a strategy of "pre-adapting" the social systems of the candidate countries.

At the conclusion of the Berlin summit in March 1999, the Heads of State agreed that enlargement remained a historic priority for the European Union. It will result in 500 million citizens in a 28-member European Union, giving existing E.U. members a more influential European voice in world affairs. Such a Union would enjoy broader cooperation levels for dealing with challenges like environmental pollution and organized crime, as well as open opportunities for businesses to develop new markets and new economies of scale. Central, eastern, and southeastern countries, in turn would benefit by greater democratic and social stability and enhanced prosperity (*Europe's Agenda 2000*, 1999).

The enlargement of the European Union was debated again during the Nice summit in December 2000. Present E.U. members, and particularly large countries, worried that the enlargement might dilute their influence and decision-making power. Policy procedures would risk becoming even slower than they currently are. In response to these fears, a re-weighting of voting power was approved in Nice. The size of a country's population will determine the weight of its voting power in the European Union. Larger countries (Germany, Britain, France, Italy, Spain, and Poland, when the latter joins the Union) will get more votes in the Council of Ministers in absolute terms. Small countries will get more votes in proportion to their populations. Pro forma vote totals have been set for aspiring members.

In order to facilitate integration, the Treaty of Nice, signed in December 2000, proposed that groups of eight countries or more might pursue greater integration in certain policy areas. This could facilitate, for example, a better coordination on financial and tax policies among the countries in the Euro zone ("The Nice Summit: So That's All Agreed, Then," 2000).

However, creating such groupings within the countries of the Union risks overempowering some countries and marginalizing others. This was one of the reasons why the Nice Summit was met with intense public criticism of the European governors in demonstrations that resembled earlier protests in Seattle, Washington, and Prague against the World Trade Organization (WTO), the International Monetary Fund (IMF), and the World Bank.

How the Treaty of Nice weighted the votes of "large" and "small" countries in the qualified majority also came under fire, along with the new ways of voting for the qualified majority and other issues of cooperation. Some members that entered the Union as small and weak countries, such as Ireland, but became economically strong are unwilling to reduce their power and influence in Brussels.

The Historical E.U. Treaties

The Treaty of Maastricht, signed in 1992, gave birth to the European "Union." Its purpose was to integrate and modify the former Treaty of Rome, signed in 1957, which had created the European Economic Community.

The Treaty of Maastricht was based on two ideas that are basic principles in Europe: the right to vote and the right to work. Its overall aims were to strengthen European citizens' feeling of belonging together and to recognize the Union as having a political dimension. However, E.U. citizens are only those who are nationals of a Member State. Therefore, citizenship and nationality are equivalent in the European Union.

Since not only E.U. citizens live in the European Union, the treaty established three other categories of members of the Union: denizens from E.U. countries, denizens from non-E.U. countries, and foreigners. Denizen status is not the same as citizenship. Denizens have the same civil and social rights as citizens, but without the same legal guarantees. Foreigners are those without full rights of residence (Rea, 1994). Women denizens and foreigners acquired their rights directly, without the intermediary of their husbands, only very recently. Freedom of opinion, the right of association, and the right to demonstrate are restricted for denizens and foreigners (Rea, 1994).

The subsequent Treaties of Schengen and Amsterdam, the latter signed in 1997, relaxed borders between several European countries. It is now very simple to move without a passport between the countries that signed those treaties to date: Austria, Belgium, Denmark, Finland, France, Germany, Greece, Iceland, Italy, Luxembourg, the Netherlands, Norway, Portugal, Spain, and Sweden. This simplifies life for the nationals from those countries and for others with residence permits in those countries. However, other people who want to enter in the Schengen/Amsterdam territory face more complex and often slower procedures.

The Treaty of Amsterdam also defined the so-called European social model. It is based on the belief that enterprises need strong competition in order to improve their productivity and growth, but also insists that citizens require a strong sense of solidarity if there is to be a stable society and prosperity for all. E.U. social policy is built on the principle of subsidiarity. According to this principle, Europe only deals with issues that concern the whole of Europe, such as defining minimum standards and minimum rights. NGOs are important partners in the E.U. social policy. The European social model aims to encourage and support transnational initiatives by co-financing projects involving partners from at least two Member States, such as the EQUAL program of the European Social Fund for the 2000–2006 budget. (See Appendix 2.)

Illegal Migration

In addition to mobility within the region, immigration from outside Europe has reached record highs. Europe is the most populated continent in the world with respect to its size. Nonetheless, the number of people living in Europe is bound to increase. Immigration is caused by economic needs and opportunities from within, as well as by economic and political asylum seeking immigrants from without. People move where they can find work. Consequently, there is no reason to forbid mobility, and this makes demographic shifts unavoidable. This provides both cultural challenges as well as fresh opportunities to both private and public sectors.

In addition to high-tech and professional talent, large numbers of immigrants from third-world countries come as low-cost hand labor, to work in agriculture and factories and to serve as domestic help. Europe needs this working population, because the more highly educated European population generally refuses to engage in repetitive production-line jobs and agricultural work. They aspire to value-added tasks and to professional careers that they believe will raise their quality of life.

The immigration challenge should be tackled at political and legal levels. Since it is impossible to stop immigration, every effort should be made to extend the right to be legal. Having a large number of illegal residents threatens the citizens' right to security. It also creates uneasiness and unhappiness. Legal immigrants are few in number in every European country, mostly because immigration is discouraged by complicated bureaucratic procedures.

Even though immigration is now controlled at the international level by the countries signatory to the Schengen and Amsterdam Treaties, no measures have been successful in stopping illegal immigrants from entering the European Union. Their number increases constantly each year. Freedom of movement of peoples conflicts with the will and the resources to integrate newcomers in a meaningful way and thus head off major social disruptions.

Despite international agreements, immigration procedures in some countries remain extremely bureaucratic. In Italy, for example, the complicated process for becoming a legal immigrant encourages illegal immigration. Illegality is tolerated more in southern Italy, while northern companies offering a wider range of working opportunities tend to favor legalized immigrants. Therefore, there is a tacit agreement that immigrants enter in the country through the south and accept very poorly paid jobs for such time as they need to obtain a residence permit. Then they gradually move north in search of better-paying jobs. As the south provides the requirements expected in the north, this system relies on the prevailing economic and social conditions in both the south and north.

Racist extremist groups are another negative response to the increasing waves of immigration. Despite the fact that immigrants and asylum seekers are generally better received and cared for in Germany than most other European countries, awareness of the country's National Socialist past still causes the press to pay special attention to racist activities there. Highly visible extreme right-wing parties discourage foreign investment. Ludolf-Georg von Wartenberg, one of the heads of the Bundesverband der Deutschen Industrie (BDI), the German Federation of Industry, suggested measures that would allow companies to fire known extremists ("Germany: Fighting Racism," 2000, p. 32). When the German government ratified a plan to issue work and residence permits to foreign information-technology experts, the right reacted with the slogan, *"Kinder statt Inder"* ("Let's have children, not import East Indians"). Even a critical lack of professional expertise among the national population does not seem sufficient to prevent racial attacks against foreigners or foreign businesses.

No Land Workers

European economic systems make high demands for foreign labor. However, the political and social systems seem to be unable to respond to these demands by providing the kind of systematic support needed to facilitate and manage immigration flows. The high tide of immigration in several E.U. countries comes crashing against the reefs of inexperience and stagnates in the shoals created by the lack of knowledge and practical policies for dealing with immigrants.

Immigrant children can be in an even worse position than their parents. When their parents are marginalized, they are automatically marginalized too. Their exclusion is said to be socially inherited and is normally remedied only when one or both parents are socially integrated.

During the summer of 2000, Coldiretti, the largest Italian farmers' federation, called for 65,000 foreign seasonal workers to harvest grain, vegetables, and fruit. Despite a 9% unemployment rate, Italians despise this type of work and refuse to take it ("Europe's Migrants: Riding the Tide," 2000). Still, Italy's immigrant population is among the lowest, being a scant 2% of the total population. Currently, the Italian government has set the legal limit of 85,000 immigrants per year, even though, in 1999, 220,000 foreigners obtained residence permits. This figure refers to the number of permits officially issued by Italian authorities. The real number of foreigners who enter the country, often with the idea of moving on to more prosperous countries, is uncountable, probably over 300,000 per year.

The Catholic Church plays a significant role in immigration policy and settlement in Italy. It generally favors immigration, and many volunteer organizations providing assistance to immigrants who are Catholic. However, the Church has a declared fear of a strong Islamic influence in Italy, and this is supported by extremist politicians of the Northern League ("Italy: A Few Bad Apples," 2000). In terms of real numbers, about a third of the immigrants are Muslim and a half of them are Christian.

Spain is another country that was a net exporter of labor until the 1970s, but as its citizens became richer and better educated, they, too, began to refuse humble jobs in farming, domestic service, and construction. In 2001, legal immigrants accounted for about 1 million out of a population of 40 million, but at least 500,000 illegal immigrants should be added to the total number of newcomers. A new 2001 law regulates immigration in Spain. It aims at discouraging employers from taking illegal workers and smugglers from bringing them into the country. It also defines strict conditions for expulsion of illegals. However, expulsion requires bilateral agreements between the hosting and the sending countries. Considering that immigrants to Spain come from over 50 countries, securing such agreements is a long, painstaking, and often unsuccessful process. Some sending countries are not willing to take their citizens back due to their local social, economic, and political situation. Therefore, illegal immigrants have neither a place to go to nor a place in which to stay. At the same time, employers urgently need workers and feel that Spanish regulations are too tight and irreconcilable with the country's labor needs ("Europe: Unwelcome to Iberia," 2001).

The situation in Portugal resembles that of Spain. In the past, a high emigration rate resulted in an exodus of 2.5 million Portuguese, with about one-fourth of the population still living abroad. About half of the immigrants come from Africa, as a consequence of the freedom granted to the Portuguese colonies in Africa in 1975. Illegal immigrants number about 200,000, about the same amount as legal ones. They live in dreadful conditions and are brutally exploited by different Mafia groups. A new law proposes to reduce illegal immigration by issuing temporary work permits. Major constructions for the Euro 2004 soccer championship include a second airport and a new stadium, both of which require lots of labor. No one knows what will happen to these workers when their temporary work permits expire ("Europe: Unwelcome to Iberia," 2001).

Other European countries with little tradition as immigrant destinations also face a new influx of immigrants, but at a much lower rate. Finland, for example, has a total of 85,000 immigrants, which is equivalent to the number of people officially entering Italy in a single year. Unemployment of immigrants in Finland is extremely high. It can reach 75 to 80% for some groups as the private sector is unwilling to give employment to immigrants. Therefore, they more often hold government-subsidized jobs or jobs related to services for immigrants, such as interpreters, cultural mediators, and native language teachers.

But even in a country like Germany, with an older immigration tradition, only 9% of the population is made up of legal immigrants. Since the fall of the Berlin Wall, a new type of immigrant has appeared in Germany and Austria. They are called "cross-border commuters," "labor tourists," or "incomplete migrants." They go abroad to work for a few weeks at a time and bring the money they earn back to their home countries in Central Europe ("Europe's Immigrants: A Continent on the Move," 2000).

National versus E.U. Directives

Developing an employment framework for immigrants is a momentous challenge for Europe. Decisions need to be made at supranational, national, and local levels about how to include and incorporate these new populations into the local cultures and legal structures. Norms should be both clear as well as sensitive to cultural values of both nationals and newcomers, and they should take into account international economic shifts.

The restriction of immigration policies violates E.U. directives. Prodi has stated that the European Union needs to foster labor mobility in order to fill the gap of qualified workers. Recruitment agencies, European managers, and industrialists realize the serious negative effects of immigration restriction on their business and try to influence

European ministers on the matter. Excessively restrictive regulations for obtaining legal work permits do not only affect the simple worker, but also hinder the entire mobility system.

Antonio Vitorino a member of the European Commission, has stated that the European Union needs to adopt a more open and transparent policy, with clear rules and procedures, allowing potential economic immigrants to apply for entry in their countries of origin informing them about the conditions that will apply to the candidates who are accepted (Vitorino, 2000). Such a policy would reduce the illegal traffic of immigrants. It would also set up agreed upon procedures for immigrating into the European Union and recognize the contribution that immigrants bring to Europe's economy and society.

The European Union supports and finances several programs to develop intensive trade with countries outside Europe. The most important ones focus on the Mediterranean countries (Morocco, Algeria, Tunisia, Egypt, Jordan, Israel, Lebanon, Cyprus, Syria, and Turkey). This is a vast and heavily populated area with 700 million inhabitants. The European Commission is their chief economic and trading partner, accounting for over half their foreign trade. The majority of the Union's exports include manufactured goods and agricultural products. The Mediterranean countries supply almost a third of the Union's fertilizer imports and nearly a quarter of its imported energy (particularly oil and natural gas). Unfortunately, unstable oil prices have left the Mediterranean countries with a considerable deficit toward the European Union. This imbalance has been attributed to the fact that the Mediterranean countries' exports are concentrated in a limited number of products, with little diversification in the agricultural sector. Currently, the European Union is negotiating new trade agreements with Mediterranean countries that aim at establishing a free-trade area uniting all European and Mediterranean countries by the year 2010.

Managing Ethnic-Focused Civil Unrest

The numbers of laborers with families originating outside Europe have become significant and visible, and can no longer be ignored or quickly assimilated. The potential for unrest is particularly acute when unemployment is high and in times of economic downturn. Therefore, Europe has to be prepared with measures that realistically address both the unrest of the newcomers and the sense of disenfranchisement on the part of the traditional population.

The educational level of Europeans, generally speaking, has been on the upswing. As a consequence, employment expectations are also rising. This phenomenon is rarely considered when the unemployment rate is compared with the number of foreign laborers seeking jobs. There are many jobs that have become undesirable to youngsters with at least a high-school diploma. Therefore, employers, whether they like it or not, are often compelled to hire foreign laborers. Immigrants often take jobs that local workers refuse. The same dynamic affects other social resources. In the East End of London, for example, Asian families were housed in run-down council apartments whilst numerous members of the white working class waited for rehousing. Though the whites would never have been housed in these dilapidated dwellings, some political groups used this issue to stir up discontent.

In many European countries, unemployment is not a significant issue. On the contrary, immigrants are needed due to a lack of workers. As a consequence, xenophobia can be a serious threat to economic growth, not only because workers are needed numerically, but also because immigrants bring entrepreneurial skill and spirit to their new home countries. Even business professionals recognize that immigration has played and still plays a positive role in many countries. Immigration is a way for European countries to acquire skilled people and, in part, to offset the demographic consequences of their aging population. However, when governments pander to thinly disguised racism, they do not appease it but rather both fuel it and give it a guise of acceptability.

There is an additional social integration problem in that immigrant labor tends to be hidden in the "black" economy, or what Americans would describe as the "underground," economy. This problem is intensified when bureaucratic procedures for legal working permits are too slow or too complicated for foreigners, especially when they speak a different language. As a consequence, an uncountable number of immigrants are forced to accept extremely low salaries without job security during their period of illegal stay. Such a practice is easily tolerated by those employers who take it as an opportunity to evade taxes on their foreign employees' salaries.

To respond to the new diversities created by trans-European mobility, social institutions must develop a new framework for working and for dealing with business. Trade unions will have to come to terms with new ways of working that are appropriate to the new needs of the population on the one hand, and meet the need for higher corporate efficiency on the other. The issues at stake include both traditional jobs as well as newly emerging forms of employment, such as distance work and time-sharing. Legislation will also have to review its present bureaucracy, as more small- and medium-sized enterprises (SMEs) are woven into the true socioeconomic fabric of the system.

A young Italian manager who responded to our survey summed it up well: "Immigrant workers have the right to participate in the distribution of European wealth. Needs should sometimes be considered before merits."

The Aging of Western Europe

Young Europeans

Cultural shifts are accelerating on two age fronts. Firstly, the indigenous peoples of Western nations with their low birth rates are quickly growing older. The ratio of the pensionable population in Europe was about 5% higher than in the United States in 2000 and is expected to remain constantly higher for the next 50 years. Secondly, newcomer minorities are replacing aging Europeans. Diversity along the age line is driving a deep wedge between the fixed older population and the under-35s who enjoy freedom, mobility, and career flexibility. Furthermore, as life expectancy has increased, the period of time dedicated to work in a person's life is also likely to increase (Exhibit 3.2).

People between 50 and 60 are still active, with a longer life expectancy and with longer working life capabilities than in previous

Exhibit 3.2

Replacement Migration Trends

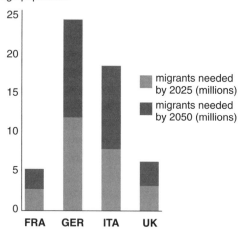

Number of immigrants needed to maintain working-age population

migrants needed by 2025 (millions)

migrants needed by 2050 (millions)

Source: UN Population Division.

times. Therefore, systems need to be devised that will allow the elder generations to continue working and actively participate in mentoring and interacting with the new generations. It is vital to keep them active, as the socioeconomic system cannot afford their early retirement. One of their problems is that they find it more difficult to readjust in a world of rapid development in technology, computing, and mass communications. In most parts of Europe, the Internet has far fewer users over 60, whether retired or not, than in North America.

On the other hand, the social security system of Western Europe appears inadequate to cope with new realities. Pension systems are encountering demographic crises due to the aging of the population. Young working generations will probably not support a growing retiring population in the way the system was originally conceived.

In Europe, more than in North America or the Far East, freedom, mobility, and career flexibility for those under 35 also includes a great deal of insecurity. This age group lacks respect from older colleagues and lacks support for career planning, which is often still done in a very paternalistic and restrictive way. They are frustrated by poorly designed organizations. According to research carried out in 1999 by the Economic Department of the Organization for Economic Cooperation and Development (OECD), barriers to entrepreneurship are very high in Western Europe. They are found in administrative burdens, regulatory systems, and competition practices. Add to these high taxation, a lack of harmonized rules about share options, and the threat of draconian bankruptcy laws, and it is easy to see why entrepreneurs and startups are less in evidence.

Italy tops the list of administrative complexity discouraging entrepreneurs. It is followed, in order, by France, Belgium, Germany, Sweden, Spain, and the Netherlands. All these countries scored higher than the United States in terms of complexity, with Britain as the only European country below the United States ("France's Economy: Now for the Hard Bit," 2000). The civil service in France and in a number of other E.U. countries represents a quarter of the workforce.

Older Europeans

The OECD produced several publications and surveys on aging populations in Europe. They also developed policies for maintaining prosperity in aging societies. In the past 25 years, the number of people of pensionable age (65 and over) in OECD countries rose by 45 million, while the population of working age rose by 120 million. In the next 25 years, the number of people of pensionable age will increase by 70 million, but the population of working age will only rise by 5 million. Average age is increasing because people live longer and birth rates have fallen. Less people will produce the goods and services necessary for both the productive population and the retired population. As a consequence, average living standards are bound to diminish (Kohl and O'Brien, 1998).

The United Nations Population Division estimates that the Italian population over 60 will rise from its present level of 24% to 35% by 2025. Germany's will shift from 22% to 33%. The number of workers per pensioner will go from two to one. Therefore, either pensions must decrease considerably or contributions will have to increase. German chancellor Gerhard Schroeder has developed a totally new pension system. According to this plan, state pension payments are expected to rise from 19.3% of gross earnings to 22% by 2030, and benefits would drop from 70% to 64%. Tax breaks and subsidies will, it is hoped, balance the expected loss. The government's plan is to encourage workers to put an extra 4% of their earnings in private pension funds, which are expected to eventually cover about 40% of the total pension ("Germany: Radical Pensions," 2000).

The OECD has pointed out that state-run "pay-as-you-go" pension systems in many countries either need to be or have already been reformed. This system implies that workers pay the pensions of retirees. Reforms involve both the contribution and the benefit sides. The effect of pension systems on public and private saving is important. The OECD calculated that unfunded public pension schemes reduce national saving by up to 30% of the funding, while tax-favored private saving schemes could increase national saving, although fiscal effects reduce savings. (See Kohl and O'Brien, 1998. For discussion of a gradual removal of the pay-as-you-go pension systems, see Hviding and Mérette, 1998.)

The European pension systems of the mid-1990s made it financially unattractive to work after the age of 55. The frequency of early retirement is higher than that of normal retirement in most of the countries of the European Union, except for Finland, Greece, Italy, Luxembourg, and Spain. At the same time, taxes on continued work have continued to rise since the 1960s. These financial disincentives to continue work caused a decrease of older males in the labor force and further deteriorated labor market conditions (Bloendal and Scarpetta, 1998). The result is that Europe is sitting on a "pension time-bomb," as the *Economist* put it ("Pension Funds: Old Hopes Stirring," 2000). The over-60 population is expected to rise by about 10% in most E.U. countries by 2025.

Despite these figures, European governments have still been discouraging private investments by limiting the returns from pension funds. In Germany, for example, pension funds cannot invest more than 30% of their assets in equities. In the United Kingdom and the Netherlands, there are no such restrictions. Other countries, like Spain and France, are even more restrictive than Germany. Some E.U. commissioners are more favorable to private pensions and have been trying to reform the European rules on pension funds. A reform aimed at supporting the multinationals that provide unified pension plans to their employees is planned for 2005.

In France, at the moment, the contributions necessary to cover one person's pension must come from 1.7 workers. By the year 2030, they will have to come from only one worker as the number of pensionable French seniors will rise from about one-fifth to more than one-third of the population ("France: Strike to Retire," 2001). In Germany and Italy, the figures are even more alarming. Their percentage of pensioners will increase from a little more than 20% to almost 50%.

Neither Young Nor Old

Several European professionals have observed that companies tolerate biases against the aged more than they do racism or sexism. This indicates that ageism prejudices are still largely unconscious.

The United Kingdom has a cultural tradition imported from North America where youth is worshipped and age despised. Old people are perceived as a burden on the state and are treated badly by health services, social services, and the commercial sector. For example, breast screening ceases for women over 70, even though they are a high-risk group. Old people are treated like jobless mothers; they are not seen as an economic force and are, therefore, considered worthless. We wonder if the new license for euthanasia in medical practice in the Netherlands is not as well a part of this cultural shift toward valuing youth and devaluing old age. Other countries, such as those in southern Europe, traditionally have more respect for older people, who as a result tend to have more power and receive more respect than in central and northern Europe.

Europe suffers from ageism at both ends of the age scale, leaving only the people in the middle untouched. Occupational criteria still rely far too much on "experienced" people, measuring experience by years rather than skills. It should also be noted that today's well-educated young people, who have already made considerable investments in terms of money and labor, have much greater career expectations than the job system is prepared to meet, and that the best young people are no longer willing to be treated as second-class employees for the first 15 years of their career.

If work expectations are not met, older people prefer to retire. A 1995 survey of male workers aged 55 to 64 showed that the percentages of employed people with a vocational education was lower than that of retired people with the same type of education; this was true in most E.U. countries except for Denmark, Sweden, and the United Kingdom. The ratio is reversed for men with a university, technical school, or college education.

In the aspirant E.U. countries of Eastern Europe, the challenge is even greater, as many of the younger generation grew up expecting that the State would provide them with health and employment guarantees. This is no longer possible in a competitive free enterprise economy. In the former East Germany, for example, the over-50s tend to be ill-equipped for working in the new economy. Further east the social security system has evaporated for those who reach pensioner age. Private insurance systems may be an interesting opportunity for business in the Eastern European countries that are going to join the European Union. Such systems are also gradually entering the market in those Western European countries, such as Italy, Spain, and Portugal, that used to rely almost entirely on accumulated wealth or public welfare.

Many Europeans believe that Europe should have a social free market economy where the governments still hold a certain responsibility for a new type of welfare state. European citizens are still used to relying on the State as the great provider. This mentality will no doubt continue to hold for a while, particularly until the Central and Eastern European countries are fully integrated. In most European countries, there is still a large wealthy and powerful pensioner class with money and property. Even recent pension reforms in Germany seem to favor the older generations. Public pensions are still granted in Italy. Realistically, this cannot continue for coming generations, for whom a totally different saving and private insurance system will need to be developed in the next 10 to 20 years.

Using the Whole Workforce

It is estimated that about 19 million working-age Europeans have a disability in a labor market where they are three to four times more likely to be unemployed than non-disabled people. Increasingly, training and appropriate technology enables disabled people to demonstrate their ability to work to the same standard as non-disabled people. Changes in work structures and technologies challenge the existing discrimination toward disabled people. There is growth in sharing knowledge between specialist organizations and businesses in order to eliminate these barriers. Although legal requirements vary from one country to another, a number of employers are developing practical responses to provide access to employment (Shaw, 2000).

Managing Diversity to Create Marketable Value Added from Difference

4

Elena A. A. Garcea

> I want a BBC where diversity is seen as an asset, not an issue or a problem; a BBC which is open to talent from all communities and all cultures; a BBC which reflects the world in which we live today, not the world of yesterday.
> —*BBC Director General Greg Dyke, in a speech given April 7, 2000 in London at the Race in the Media Awards, organized by the Commission for Racial Equality*

Managing Cultural Stresses and Strains in the Present and Future European Union

In this chapter, we will continue to look at the demographic and sociopolitical conditions developing in and around the European Union countries. We will focus particularly on how culture plays a role in both promoting and hindering change and how it impacts Europeans' present and future attitudes toward cooperation and integration. As this chapter demonstrates, these fundamental dynamics will either allow diversity to add value and productivity to European enterprises, or hinder them from doing so.

The Cultural Challenge of Adding New Member States to the European Union

Managing cultural stresses and strains is essential for the development of Europe, particularly as its complexity increases through new membership and the eastward shifting center of gravity that this implies. Firstly, not all Member States see the European Union in similar terms. The French, for example, see the European individual as embodying a way of life to be nurtured and protected as essential to the purpose of the Union. The British, on the other hand, who regard themselves as least attached to Europe, take a much more pragmatic view of the Union, seeing it as something to participate in to the degree that it benefits them. The Dutch, equally individualistic and pragmatic in their own way, are inclined to see the European Union as an act of enlightened self-interest, and the Germans, often unconsciously, see European citizenship as freeing them from the burden of an all too recent history of conflict with their neighbors.

If the 13 nations currently applying to enter the European Union were all to join, the population of the European Union would increase by over 25%. These countries average a farming population of 20% compared to the 4% of the current 15 Member States. The risk of including all other countries in the European Union is twofold: they have large workforces, but they presently have weak economies. This combination stokes fears of a destabilizing migration of cheap labor westward.

Nor does integrating Eastern European countries into the European Union necessarily imply that they will fully embrace the same sociopolitical-socioeconomic model that currently exists in the European Union. Either there will be a process of mutual influence, or Europe will evolve in concentric circles with different levels of integration. In the second case, a minimum common ground will need to be established, but then these countries will continue at different stages of socioeconomic development and use different political, social, and economic models.

At present, the speed of integration depends on the capacity of the people and institutions in each country to shift from their present social behavior and governance style to more multiparty governance structures and higher levels of private enterprise. This will entail a major culture shift for many organizations and institutions. The European Union will be formed by the countries that meet the "spirit" of the European Union (i.e., "free movement of people, goods, and capital") as first envisioned in the foundation of the European Community. Peripheral nations will advance to join the core group as their capacity to honor human rights grows and their multiparty political system develops. Presently, it looks as if the future Union will be formed by the current Euro countries and those whose convergence policies allow them to join this club.

Current Cultural Challenges and Strains among Existing E.U. Member States

Stresses and strains are already present among the current E.U. countries. Tax harmonization, agricultural subsidies, bolstering of financially threatened industries, and salaries are among the problems that worry the citizens of the European Monetary Union (EMU). European citizens hope that the new single currency will bring similar tax systems, similar subsistence means, and similar economic subsidies. As a matter of fact, each country has its own cultural and historical past with different economic assets and values about those assets that will necessarily affect the economy of each individual country, even with the recent introduction of the common currency.

Harmonizing Existing Diversities in the European Union

The European Union originated in the effort to create and share a common market economy and has been a single economic space since that effort began to succeed. However, policies and laws remain quite different in the various E.U. countries. In order to adopt a truly common market economy, policies should become more uniform and coordinated. Although these adjustments are necessary to improve the efficiency of the Union, they will continue to be difficult to achieve. Each member, new and old, will be required to make cultural adjustments for each step along the road to achieving a satisfactory unity in diversity.

To achieve this by peaceful and voluntary means is a diversity challenge of the highest order and, should it be accomplished, will stand as an outstanding accomplishment in the history of human civilization. The United States boasts of having the longest continuous system of government in the world and of being a successful multicultural democracy. Nonetheless, it got to its present level of cultural integration by acrimonious debates over states' rights, by the use of force in a prolonged fratricidal civil war, and through the coercive assimilation of native and immigrant groups. It labors for equity today in a climate of litigious diversity initiatives while the widening gap between its rich and poor goes largely unattended.

Today the European Union has constitutional arrangements and a series of treaties, but a European constitution does not exist yet. Attempts and suggestions have come from different sources. The European University Institute in Florence drafted a "Basic Treaty" for the Union at the request of the European Commission. In order to open a discussion, the *Economist* suggested a review of the Basic Treaty combined with the previous E.U. treaties ("A Constitution for the European Union," 2000). No formal decisions have yet taken place.

In the 1990s, the communal principle was further extended to political, legal, financial, and social issues. As there are so many different cultures that produce different political, legal, and social organizations, it became necessary to imagine and design a union with a wider perspective—one specifically created to harmonize European diversities. Now, many Europeans are beginning to see that cultural diversity should be seen as an important resource and are learning to use it to develop alternative models to North American ones.

Market Regulations

Competition in Europe, while regulated at national levels, has flourished internationally. This discrepancy both complicates doing international business and weakens competition at the international level.

Germany, for example, has the biggest European market, and its citizens are among the richest in Europe. However, Germany still maintains market regulations within Europe that are intended to limit local competition and are not applied to the rest of the world. Retailing, for example, is regulated by laws that prohibit clearance sales from taking place more than twice a year. Opening hours are also set by law, despite the fact that it is getting harder to shop as the average person's working hours are becoming longer and more irregular. In addition, Sunday closing remains sacred in conformity with the religious cultural tradition, to the dismay of many German citizens and even international economic commentators like the *Economist* ("Germany: The Church Victorious," 2000; and "Six Days Shalt Thou Shop," 2000). German business people suffer from the competitive pressure created as German customers cross the border to shop in countries without such restrictions.

Metro, the biggest German hypermarket chain, has had considerable losses, particularly in the food market, due to competition from other European rivals. Profit margins (just over 4%) have been lower for Metro than for other European chains. The Portuguese Jeronimo Martins, British Tesco, Dutch Ahold, and French Carrefour, for example, all have profit margins over 6%. In addition, German hypermarkets have more selling space than do those in France and Britain, which creates higher costs; at the same time, hard discounts have a larger market share in Germany ("German Retailing: Cheap and Cheerless," 2000).

Tax Harmonization

The Lisbon summit of March 2000 took the first steps toward tax harmonization among EU countries. They agreed to tax nonresidents' savings, a step that will eventually harmonize bank secrecy laws and improve transparency in international financial markets.

Sweden has the highest taxes, averaging 52.9%. Its economy is doing very well with an unemployment rate that hovers around 5%. However, the IMF (International Monetary Fund) urged Goran Persson, Sweden's prime minister, to lower taxes in order to encourage investments and savings. Most E.U. countries have cut their taxes and increased their competition. So far, Swedish politicians have preferred to invest their country's budget surplus in welfare, particularly health care, on which Sweden spends more than most western countries. This may be an attractive factor to foreign professionals, but high taxes scare top managers who would otherwise move to Sweden. For this reason, some Swedish companies, Ericsson for example, moved key corporate and production functions abroad. They created their major headquarters in London precisely created to recruit foreign managers ("Sweden: Taxcuts? Why?," 2000).

In the United Kingdom, the welfare state was to some degree dismantled in the 1980s, during Margaret Thatcher's term of office. Social security expenses were reduced in order to limit public debt. As a consequence, the percentage of the population living below or at the minimum subsistence supplementary benefit rose from 12% to 19% (Rea, 1995), a direction that seems contrary to the well-being envisioned as a result of E.U. policies.

Agriculture

A large number of agricultural products (e.g., olive oil and citrus fruit in Italy, Spain, and Portugal) have long received economic support from the European Commission. Their production is protected but also subject to control. Such a policy sustains producers when

Exhibit 4.1

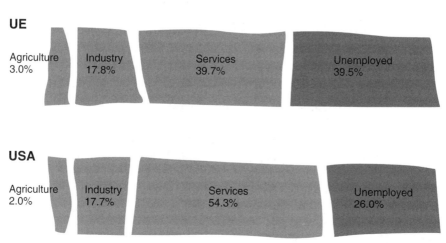

Occupations by Sector, 1997

UE

| Agriculture 3.0% | Industry 17.8% | Services 39.7% | Unemployed 39.5% |

USA

| Agriculture 2.0% | Industry 17.7% | Services 54.3% | Unemployed 26.0% |

Source: European Commission, Directorate General for Education, © 2000 European Community.

production is low, but it also penalizes overproduction by a system of fines. This is done to provide equal opportunities to farmers in all countries of the European Union. In 2000, roughly 45% of E.U. subsidies were earmarked for agriculture. This percentage will be gradually reduced: the estimate for the year 2006 is 41,660 million out of 103,840 million euros (Directorate General Education and Culture, 2000). Nevertheless, agriculture remains one of the main focuses of E.U. concern. The goals of *Europe's Agenda 2000* (1999) are summarized in one of its headings: "A leaner, greener European model of agriculture: contented consumers, cleaner countryside, competitive farmers, stable spending" (*Europe's Agenda 2000*, 1999, p. 6).

The cost of agriculture for the European Union is particularly appalling when compared with the number of people actually employed in the agricultural sector: a mere 3% of the total working population. Nor does this sector even begin to appeal to the 39.5% of the total population of unemployed people living in the Union (Exhibit 4.1).

Agricultural employment has dropped even in the countries traditionally based on this subsistence economy, such as Greece, Portugal, Ireland, and Spain. At the moment, the European Union spends about 47% of its budget on farm subsidies. The Common Agriculture Policy (CAP) provided between 70 euros in Luxembourg and 164 euros in France per person in 1998.

In the larger perspective of global markets, this system of subsidies will probably need to be revised to give European goods greater opportunities to extend their markets beyond the E.U. borders. All of these factors require revising traditional organizational cultures and thinking patterns.

The twin plagues of BSE (Bovine Spongiform Encephalopathy) and FMD (foot and mouth disease), which we discussed at length in Chapter 2, required emergency measures that, during the first trimester of 2001 alone, cost about 1 billion euros out of a total budget of 42.8 billion. CAP spending is mostly oriented toward agriculture. Beef and veal were only 11.7% and dairy products 6.4% of the total budget.

If more subsidies are going to be required there will be less support for agriculture. Germany would like to change the system of CAP spending to favor organic farmers. Austria is well advanced in organic farming and supports this position. Other countries, who are used to relying on the present CAP system, like Italy, Spain, Greece, and France, are much less keen on this proposal ("Europe: From Bad to Worse, Down on the Farm," 2001).

Internet Investment

Until April 2000, it was easy to raise funds for an Internet venture in Europe. However, several European Internet companies have not been as successful as they promised and went bankrupt. When the high-tech stock markets started to deflate, only the best conceived Internet business could obtain startup funds. In this respect, pan-European companies have more chances to compete with American business organizations, even though there is no guarantee of success ("Europe's dot.bombs," 2000). Some European Internet companies that have been unable to maintain needed cash flow have put themselves on the market to be bought by bigger corporations. This consolidation reduced the number of weaker organizations. Even old economy European businesses, such as car manufacturers, were expected to show interest in buying weak Internet companies ("Europe's Internet Drought," 2000).

The consolidation of the European Internet companies poses several cultural challenges to their owners. They have to give up the idea of being their own employers and accept being part of a bigger entity. Not all Europeans are used to teamwork, being traditionally more individualistic. Furthermore, one of the cultural differences between U.S. and European managers is that Europeans are much less used to business failure. Although the Internet business has actually shaken even the stiff European entrepreneurial culture, European business people are still not ready to take too many risks, and the European labor market operates too slowly to recycle workers quickly and efficiently.

According to a recent E.U. law, European consumers have the right to sue E.U.-based Internet sites in their countries. If they win, the rule may be extended to the rest of Europe. Such questionable rights should not be confused with the sacrosanct necessity to elaborate common laws against hacking, Internet fraud, and child pornography, as indicated in the Council of Europe's treaty on cybercrime and endorsed by the United States.

Moving Toward a More Transparent Business Culture

Globalization requires more open actions and transparent decisions, which are not habitual in all European cultures. Yet the concept of good corporate governance derived from U.S. companies has become attractive to many Europeans, though it is not always reflected in practice. Vivendi, for example, a French media-to-utilities group, promised improved corporate governance upon embarking on a merger with Canadian Seagram. A few months before the merger, it changed voting rights to reduce the power of its shareholders under the pretext of protecting the company from takeover. This, in fact, reduced the power of small shareholders and doubled that of big ones. Observers saw this as manipulation and attributed it to the culturally typical French ambivalence to outside evaluation ("French Corporate Governance: Ambivalent," 2000).

Marketing to children is also growing in Europe. Advertisers realized that children, who tend to watch lots of television, represented a very lucrative target population. In reaction to this, Greece banned all toy advertising between 7:00 A.M. and 10:00 P.M. and has considered banning all advertisement directed at children. In Sweden, television advertising aimed at children has been illegal since 1991. Sweden is even planning to review the E.U. rules on television advertising during its six months of E.U. presidency. Italy, Belgium, and Ireland have been discussing regulations on marketing aimed at children ("Advertising to Children: Kid Gloves," 2001).

Unemployment

High unemployment seems to have become a structural feature of European economies. Unemployment affects the various social strata with a disproportionate bias toward youngsters, women, school graduates, and those from less developed regions. This not only threatens the social equilibrium, but also feeds the crisis in the welfare system by increasing the number of unemployment subsidies that must be paid out.

In Japan and the United States, as well as in emerging countries, unemployment rates, in a comparable period, have significantly dropped. Such unemployment is not a problem in most of the world, but it is endemic to Europe. Manuel Castells (1996), a Spanish sociologist, agrees with many economists who suggest that this problem arises from the ethnocentric conviction of most Europeans that their work and social state models are much better than those in the rest of the world. A contradiction is apparent as Europe pretends to preserve its competitive position in the global economy while, at the same time, seeking to maintain better working conditions and better welfare benefits than the rest of the world. To aggravate matters, Europe has been reluctant to embrace flextime and part-time jobs that are a rapidly growing feature of the new economic system.

The Weaknesses (and Strengths) of the Euro

The European Union has been further plagued by the now chronic weakness of the euro against the dollar. At the outset, the euro's weakening exchange rate seemed to be an asset to substantial economic recovery. After the first year, its decline became serious. Even the European citizens who welcomed the euro as a way to overcome the economic disadvantages of their weak national currency, such as the Italian lira or the Spanish peseta, started to doubt the protection that the single currency promised to provide. The weak euro was beset by the fact that the United States grew much faster in the year 2000 than did Europe, and it was able to sustain an unemployment rate less than half that of the Euro zone.

At a macroeconomic level, on the other hand, the Euro zone has benefited from some favorable conditions. Inflation has been under better control than in the United States. Growth of industrial production has accelerated. The account deficit is better in the Euro zone than in the United States. However, one structural weakness remains: the rapid decline in value of the euro has severely limited the gains and interest of outside investors ("The Euro's Chronic Weakness," 2000).

Even as the European Central Bank (ECB) kept raising interest rates, the weak euro and higher oil prices brought inflation up to 2.4%, despite an expected ceiling of 2%. Europe does not offer the same incentives as the United States for companies to invest in cost-cutting technology. The higher costs of firing employees and static labor markets hinder labor mobility and flexibility.

In spite of all this, signs of improvement seem to appear in the European skies. In the second quarter of 2000, Germany's GDP grew by an annual rate of 4.7%; this is comparable to the 5.3% registered in the United States, particularly in the light of the more rapid U.S. population growth. Many E.U. governments have been taking action in favor of flexibility of their labor markets. Even in the stiffer countries, like Italy and France, companies have been able to hire more workers, often on short-term or part-time contracts, with less job protection and lower social-security contributions. Employment has, until recently, grown in the Euro zone faster than in the United States. Furthermore, Germany announced that they will reduce income and corporate tax rates, and Italy and France have followed the German plans ("Old World, New Economy," 2000).

Even though inflation in the European Union is above its expected ceiling, and the downturn in the economy at the end of 2000 has slowed growth, there is optimism about the European economy. At 2.4%, inflation is still well below that of the United States at 3.5%. Economic growth can be measured in different ways and over different time periods. If the last decade is taken into account, the overall GDP is higher in the United States, but the labor productivity is very similar in both areas. The adoption of the single currency in the European Union impels governments to make structural reforms in their economic systems and labor markets. Employment is expected to increase at a higher rate in the Euro zone than in the United States.

The euro has already facilitated the integration of European financial markets and brought the elimination of currency risk on cross-border investments. Cross-border mergers doubled as soon as the euro was adopted in 1999. Nine countries in the European Union had a budget surplus in the year 2000, giving the whole euro area its first surplus in at least half a century ("Europe's Economies: Stumbling Yet Again?," 2000).

The euro's weakness has another positive side. It favors increased exports, sustains a market that needs to expand, and supports employment of the growing population. The value of the euro became of even greater concern with the assimilation of Greece into the Euro zone at the beginning of 2001. Greece's GDP is less than 2% of the total Euro zone, and therefore its assimilation did not seem to be a major challenge for the ECB. However, its higher growth and inflation rates remain a constant challenge for the single monetary policy. Nevertheless, the hope is that by joining the euro, Greece will pursue its commitment to reform its economy, much as Italy, Spain, and Portugal had to do and did.

The division of responsibilities between the ECB and the national central banks is one of the main challenges for the monetary union. Monetary policy is developed in Frankfurt, but national banks still hold control over their banking customs and policies, including bank supervision and financial stability. The Eurosystem composed of ECB and the 11 participating national central banks (NCBs) is supposed to coordinate European and national banking policies, but apparently at least 50% of the Eurosystem balance sheet lies outside the ECB's direct control ("The European Central Bank: The Terrible Twos Begin," 2001).

Stock Exchanges

Today investors can cross virtually all borders through electronic stock exchanges. However, even with the introduction of the euro, it still costs more to trade across the Euro zone than within national markets. Some major European exchanges have merged in order to offer more appealing opportunities to their investors. The French, the Dutch, and the Belgian exchanges created Euronext in 2000; the London Stock Exchange (LSE) and the Deutsche Börse had planned to merge into iX (for "international exchanges") and started negotiations with the Milan and Madrid exchanges, which wanted to join. Even Nasdaq tried to create an alliance with iX.

However, the owners of the LSE were also its customers, and many of them had conflicting interests. The LSE abandoned its mutual ownership in March 2000, preferring to be a company owned by its shareholders. However, shareholders come from the mutual structure anyway. Stresses derive from two opposite tendencies: one demanding cross-border trading, the other preferring national exchanges ("What? Sell the Exchange?," 2000).

At the same time, Sweden's OM Group, a technology and exchange company, promised a takeover bid and the LSE had to postpone a vote on its merging with the Deutsche Börse. Different national rules and behaviors left many investors unhappy or perplexed ("Shocking Times in Throgmorton Street," 2000). In the end, the LSE gave up its plans to merge with the Deutsche Börse. The Germans lost trust in the LSE as the British seemed open to other offers, and at the same time the British suspected the Germans. Brits did not want all the growth market to go to Frankfurt, and Germans were not happy that all the blue chip market would go to London. The third party, the Swedish OM, launched a new offer based on their successful experiences in technology, suggesting changes in the entire organization of the exchanges ("Europe's Stock Exchanges: Beating a Retreat," 2000). This offer was put down a few months later.

Facing the Challenges of Globalization

The Culture of Power, Protectionism, and Prestige

Many Europeans view the challenges of globalization as direct results of the power of the U.S. economy and its media. Other European citizens feel less threatened and are more open to the U.S. market. As one Austrian put it, "Going to McDonald's in Graz does not mean that I will stop wearing *Lederhosen.*"

More than anyone else, the French have played the role of Europe's bellwether in respect to the invasiveness of the global mentality into the culture of peoples. In France, attacks on global organizations by individuals can confer the status of folk heroes on their perpetrators. An outstanding example of French resistance to globalization occurred when a French judge ruled that Yahoo!, the American Web portal, must either stop French users from looking at or buying Nazi memorabilia from its auction site, or pay a daily fine of $13,000 ("The Internet: Vive la Liberté," 2000). Even the French judge himself must have known that his decision was unlikely to be implemented, both for technical and legal reasons. Still, he wanted to send a clear message of French non-submission to the global, uncontrolled market. And, in fact, Yahoo! did stop selling Nazi memorabilia ("The Internet and the Law: Stop Signs on the Web," 2001).

For several decades, three "Ps" have obsessed the European business elite: power, protectionism, and prestige. What they say they mostly lacked was another "P": profit. This is gradually changing as power is transferred from politicians to stockholders. A new generation of managers is more inclined to turn down guaranteed government positions and take the challenge of entering private business. They are changing the old European economic model based on large companies. In the past, having a job in a large company was like having a job in a government institution. It offered lifetime employment and national prestige of a kind that one could not get by working in or owning a smaller business.

Companies in the European business system sustained themselves by holding portfolios in each other's companies. For instance, the Deutsche Bank held a 25% stake of Daimler-Benz. Groups were rewarded for their support with large holdings in each other's securities, and managers were selected from within the companies that protected each other.

Globalization has come to involve all types of products, even those, like beer, preeminently created for local consumers. Dutch-based Heineken is the world's second-biggest brewer. More than 170 countries drink its product. Nevertheless, beer continues to be mainly distributed in local markets. Heineken sells about 61% of its product in the European Union, and Denmark's Carlsberg sells 68% in the European Union. Taxes on alcoholic beverages can be very high in some countries. Other countries like Germany, with its *Reinheitsgebot* (purity regulations), apply strict production rules that may discourage imports. As a result, the growth of its beer market is not expected to go beyond 1.5% to 2%, which is only a quarter of the expected rate for soft drinks. Many international mergers of beer companies turned out to be failures, confirming the local character of beer markets. Apparently, brewers lack marketing traditions and do not have the skills to compete in the global markets ("Beer Makers: The Big Pitcher," 2001).

The "three Ps" system worked very well during the 30 years between 1950 and 1980. Economies were dominated by large enterprises, and the competition with Asian and North American businesses was still limited. Personal interests dominated. European citizens paid the cost of this system with high taxes that were used by their governments to shore up failing businesses. Paris spent billions to support Air France, Renault, and the Bull group. In 1986, Fiat asked the Italian government to prevent Ford from buying Alfa Romeo. After Ford withdrew its offer, Fiat took over Alfa at the government's expense, offering much less than the U.S. company. The Treaty of Maastricht obliged governments to reduce their deficits. Therefore, they could no longer support losing companies and were forced to privatize many of them. Now, in order to obtain capital, European enterprises have to seek international investors who impose stricter rules and greater transparency (Ernsberger, 1998).

The European Union and the United States: Culture Gap or Field for Cooperation?

Several European managers working for multinational companies recognize that, in cultural terms, the United States continues to set the agenda for business trends, including downsizing, core business, transformation, coaching, and e-commerce, all of which have had a very mixed impact on financial performance in Europe. They believe that European companies should have more confidence in constructing their own business models and initiating their own business trends, which should not be confused as conservatism in business.

Some European professionals in the field of diversity management see that the struggle for leadership of a socioeconomic block will pit American and Europe cooperation against the Asian countries, who have clear demographic supremacy and a cultural discipline that may give them a strong competitive position against the liberal Western model. This may be inevitable on the basis of the perception of cultural similarities.

Many younger Europeans no longer see a choice. Europe will either learn to globalize in a satisfactory way or will fall further behind the United States and be overtaken by Asian economies. The energy, involvement, and hard work of many Asian immigrants to Europe remind us of this specter daily.

Presently, the gap between the United States and Europe is mainly based on the rapid deployment and use of technology. The speed of technical innovation in the United States and the speed of its population to assimilate and implement these macro changes seem well beyond the ability of Europeans. There is also a possibility that this technological cultural gap will widen, unless intercontinental mergers and alliances contribute favorably in bridging it. Therefore, the impact of technology, primarily information technology, should be high on the list of priorities for the European Union in the new global socio-economy.

While technology is global, techniques are local. Technology can be easily disseminated at an international level. However, the techniques for using and managing it are culturally different. This is a significant issue in the European Union, although it is hardly of concern in the United States. Economic globalization, as well as the internationalizing business enterprises, seems to work best when systems can be adjusted to specific local contexts. Even the European economic, legal, political, and administrative union has to face the challenge of functioning at both levels.

A significant example comes from the European companies operating in the soft drink market, where U.S. brands command the market and are extremely focused on global domination. There is an internal contradiction in the behavior of the European companies in this market. In some countries, like the United Kingdom, they act as the bottlers for U.S. brands, while at the same time competing with U.S. companies in their international divisions by distributing their brands around the world. This is a difficult scenario to emerge from, especially because the U.S. model is so attractive. Moreover, U.S. culture is sold through brands like Coke and Pepsi. Finding appealing alternatives is very difficult and often far too costly for Europeans. The United States has succeeded better than Europe in successfully selling quality products at better prices around the world. However, global success has an Achilles heel. When a product is too ubiquitous and easy to come by, it can lose its appeal and thus open the way for other, more unique offerings. Some Europeans see and use this dynamic as a strategic advantage to challenge the primacy of U.S. product images. Examples of this can be seen in transatlantic M&A, as well as the European efforts in aviation, space technology, high-speed trains, cell phones, and other fields.

On the other hand, the success of the U.S. economy has been abetted by the growth of some European economies. Ireland, for example, has been enjoying the fastest growth in the European Union. It grew by about 9% in 1998, by around 10% in 1999, and was expected to grow significantly in 2000. Irish per-capita wealth may now exceed that of Britain. Unemployment decreased from 15% in the early 1990s to below 5% in the year 2000. The local population can no longer fill available jobs. Ireland became another country where the pattern of emigration has been replaced by one of immigration. Its new workforce comes mainly from Central Europe, but also from the United States. The United States is also the source of much foreign investment, especially in computing, which has a particularly favorable corporation tax. Inflation, an undesirable side effect, runs the risk of being the highest in the Euro zone ("Hot and Sticky in Ireland," 2000).

Furthermore, globalization needs to be seen as more than the sole result of U.S. economic power and its media penetration. Europe could be an ally, rather than an opponent, of the United States in globalization. To do so, large European enterprises will have to take on an aggressive economic role if they want to compete with those of the United States. Products have to be adjusted to a larger variety of market needs. This implies new market opportunities and a wider exposure to cultural diversity. However, globalization should be seen as an economic vehicle for cross-cultural outreach and distribution. Intelligent globalization should focus on the integration and localization of global products, instead of selling global cultures as is.

At present, it is still harder to start a business in Europe than in the United States. It can take 10 times as long and it can cost 4 times as much. Structural rigidities slow productivity. This is particularly evident in the business related to IT and the Internet. The only market where Europe has had the lead is in mobile telephones, which, despite the slowdown of 2001, may become the main gateway to the Internet ("Catch up If You Can," 2000).

Foreign Investments in the European Union

The 2000 report of the United Nations Conference for Trade and Development (UNCTAD), indicated that Europe has surpassed the United States in international investment. In the year 1999, there were 109 mergers and acquisitions valued at more than a billion U.S. dollars each. The British Vodafone bought the American AirTouch Communication for $60 billion, the French Havas/Vivendi bought Cendant Software, another large American corporation, for $1 billion. In total, the United States made 21 acquisitions; the United Kingdom, 20; France, 17; the Netherlands, 12; Germany, 9; and Spain and Italy, 1.

Between 1999 and 2000, foreign investment in the United Kingdom rose by 23% to something like 379 billion U.S. dollars. Foreign multinationals employ some 2 million workers in Britain. This certainly represents a sign of confidence in the British economy. On the other hand, criticism for its reluctance to adopt the euro is coming from several sources, including British ones. Invest.UK was the first agency to notice risks of disinvestments in the manufacturing sector. Even if others doubt that British monetary independence could influence foreign investments, it is an open discussion. Those in favor of joining the single currency are afraid that independence will have heavy costs in the loss of foreign investment. Those against the monetary union fear that heavy E.U. taxes and regulations will discourage foreign investors ("Britain: Sunshine, with a Chance of Showers," 2000).

The Mobile Communication Business

The use of third-generation (3G) mobile telephones promised to be a highly profitable business, although it has been a very expensive issue for European governments. The cost of licenses in national auctions may go up to a total of $150 billion. Prices are higher than what bidders expected and are able to pay. The former national monopoly telephone companies, including the biggest ones like Deutsche Telekom, British Telecom, and France Telecom, lost half of their value in 2000. In France, for example, the two big companies, Suez Lyonnaise des Eaux and Bouygues Telecom, refused to buy 3G mobile phone licenses from the government. As a consequence, the French government lost some 65 billion French francs, planned to have been put in the pension system's reserves ("France: Strike to Retire," 2001). Meanwhile, the cost of these licenses has severely taxed the liquidity of the buyers.

The costs of opening liberalization and competition and introducing new technology are higher than in the past, and the revenues are lower than previously. High-quality services, such as broadband for Internet users, mobile voice, and data and data-based services for corporate customers, have shown to be highly expensive and slow-return investments at the moment. This is happening despite the considerable flows of cash resulting from the privatization of government-owned companies.

In spite of liberalization, European telephone companies remained national businesses. Although they do take significant holdings in foreign telephone companies, they can rarely take control. Deutsche Telekom tried to buy Telecom Italia, but failed due to heavy pressures from the Italian government and employees.

Although big companies face higher investments and lower returns, local exchange carriers are not having it much better. Created both in the United States and in Europe to compete with gigantic, expensive, and monopolistic companies, these carriers often discovered that offering alternative and cheaper services was not so simple. In Europe, shares of Spanish Jazztel and French Completel bottomed out. Some other British companies, however, like Colt, Energis, and Cable & Wireless, have been more successful. So has British Vodafone, the biggest mobile-telephone operator ("Telecoms in Trouble: When Big Is No Longer Beautiful," 2000).

The Automobile Business

The car industry provides examples of the importance of managing cultural diversity while globalizing markets and merging companies. General Motors was accustomed to producing large cars for its U.S. buyers, but had to restructure its product line to meet the European and Asian demand for smaller cars. In order to do that, foreign expertise seemed indispensable. GM's policy was not to buy entire companies, but to take a solid stake in them. Despite numerous subsidies from the Italian government, Fiat was forced to sell 20% of the company to GM, taking its chance with a 6% stake of the world's biggest carmaker. In this way, GM entered the European and South American markets and could compete with them through the Fiat brand ("The Global Gambles of General Motors," 2000).

General Motors already had two European subsidiaries, Opel in Germany and Saab in Sweden. Opel had consistent operating losses in recent years, partly due to a greater decrease in the German car market (11% in 2000) than the European average (2.2%). In addition to the German decline of car sales, part of the blame was put on Robert Hendry, Opel's chairman, an American who spoke little German, although operating from Germany. GM's management and Hendry himself realized that the company needs a German-speaker, and Hendry resigned from his post. The German unions as well admitted that they could not understand Hendry's American management style and asked for a German chairperson ("Opel Loses a Packet, and Another Boss," 2001).

Knowledge of a foreign language can seriously affect the success of a company. Hendry was not successful in a German environment, but he was much more effective in Sweden. In fact, he was Saab's chairman in 1998 and succeeded in managing the company profitably. English is regularly accepted and commonly used in the business world in Sweden, whereas it is usually understood but not habitually spoken in Germany.

Cross-border mergers did not seem to be a big deal when Daimler-Benz and Chrysler first approached each other in 1998. Differences in nationalities and corporate cultures did not seem to be a significant liability for the headquarters in Stuttgart and those in Auburn Hills, Michigan. Daimler's pre-merger planning paid little notice that this was an international and intercultural deal. The managers involved in the pre-merger discussions apparently raised no questions in this regard. Their main preoccupations concerned the ways, the possibilities, and the potential successes of combining two companies, each with a strong and distinctive heritage in the car industry. Even though these business concerns are intertwined with international and intercultural factors, these latter elements did not seem to be relevant. Of course the pro forma diversity policies (see sidebar) were set forth, but efficiency and planning appeared as the only preoccupation and responsibility of the Daimler managers.

DaimlerChrysler is committed to enhancing the value of our enterprise by creating an inclusive environment that encourages and values teamwork and inspires all employees to work with passion and enthusiasm. The success of our business depends on a well-qualified workforce that is reflective of the customers who use our products and services and of the communities in which we operate.

Only people are capable of creating the value that will ensure the success of our company.

DaimlerChrysler is people-driven. Being a people-driven company demands equal opportunity in our employment policies and programs. In this context, it is of utmost importance to have initiatives that create a flexible workplace and harmonize professional and family interests.

Building globally competitive products and offering future-oriented services requires that we use the unique talents of every employee in our workforce worldwide. The best decisions result when all perspectives are considered.

Therefore, we must value all employees for their unique talents, backgrounds, cultures, and experiences.

We also believe the scope of equality extends beyond the walls in which we do business. We are committed to promoting diversity among our suppliers, dealers, investment managers, customers, and communities.

Diversity creates value and is an integral part of being the premier global company. Diversity makes good business sense.

Robert J. Eaton and Jürgen E. Schrempp

November 17, 1998

However, questions regarding the difficulties of differing locations and cultures were eventually raised in the discussion of the post-merger integration. They came especially from the U.S. side, which protested that their German colleagues were not treating the two sides as equals. U.S. managers and employees even felt it was going to be a sell-out to the German company and consequently feared that they had to give up their flexible U.S. management style and would need to put up with a "Teutonic" type of organization. Daimler had a formal and bureaucratic organization. The German senior mangers were used to long reports and detailed minutes. The American ones were more familiar with short memos and oral presentations.

According to the *Economist,* the fact that the DaimlerChrysler merger pressed on in the face of such neglect can be considered "miraculous." Share prices of both Daimler-Benz and Chrysler kept rising until the time of the merger. At that point, with some brief ups and downs, they started into constant decline.

Jürgen Hubbert, a board member responsible for Daimler's Mercedes-Benz car division, declared, "One company, one vision, one chairman, two cultures." The main worries seemed to regard practical adjustments, including a specially converted aircraft that would reduce the inconvenience of jet lag for company personnel who constantly had to cross the Atlantic. However, significant cultural questions were still unresolved. Until fall 1999, two head offices seemed necessary to represent the two companies. Then Hubbert suggested that DaimlerChrysler have a single headquarters in Stuttgart, thus reaffirming German dominance.

At the time of the merger, share options increased, favoring Chrysler managers, who earned two, three, or even four times as much as their German colleagues. On the other hand, the Americans considered that the Germans were squandering money by traveling first class to go to all their meetings and staying in five star hotels even during their weekends ("The DaimlerChrysler Emulsion," 2000). As a consequence, all

U.S. top managers were replaced by German ones, resulting in tremendous losses in the U.S. market.

The differences of attitude toward the company affected the workers' motivation and loyalty, a factor too often taken for granted. Furthermore, the cultural situation was so acute that language and culture differences were made the scapegoat for all kinds of misunderstandings and failures that were not necessarily related to intercultural issues. The situation collapsed at the end of 2000, when the top executive of Chrysler, Jim Holden, was practically fired by his German boss, Jürgen Schrempp. Americans felt that their talented U.S. team, which had built successful car models and created big profits in the 1990s, was kicked out of the company by their German colleagues.

Cultural misunderstandings and biases came out all at once when the new Chrysler CEO, Dieter Zetsche, was depicted as Sergeant Schultz, the buffoonish Nazi prison camp guard of the 1960s American TV sitcom *Hogan's Heroes*. When Schrempp was invited to meet with the Chrysler board before the merger, he refused, and Americans felt it was a slap in the face (Naughton and Lowrey-Miller, 2000).

Ford provides a different example of how to manage cultural issues in a globalizing economy. The value of its shares did not have the same shocks as those of GM and DaimlerChrysler, although Ford's prices slid lower in 2000 than in 1998 and it continued to decline in the ensuing shrinking economy.

In Britain, cars used to cost about 30% more than they did in the rest of Europe. This discouraged car ownership and made company cars an important perk. The British government finally reacted to this situation by imposing a price reduction on car manufacturers. Therefore, Ford reduced its prices by 11% in October 2000, even though its sales in Europe were decreasing and were much lower than in North America. Its profits were $1.8 billion in North America and $157 million in Europe. The difficulties in Europe are due to competition in the different types of autos offered on the European market.

Volkswagen, Renault, and Peugeot Citroën are able to offer products that are much more successful for the European market. Mini people-carriers, like the Renault Megane Scénic or the Citroën Picasso, doubled their sales in 1999 and 2000. American GM was successful in responding to the European demands by producing its Zafira model. Ford, on the other hand, produced the Scorpio, which did not sell very well. According to the *Economist*, the reason for this failure was that the Scorpio looked American in the front and German in the back ("Ford in Europe: In the Slow Lane," 2000). Furthermore, Ford did not respond to the switch from overtaxed gasoline to more economical diesel as did other car manufacturers. As a result, Ford is not present in that segment of the market that now occupies 35% of Europe's total car market. Ford engineered a corporate reorganization in 2000 and headquartered Ford Europe in Dearborn, Michigan, just outside Detroit. Its president, David Thursfield, admitted that it has been difficult to run a company for the European market from Detroit.

A European Military Force?

The need to provide alternatives to the U.S. culture and economic forces may be one of the most compelling reasons for European unity and for the development of an independent military and concomitant capability. In addition to the United States, the emerging power of China and other Asian countries represents a real threat for Europe.

The geopolitical deployment of overseas military forces also ensures that the United States will continue to have a major role in the energy-rich countries of the world, notably around the Persian Gulf and the Caspian Sea. The European Union cannot, at the moment, match this military presence, even though its total military spending is comparable to that of the United States.

European managers hope that the European Union will develop economic power comparable to that of the United States, and possibly an equivalent, independently deployable military force to deal with those military issues that do not interest the United States, provided that this does not lead to protectionism or the creation of opposing blocs.

This issue is of particular interest to British companies that work in countries that lie under U.S. sanctions. The European Union does not recognize these sanctions, and E.U.-based companies seem, in practice, to have largely ignored them. However, it remains possible for the United States to visit severe economic harm on these companies, and it is not clear that the European Union could do a great deal to protect them. Business could be negatively affected when multinational enterprises have both U.S. and E.U. partners.

How American Does Britain Want to Be?

The most Americanized country in Europe is doubtlessly the United Kingdom. American culture in the area of fashion has reached niches that none would have ever guessed until a few years ago. London is a good example, as the city once known as the place of bowler hats and black umbrellas. Now, even some of the most notable British businessmen seem to be attracted to informal American clothing styles. Savile Row's Gieves & Hawkes, a tailoring enterprise in the business for 215 years, reported a consistent loss in 2000 due to the revolutionary change in clothing styles. Such a change is so permeating that some traditionalist businessmen are even turning to image consultants for advice on their clothing. Adapting the American style to the British business life has become a new successful business. Color Me Beautiful, Britain's biggest image consultancy, registered a 40% increase in the number of men requesting advice on shopping trips. Another company, Image Works, is particularly busy in restyling various legal firms to make them more approachable. Even the London offices of major investments banks, such as Goldman Sachs and Morgan Stanley Dean Witter, have adopted "business casual" wear ("A Suit and Case for Treatment," 2000).

Even in more serious issues, many anti–European Union people in Britain are notably pro-United States, even to the point of suggesting that the United Kingdom should join NAFTA, even if this would mean leaving the European Union. This was supported recently in a speech made by U.S. senator Phil Gramm while on a speaking tour in England. In reality, Britain is culturally much closer to Europe than to the United States, although the fact of sharing a common language makes the British feel more like Americans than they really are and vice versa.

Even though the United Kingdom and the United States have been economically and politically close throughout most of their common history, people had different cultural perceptions of each other when they met. World War II was undoubtedly an opportunity for bringing together even some people who had never traveled before. They discovered for the first time that speaking the same language was not equivalent to living with the same values and behaviors. For example, Brits at the time jokingly remarked that there were three things wrong with American GIs—they were "overpaid, oversexed, and over here." Prime Minister Winston Churchill described the United Kingdom and the United States as "two great nations *separated* by a common language."

Diversity: Where Is the Value-Added?

The diversity of European cultures adds value when managing issues of intercultural communication, cooperation, and synergy. This means getting beyond current crises and conflicts and making things work better because of, not in spite of, diversity.

People who do not live in Europe may be surprised to know that every publication by the European Commission is published in all official Community languages: Spanish, Danish, German, Greek, English, French, Italian, Dutch, Portuguese, Finnish, and Swedish.

On the other hand, one should also say that Europeans are more similar than they think. The variety of languages and nation-states tends to obscure some other great similarities. British and Dutch engineers, for example, say they can work better together than either can with Americans.

It may be thanks to the Europeans' similarities that the employment rate is rising faster than in the United States. This is not an easy task, particularly when considering the strict E.U. employment regulations, such as high social-security contributions, job protection, and high unemployment benefits. One hypothesis is that the potential growth is higher in Europe than in the United States, where the economy seemingly peaked in the last decade of the old century. Labor market reforms are expected to favor a more job-intensive growth ("European Economies: Working Wonders," 2000).

Diversity represents richness. The possibility of having several points of view, multiple cognitive and operational paradigms, and different decision-making patterns is considered a competitive advantage, particularly in an environment dominated by uncertainty and variability like that of the present. Communication is born from difference and creates more variety.

Creating value implies a high awareness of the value contributed by all members. This is still a dream in Europe, although some steps have been taken to increase this awareness. Student and teacher exchanges at both school and university levels have become a common practice. They are often sponsored by European institutions. Some of them operate as non-governmental organizations (e.g., AFS [American Field Service] International Programs for secondary school students and teachers), while others operate as European Union initiatives (e.g., the Socrates and Erasmus programs, for secondary schools and universities, respectively).

The creation of new infrastructures has contributed to changing people's perspective of Europe. The Eurotunnel that now connects Britain with France has made a big difference in the way people in the South of Britain feel about France, Europe, and themselves. The barrier of the Channel has meant that many Brits never felt fully European. The tunnel has begun to change the meaning of that frontier.

The private sector has learned to move, operate, and leverage the advantages of a European Union space. Companies have also learned that scale economy in Europe is counterbalanced by the costs of culturally diverse consumers' personalization. They now have to apply the same diversity insights in treating their human capital as preferred clients.

Multinational European companies are out in front of their governments in their awareness of the cultural differences within their regions. They can deal with them only if locals, who are the ones best able to perceive such differences, take part in managing the system.

Some people in business find it difficult to understand the benefits of diversity. Such people are usually unaware of the compromises being made by others in their favor. A Swiss team leader, for example, may think he has a great international team benefiting from its differences, while a Greek team member struggles to deal with frequent direct confrontations that she is not used to as part of a team.

Multicultural Resources at Close Hand

Many local and international business are totally unaware of the vast resources they have at hand in doing multicultural and international business, namely the large number of businesses and services that have been created by and are owned by resident ethnic minorities. It is estimated that somewhat over 10% of the entrepreneurial startups in the city of London alone are created and owned by members of minority groups.

Turks and Moroccans are doing the same thing in the Netherlands and in Germany, where many Turks came as *Gastarbeiter* (guest workers). There were gastarbeiters in Europe in the mid-1950s. West Germany invited the first Turkish gastarbeiters to Berlin in 1961 to counter a labor shortage and their success is attested to by the 50,000 plus businesses they now own and manage. The same phenomenon is occurring in varying numbers in many major European cities, where Turkish entrepreneurs perform needed services and feed the local economy, and can also be resources in creating and serving markets that are not being effectively reached today.

Europeans are not only different in their cultures; they also have practical differences. For instance, in multinational business, most non-British Europeans speak English as well as their native language, and often another language or two. The European Union recommends that every young E.U. citizen should be able to speak at least three languages spoken in the Union. This is far less common amongst English-speaking people, and the choice of English as a corporate language by European organizations is starting to create a hiring and promotional divide between those who can and cannot speak English—a new distinction between "haves" and "have-nots."

Standards of business ethics also vary among European states, and this causes both debate and distress within companies. Conflict resolution and conflict management are increasingly important factors in business organizations involving diverse European staff, and courses and conferences on business ethics are starting to appear. E.U. members have often agreed on policies that they ignore when they are disadvantaged by them and respect when they are benefiting from them. This is possible because policies are not laws and members are not obliged to follow them. The creation of E.U. policies, however, serves as a fundamental means of negotiation amongst E.U. members.

In sum, we can say that the value-added by diversity is still largely economic, in the form of trade opportunities and economies of scale rather than in the more highly refined dimensions such as problem-solving and creativity. There is still much unfulfilled promise in diversity and much work needed to realize it.

We opened this chapter with a quote from Greg Dyke of the BBC. Shortly after he took over his position, Dyke appointed Linda Mitchell as head of diversity and had her report directly to him. He also tied part of his managers' compensation to creative leadership achievements in diversity issues. Said Dyke, "We need a new model that reflects today's world that sees the valued contribution of all peoples to shaping today's Britain" (Frankel, 2000).

In varietate concordia is the Latin motto chosen by the European citizens in 2000. Its official English translation is "Unity in diversity." It is difficult to say whether concord or unity appeals more to the European spirit. Whatever term or attitude one wants to take, Europe will, and should, remain a land where differences are represented and respected as part of the people's patrimony.

Europe Online: The "New" Economy and Virtual Collaboration from a Cultural Perspective

George F. Simons

5

> The paradox of global culture is that, whilst it offers everyone the same products and stories to consume, it is also constantly looking for points of difference, something new to sell, or exploit. In the knowledge economy, cultural complexity doesn't simply produce wealth: it is wealth. The more you have of it the better. "Poverty of identity" has become a handicap.
> —*Andrew Marr, "Perils of Ethnic Purity,"*
> The Observer, *July 4, 1999*

Although this chapter is being written at a time when a number of European dot.coms are becoming dot.bombs and serious regrouping is going on in the mobile phone industry, it is undeniable that a new business environment has been and will continue to take shape worldwide as a consequence of the technological boom, whatever the mood swings of the financial markets. The explosion of business-to-business and business-to-consumer e-commerce is changing the ground rules of marketing and sales as well as the definition of assets. "Bricks and mortar" businesses either become "clicks and mortar" enterprises or risk being left out of the new Net economy. Virtual organizations—clicks without the mortar—also need to be seen as serious competitors for traditional ways of doing business as more and more intangible assets become the locus of value and many tangible ones become increasingly irrelevant.

It is hard to measure the cultural impact of the speed and magnitude of change enabled by information technologies because, like the media before them, they are capable of reinforcing culture and redefining it at the same time. Change is no longer a matter of periodic evaluation and bursts of activity, but a constant companion to our work and indeed a strategy for carrying it out. This goes down harder in Europe than it does in North America, because rapid change does not automatically respect deeply rooted diversity and its traditions and accomplishments. At first Europe gave the impression of being dragged into the electronic age, kicking and screaming, and "blaming America." This cultural resistance was not necessarily a bad thing. It assured that the diversity of Europe would add its own value to the debate about what the future would be. In Chapter 3 we noted the hindrances to entrepreneurship in the European Union. Risk avoidance has been particularly responsible for slowing development in the European high-tech sector. Specifically, the capitalization and startup of high-tech ventures have been hobbled by:

- Excessive regulatory demands on startups that can take up to 10 times as long to pass through as in the United States;

- Heavy taxation of stock options that prevent their being used as incentives for employees in high-tech startups, and heavy social charges for those same employees;

- Draconian punishment for failure and little relief from creditors; and

- Lack of connection and collaboration between academic and research institutes and businesses, and the lesser availability of academics for consulting and involvement in enterprises. ("New Economy, Old Problems," 2000)

Despite all this, however, Europe, already leading in mobile technology, is now speeding toward an Internet business culture. By the time this book is published, if predictions hold, there will be more Internet users in Europe than in the United States. As mentioned in Chapter 3, hindrances to entrepreneurship in European States have slowed the development of e-commerce, but it too should surpass that of the United States in the next several years. Starting with the "Declaration on a European Policy for New Information Technologies" by the Committee of Ministers of the Council of Europe in

1999 (see Appendix 3), both E.U. and national governments have set agendas and goals for the digital society.

A More Temporary and Flexible Workforce

Meanwhile, the European workforce is changing along with the technology and the economy. Economists at Morgan Stanley Dean Witter indicated that most of the new jobs created in the European Union in the last half of the 1990s fell in the part-time or temporary category and had grown to over 25% of all jobs. They projected that this figure could rise to as much as 40% by 2007. Only about 25% of European women would prefer to work full-time. They already hold 80% of the part-time job market. Of the Dutch workforce, 40% is already part-time. The *Economist* recently summarized this development:

> In short, what seems to be happening is the creating of a two-tiered job market. On the one hand, there are the existing jobs, which still carry many of the perks, privileges, and protection that Europe's labor market is famous for. On the other, there is a less-protected job market, which consists of most new jobs, whether part-time or temporary. ("Western Europe's Job-Seekers Limber Up," 2000)

The consequences of this development for gender mainstreaming and equal access for women remain to be seen.

Globalizing Means Catching Up Socially as Well as Technically

The theme of the 2000 Lisbon Summit was Employment, Economic Reforms, and Social Cohesion—Toward a Europe Based on Information and Knowledge. Portugal's Prime Minister Antonio Guterres announced the "Lisbon strategy," which aims at combining business competitiveness, employment, and the fight against social exclusion. Government leaders agreed to develop measures and deadlines by the year 2010 in order to increase economic growth by 3% annually; create 20 million jobs; increase the number of employed women from 51% to 60%; identify common indicators to exchange best practices in education and in fighting social exclusion; cut in half the number of 18-to-24-year-olds without higher education or training; and build partnerships between educational and training institutions and companies and research institutes. They also agreed on the need to create an "eEurope," an electronic Europe, in order to improve both the economic and the social systems. In particular, they fostered adopting a legal framework for e-commerce; liberalizing telecommunications markets; increasing the competition in local Internet access networks; cutting costs of Internet use; and providing all schools with Internet access and teachers skilled in using information technology. (European Commission. "An Information Society for All of Europe." *eEurope 2002*. Available at http://europa.eu.int/information_society/eeurope/index_en.htm. This site contains updates to the action plan and a benchmarking strategy on the use and quality of Internet access for key groups of the population.)

The European Union is making efforts to reduce the gap in information technology between its members and their competitors. In 1996, they created an online Market Access Database (http://mkaccdb.eu.int/). It has three main aims: (1) to list trade barriers to European exports in the different countries outside the European Union and guarantee constant monitoring and intervention for each identified barrier; (2) to provide basic information to European exporters on applicable taxes, trademarks, export licenses, and so on; and (3) to provide an interactive communication tool for an online exchange of information between enterprises and European authorities. The main sections of the database are sectorial and trade barriers, applied tariffs, and the exporter's guide to import formalities.

On the other hand, people who express skepticism over a globalizing Europe, or even a globalizing world, are not only those who invaded the streets in Nice in protest when a new treaty had to be signed at the end of 2000. Some business managers and economic scientists have trouble finding agreement on global rules. The Multilateral Agreement on Investments (MAI) failed, the World Trade Organization was heavily contested in Seattle, and the Conference on Climate held at The Hague was one more failure in the attempts at globalization at the turn of the last millennium.

Portugal Finds a Forefront

The enthusiasm of Portugal for a digital future is perhaps unmatched elsewhere in Europe. The first e-learning conference in Portugal focused not on technical problems and needs, as is common in the United States, but on how e-learning would change the shape and culture of organizations and learning establishments, and the effect that collaboration might bring to bear on the development of openness and trust in user groups. The conference gave impetus to the development of AcacemiaGlobal.com (http://academiaglobal.sapo.pt/np/index.jsp), a major European learning joint venture between Tracy International and state-owned Portuguese Telecom. Its objective is to become the de facto learning portal for the Portuguese-speaking world, which has the fifth largest language presence on the Internet.

The discussion of e-learning* in Portugal, as we have observed in other E.U. countries, is not discussed solely in commercial or academic contexts, but is also intimately linked to broader economic, societal, and political agendas. The national priorities for developing capabilities were proudly expressed and sounded much like objectives in a corporate mission statement. Elliott Masie, President of the Masie Center, a U.S.-based e-learning think tank, who keynoted the conference underlined the significant objectives of the Portuguese initiative:

- To provide lifelong learning to a broader range of citizens, regardless of location;

- To provide strategic training to fill a current or sudden skill gap in the labor marketplace;

- To provide access to international expertise with a localization of both language and context;

- To export subject matter expertise from Portugal to the global economy;

- To use e-learning across the entire supply chain, from customers to suppliers to partners, allowing companies in Portugal to be more agile in competing in e-marketplaces; and

- To leverage collaborative technology to link learners throughout Portugal and Portuguese speaking countries. (Masie, 2000)

The Inevitable Shifting of Culture in the Media and on the Net

A recent ad for a European high-tech service company pictures an aged couple earnestly focused on something in front of them while

---

* E-learning or online learning, as it is also called, is the latest development in instructional technology for home and workplace computer users. Users can access both recorded and live classroom learning as well as participate via the Internet or their local server in instruction that furthers their education and job skills.

the voice-over talks about serving the diversity of customers not as groups but as individuals. As the camera backs away from the couple the viewer sees from the game controllers in their wrinkled and liver-spotted hands that they are passionately playing a video game together. In a world where we are promised "anything we want" and that we can "have it our way," the cultural component of our personal desires, no matter how unlikely, becomes of enormous interest to suppliers of goods and services. The glory of the industrial age was mass production. Henry Ford made it possible for the average person to drive a Model T—as long as it was black. It didn't take too long, however, for this to give way to lines of customization to fill multiple market niches. Today you may build your own car or computer on the Internet and have it delivered in a couple of days. Mass personalization is the latest trend in the evolution of product development, and is perhaps best positioned both to serve and take advantage of cultural diversity.

In the small Mediterranean town of Mandelieu-la Napoule on the Mediterranean coast of France, there is a large commercial center dominated by a Géant hypermarket. Géant is, true to its name, a giant store where one can buy virtually everything for the table, the home, the office, the playroom, the wardrobe, or the garage. You can also pre-shop for bargains online to get discounts when you arrive. Unlike stores of this magnitude in North America, such as Costco, there are not only the standard shelves laden with products and produce from Europe and the rest of the world, but also regular feature presentations where several aisles are created to promote the cuisine or products of a specific country. What really catches one's attention, however, are the almost weekly appearances of stalls or sales areas specifically set up to promote the delicious, high-quality products of *terroirs* or regions of France. While I was working on this chapter, I took a break to get the mail. Not to be outdone, Carrefour, among the largest of French grocery chains and a competitor to Géant, had deposited a flyer in the mailbox advertising a France where "the regions treat us to their flavors." Every region was represented on a large map of the country with a specialty sale item during the coming week.

Next door to the Géant is a McDonald's restaurant complete with a large indoor play area for children. Sensitive to its situation as a global and very American organization in another culture, *MacDo* (pronounced *Mac doh* with a long o) has taken up the challenge of marketing to the French palate. It, too, has regular campaigns in which Big Macs are transformed for worldwide tastes (Mexican, Chinese, East Indian flavored burgers). *MacDo* bravely tackled the French *terroirs* using a dozen varieties of local breads, condiments, and sauces from all

Exhibit 5.1

In La Napoule, France, You Can Order Your Barbecue in Four Languages on the Web at La Maison du Bon Poulet

Source: http://www.aubonpoulet.free.fr.

corners of the *Hexagone*,** to dress up the humble Mac *à la Provençale*, *à la Bretonne*, and with half a dozen other regional guises. *MacDo* is the symbolic target of resistance to globalization on the part of many French activists, perhaps because it is almost always full.

Meanwhile, a kilometer away in the old town of La Napoule, La Maison du Bon Poulet (The House of Good Chicken), a traditional *traiteur* with a scant 25 square meters of floor space that specializes in roast chickens, has designed its website in six languages to take orders from the laptop-toting tourists and the resident international community (Exhibit 5.1).

The real question here is whether, in the case of *MacDo*, Géant, or even La Maison du Bon Poulet, we are looking at the propagation or dilution of cultural values. The realistic answer is probably both. Culture is a living thing that changes with all forms of contact and has always done so. The difference today is that there is infinitely more contact than before. That puts the responsibility on us either to debate intelligently and try to guide its course, or dig in and resist contact to preserve what we want, using some prototype of what we (subjectively) as individuals or a group feel to be the correct or best expression of the culture. This, too, inevitably changes culture. Whether one is a radical constructionist who believes that saying things creates them

---

** *Hexagone* is often used by the French to describe the shape of their country, which is roughly six-sided.

in reality or an Islamic cleric enforcing the strictest *sharia* (sharia is the law of Islam, based upon the Koran, the Sunna, parallel traditions and work of Muslim scholars in the two first centuries of Islam), one is in fact changing culture. This is why the active search for value-added by diversity is the safest and most substantial means for sustaining culture and cultural life. It is also why we need both real and cybermuseums of all kinds to preserve strains of culture that both give us comfort about who we have been and are, and that may be rediscovered to add value at a future time.

Getting It Right

When it comes to crossing cultures, the advertising industry, because of its enormous stake, has got to get it right. They need the value-added that comes of diverse perspectives to succeed at their job. Unlike many other undertakings, advertisers receive relatively quick feedback, at least in the form of sales response. They need to be in touch with the stereotypes that move people as well as the ones that annoy them, and constantly monitor the cultural fads.

The truly pan-European ad is a rarity, and for advertisers it may be a "Holy Grail" that in many cases does not merit the quest. In spite of globalization, very few products seem identical all over the world. Among them are Coca-Cola, Mars, Mach3 by Gillette, Pampers, Pringles, Ariel detergent, Nivea cream, and Ajax scouring powder. According to the AC Nielsen company, a leading expert in marketing and market analyses, these products succeeded in becoming global for they can have similar prices and customers perceive them through the same types of advertisement (Dipollina, 2000).

For other products, it is the skill at adaptation to local culture that counts. Here is how it works: develop a marketing strategy that attempts to identify the essence of the brand, and then pay attention to local values and preferences in its storyboard and execution. Let's look at McDonald's once again. The Leo Burnett agency in London created campaigns that characterized the McDonald's brand as a safe family place for sharing food and intimacy. In the Belgian ad, a mother brings her young son to McDonald's. He is distressed by having to wear new eyeglasses. At the restaurant he brightens up as the new glasses make the hamburgers bigger and he gets to flirt with a girl his own age. The Swedish ad features a working mother, who avoids a business meeting to take her daughter to McDonald's. There she runs into her boss, who has cancelled the meeting, with his son. The British ad tells the story of a lad who gets his dad to take him to McDonald's in order to run into his mother. The couple, whom had been separated from each other, have a warm conversation to the delight of the boy who has engineered the meeting. The ad is called, "The Go-Between." In Norway, a boy is led safely through scenes (in grim black and white) of strange and (to the child) fearsome mod and punk characters to the safety and familiarity of McDonald's.

New Yorker commentator John Heilemann, who described these ads, observes, "In advertising, narrative is inherently local. Burnett's office in Norway had considered running the Swedish ad, since the people look alike, but discovered that it "jarred" . . . because of the perception that "family units are more intact in Norway." Similarly, "The Go-Between" would be awkward in Ireland, because divorce had only just been legalized there.

One recent McDonald's ad in Britain was called "Birds and Bees." . . . [A] little girl is potting a plant. She looks up and asks her father where babies come from. After hemming and hawing, he tries to distract her by offering to take her to McDonald's. She happily accepts and then, as the father sighs with relief, she announces that they can talk about babies over Big Macs. By playing on a father's unease in discussing sex, the ad . . . is "quintessentially British" (Heilemann, 1997, p. 181).

Speaking to, Hearing, and Reading Each Other

In Chapter 1 we discussed the impact of language on diversity and the maintenance of boundaries between Europeans. The year 2000 had been declared by the European Commission to be the "European Year of Languages," giving emphasis to language education programs and urging all citizens to speak at least two languages in addition to their mother tongue. Although the smaller northern European nations such as Luxembourg, Denmark, and Holland have been good at multiple languages, German speakers and the Mediterranean nations have developed language competence to a lesser degree.

On an operational basis, the language issue, according to Tony Norman, a Frankfurt-based interculturalist, "can be broken down as follows: mother tongue supremacy, dialects, speed and delivery, slang and idiom, and people do not like to admit they do not understand." These factors are often either not visible in online work, or are accentuated when the telephone or computer voice technologies are used. Reporting on a recent face-to-face intervention, Norman

> put the issue on the table. The delegates from the U.K. were singled out for intensive treatment and were persuaded of the benefits of Euro English or Neo-English (promoted by Daniel Goeudevert, former Ford executive and a director of The Green Cross) compared to a near incomprehensible dialect from Ulster. This language issue was explicitly monitored and facilitated throughout the conference. Perhaps most important was the pre-conference coaching of the main speakers, covering choice of language, style, and how to run effective question-and-answer sessions. (Norman, 2002)

Recently, I was also called on to do a cultural briefing at the initial meeting of a pan-European works council of a large multinational corporation. Twenty-four people speaking six languages in a two-day meeting needed to get to know each other, learn to recognize and respond appropriately to each other's intercultural behavior, elect a governing body, and start to create an agenda for their responsibilities as an active council on a day to-day-basis. In addition to myself, the trainer, this meeting alone required a facility with a vast outlay of electronics, including 12 interpreters spelling each other off. The cost of comprehension and democracy runs high when Europeans need to work together across linguistic barriers.

Such events make it interesting to speculate about the impact that machine translation is making, and along with it, the impact instant voice interpretation will make as it comes into service to varying degrees in telephony and broadcasting in the next 4 to 12 years. Europe, with its large population, its multiplicity of languages and cultures, and its high level of affordable technology, stands to reap the biggest gains from these new developments. Already on the Internet multiple language sites are common, and search engines offer immediate translations of the pages one searches for. Knowledge of how to write for machine translation is an important and time-saving skill of which few are aware. Excellent resources for such writing in English and French are *Plain Language, Pure and Simple* (1993) and *Pour un style clair et simple* (2000), both available from the Minister of Public Works and Government Services Canada.

The ability to hear and read everything in one's own language will affect everything we are talking about in this book, but raises more questions than it can answer. Will hearing and reading each other in our own language make us less or more inclined to acquire cultural skills? What will it do to our motivation and efforts to learn to communicate with each other? Will this slow or even reverse the dominance of English and other principal languages now used as second languages? Does it lead in the direction of greater or lesser connections with each other? Will it revolutionize cultural exchange or stagnate it?

As with most technological revolutions, this one too will probably depend very much on what values we bring to it and what uses we make of it.

E-Commerce and the "Hidden" New Economy

"Having it our way" is a business-to-consumer challenge that is more and more evident in the way products are advertised, designed, produced, and delivered, and therefore the cultural shift involved is relatively easy to see and discuss. On the other hand, the vast percentage of e-commerce goes unseen by the average person. It lies in the broadband communication webs in which business-to-business transactions take place. A recent TV commercial advertisement shows a harried manager beleaguering his subordinates because a supply of plastic parts for the company's mobile phone product is desperately needed. He paces the floor and barks orders to them to find out where a new supplier can be had immediately. One young manager is calmly but busily typing at his laptop. The annoyed manager asks him if he is paying attention. He says, "No." He has in fact just ordered the needed parts on the Web.

In the Net economy, traditional roles of suppliers, customers, and partners are blurred. This does not mean confused. It means that organizations and parts of organizations are playing multiple roles simultaneously in the new marketplace made possible by new technology. (For a good look at these cultural shifts in doing business, see Davis and Meyer, 1999.) It is almost possible to think of information as the only real commodity, and it only takes a few minutes looking at business sites on the Web to see that traditional market brokers are few in evidence, but that in addition to specialized industry portals, virtually every organization sees itself online as a portal that is brokering information.

The New Workplace Is Everywhere

For the past several years, I have been spending most of my time working in two areas, training largely European groups in how to succeed at virtual teamwork, and collaborating as part of a virtual team in the creation of e-learning capability for Management Centre Europe. While these activities are Eurocentric in terms of their primary

Exhibit 5.2

Virtual Teamwork Model

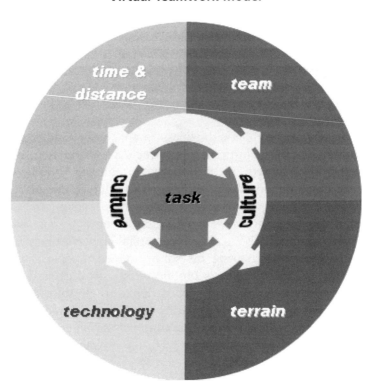

markets, they become culturally global almost immediately, because nearly all of the European businesses and business people involved are either transnational or global in their markets, personnel, and activities.

In addition to the capability of worldwide synchronous and asynchronous team cooperation, the simple fact is that most work is being transformed by the same technology. The *15-meter* or *50-foot rule,* as some virtual working consultants have called it, means that in addition to virtual teams and dedicated teleworkers, most of us in today's workplaces work virtually most of the time if we are more than this distance away from each other.

Working virtually does not make cultural differences disappear; it simply makes them invisible and harder to manage. To see how culture plays out in virtual collaboration, think of virtual global teamwork as a wheel (Exhibit 5.2) with these following characteristics.

At the center of this wheel is the *axle.* This is the task or set of objectives whose successful performance by the team contributes to how the organization reaches its goals and fulfills its mission.

Surrounding and supporting the axle are four sets of challenges that must be dealt with successfully if virtual teamwork is to roll along smoothly and in balance. They are:

1. How *time and distance* affect the ways in which we must communicate, lead, work, and manage people and projects in a distributed environment.
2. How we define, select, form, and maintain a high-performing, diverse, distributed *team*.
3. How we manage the *terrain* or contexts in which our distributed team works. This means making sure the parent organization(s) and other stakeholders recognize, understand, support, cooperate with, and reward virtual teamwork and virtual team workers.
4. How to choose the right *technology* or virtual working tools, and then learn to use them appropriately, both to do the team's assigned business task as well as maintain the social cohesion and motivation of the team.

Culture is a key factor, because it deeply affects not one but all of these four virtual teamwork challenges. Culture can either be "grit" or "grease" that gets between the wheel and the axle, that is, between the team and its performance of the task. It can slow down or even halt the virtual team, or it can be turned into added value for even higher performance. Culture is an essential part of every discussion of these challenges, as one can see in the diagram. Even the definition of the task, the importance with which it is seen, and its feasibility and difficulty will differ by culture, and the outcome will either be enhanced or endangered by the diverse perspectives of the team. In addition, each of the four team challenges needs to be culturally considered or it will run the risk of being derailed:

1. *Time and distance.* Differing concepts and expectations about how time is or should be used, and the absence of face-to-face contact, can quickly cause breakdowns in communication, authority, and commitments.
2. Multicultural *team* formation, difficult in intact teams, demands an even higher level of attention to the social and interpersonal dimensions of work when working virtually. Culturally, there may be a range of understandings of what a team is, and extremes of attitudes toward what requires individual initiative and what demands group cohesion.
3. The *terrain* or contexts in which our distributed teams work may be in different countries with different styles and levels of man-

agement support, and differing approaches to decision-making and delegation. Leaders and team members need to know how to strategize to get what they need to function well together across a variety of organizational and regional cultures, particularly when there are local pressures and demands.

4. Even *technology* is not culture-free. How one uses what tools, and when they are used, can differ significantly among team members and working locations.

The cultural issues surrounding virtual teams are not essentially European but are global in nature. One working team that I was training consisted of three Europeans, one Australian, one American, and one Canadian. It took several months of exchanges online to identify, define, and discuss the cultural factors that were likely to affect their collaboration with each other, their customers, and other business contacts. Their final list of tips and best practices for virtually working together ran to 18 pages when printed out.

The point to be made here is that in dealing with Europeans, and when Europeans are dealing with each other, one needs to explore differences by having conversations focused on cultural issues on a regular basis to keep the team functioning smoothly and on track. We have found that one best practice for getting this conversation going is to use an instrument that gets the team discussing and comparing for understanding, either face-to-face or online, their individual differences. There are a number of cultural instruments, such as the Cultural Orientation Inventory (COI), which enables the user to get a sense of his or her own cultural profile and compare and discuss it with teammates. (See www.tmcorp.com. The Intercultural Management Quarterly maintains a list of such cultural testing instruments at http://www.imquarterly.com/assesstools.htm.) If starting to discuss culture directly is too sensitive for a particular team, we recommend leading up to it by using and discussing a role-oriented survey such as the Belbin (www.belbin.com/) or even the Myers-Briggs Type Inventory (MBTI) (www.cpp-db.com/).

Radical Continuity—All Aboard the eTrain!

Outside of the U.S. East Coast commuting corridor and several urban metro systems located in the biggest cities, trains in North America are a remnant of the past, a touch of nostalgia. Not so in most of Europe where many high-tech trains provide reliable, abundant, swift, and timely connections to where people want to go.

It is not surprising then that Management Centre Europe (MCE) (www.mce.be), the Bruxelles daughter of the American Management Association (AMA), chose the metaphor of the eTrain to carry its management education efforts into the future. For many years, MCE has provided high-quality management education, briefings, and conferences in the heart of Europe, with spin-off efforts in the Middle and Far East and, most recently, in Central Europe. Hiring the best of the best faculty and lecturers for its programs, it, like many other institutes, training centers, and universities, both corporate and academic, faced the explosion of e-learning worldwide with the question, "Where do we go from here?"

With a veritable revolution in learning underway, some organizations have decided on e-learning as their primary focus, and others have allowed it to develop separately and alongside their more traditional offerings, as did the AMA and many other institutes and academic organizations. MCE opted for a third solution that would answer the question, "How does one blend radical innovation and continuity?" It chose to enter e-learning in such a way as to enhance and add value to its core business. The solution was one of what we might term "radical continuity," and is called hybrid, blended, or balanced learning.

MCE's strategy focused on creating a "digital surround" for its courses. Digital surround means that the core value of bringing the best faculty together face-to-face with learners is retained, but dramatically enhanced in several ways. Courses are being designed in phases. The first is the *assessment phase*, in which questionnaires, surveys, and other instruments help the learner see what she or he already knows and where his or her learning objectives might lie. The faculty is likewise alerted to the strengths and weaknesses of the class so that they know what parts of the course may need special emphasis. Depending on their readiness, learners with deficits in certain areas may be instructed to prepare themselves further by the use of online modules or courses before coming to the *tutorial phase*, where they are guided by a professional faculty member in digesting and integrating the core material into their thinking and practice. With the basic terminology and ideas in place, this phase can concentrate on the kinds of live experiences of discussion, role-playing, case study explorations, and above all, nuanced discussion with a top professional in the field. The face-to-face tutorial is followed by an online *application phase* of 10 weeks or more, during which course participants can test and review their knowledge of what they have learned, discuss and receive coaching on the issues that arise for them in their application of what they have learned, and receive, as needed, additional information or resources from the faculty or course facilitators.

The vehicle MCE created to carry this effort to its destination is called the "eTrain." The eTrain is an online community platform that serves not only to meet client and participant needs in the online phases described above, but also serves as a community of practice for various groups involved in the ongoing design and development of e-learning.

Though its in-house language is English, MCE's staff and faculty are from 47 countries and have customers worldwide. The eTrain project faces a number of formidable challenges, including educating faculty in how to create digital surround that is both pedagogically sound and culturally appropriate; refitting and reeducating existing approaches and personnel on how to market this new form of learning to a multi-cultural European and global clientele; and, of course, educating its clients in how to build, market internally, and benefit from the newly available tools and approaches to mastering management and business skills.

In addition, a new role has appeared. Herman Coquel, IT manager at MCE, describes it as follows:

> Facilitating online discussion forums clearly requires special skills, particularly in a multicultural online environment. Having trained online facilitators will be the primary key-success factor for the project. While it is not necessary that the facilitator is an expert in the subject-matter, she or he must be conversant with it as well as having the ability to recognize communication styles and learning patterns in other cultures. Above all he or she needs to have the ability to keep the discussion going on by stimulating every student to participate. A moderator or facilitator stimulates the discussion by raising challenging issues and puts participants back on track when the discussion is drifted from the subject. Fast-moving participants are given the challenge to coach their less-active co-students, which enhances the team-spirit and moves the whole class forward at the same pace. (Coquel, 2001)

MCE's approach is a very timely solution to incorporating e-learning into one's core business. MCE's organization and approach is also a good example of the best European tendency: it solidly addresses diversity in the context of a past that has brought us to this point in history, it had a full view of what is going on in the present, and it takes advantage of the possibilities found in a global future. It is far too soon to tell whether MCE's efforts will be a great success or not, but they are indicative of the kind of transitional thinking that European organizations are doing and that should be taken into account when proposing organizational change such as what diversity initiatives entail.

Online Support for Diversity

This morning, www.google.com, my favorite search engine, reported that it was searching 1,610,476,000 Web pages—a number, no doubt, far far less than it will be searching on the day that you read this line. The authors of this book have been overwhelmed by the amount and quality of information, links, online courses, and other resources available for pursuing diversity information and initiatives on the Internet. This revolution of information distribution calls into question the very nature of publishing a book on the topic of diversity. Because the choices of media are so large and varied today, one has to ask a couple of questions: What is it that books and other print media do better that cannot be done via other media? What is the blended solution? This is not the forum to discuss this question in detail. However, we feel that one of the things print media can do, and what we attempt in this book, is to open the eyes of those who have not yet explored online diversity resources to the possibilities that the Internet, intranets, and extranets hold for them, both in the information they provide as well the support they offer to diversity initiatives.

For those unfamiliar with these distinctions, the *Internet* refers to the public network that is accessible to anyone with an online connection and a browser; *intranets* are similarly constructed pages that belong to a company or organization and are generally accessible only to authorized individuals or to the members or employees of the organization; *extranets* are websites that an organization creates for its customers or a specific group of outside users. Discussed below are some of the ways in which each of these media can and should contribute to diversity initiatives:

1. The *Internet.* The first thing to remember is that the Internet is a dynamic medium, an organism that reflects the dynamism of the world it represents. It is ever-growing and ever-changing—one of the reasons why it is necessary to restrict the URLs (Internet addresses) that we provide you with to the home sites and more stable locations of the organizations and topics we refer to. Therefore it is important for those working in the intercultural and diversity field to learn how to search for what they need. At www.yahoo.com, another major search engine, for example, fol-

lowing the search path of "Home > Society and Culture > Issues and Causes > Multiculturalism >" provides hundreds of listings of Governmental services, NGOs, and other enterprises concerned with cultural diversity that is searchable on a country-by-country basis and in various languages, not just in Europe, but worldwide.

2. *Intranets.* Online support for diversity initiatives is becoming the second most important success factor to top management support for the implementation of the organizational change required to derive value from a diverse workforce. This support largely occurs on intranets, where organizations can project the organization's commitment to diversity and develop its multicultural identity and image, as well as disseminate information, manage diversity projects, create and sustain affinity and special interest groups, carry on discussions, poll their employees, manage expatriation and repatriation, and deliver e-learning for multicultural competence on a companywide basis. The possibilities seem limitless and realizable as long as the organization makes the effort both to market its intranet to its stakeholders and to construct a user-friendly environment that is truly of interest and use to its employees. The diversity parts of the intranet, generally speaking, should be well integrated into the organization's online intranet and workspace to emphasize that culture and multiculturalism are an essential aspect of everything the organization does.

3. *Extranets.* The *PC Webopaedia* defines an extranet as follows: "Whereas an intranet resides behind a firewall and is accessible only to people who are members of the same company or organization, an extranet provides various levels of accessibility to outsiders. You can access an extranet only if you have a valid username and password, and your identity determines which parts of the extranet you can view" (see http://www.pcwebopaedia.com/TERM/e/extranet.html). Extranets allow organizations to project their diversity commitments to their partners and customers in the conduct of everyday business. They also offer a medium for specific diversity projects that one is willing to share with others in terms of information and processes, such as diversity benchmarking.

Although benchmarking surveys of European diversity efforts are under way, and the next chapter reflects a benchmarking survey undertaken in the context of preparing this book, there is a great need for an ongoing online benchmarking resource focused on EuroDiversity, particularly in languages other than English.

The Changing Face of the Expatriate

While I was preparing this book, I conducted a small survey of largely European HR (human resources) professionals. Essentially I asked three questions:

1. How are expatriation processes and procedures in HR departments and in the relocation profession changing due to new technology?
2. Precisely, how are you and companies you work with using new technology in the selection, preparation, and support of expatriates?
3. How has the expatriate's experience of expatriation been changing as a result of new technology?

The answers we received not only pointed to some remarkable uses of information technology to manage various aspects of the expatriation process, but even to whole systems approaches like those offered by www.propelleronline.com, and especially that of www.gpslink.com. The latter (Exhibit 5.3) manages the expatriate process for the company HR and accounting functions, the vendors and suppliers, as well as the expatriate and his or her family, from the process of recruitment to reintegration after returning from abroad, providing assistance and coaching throughout.

Such solutions not only lower costs by reducing administration efforts, but actually provide greater efficiencies in transferee management: they provide the transferee (and family) with more personalized and accurate services, including both practical and cultural information, than were available before. In addition the users of such systems can make accurate and integrated data accessible to all stakeholders around the world.

The Lines Are Blurring . . .

As a result of the new connections provided by technology, and the new mobility of not only hand labor but also skilled labor, the lines are blurring between:

- who is an expatriate and who is an immigrant
- who does what in HR management
- what is intercultural training and what is diversity training

Exhibit 5.3

The GPS Link Expatriate Management Software Integrates the Full Range of Expatriate Management Activities in a Single Online Support System

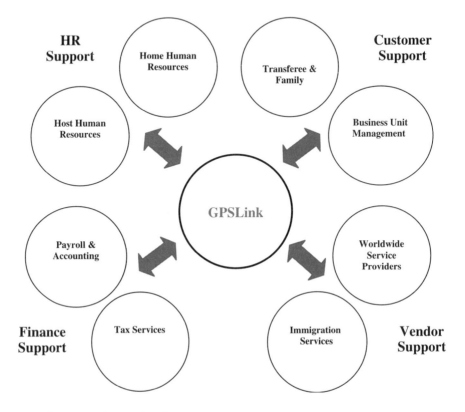

HR Support — Home Human Resources, Host Human Resources

Customer Support — Transferee & Family, Business Unit Management

Finance Support — Payroll & Accounting, Tax Services

Vendor Support — Worldwide Service Providers, Immigration Services

GPSLink

Who Is an Expatriate?

It is still very true at an upper management level that,

> Top performing multinationals not only demand superb performance from expatriate managers, but also accept some responsibility for ensuring that their families are happy in the host country and that the expatriates themselves remain well-connected to the organization and enthusiastic about their career development. *All three are prerequisites for success.* (Hsieh, Lavoie, and Samek, 1999, p. 71–82)

On the other hand, we are now living in a world in which expatriates and impatriates, virtual and real, abound, and the business of recruiting abroad has become a key survival strategy in some industries and a primary concern of human resource professionals. Mobility within the European Union is growing, and it is common to live in one country and work in another. Is this expatriation anymore?

Who Does What in HR Management?

These shifts are occurring at the same time that the aforementioned strides are being made in the technology available for HR work. John Sullivan, professor of Human Resources at San Francisco State University, suggests, "75 percent of the current workload in HR could be taken care of by IT systems. Even worse, the remaining 25 percent could be outsourced. Unless HR finds itself a new agenda to fill the void, it will find it is history" (Sullivan, 2001).

Gone are the days when a foreign assignment was tantamount to a disappearance (and in some cases banishment of the unpopular employee) and a phone call home cost a day's wage. Today people can work anywhere from anywhere as well as moving to new locations. In this environment, self-service initiatives, technology solutions, virtual working, and HR portals proliferate, and the tendency of HR departments is leading to hands-off administrative procedures (outsourcing or co-sourcing) due to the demand for both cost-reduction and better customer service. All this leads to less localized HR and more and more transferee self-responsibility, and away from the cozy and costly practices and perks derived from the colonial era of Europe.

The self-directed process often starts with an online job search. Once recruited or chosen, the transferee (and family) is offered a menu of support options from which to shape a support package. He or she is encouraged to research the job destination, and make virtual visits to the culture. Even the orientation tour is gone as relocation companies use e-mail and the Internet to "show" properties to employees being transferred.

Once the transfer has taken place, constant two-way information flow is likely to occur. Colleagues, coaches, and mentors feel like they are in the office next door via e-mail, phone, and wireless technologies. It is no longer necessary to be or feel out of the loop. Individuals can be constantly updated on their role and job back home, and stay abreast of corporate politics. They can enter an e-learning environment to support their foreign adjustment, or take expatriation workshops online as well as participate in in-country communities of practice. Individuals and their families are integrated into virtual teams and electronic communities even before departure, and these e-environments can well support the expatriate during the entire cycle of expatriation.

What Is Intercultural Training and What Is Diversity Training?

At some job levels, individuals are moving directly from college to overseas. This is creating a younger, more flexible, as well as more culturally alert and culturally diverse workforce. The concern is to be able to function in a new culture, and it seems that organizational assimilation is the key to success and to social assimilation. Not surprisingly, the management of cultural issues in such circumstances becomes an everyday matter that can benefit from intercultural training and learning. It seems that there is more of a natural flow from the intercultural objectives of learning to survive and succeed in another culture to taking advantage of the available cultural diversity for enhancing organizational and individual social success.

Both kinds of training are tending to pass more and more into just-in-time learning resources and job enhancement tools, in short, into effectively managed intercultural knowledge. In one organization it has become standard practice to interview each expatriate upon return home, and enter that person's key learnings into a central database, so that others can learn from the wisdom and experience gained in both expatriation and repatriation processes. This is not new, but it is being done with new technology that enables information to be turned into ready-to-apply knowledge. Short case studies or critical incidents from expatriate experiences can be developed and posted as well, and these in turn can be transformed into readily available learning objects and learning sets. Customizable intercultural and diversity learning games can also be customized and integrated into training or e-learning, or folded into corporate intranets that are available in many European languages from www.diversophy.com.

The self-service mentality created by online tools makes it up to the individual expatriate to manage culture, and this in turn is influencing the face-to-face behavior of multicultural work groups and creating corporate cultures that have their own processes for dealing with cultural difference, sometimes by choosing deliberately to ignore it. Tony Norman, whom we cited earlier about ESL issues, following U.S. researcher Kovacs, who asserts that multicultural groups tend to be either "top" or "flop," is shifting the focus in his training and consulting work from intercultural education to group process: "The difference between success and failure can be found in a handful of not unfamiliar factors: agreed common goals, clarity of and focus on task in the group, clear conference and group ground rules, mixed and changing groups, putting issues on the table" (Norman, 2002). Even with little explicit input, employees and teams, are given time, space, and the opportunity to grow together by engaging in evaluation and reflection, can live and learn intercultural interaction.

Can We Actually Leave Home Anymore?

Immediate connectivity with "home," with family, and with friends in the home country or the previous assignment country, is becoming normal for not only European and North American expatriates. For long periods one can maintain the feeling that "I am still a part of their lives even if I don't see them every day." From an intercultural perspective, this may have some major drawbacks as well. For expats or those who don't have as much of a spirit of adventure, it is possible to have too great a reliance on what was left behind and to avoid settling into and acculturating to the place to which they have relocated. Further, one can even live in two worlds without a complete commitment to either. Given the short-term nature of many assignments, it might be interesting to think of home as a culture that one carries about in an electronic rucksack rather than being located in one special geographical place.

Perhaps the children of expats who have grown up and been educated in several different cultures, as is becoming so common in Europe today, will be the harbingers of what this future culture is like. As one young man noted, "I am at home almost everywhere, but don't really belong anywhere." His parents are British and German; he was born in Germany, grew up in France, went to University in Britain, and now works for a major U.S.-owned international publishing concern in Paris.

I discover that in my sixth decade of life I am now learning faster and more than I did in my best university years, so I can only wonder about the perspectives of these multicultural young people entering the workforce and their perceptions, hopes, and ideals.

As virtual reality becomes real and reality becomes virtual, we clutch at the familiar things, such as the computer desktop that convinces us that we still have "files," "folders," and "trash baskets" that ground us in physical images. At a recent convention I was telling a resistant trainer of the possibility of creating solid learning relationships online. She didn't believe me, that is until a participant in one of my courses whom I never met face-to-face before interrupted us to give me a warm embrace. This chapter has contained some thoughts and examples of the implications of technology for business and culture. We turn now to more of the specific activities and best practices for organizations and people working in this new world.

Corporate Best Practice: What Some European Organizations Are Doing Well to Manage Culture and Diversity

6

Michael Stuber

In the previous chapters we looked at what makes working with diversity in the Euro zone distinctive and examined the challenges that it offers. We are now in a good position to ask what diversity means to corporate Europe in terms of how they have responded to it, and to examine the lessons that can be learned on the basis of what we have heard from them so far.

To gather substantial new insights, mi·st [Consulting carried out a pan-European corporate practice survey and identified approximately 60 companies to invite to participate in the fall of 2000. Multiple methods were used to identify potential participants:

- Internet research
- Companies featured in the press or on diversity websites
- mi·st [Consulting's clients and contact network, and clients of British diversity consulting companies
- The Centre for Diversity and Business actively contacted companies across Europe

- Companies mentioned in a 1997 British best practices report
- Companies from relevant contexts, such as EBNSC (European Business Network for Social Cohesion, now called CSR-Europe, or Corporate Social Responsibility Europe) British Diversity Awards, German *Total E-Quality* label

The public sector and nonprofit organizations were excluded to strengthen the business focus of this initiative. However, some publicly owned companies from the private sector were included.

During two rounds (November 2000 and April/May 2001), participants completed a questionnaire of 12 pages; some gave additional telephone interviews. At the end of the process, 20 corporations had contributed to our sample. They were split into two groups that were compared, if possible and appropriate: 10 European subsidiaries of global companies headquartered in the United States, and 10 European companies:

Air Products Europe
AerRianta
American Express Europe
Bausch & Lomb
British Airways
British Telecom
Cable & Wireless
DuPont Europe
Ford of Europe
GE Plastics Europe
General Motors Europe
IF/Skandia
Kraft Foods Europe
Lucent Europe
Lufthansa
Procter & Gamble Europe
SaraLee DE
Shell Europe
Telia
Virgin Retail

What the remainder of this chapter contains are the insights and best practices emerging from this inquiry.

What Does "Diversity" Mean to Corporate Europe?

Ever since the idea of diversity began to spread in the business world in the 1980s, extensive discussions have taken place as to what the word "diversity" actually means in its new context. Although early definitions focused mainly on differences of race and gender, more dimensions were later included. More recent and more sophisticated perspectives embrace differences and similarities, or highlight "individuality" as the most inclusive and broadest possible paradigm.

In addition to describing the phenomenon of "diversity," organizations position the issue in relation to their policies, their culture, or their day-to-day business. This may either result in integrating diversity as part of their managerial tool-kit, or seeing their diverse stakeholder base as a value-added for the business at large. One respondent to the survey on which this chapter is based gave his personal definition of diversity in the phrase, "appreciating, valuing, and utilizing difference for competitive advantage."

A third way to look at diversity is as a basic attitude reflected in everything an organization and all its members do. This could be called, "Diversity with a capital D." This definition avoids the risk of diversity being seen as "positive discrimination" or "yet another program."

In European companies, three major questions emerge from the definitions above. The differing approaches of these companies to diversity seem to correspond to the developmental stage that each finds itself in regarding diversity.

It is perhaps obvious but also interesting to look at whether differences or "dissimilarities" between people were even mentioned as an aspect of diversity. Two-thirds of our respondents mentioned some or even a wide variety of differences when defining diversity. They pointed to factors like "family status, military service, religious belief, education, etc." On the other hand, the remaining one-third did not explicitly point to how people were different when talking about diversity, but simply said things like, "all the ways people differ." *Looking at the historical development of diversity, can we argue that the latter approach is more advanced, as it is more inclusive and it serves better to avoid special interest discussions.*

Irrespective of whether *how differences are defined* is itself a question of diversity, some companies do refer to "uniqueness" or "individuality" in this context, while others do not. Respondents are evenly split on this issue. *Again, can we assume that highlighting indivi-*

duality is a more advanced approach to diversity because it actively avoids a they-versus-us backlash and makes it easier for everybody to relate to the definition, or is it a way of avoiding critical issues. A third element found in the various definitions of diversity in Europe concerned how diversity was linked to business. Half of the participants referred to the potential and economic benefits of diversity, while the other half did not mention any business perspective in their definitions. *Should we see this as convincing evidence that some companies position diversity as a business initiative, while others stress fairness, ethics, and the moral dimension of diversity as paramount?* One organization, SaraLee DE combined parts of all three perspectives by asserting that, "diversity encompasses all the ways that people are different from each other and calls for recognition of the contribution that every individual can make."

No differences between U.S.-owned and European companies could be identified regarding their definitions of diversity in Europe. Two major explanations can be given for this finding. First, some aspects, such as the "core dimensions" (gender, ethnicity, age, disability, sexual orientation, and religious beliefs) of diversity, are in fact based in human nature and have universal relevance. Secondly, European companies do look at what other companies have done when developing their framework. Even if they do not copy North American approaches, some basic considerations are likely to be reflected in their initiatives.

In a pre-test of the survey, we asked concrete questions about which explicit dimensions of diversity were addressed. We found that quite a few companies limited their European diversity initiatives to gender and differences of ethnic or national culture differences. In order to identify developmental gaps, we asked separate questions about whether or not these core or external dimensions of diversity were actively addressed.

Gender and ethnicity are most often explicitly mentioned, and age ranked third. When we looked at how European companies were "actively addressing" different dimensions of diversity, we found that they tended to embrace more dimensions than U.S.-owned companies did. That Europeans are more inclusive in this respect could be seen as a "lesson learned" from the pioneers in the United States. On the other hand, American companies working in Europe might feel that it is not as important or relevant to address the entire range of differences found on their side of the Atlantic. This appears shortsighted, and ignores the clear commitments to all six core dimensions of diversity that the European Union has repeatedly made. Gender, ethnicity, age, disability, sexual orientation, and religious beliefs are all mentioned in the new Article 13 of the Treaty of the European Union, in the E.U. Charter of Human Rights, in the antidiscrimination directive, and in the EQUAL program.

As diversity developed in the United States, sexual orientation and religious beliefs were often not explicitly acknowledged, and, when mentioned, were even less likely to be addressed actively. This may be due to the natural inclination of organizations to steer clear of divisive emotional issues and historic taboos. Even in the field of diversity, there seems to be a tendency to perpetuate mainstream heterosexual and Christian norms. Culture has a tendency to reinforce itself, even when it is trying to change.

Work style, lifestyle, languages spoken, and, to some extent, education, are mentioned as relevant external dimensions of diversity. Yet, parental status, life experience, and professional background do not rank high in this context, while differences in education are rarely addressed actively. On the other hand, organizational differences such as seniority, compensation and benefits, function, level, sector, and location are widely acknowledged as relevant dimensions of diversity.

Overall, there is a certain discrepancy between the declared intent to embrace all kinds of differences and acknowledge individuality, and the organizations' active efforts to address a wider variety of differences. Companies are reluctant to "admit" that some issues like being a parent affect employees differently and actually exist, while at the same time, they place a high priority on and explicitly address related activities such as work/life balance.

The following lessons were extrapolated from our survey results. They are lessons that North American and other business people interested in diversity issues can use while working in Europe.

Lesson 1: Be as inclusive and as business-focused in Europe as you are in the United States.

The European Business Case Behind Diversity

To identify precisely why companies chose to address diversity in Europe, we reduced the so-called "business case" into three basic components using a framework (Exhibit 6.1) developed earlier by mi·st [Consulting:*

---

* Michael Stuber, the author of this chapter, belongs to mi·st [Consulting and has provided these findings.

Exhibit 6.1

The Business Case for Diversity in Europe

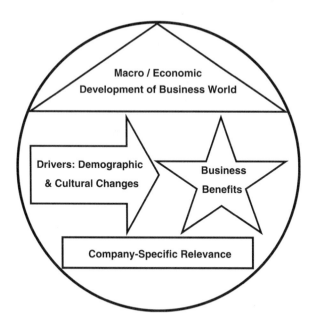

- Strategic fit with economic or macro developments in the business world
- Business drivers—the bottom-line costs of not addressing societal and cultural changes
- Business benefits—the return on investment companies could reap from their diversity work

Obviously, company-specific elements of the business case were not included in the survey. Such might include an analysis of concrete business goals and challenges. If these could also be addressed by diversity, they would add elements to the business case.

The Strategic Fit of Diversity in Europe

Almost every quarter sees a fresh list of key challenges for the corporate world that includes macroeconomic, demographic, technical, or strategic issues. Our survey focused on developments relatively new to companies in Europe, but whose pace have increased over recent years.

The most important trends were found to be:

- Ongoing organizational changes, such as restructuring, reengineering, general flexibility, and multidimensional matrixes
- International shifts, like European integration, globalization, and changing conditions in Eastern Europe
- The strategic need for market differentiation

Although internationalization is obviously associated with diversity, to find it linked with organizational change is more surprising. This suggests that companies are not only aware that organizational flexibility is and will be key, but also that diversity efforts may help employees adapt more easily to new roles, responsibilities, and colleagues. The strongly held view that diversity is a *potential* strategic differentiator shows that the issue is still quite new in corporate Europe. In North America, diversity has become a clear business imperative during the past decade.

Two developments held medium relevance for diversity:

- Increasing numbers of mergers and acquisitions, strategic alliances, and other forms of cooperation
- Technological innovation

To some extent, it is remarkable that the increased cooperation between companies is only ranked as "of some importance," as this issue has been driving many sectors and even some national economies over the past year. It would seem obvious that diversity efforts support cooperation by helping to bridge diverse corporate cultures. Business trends perceived to be least connected to diversity were:

- Pressure on productivity and costs
- Pressure on market, client, and revenue side
- The need to increase shareholder value

The most noteworthy, if not the most worrying, aspect of these results was the implied lack of awareness of the business and financial benefits that diversity can bring. Although the business importance of market share, cost-cutting, gains in productivity, and resulting shareholder value are universally acknowledged, diversity does not seem to be associated with any of these, at least in Europe.

Shareholder value was mentioned by quite a few European companies, while U.S.-owned companies, whose shares are usually not traded in Europe, did not place much emphasis on this issue in Europe.

The Drivers for Diversity in Europe

In the United States, the famous report *Workforce 2000: Work and Workers in the 21st Century* (Johnston and Packer, 1987), which was widely distributed in the 1990s, triggered far-reaching discussions on how to respond to increasing diversity in the labor market, and subsequently in consumer and financial markets. This report gave solid facts about the rise of women and minorities in importance and numbers in the overall group of external stakeholders. It sent a clear message to companies that they needed to improve relations with many groups and change attitudes toward differences that were no longer tenable. There was no choice but to accept the new realities. Valuing and managing diversity became a necessity.

Do similar drivers exist in Europe? Are corporations seeing and responding to them? We raised these questions in two areas of our survey. We inquired how people saw demographic and cultural changes. In the area of demographics, we looked at the concrete numbers and percentages of people from diverse backgrounds in terms of the six core dimensions. With respect to culture, we inquired about values, attitudes, and lifestyles.

For all intents and purposes, the companies surveyed agreed that the most important shifts were in the areas of gender and ethnicity:

- Women are becoming increasingly important both in the workplace and the marketplace as they more often obtain higher professional degrees and qualifications and earn more money. They are increasingly self-aware as customers, and their needs reach far beyond the purchase of traditional "household goods."
- Ethnic minorities provide a growing workforce and customer base.**

These findings directly explain why companies actively address these diversity dimensions in Europe. Finally, the statement that ranks third is in line with the above "definitions of diversity." The workforce is becoming much older on average.

** As almost each country in Europe has its own specific mix of newcomers and traditional minorities, and thus their own priorities for managing "ethnicity," details of these were beyond the scope of our survey.

Almost no relevance was attached to ongoing changes in the other three core dimensions:

- Mental and physical disabilities are getting less important due to technological improvement;
- Religious diversity is increasing in certain areas and specific regions; and
- Gays and lesbians are becoming more visible and proud, demanding active integration.

These findings appear in a different light when contrasted with the actual numbers. Although the coming decades will probably be dominated by age issues, research by mi·st [Consulting suggests that the most dramatic changes in recent years may concern sexual orientation issues in Europe (see Exhibits 6.2A and 6.2B).

It is also inexplicable that religion is not seen as a significant issue, given the severe conflicts in Northern Ireland and Southeastern Europe that are based on or draw heavily on religious issues.

The demographics of gender and ethnicity are steadily evolving in Europe, as they have done for many years. European politics has acknowledged these developments while paying less attention to other changes. The business world seems to pick up issues that are politically accepted and publicly featured.

Yet the cultural shifts that companies see as the most important reasons for engaging in diversity work turn out to be:

- Self-fulfillment and flexibility are increasingly preferred to status and hierarchy
- Younger workers tend to prefer an open and multicultural environment

These two shifts highlight one key issue from different perspectives. Changing relationships among people are causing shifts in their interactions with each other. Companies recognizing these as significant societal shifts can be expected to change quite a few of their organizational structures and processes.

Developments describing new ways of living scored in the middle ranks:

- Alternative lifestyles are becoming mainstream models of living
- Traditional values and roles are losing importance

Surprisingly, single parenting and smaller households were not highly ranked, despite the intense discussion of work/life issues and the number of marketing initiatives targeted at small households.

Exhibit 6.2

(A) Growing Visibility of Gay Pride in Europe; (B) Growing Size of Gay Pride Events in Europe

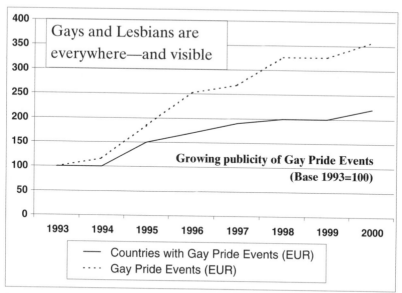

(A)

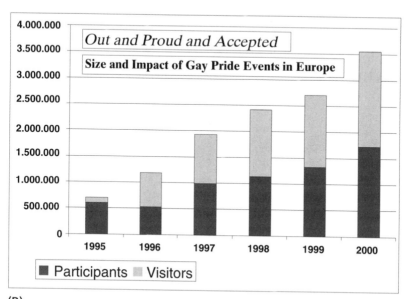

(B)

Source: EPOA (European Pride Organizers Association) data, and mi·st [Consulting data, analysis, and graphs.

The Benefits of Diversity in Europe

In our survey, three internal and three external categories of benefits were mentioned (Exhibit 6.3). Respondents were asked to select the three most important aspects, both external and internal.

Grouped by categories, the biggest benefits were expected in recruitment and for individual employees. These results were linked directly to the ability to better meet personal needs. In other words, companies expect to use diversity efforts to interface better with some of their stakeholders. But this finding also suggests that diversity is seen as a soft issue, "one that does not necessarily provide business benefits.

Expectations for interpersonal, consumer, market, and organizational benefits were less highly ranked. Investment benefits were least frequently mentioned. This suggests that companies fail to see diversity as a primary resource for enhancing the overall performance of the organization. Counting the responses in terms of benefits, a slightly different picture emerges. The most often mentioned benefits were:

- Improved team effectiveness and cooperation (interpersonal)
- Increased productivity (individual)
- Improved customer intimacy (consumers and markets)
- Broader access to labor markets (recruitment),

Exhibit 6.3

The Benefits of Diversity in Europe

Externally		Internally	
Consumers/ Markets	• Increased market share • Ease of entry into new markets • Improved customer intimacy	**Individual**	• Increased productivity (quantitative and qualitative) • Improved morale, commitment
Shareholders	• Enhanced rating • Improved attractiveness	**Interpersonal**	• Improved team effectiveness and cooperation • Easier integration of new staff
Labor Markets	• Broader access to labor markets • Improved employer image	**Organizational**	• More openness to change (restructuring, mergers and acquisitions, etc.)
Community	• Improved public image		• Enhanced effectiveness of complex organization

Source: mi·st [Consulting.

Moderately ranked benefits were:

- Improved employer image (recruitment)
- More openness to change (organizational)
- Improved morale and commitment (individual)
- Ease of entry into new markets (consumers/markets)
- Enhanced effectiveness of complex organization (organizational)

The benefits given least importance were:

- Increased market share (consumers/markets)
- Improved attractiveness (investors)
- Enhanced ratings (investors)
- Easier integration of new staff (interpersonal)

Analyzing the three elements of the European business case from an overall perspective, it can be seen that some of the top aspects of each building block match while some do not.

In a next step, we wanted to find out how clear and coherent this business case was for the sample of our study. To do this, we compared elements from the three different areas of the business case that are interdependent or at least related to each other. The idea behind this is the following: If an issue is seen as of great strategic fit or as a strong driver for diversity but no great benefits are expected in that very area, an organization is not likely to focus its diversity work on such issues. On the other hand, if certain aspects are coherently rated as high or low across different areas of the business case, related activities will be given accordingly high or low priorities. In the light of this, we analyzed whether related issues were rated on comparable levels.

Matching Results: Aspects Given *Low, **Medium, or ***High Priority		
Strategic Fit	**Drivers**	**Expected Benefits**
Strategic differentiator***		Access to labor markets***
	Women and ethnic minority workforce potential***	Recruitment benefits***
International shifts***	Increased open-mindedness**	
Shareholder value*		Investor relations*

Some issues appear to be clearly positioned on the map of European diversity managers. They place high importance on recruitment issues, and they see medium/high relevance for multicultural aspects. Shareholder and investor issues are consistently ranked low.

Conflicting Results: Aspects Given *Low, **Medium, or ***High Priority		
Strategic Fit	Drivers	Expected Benefits
Organizational change***	Flexibility***	Openness to change** Organizational effectiveness*
Cost/productivity pressure**		Teamwork*** Individual productivity***
Market pressure*	Aging population**	Customer intimacy*** New market segments**

Looking at some of these inconsistencies, we feel that more work needs to be done to highlight the linkage of diversity with issues such as market pressure, or make clear how diversity can improve organizational effectiveness. Overall, Corporate Europe does not yet seem to have clearly positioned diversity in the business nor has it created clear-cut business rationales and set expectations for directly related business benefits. Perhaps this is due to lack of research, public data, resources, and internal monitoring systems to substantiate the above-mentioned facts. Such activities would help companies better understand the potential impact of diversity work and make it easier to link it to key business issues.

Unfortunately, the absence of a sharply outlined, coherent business case might imply that diversity strategies, priorities, and action plans in Europe simply lack business focus, and that their success is being measured by criteria not linked to the key elements of the business case. This will be discussed in more depth in the next lesson.

Lesson 2: Make a rigorous European business case, related to the European business environment and to your European business goals and challenges.

Diversity Aims and Objectives

Having looked at what diversity means to companies, our logical next step was to find out what organizations were trying to achieve with diversity efforts. This was an open question in the survey, and participants usually wrote a few sentences. When these responses were analyzed in terms of the aims of each company, four key objectives emerged:

1. To have a diverse workforce.
2. To have an environment that includes everyone and values and respects diversity.
3. To reflect or relate to and understand diverse customers and stakeholders.
4. To benefit from different stakeholders and the potential in diversity.

These four aspects directly reflect the paradigms of diversity described at the beginning of this chapter: (1) the phenomenon of diversity; (2) the individual mindset of "valuing diversity"; (3) the organizational perspective of "managing diversity"; and (4) the comprehensive business attitude of "leveraging and nurturing diversity."

In combining these features, companies commonly embrace one or two, and sometimes three or even all four aspects to describe their diversity objectives. The one contribution that included all four wasn't clearly phrased as a set of aims, but in fact sounded more like a mission statement.

Though the questionnaire offered "being known as a company leading in diversity" as a choice, none of the respondents mentioned it. This finding does not correspond with results showing that most companies see the strategic value of diversity in its external aspects, and that they expect to reap significant external benefits from it.

Differences of focus showed up between U.S.-owned and European companies. Americans tend to be shorter and clearer in describing their aims. They emphasize "providing an environment where no potential is lost." European companies, on the other hand, actually desired to become more diverse, and to use that diversity in a positive way. Clearly, this finding reflects the fact that European subsidiaries of global companies tend to be quite diverse as a result of where they are located, while European firms operate in a home region that tends historically to be more monocultural.

Lesson 3: Set comprehensive diversity objectives that relate to all elements of the business case.

Changing the Organization, Its Culture, and Its People

How can comprehensive diversity objectives be reached? How to identify the factors involved in successful diversity-related change remains among the last mysteries in management. The mere complexity of the issue seems to be a prime obstacle to a comprehensive scientific answer to this question. Our survey, while providing data for this publication, covered in an albeit limited way three major aspects of this topic:

1. The principal approach chosen to change people and systems.
2. Implementation strategy in complex organizations.
3. Individual accountability for engagement and action.

An Approach to Change

One of the common ways to describe different strategies for triggering change shows three approaches to impel an individual to think, feel, and act differently:

A. **Address the "*head*"—Provide information to change a mindset.** This strategy assumes that people lack basic information or experience about those different from themselves. This leads to prejudice and behaviors that keep a company from leveraging diversity. Concrete facts about the potential benefits, internal and external drivers, and other information on diversity will, for rational and business reasons, eventually change attitudes and behaviors. Activities related to the business case belong in this category.

B. **Address the "*heart*"—Use personal messages to trigger emotional responses.** This strategy assumes that people are unaware of how people different from themselves feel about specific situations. Providing them with comparable experiences and showing the positive benefits of sensitivity and fairness will eventually lead to more correct behaviors, usually for moral or ethical reasons. Most training and the use of personal case studies belong in this category.

C. **Address the "*hand*"—Give clear directions to change concrete behavior.** This strategy assumes that many people lack the motivation, energy, or curiosity to try out new ways of dealing with "otherness." Simply instructing them to do things differently will eventually give them the experience that things can be improved by valuing diversity, and will subsequently make them change their behavioral patterns. Policies, legislation, and target-setting belong in this category.

Participating companies were asked to name the approach they felt was most promising to trigger diversity-related change. *Head* and *heart* strategies were both favored, but the *hand* approach was not seen as relevant. Further analysis showed that some strategies that were seen as successful actually fell in the hand category but were listed elsewhere. Nonetheless, the low ranking of the hand strategy is surprising, given that:

- Those European countries most advanced in the field of equality, equal opportunities, and diversity have all introduced targeted legislation at an early stage (United Kingdom, Scandinavia, the Netherlands). Public legislation is a hand strategy because it does not leave companies and individuals with a choice. Legislation, in the long run, results in positive experiences, and gradually changes not only behavior but also attitudes and ethical values.

- In a European best practice survey on "public initiatives to combat xenophobia and racism" carried out by mi·st [Consulting (September 2000, unpublished internal report), all key interviewees stressed the importance of legal pressure in triggering diversity-related change.

- Preferred activities and perceived success factors for diversity that will be detailed below highlight the need for leadership and an element of pressure from the top.

Overall, our respondents saw relevance to all three aspects, but there were differences between U.S. and European organizations. U.S.-owned companies tended to prefer one specific approach—either training or workshops to address the "*heart*," or business case models and data to address the "*head*." On the other hand, almost all the European companies said a combination of the two strategies was needed, and they gave examples of such efforts. Probably, Americans tend to transfer their internal domestic best practices to the European arena or operate under a global set of diversity standards.

Air Products gave a detailed description of their heart approach: "Our training sessions included the use of videos that demonstrate classic discrimination problems, the ease with which groups can be set up against each other, and some examples of employees who have not been valued."

SaraLee DE describes its head approach as, "clearly defining the business case behind valuing diversity and highlighting the risks of not taking action."

Organizational Strategy

Most companies organize themselves in a multidimensional matrix when operating in Europe. This includes at least a business and a country dimension. Many add functional or specialized dimensions such as HR management, recruiting, training, organizational development, or corporate communications for public or internal affairs.

Besides asking about the different approaches used to make people change, our survey also asked what organizational structure was primarily used to drive the implementation of diversity. Was it done along business divisions, by countries, or using specialized functions?

The majority of companies replied that business divisions were the usual structures for implementing diversity. This would mean that most of the work was done across national borders and cultures, and that different specialists were involved in different businesses.

This finding conflicts with two other observations:

- Most diversity work is still somehow connected to those HR functions that are centralized or have strategic responsibilities; and

- For legal reasons and for market purposes, most businesses in Europe are still to some extent driven nationally.

It could be argued that although the declared strategy is linked to business divisions, the actual work is done by specialized functions and in the country organizations.

Many respondents saw problems with specific strategies. Spreading ownership and creating buy-in was reported as an overall work problem, but this was particularly challenging for those working with a HR or with an in-country strategy. Some companies with a business division strategy highlighted how important it was to acknowledge the differences between European countries.

These considerations highlight one of the most important differences between the United States and Europe. The old continent is simply not as unified as the United States, politically, culturally, or even in business terms. Different countries with differing nationalities, languages, and histories provide critical layers of diversity that do not exist in the United States. Any European implementation strategy will have to acknowledge these national differences at some point. Paradoxically, experiences and observations in past years suggest that purely national strategies are not successful in Europe, as they lack the value-added that can be created by pan-European work.

Commitment to Leading the Change

In addition to identifying strategies used for personal and organizational change, we wanted to know how companies ensured that individuals from all levels became personally engaged in diversity initiatives. In asking about this, we divided personnel into three categories, individual contributors, managers, and senior or top management. To this, we added one function: human resources.

Companies seem to have many mechanisms for involving nonmanagement staff, but few for managers and HR, and even fewer to ensure that top managers participate in a change process. This runs afoul of the widely acknowledged notion that engagement on the part of an organization's leadership is the key to successful diversity initiatives. Involvement of senior managers varied considerably among the companies surveyed. Although commitment seems to provide visibility and credibility, there is little emphasis on accountability or targets. This suggests that diversity is not yet on the serious business agenda of corporate Europe. An exception is Ford of Europe, where both top-executive level and vice-presidential level objectives for diversity were introduced, indicating that top management has committed itself to addressing diversity as a business priority.

At all levels, personal interaction and involvement seems essential for creating employee buy-in. On the lower levels, networking and feedback are important mechanisms, while training and accountability are more characteristic of the middle ranks.

Several strategies are used to make sure that HR actively supports diversity. While U.S. companies favor data and measurement driven reporting, European companies put their emphasis on mainstreaming diversity. This approach aims at integrating diversity into all systems (policies, processes, structures, etc.) of a company. It requires an in-depth review of existing mechanisms and a comprehensive realignment if needed. The long-term goal is that the company's day-to-day business clearly reflects the diversity mindset in all respects. In this case, only marginal diversity work (updates, etc.) would be needed thereafter. This concept competes with diversity programs and initiatives that seem to be more widely spread in the United States.

Clearly, this difference between the American and the European approaches can be explained by the legal requirements for such data in the United States. In Europe, on the other hand, compliance in terms of data-based evaluation is unknown, despite the fact that equal opportunity legislation does exist for different fields in different countries. European organizations prefer to align all HR policies and procedures with diversity so that the "system" supports the needed changes.

Making "Change" Happen

Considering the many different ways companies choose to start their diversity journey, one may ask which strategies have proven most successful. In response to this question, we found more differences between U.S.-owned and European companies.

The Americans place a strong emphasis on training and workshops, as well as on networking. European companies list some of these tools as successful strategies, but also insist that business-related strategies are required, a fact not mentioned by U.S. participants.

Many respondents pointed out that involving senior managers, a clear business case, and sound strategic priorities were key to successful diversity initiatives. This was the case at Ford of Europe, where top managers chair diversity councils on the European level, in different countries, and in different business divisions.

Overall, the different legal environment in Europe seems to lead to different approaches of implementation. Here, linking diversity to the business is more important than compliance with the law. But this finding also has another more subtle aspect—the European business environment seems to prefer facts-oriented work over soft, cultural approaches.

Lesson 4: Accept and actively manage the complexity that implementing diversity in Europe implies. Neither legal nor moral considerations should be at the forefront of a European strategy.

Communicating Diversity

Implementing any of the strategies described above requires communication, mainly with employees. External communication will be discussed later in this chapter. This activity can either aim at getting messages across (one-way) or at obtaining feedback or input (two-way). Various means of communicating diversity can be used internally:

- Basic communication, such as a mission statement
- Explicit communication on diversity, such as a diversity brochure

- Diversity features, such as an article on diversity in the company magazine

The survey asked about which tools were actually used, and which were seen to be most effective or valuable.

Diversity Vision, Mission, Policy

When asked whether they had any of these statements, practically all participants from U.S.-owned organizations said they had at least one of these tools, but only 50% of the European companies had them. This finding is not surprising as, generally speaking, visions, mission statements, and explicit policy documents are more widespread in the United States than they are in Europe (Exhibit 6.4). But this also confirms that U.S. companies are more likely to use the *hand* approach to address a new issue. A strong message from the top gives clear directions as to what and how certain things, in this case diversity, are supposed to be handled in the future.

As top-down implementation is widely accepted as an important work stream for diversity, the survey results suggest that quite a few European companies are not using all the available and effective tools for implementing their diversity efforts. There was a difference in how communication of an existing vision, mission statement, or policy and internal and external communication were evaluated. Overall, a third of respondents said they still needed to do more work in this field, or they were still developing appropriate activities.

The tools listed for internal communication included presentations, forums, websites, and printed media such as leaflets, brochures, and articles. Special brochures or presentations were directed to specific audiences, such as senior or line managers. On average, U.S. companies tended to do more of this than did European companies.

External communication activities were very limited. Some organizations include their vision or mission statement on the website or in company brochures. The fact that the diversity statements are not used very much for external communication contrasts significantly with the business emphasis on consumer and labor market relations that we discussed earlier.

Exhibit 6.4

Diversity Policy of Ford of Europe

Ford of Europe
Diversity Policy

Ford of Europe is committed to equal
opportunity, fairness, work-life balance,
respect and dignity at work for all. Ford
values differences of culture, ethnicity, race,
gender, nationality, age, religion, disability,
marital status, sexual orientation,
education, life experiences, opinions and
beliefs.

Diversity adds a clear value to our
employees, our business, our customers,
our company, our shareholders and the
communities in which we operate.

As a result of this policy, we aim to:

- become an Employer of Choice by
  recruiting, retaining and developing the
  best people;
- provide the best possible customer
  service to all our employees;
- provide excellence in customer service to
  ALL our external customers in ALL their
  diversity;
- access the supply of goods, facilities and
  services from a diverse business
  community;
- show responsibility to and reflect the
  communities in which we live and work.

David Thursfield
Chairman, CEO and President Ford of Europe

Ford of Europe
Diversity

Source: The European Diversity Team developed this specific policy at Ford of
Europe. It was first published May 2001 in the special section diversity@ford of the
employee magazine @*Ford*.

Communication Tools for Diversity

In order to communicate diversity to employees, corporate Europe mainly uses the following dedicated tools as implementation strategies:

- Intranet
- Newsletters and magazines
- Surveys

The following tools are also sometimes used:

- Speeches
- Employee networks
- Focus groups
- Posters

The list of tools that are rarely mentioned includes:

- Leaflets
- Workshops
- Stickers and badges
- Diversity offices or hotlines

The top group includes three different kinds of communication tools: one-way (print and personal), interactive, and feedback tools. Though there is probably no "best way" to communicate diversity, the golden rule of using a good mix of tools is likely to be valid still. What also stands out is the relatively low importance given to printed material (Exhibit 6.5).

In communicating about diversity, U.S. companies are again significantly more active than their European counterparts. But this may change soon. European company respondents, more often than American ones, reported plans to expand current activities. In addition, European companies seem to have a strong liking for newsletters and magazines. Quite a few plan to install a diversity hotline or office. U.S. companies prefer management speeches. This is consistent with their tendency to set policy and use similar top-down implementation tools.

Featuring Diversity in Internal Communication Tools

In addition to producing material dedicated to communicate diversity values, these can also be inserted into already existing communication media.

Exhibit 6.5

The European Diversity Brochure of SaraLee DE

Source: This 12-page brochure was produced by SaraLee DE for both internal and external distribution.

Exhibit 6.6

Report on diversity in the employee magazine of Deutsche
Lufthansa. The headline reads, "Lufthansa: Multicultural
and Open to the World."

Source: This article was part of a two-page spread published in the internal
newspaper *Lufthanseat* in January 2001.

Respondents ranked these media about the same as they did the
dedicated communication tools. Most common were management
speeches, employee magazines (Exhibit 6.6), and the intranet. Diversity
found little integration in business presentations and job postings.
One-quarter of our respondents said that they never featured diversity
in the latter context.

Once again, U.S.-owned companies were more active and make more
efforts to mainstream diversity into their corporate communication.

The Most Effective Communication Tools

After reviewing the variety of communication tools companies were
using to communicate or feature diversity, we tried to identify which
were most effective. The result of this question was clearer than in
any other case. Both European and U.S. companies saw management

speeches and the intranet as the most effective tools for communicating diversity. This finding supported once more the strategy of applying top-down and bottom-up implementation mechanisms simultaneously.

Employee magazines, personal meetings, and business presentations were accorded some relevance, while other tools such as the Internet, advertising, employee networks, and e-mail received only marginal attention.

Lesson 5: Make sure your communication strategy contains one- and two-way multifaceted approaches: personal, printed, and electronic, as well as top-down and bottom-up approaches.

Organizing Diversity Work

Does strategy follow structure, or does structure follow strategy? One of the oldest questions in management comes back to haunt the diversity arena. Theoretically, the decision to change a company culture in the spirit of diversity and the strategies chosen should determine how the process will be organized.

In a way, this seems to be true. What the survey found, however, is a relative lack of resources in European diversity management and a strong emphasis on HR issues. Almost all U.S.-owned companies we surveyed had a global or corporate diversity manager or office. Only half of the European respondents could point to this. Half of the U.S. corporations also have at least some regional diversity managers, compared with only a third of European companies. Many U.S. companies have installed a European diversity manager, some full-time, some part-time, but only one global European company listed this position. This result should be seen in the light of the fact that global European companies usually have their global headquarters in Europe. If they have a global diversity manager there, they might not see the necessity to have a European diversity manager in addition. This would compare to diversity managers for the United States or for the Americas that few global U.S.-based companies have in addition to their global diversity manager.

The assumption that diversity is still more a soft-side activity than a business initiative seems confirmed by the fact that only one-quarter of all participants said that they had diversity specialists as internal consultants for business divisions. This causes some wonder as the business divisions were earlier pointed to as the critical drivers for diversity implementation.

European companies are also more likely to use diversity specialists (or internal consultants or competence centers) for specific functions or implementation tools, mainly in human resources. Roughly half of the organizations surveyed had specialists for training and one-third for communication, but experts for success measurement or networking were rare.

In addition to having a dedicated diversity function, the whole organization also needs to be involved in implementing and integrating diversity efforts. To support this, many different structures or mechanisms can be used.

The most widespread model in Europe is the *diversity champion,* the director or high-ranking executive who takes on the role of promoting and supporting with authority the diversity initiative. This can be taken as a sign of effective top-down implementation. On the other hand, most U.S. companies said that it's mainly their HR people who champion diversity initiatives. European companies mention line managers more often. This finding is very much in line with the overall impression that Europeans tend to be more business-focused and think less in terms of fairness, morality, or legal compliance.

In addition, more than half of the participating companies use diversity councils or task forces, diversity networks or competence centers. The nature and the make-up of these networks and councils are very diverse. Some are in the countries, some are in the businesses, and some are cross-functional steering groups, advisors, and sounding boards. Half of the networks are structured around a special interest issue such as gender, ethnicity, or sexual orientation. Half of the councils explicitly involve senior managers. Quite a few companies mentioned other structures, such as European teams, learning labs, or workshops.

Lesson 6: Use a variety of structures to involve senior management, specialists, and employees.

Measuring the Success of Diversity Work

Although participants thoroughly discussed monitoring or evaluating diversity, there was no shared understanding of what success actually looks like. In general, success meant "reaching objectives." The objectives of diversity efforts included such elements as:

- Consciously employing a diverse workforce;
- Creating an environment that includes everyone, and that values and respects diversity;
- Reflecting, relating to, and understanding diverse customers and other stakeholders; and

- Benefiting from diverse stakeholders and other potential advantages of diversity.

In fact, most companies are using two measures for the success of their diversity work: workforce demographics and employee satisfaction. Practically all U.S.-owned companies apply both criteria, while European companies are less enthusiastic about "the numbers." This can easily be explained from the legal emphasis on compliance in the United States.

Even more surprising, monitoring demographics in Europe seems to be almost limited to counting women in management positions. Some also mention women in career track or expatriate programs. Such narrow measurement systems can easily derail a comprehensive and inclusive diversity initiative and turn it into a more narrowly defined equal opportunity and affirmative action effort. This has already created significant backlash in Europe as the perception of a "preference for women" is reinforced.

Also, none of the participants said they were monitoring workforce statistics in relation to the overall labor market, to competitors, or to the intake of new employees. Such more sophisticated figures would help to avoid some of the backlash.

In the realm of employee satisfaction, turnover, absenteeism, and attrition were often measured. Those who paid special attention to specific groups did so for women and ethnic minorities.

The second large category of success measurement criteria included three image-related dimensions:

- Public image
- Recruitment image
- Specialists recognition, for example, invitation to conferences, hearings, and proposals for joint projects with associations (e.g., NGOs), universities, and the like, along with nomination for or winning of awards

Of our respondents, 40% to 60% apply one or more of these measures, but none of them has included anything other than recruitment in their objectives. Although public image is measured through surveys, the recruitment image is indirectly measured by analyzing the profiles of applicants. As for specialist recognition, the only metrics mentioned were invitations to speak at conferences and special interest awards.

Generally speaking, success measurement for diversity almost exclusively relies on employee statistics and image soundings. This finding reinforces the impression that diversity is still vaguely positioned and approached from the soft side. In fact, virtually no company used a customer-related measurement tool, nor is anyone measuring how the objective of reaping the benefits of diversity is being met.

Few companies said that they were monitoring the demographics of their customer base, their market shares in different market segments, or the satisfaction of different customer groups. Again, from a business and market perspective, European companies were more active than their American peers were. The low emphasis on customer and market issues is especially disappointing in light of the high expectations that companies put on the benefits they were expecting to realize in this field.

In Europe, no company monitors investor ratings with regard to diversity. This will probably change in the near future as ethical investing is becoming a higher priority in Europe as it is in the United States, where stock indices have already shown that diversity supports stock performance.

Lesson 7: Make sure your measurement system is related to diversity objectives and to the business benefits you are trying to reap. Be sure to avoid the perception of "setting quotas" in Europe.

Mainstreaming Diversity into HR Management

Diversity can only become an integral part of day-to-day business if key systems are bias-free. One of the most important areas in which diversity should be integrated is, of course, human resources management. Most companies surveyed said they had mainstreamed diversity to a significant extent in recruiting and personnel development.

In order to integrate diversity into recruitment, participants mentioned a variety of activities. Examples of specifically targeting women and ethnic minorities, or setting hiring goals for those groups, came mainly from U.S. companies. Some respondents were consciously using new and different recruitment sources to expand their candidate base. European companies seem to focus more on removing filters in existing processes that might stem the flow of candidates. Only one participant mentioned using images and language that reflect diversity as well as explicitly speaking of diversity in the recruitment message.

To integrate diversity into personnel development, U.S. companies stress the development and promotion of special groups, particularly women, mainly because they measure the success of diversity effort with the percentage of women in management as a criterion. Europe has already experienced massive backlash to this kind of "support" activity. Respondents from both sides of the Atlantic frequently mentioned training activities that included diversity training.

Only one company explicitly reported integrating diversity into general training programs, though we had positioned this as a core question in the survey. Probably, the real integration of diversity into employee development is not yet very advanced in Europe.

This seems to be true of employee relations as well. Though over the years the diversity function in Europe has been seen as "close" to employee relations, integration of the two has not progressed very far. This is astonishing, as employee productivity is among the benefits most often expected, and employee satisfaction is a major diversity measurement criterion. Along with work/life activities and antidiscrimination initiatives, making holiday policies accommodate diverse religious schedules can certainly be regarded as a "Best Practice."

Work/Life Balance

Two of the major societal drivers for diversity in Europe are said to be the growing demand for self-fulfilling and flexible workplaces, as well as an increase in "alternative" lifestyles. Both factors strongly suggest that companies pay attention to work/life balance as a key issue in employee relations. In fact, the survey found that some activities in this field were more widespread than more specifically focused diversity initiatives.

All participating companies provided flexible scheduling in some form of part-time, flextime, job sharing, telecommuting, phase retirement, and the like. Although the levels at which concrete solutions were being implemented varied, work/life can today be seen as a standard workplace feature and no longer a target for strategic diversity work. Sabbaticals, which are mainly offered by U.S.-owned corporations, are the only benefit that is not yet commonly available in Europe.

Secondly, almost all companies acknowledge diverse needs in their paid time-off and leave policies. The responses suggest that employers have largely adapted their offers to current legislation on these matters. Apart from some family, dependent, or parental leave concerns, almost no item could qualify as an agenda item that reflected specific diversity concerns or would lead to a diversity initiative.

In the areas of counseling, such as general employee assistance, stress management, and pre-retirement, the European companies surveyed are more active than the U.S. ones. Again, practically all activities seem to be ordinary general assistance work with no specific reference to diversity. This raises the question whether such standard work does actually meet the needs of employees who might have been regarded as unusual a couple of years ago, such as those undergoing sex changes or working less than standard hours in management.

Convenience programs are a more recent response to the above-mentioned societal trends. Two-thirds of the respondents list substantial initiatives in that field. General Motors, among others, has on-site fitness facilities in some locations. A few others have off-site fitness facilities with external partners. Other widespread facilities include banking and shopping.

Half of the respondents said they offered some form of childcare, in the form of on-site, off-site, emergency cases, sickness, daycare, babysitting, or financial support for such services.

Only very few employers offer elder care or related assistance. Considering the dramatic increase of older people in the near future, it is hard to understand why the least attention of all is paid to this issue. Generally speaking, almost all diversity-related activities in the HR field are limited to gender, ethnicity, or traditional family issues. Age, disability, sexual orientation, and religion seem to be excluded from the work in this field, or initiatives are not being communicated.

Lesson 8: Mainstreaming diversity into HR will be powerful if done in a comprehensive, inclusive way.

Marketing and Customer Relations

Given the high expectations corporate Europe holds about the market and consumer benefits of diversity, one would want to believe that companies were working hard to mainstream diversity into their marketing and communication activities. The survey listed three key areas in which acknowledging differences was most likely to occur and potentially be most effective:

- Product development and market segmentation
- Advertising and sales
- Customer relationship

The latter two were mentioned by only a third of the participants, and the examples they gave appeared to be a little weak.

In advertising and sales, some companies are incorporating visibly diverse groups of people for their advertising campaigns to reflect the diversity of their markets. Some use different languages and some target specific market segments that tend to be excluded in "mainstream marketing." Only one cited the practice of employing a diverse sales staff to relate better to a diverse customer base. Given the aggressive competition most participant organizations are facing, the low level of diversity activity on the market front is curious.

Before making too strong a judgment about this, it is important to note that our finding does not tell us that marketers are not taking diversity into account in their work. They might be basing their choices on professional market knowledge, separately from any diversity function or initiative. We suspect, however, that linking it to diversity could enhance the impact of such marketing. Due to past discrimination, minorities are reluctant to be exploited as "cash cows." This negative feeling grows if it is not clear that the company marketing to them manages its workforce fairly and inclusively. Marketing to minorities in a diversity context helps to avoid this perception and turns the activity into an act of "valuing customer diversity."

Very few respondents gave examples of how they were actively integrating diversity into the key areas of marketing, market segmentation, and product development. Besides a few vague statements about "considering the whole market," only two participants mentioned marketing to special groups. This mainly referred to women or gay men and lesbians. Obviously, this lack of basic diversity marketing considerations explains the lack of related advertising or customer care activities. But again, it may be assumed that the marketing planning and strategy specialists do acknowledge trends and changes in their markets without explicitly relating them to diversity concerns.

More concrete cooperation of diversity and marketing specialists would provide both sides with value-added. Marketers will receive fresh ideas; seeing through the diversity lens may refresh their "traditional concepts." Diversity specialists will see how their issues can be used to generate additional revenues for the company, and they can learn better to include business aspects in their work. In addition, diversity experts would receive some more "education" in marketing, which they could apply to their diversity initiatives.

Overall, the minimal involvement of diversity specialists in marketing matters points to one of the biggest potentials for improvement. Diverse market segments are not only further developed in Europe than the United States, but they also remain largely untapped; there is a significant gap between what companies say about marketing and diversity and what they actually do. We can rightly ask:

- Why do companies say they want to mirror the diversity of their markets internally if they are not going to actively employ advantage?

- Why do companies expect diversity to enhance their customer intimacy if they are not prepared to work concretely on that issue?

- We believe that complexity is the crucial issue at this time, and that a lot of aspects will advance in this context once diversity is further developed in Europe.

Finally, in the field of customer relationship management, some companies are responding to the special needs of certain customers. Most such activities address physical disabilities or special language needs.

Lesson 9: Work on marketing issues with the same intensity as you do on HR issues.

There is a diversity slot in each element of the marketing value chain—from market research to promotion.

Community and Society

In addition to HR and marketing, charitable sponsorship and corporate citizenship offer a third large area for integrating diversity efforts. As all large companies conduct social programs or other outreach activities, it made sense for us to inquire how diversity influenced decisions in these areas.

Again, and once more surprisingly, only a few responses mentioned concrete activities in these fields. In general it seems that traditional social responsibility, such as for the disadvantaged and the prevention and care of diseases as well as support for local communities, is untouched by diversity. Although respondents admitted that some relationship between these elements exists, almost no concrete interplay can be found.

Sponsorship and like activities are still seen either as purely charitable or as marketing related, such as support for sporting events and the arts. Diversity perspectives could help to balance this polarized approach by encouraging a more integrated view. Companies are not detached from society; they rely on the functioning of the system as a whole. Investors, customers, employees, and suppliers are all part of this system. Companies that strive to gain maximum benefit from the diversity of their stakeholders will make sure their societal commitments reflect this attitude, knowing that doing good is a responsibility that will eventually provide a return on investment.

Communities that are traditionally linked to diversity work, like those of women, senior citizens, ethnic minorities, homosexuals, and people with disabilities, especially offer organizations new and powerful platforms for sponsoring activities that benefit both the charity and the business.

Lesson 10: Use sponsorship as a tool to communicate your commitment to diversity.

The Perception of Success

Given the variety of diversity activities in Europe, our survey sought to highlight those initiatives that participants felt had been most successful, so we posed an open question asking about the most successful internal and external activities.

Internal Success Stories

U.S.-owned and European companies alike most often mentioned two categories of successful initiatives:

- Networking, councils, and other groups explicitly formed to work on diversity issues; and
- Workshops, training, and other activities aimed at raising diversity awareness and communicating the business case.

Although workshops seem to kick off diversity-focused activities, the major effect of networks and councils was to maintain momentum once the work was under way.

It should be stressed that much of the training mentioned is not "awareness training." Many workshops are held to make people understand the importance of diversity (a *head* strategy) rather than the implications of "otherness" and how excluded people feel (a *heart* strategy).

Networks serve other purposes. They help to spread ownership, they support the development of their members, and they empower employees to give feedback on diversity issues. Additionally, networks ensure that diversity will "live" in an organization and that one can "put a face" on it.

Several successful leadership initiatives were also cited. Activities involving top or senior managers were mentioned as having made vital contributions to the work of diversity. Engaging management usually makes diversity more relevant to the business.

Concrete support activities for specific groups, mostly women, were sometimes mentioned. Mentoring was the dominant tool in that category, but respondents did not accord it the same level of importance as they did the activities listed above.

Some companies outlined innovative or unusual projects as part of their most successful work. At Lucent Technologies, a "Cultural Day" was organized in 1999, where people from different cultures told about their country, their way of life, and their cultures. April 2000 was declared a diversity month during which employees could subscribe to as many as 4 out of 14 available workshops. Topics ranged from personality types and hierarchies to exclusion and international issues. A total of 50 events took place during that month. Such a comprehensive and inclusive approach is preferable to the occasional "show and tell" about differences, as the latter can consciously or unconsciously reinforce existing stereotypes.

The Swedish telecom giant Telia has launched Job Coaching for Daddies. This project provides a forum for fathers to discuss their careers, their private lives, and, of course, parenting. Job Coaching for Daddies helps address the often overlooked male side of the gender debate and shows men that there can be diversity benefits for them as well, including:

- More time with their children via programs of paternity leave, part-time status, and the like.

- An open environment where they can reflect on and challenge both traditional and evolving male roles.

With this activity, Telia helps create an "equal" organization between men and women in leadership by encouraging men to use their 50% share of parental leave available.

One participant said about her company that introducing specific metrics for diversity in their European operations was a great success. Probably, this activity has led them to a more concrete awareness that metrics are relevant in this part of the world as well.

Exhibit 6.7

AerRianta—Respect and Diversity at Work Brochure

External Success Stories

As diversity in Europe has been more inward looking in the past, not all participants were able to point to successful activities oriented toward external stakeholders. Those who did most often highlighted initiatives in the labor market. Although not explicitly stated, most recruitment work is not seen as "diversity," but rather targets specific groups within a diverse talent base. Some European experiences show that diversity can also be used to attract "mainstream candidates" and not just women and minorities.

The second area of external diversity work that companies in Europe find successful includes activities with a strong publicity element, such as invitations to conferences, sponsorship, corporate citizenship, awards, or equality labels. Some also mentioned networking activities with other companies, for example, in women's networks and through cross-mentoring.

Although success stories from within companies included mostly long-term activities or projects aimed at creating sustained commitment for diversity in the organization, the external successes were mostly "quick wins." Perhaps this is another sign that corporate Europe has not yet opted for a truly strategic approach for its external diversity work.

AerRianta mentioned its "Respect and Dignity at Work Policy" (Exhibit 6.7) as its single most successful external diversity activity. They communicated it to external companies on the airport site, which gave them a strong positive image and improved the internal credibility and impact of their diversity work.

One should note that not one single project from the marketing or sales arenas was mentioned in response to this question. This could be an additional indicator of the lack of business focus that diversity has in Europe, or, the result might be due to missing information on relevant marketing activities and therefore to poor communication and coordination of diversity related concerns.

Lesson 11: Make sure your diversity work includes top-down and bottom-up activities, and works toward both short-term and long-term perspectives.

Future Priorities

Throughout the survey, it was possible to identify clusters of companies with a coherent approach to diversity issues. Certain clusters were found among the U.S.-owned and others among the European groups.

Regarding plans for the future, the answers were scattered over a whole gamut of issues touched by diversity. Some respondents were perhaps influenced by projects that were their priorities at the time they filled out the questionnaire. The only issue that received more attention than all others was "business linkage." A quarter of all respondents said that their diversity work needed to be more tightly linked to the core business of their company, or that business managers had to engage themselves more openly in the change process.

Overall, U.S.-owned companies more often mentioned specific issues such as gender, culture, and nationality that they felt needed more attention in the future; Europeans were more reluctant to place emphasis on "special interests." On the other hand, a few participants said they had to become more inclusive by broadening their diversity work and embracing more differences than they had before. Other future priorities included more work/life balance and making diversity work "more practical."

Final Remarks

In this chapter, I have tried to elaborate the lessons learned by corporate Europe in response to its diversity challenges, and how we might see in these lessons guidelines for approaching further diversity initiatives. Although the work has not been scientifically grounded, the other contributors to this book and I believe it has been worthwhile to look into the differences that exist between the European and the American approaches. Some of them are quite significant, and most could be explained from the existence of different legal, social, and business environments. In addition, we think that the results clearly suggest that it is appropriate to implement different strategies in Europe and the United States—under a common corporate umbrella in the case of global companies. Acknowledging and actively leveraging the different situations in various regions of the world appears to be an imperative in international diversity work.

Again, in closing, we are grateful for the cooperation of the individuals and organizations who participated in this survey and for the many useful insights they have shared with us. For us, this highlights once again the importance of benchmarking and the value of sharing best practices in this field. The chapters that follow will offer in-depth looks at the global initiatives and practices of specific organizations.

The Cross-Cultural Transfer of Best Practices: Learning from European and American Experiences of Knowledge Management

7

Nigel Holden

This chapter will examine the knowledge management practices of two Europe-based corporations, paying particular attention to how these firms address the complex cross-cultural challenge of transferring the knowledge and experience of best practices throughout their respective organizations worldwide. The two companies are Novo Nordisk, a Danish biotechnology concern, and Sulzer Infra, a Swiss concern that offers specialist environmental expertise to the construction industry. The information on these companies is taken from extensive case study material and its analysis in my book *Cross-Cultural Management: A Knowledge Management Perspective.*

Before introducing these companies in the form of short case studies, we will briefly discuss knowledge management and its relationship with the leveraging of good practice. This will lead to a short exposition about a third company, General Motors of the United States, mentioned previously in Chapter 4. This company may be responsible for the most expensive and damaging failure of the transfer of best practices in corporate history. This is a useful cautionary tale against which to place the experiences of Novo Nordisk and Sulzer Infra, because it exemplifies how well—perhaps insidiously well—cultural factors become very awkwardly intertwined with business factors.

The longer case studies of the two European companies will provide the essential company background and then focus on a key theme. With respect to Novo Nordisk, attention will be directed to a group of international change agents charged with the task of visiting its locations worldwide in order to identify valuable best practices and help diffuse them throughout the company network. Sulzer Infra's approach is mediated through its corporate university, called the Sulzer Infra Academy, which has the aim of making the parent company a full-fledged learning organization. A short analysis from a cross-cultural management perspective is provided after each case study. This perspective is based on the following guiding definition of cross-cultural management: The core task of the management of cultural complexity in organizations is to facilitate and direct synergistic inter-action and learning at interfaces, where knowledge, values, and experience are transferred into multicultural domains of implementation (Holden, 2002).

In the concluding sections, the experiences of the three highlighted companies are presented from a knowledge management perspective, which focuses on the recorded company experiences with reference to decision support, organizational learning, and knowledge sharing (Burton-Jones, 2000).

Knowledge Management and the Transfer of Best Practices

Knowledge is said to be the ultimate corporate resource, the perpetual sustainer of competitive advantage. Knowledge in this sense should not be taken to mean the equivalent of the contents of encyclopedias or reference books. In the corporate world it refers to the accumulated know-how about running the business in the widest sense of the expression. As such it includes experience, good practice, and even company values. In large corporations the total activity of handling knowledge and making it available to users ("knowledge management") is a worldwide operation, involving the crossing of organizational boundaries in ways that challenge traditional concepts of management and demand new forms of behavior at all levels. For at the root of knowledge management lies the notion of organizational learning; and organizational learning is not just about learning something new and valuable, but is a practice to break firms from the expensive and time-consuming task of reinventing the wheel (Davenport and Prusak, 1998; Dixon, 2000; Nonaka and Takeuchi, 1995).

Researchers and consultants have identified several constraints on the implementation of effective knowledge management systems. These constraints include lack of time to share knowledge; failure to use knowledge effectively; difficulty capturing tacit knowledge; lack of user uptake; failure to integrate knowledge management systems; lack of training; and lack of time to learn and understand benefits (KPMG, 1999). Other constraints identified have been lack of knowledge policy and inaccessibility of knowledge in company systems (Coles, 2000); lack of trust; different cultures, vocabularies, and frames of reference; lack of time; problem of rewards; and finally, lack of capacity to integrate knowledge into existing procedures and mindsets (Davenport and Prusak, 1998). When it comes to the cross-cultural transfer of knowledge and best practices, firms are faced with the very big challenge of handling what is called tacit as opposed to explicit knowledge.

Tacit knowledge is "personal, context-specific, and therefore hard to formalize and communicate." It is embedded in a country's language, social organization, and value systems. Explicit knowledge is that "which can be articulated in formal language including grammatical statements, mathematical expressions, specifications, manuals and so forth," and "thus can be transmitted across individuals formally and easily" (Nonaka and Takeuchi, 1995). For the sake of argument, let us not quibble with the word "easily" in that statement. Bresman, Birkinshaw, and Nobel refer to tacit knowledge as "know-how" and the "more articulable dimensions of knowledge" as "know-what" (1999).

Best practices are complex amalgams of tacit and explicit knowledge. When knowledge and best practices are to be leveraged from one location to another by combinations of technological mediation and human interaction across barriers of culture and language, the task presents major challenges to knowledge officers. And, as I have noted elsewhere:

> The challenges are even greater if those knowledge officers have very limited international experience. Global nerdism is not only no substitute; it represents a mindset that is unlikely to feel at ease

with human quirkiness in myriads of cross-cultural settings. Firms will have to rethink job profiles. (Holden, 2002, p. 309)

This minimal discussion of knowledge management will be sufficient for this chapter. Readers without prior knowledge of the field are strongly encouraged to read *Knowledge Capitalism: Business, Work, and Learning in the New Economy*, by Alan Burton-Jones. But it is important, finally, to emphasize that knowledge in management contexts seldom refers to a discrete item of information for cognitive digestion; it refers to partially organized bundles of information that represent attitudes, values, and behaviors that more often than not are outcomes of collective endeavors.

The Cost of Knowledge Mismanagement: General Motors Takes a Beating

The exposition that follows concerns the auto industry, highlighting the reaction of General Motors to meet the onslaught of competition from Japanese carmakers. The information comes from a colleague, Charles Tackney; he is a labor relations expert at Copenhagen Business School who specializes in lifetime employment in Japan. In a seminar paper he wrote:

General Motors, in the face of increased Japanese exports and reduced market share, embraced JIT (just-in-time) and *kanban* production schemes throughout its complex motor vehicle manufacturing system. In June 1998, over a dispute involving threatened plant closure, failure to provide promised plant upgrades, and threats of "outsourcing," two plants were closed in strikes involving more than 9,200 workers. By the end of that month (a matter of mere weeks), almost the entire global GM manufacturing system ground to a halt. Over 125 factories were closed and more than 170,000 workers were out of work in five countries (United States, Canada, Mexico, Singapore, and Japan, where Isuzu workers were kept busy with other tasks). By the end of the third week of the strike, GM production loss was estimated at 106,000 vehicles per week. At that rate, direct and indirect effects of the strike to the U.S. economy were estimated to cause a $2 billion drop in the U.S. GNP per week of lost production. And this obviously *underestimates* the global impact of this strike by 9,200 workers. (Emphasis in the original; Tackney, 2000, quoted in Holden, 2002, p. 8)

This seems to be another case of an American company failing to grasp Japanese organizational culture with a very high price tag and dramatic ripple effects attached to it. But when we in due course analyze this scenario from a knowledge management perspective a rather different picture emerges, as we shall see.

Novo Nordisk: Facilitating International Transfer of Best Practices

Novo Nordisk, whose headquarters are located just north of Copenhagen, is a major biotechnology company, being the world's second-largest producer of insulin (used in the treatment of diabetes) and the world's largest producer of industrial enzymes. The pharmaceutical business accounts for more than 75% of Novo Nordisk's total sales. The company turnover is in the region of 20 billion Danish krone, which is $1.8 billion. Novo Nordisk is one of the largest companies in Denmark, but by world standards, it is small for a pharmaceutical company. Worldwide, the company employs some 15,000 people, and it is represented by wholly owned operations in 68 countries. It has manufacturing facilities in seven countries. As such, Novo Nordisk is one of Denmark's most internationalized companies. As a small player in an industry almost notorious for large-scale mergers and failed mergers on an equally large scale, the Danish concern knows that it must be nimble and innovative if it is to rebut the unwelcome attention of one of the big corporations.

In the early to mid-1990s the company, which had been created out of a merger of two rival companies in 1989, began to suffer from a creeping paralysis. It was becoming top-heavy and over-administered. As a consequence, its corporate management was being perceived as being out of touch with employees, even in Denmark, and it was recognized that many of the company's employees in other countries felt equally detached. This triggered a number of initiatives to reduce the sense of remoteness and improve both vertical and horizontal communication. For example, the corporation developed the concept of the Novo Nordisk Way of Management and other ideals to encourage better practice throughout the company at every level and every location. One initiative, focusing on an identified need to make the international subsidiaries feel more involved and valued within the company, is the subject of this case study.

This initiative, launched in May 1996, aimed to improve communication and the transfer of values throughout the company worldwide through a special, internally appointed, 14-member task force called Facilitators. As the name implies, they are change agents acting more as catalysts than enforcers. Part of the Facilitators' task is to promote conformity—and, if necessary, enforce compliance—with the company precepts. Compliance is a strong word, but it should not be forgotten that, as a biotechnology company producing health-care products, its staff must always be aware that a shortcut here or a condoned malpractice there can easily bring the company into disrepute, expose it to press scrutiny worldwide, or even land it in a court of law.

The Facilitator Concept

By January 1, 1997, the company had appointed its Facilitators from within its own ranks. The team consisted of seven Danes, two Britons, two Americans, one Malaysian, one Japanese, and one South African. Between them, they had more than 200 years of experience within the company, with professional backgrounds covering general management, logistics, R and D management, organizational development, international marketing, and production management. Their main task was to assist corporate management in transferring the values associated with the Novo Nordisk Way of Management to all units throughout the world.

But there was more to it than that. It was realized that if all units complied with the company philosophy and precepts and conscientiously lived up to the goals and values, that would make communication amongst units smoother and faster. That, in turn, could reduce barriers to the sharing of knowledge and stimulate more innovation and cooperation among units. It was also believed that the synergy would contribute to the same standards of ethical conduct wherever Novo Nordisk did business: customers could always be sure of obtaining the same kind of service and quality when dealing with Novo Nordisk, no matter what unit they were dealing with.

The Objectives and General Operations of Facilitation

Facilitation is a process consisting of three phases: pre-facilitation, the actual facilitation, and post-facilitation. As a rule of thumb a facilitation takes roughly a working week, beginning with the pre-facilitation encounter with the unit manager in situ and concluding with the agreed final report and action plan. According to company guidelines, a facilitation is described as "a structured, planned assessment of the status of implementation of the Novo Nordisk Way of Management with a unit or within a project or process with the aim of developing agreed actions for improvement." In line with this process, facilitation is focused on two main objectives:

1. Assessment of the status and application of the Novo Nordisk Way of Management.
2. Ensuring a balance between business objectives and targets and the methods by which these business objectives are met.

When it comes to the facilitation of a unit, all arrangements including its scope and fact-finding methods (i.e., interviews, observation, verification) will be made with the unit manager. The owner of a facilitation is the unit manager *not* the Facilitators. The unit manager ensures that the Facilitators obtain sufficient background information, interview a representative number of staff, and agree to follow-up action with the Facilitators. The work of facilitation can be said to comprise three main components that are expressed in the key words *assess*, *assist*, and *facilitate*:

1. Through on-site auditing and facilitating of departments, factories, and affiliates, to *assess* whether or not the companywide minimum standard requirements or "ground rules" as specified in the Novo Nordisk Way of Management have been met.
2. Through on-site advice and help, to *assist* the unit in question in correcting identified nonconformity with these requirements.
3. Through on-site identification of "best practices" applied, to *facilitate* communication and sharing of these across the organization.

Facilitators always operate in pairs, which they refer to as duos. Membership of the duos is perpetually changing so that wherever possible a given pair embodies the best combination of professional competencies, language ability, or cultural knowledge for facilitating a particular unit. In Facilitator terminology, the first aspect of their function is called *fact-finding*. This phase, which involves interviews, observation of procedures, and possibly verification of results (technical, commercial, or administrative), is more concerned with the corroboration of facts or otherwise. Generally, interviews are the most productive form of inquiry. There is no agreed format. A second aspect of the process involves the *perusal of unit documentation*. Facilitators are within their rights to request units to supply information on job descriptions, development plans, performance evaluations, business plans, or minutes of meetings.

The third aspect of a facilitation is concerned with *identifying better practice*. When the Facilitator concept was being disseminated throughout Novo Nordisk, many who were skeptical about its chances of having a real impact easily overlooked the fact that a major task of the Facilitators was to identify examples of better practice so that good ideas, new applications, and new marketing ideas could be picked and transferred to other parts of the company. The fourth aspect of facilitation is described as *closing and reporting*. The Facilitators prepare a report listing action points, which they discuss with the unit manager and possibly members of his or her staff. A final report incorporating jointly agreed action points is prepared and is be signed by the Facilitator and the unit manager. The parties also agree on how best to communicate the facilitation results to relevant unit members.

Post-Facilitation

One of the Facilitators will be designated as responsible for follow-up of the facilitation. It is the responsibility of this Facilitator to follow up with so-called action nominees of the given unit in order to verify that the agreed action plan is being implemented (or has been completed). If the unit has problems in complying with a specific aspect of the action plan (for example, meeting a deadline), the manager is required to notify the appropriate Facilitator in good time with an explanation. This may require further discussion with the Facilitator team to agree to a modified action item. In the event of complete compliance with the action points, the responsible Facilitator will notify the unit manager that there will be no further follow-up and that the facilitation is concluded.

Cross-Cultural Management Issues

The Facilitators constitute a complex multicultural task force, challenged to ensure that any unit of Novo Nordisk on this planet is complying with the company's business philosophy and management precepts, and assigned to make better practices, identified in any unit, available throughout the company. From a cross-cultural management perspective there are two key dimensions:

1. Their self-management as a multicultural, multilingual team (an important issue which is not further discussed here).
2. Their interactions with units they facilitate.

In all the phases of facilitation that bring them into direct involvement with units, Facilitators are aware that their function requires not only exceptional communication skills and listening skills, but also a capacity to adapt behavior—and dress—according to circumstances. Regarding language issues, the normal language of facilitation is English, but it is Danish if a Danish duo happens to be conducting a facilitation in Denmark. In some countries where the knowledge of English is relatively weak among members of a particular unit, the facilitation may require the services of an interpreter. A facilitation in Moscow, despite some language problems, proved to be one of the most productive interactions of its kind. This suggests that an approach based on listening and consultation may be a valuable way of developing collaborative learning with Russians, who have a well-known aversion to being treated by "wise" Westerners as second-class citizens in their own country.

Regarding personal adaptations, the two Asian facilitators have found it difficult to adjust to the less formal, more relaxed style of things in Scandinavia. In Denmark these meetings can proceed with casual dress (non-Danish facilitators have bought casual business wear for facilitations in Scandinavia), but in more formal business cultures like Japan or Germany, more formal attire is expected. The appropriate use of first names, surnames, and titles has proved to be an intricate cross-cultural learning experience. The Facilitators might use the first name of their fairly Westernized Japanese colleague, but would not dream of using that name even with the de rigueur "san" after it in front of Japanese staff who are junior.

In India, it seemed, there had to be meticulous use of titles in front of "lesser mortals." For example, it was found fairly early on that facilitations in Asia (including India) proceeded better if one of the duo were either the Malaysian or Japanese facilitator. Duos consisting of Europeans and Americans came across as somewhat tutorial and assertive. For all the European and American Facilitators, the handling of interpersonal relationships in more hierarchically organized cultures, especially when junior people are present, has proved a difficult learning experience. The Danish Facilitators, brought up and educated in a country where informality is (generally) a way of life, found the adjustment to more formal cultures quite difficult. Furthermore, the relaxed Danish style *can* be interpreted as lack of professionalism in more assertive cultures.

How has Novo Nordisk judged the success of the Facilitators? Now that they have been an operating group for three years it is possible to pinpoint precisely in what ways they have had a significant impact, as follows:

- First, the company has recognized that compliance simply does not happen by itself, and the Facilitators have had considerable success worldwide not only in securing compliance, but pin-pointing why it was difficult for particular units to adhere to company guidelines.

- Second, facilitation has helped the company identify where it lacks competencies for handling particular issues.

- Third, they have acted as a catalyst for setting up communication between various domains of the companies that in the past may not have known that another entity in the company had grappled with a similar problem and found a solution. This has even resulted in the setting up of cross-functional interest groups, which would not have otherwise come into existence. Thus the Facilitators are a pragmatic force for localization and empowerment.

- Fourth, the units discovered that if they entered into a frank and open dialogue with the Facilitators, the outcome was almost invariably constructive.

- Fifth, units that had been facilitated were contacting Facilitators to ask for advice on other issues. Hence, they had become a very valuable resource of knowledge and experience, valued not just in corporate headquarters but throughout the Novo companies worldwide. All this is acknowledged by the CEO, Mads Ølivsen, who has proudly described them as "the global messengers of the (Novo Nordisk) culture." (Rosen, 2000)

How important are the Facilitators to the transfer of good practice? The Facilitators have become very knowledgeable about examples of good practice in virtually every corner of the company. It has been found that when a Facilitator says to a particular unit, "I have seen this instance of good practice," *it has more impact than any other method that the company has devised.* Indeed, the personal interaction has led, literally, to the dismantling of the internal IT support system for transferring good practice. As it became known that the Facilitators were seeking examples of good practice, it proved an incentive to units to make certain that they had something to offer other parts of the company.

The company can also thank the Facilitators for rooting out mal-practices, which affected the company worldwide. In a certain country a Facilitator duo was able to unearth a malpractice that was not only a serious breach of company rules but also a punishable crime in that country. This particular breach was well known to the company (and not unfamiliar to other major pharmaceutical companies as well). For the first time, the company was able to identify exactly how the malpractice was being perpetrated. Once this information was transmitted to headquarters, a meeting of *all* senior managers responsible for regional businesses was immediately called. As a result, Novo was able for the first time to take corporate action to stamp out the scam.

Sulzer Infra: Creating *One Winning Team*

Modern international business requires teamwork, which means that the company must assemble teams of specialists within their globally spread companies to pool knowledge and experience. Differences in language and national or cultural background can make it difficult to create international teams and ensure that all members cooperate and communicate straightforwardly *unless they can all identify with the company and what its stands for.* This means that a successful multicultural team cannot merely focus on the project that has, as it were, created that particular team, but it must learn to cooperate within itself. But how does it learn this? If it has positive learning and knowledge-sharing experiences—and negative ones—how can these experiences be made available to other beneficiaries in the company? And what is the role of headquarters management in ensuring that the groups are well motivated, task-oriented, and inclined to knowledge sharing?

Some answers to these questions are provided in this short account, which highlights the Swiss industrial concern, the Sulzer Corporation, a diversified engineering group. Specifically, we will study a constituent company, Sulzer Infra, which provides engineering know-how to the construction industry. This company has a vision of being a knowledge-based company and it sees special-purpose teams drawn from several of its European subsidiaries as the catalysts for realizing this vision and consolidating the company's competitiveness. It employs just over 5,000 staff, making it the second-largest divisional employer in the Sulzer Corporation; and, with a turnover of about $1 billion, accounts for about 20% of the entire corporation's revenue. Unlike the other Sulzer businesses, Sulzer Infra provides specialized services; it does not manufacture. It is best seen as a technical consultancy company. It has 13 offices in Germany, 1 in Brazil, 2 in the United Kingdom, 2 in Austria, 11 offices in Switzerland, and 1 each in the Netherlands, Italy, Portugal, and Hungary.

Sulzer Infra describes itself as "an internationally active services provider, concentrating on specialized infrastructure solutions for work and production processes in buildings, and aiming at long-term partnering with customers . . . Our professional coworkers create economic solutions for customers' needs in the field of engineering contracting, building services, and communication technology." Sulzer Infra also provides expertise relating to air conditioning, energy optimization, facilities management, acoustics, and refrigeration. Well-known clients include the Tate Gallery and British Museum in London and the Bank of International Settlements in Basle, as well as Bayer, Novartis, and Andersen Consulting. Major projects have included the design and installation of an ice rink at Hanover Expo 2000, the installation of air-conditioning systems in restored fire-damaged rooms of the Hofburg Palace in Vienna, and the modernization of production facilities in Brazil for the Roche pharmaceuticals concern.

In the early 1990s, there was a major recession in the European construction industry. This affected the company, which was found not to have the flexibility to cope with severe business conditions. The McKinsey firm was invited to diagnose the company and its problems. The result was the closure of small affiliated companies and a recognition that Sulzer Infra had been running its European operations in a decentralized manner, which meant that branches in various European cities were too often competing with local companies and not exploiting the wider pan-European business opportunities in a coordinated fashion. This necessitated not just centralization of control from headquarters, but also the setting up of mechanisms for exchanging technical and commercial information among the European affiliate companies.

But there was no habit in the company of cross-border exchanging and sharing of information. The local companies, although belonging to the same group, were accustomed to working independently under the general control of headquarters in Zürich. But the business logic demanded a pan-European approach to projects and market opportunities. Such attitudes, and the ingrained parochial practices that they engendered, were not only incompatible with a pan-European business strategy but could also undermine it. Sulzer Infra had no alternative but to introduce initiatives to create a new mindset among its employees throughout Europe.

In 1997 therefore, Sulzer Infra embarked on its scheme of centralization, which was created on the basis of a vision that gave new concepts and was underpinned with strategic aims. A key aim of this vision-led centralization was to encourage the company to bid for big contracts that smaller local companies would not be able to compete for; in other words, contracts of the type highlighted above. The plan entailed reorganization, the cultivation of new values, and the recognition that the key to success lay with developing a new pan-European teamwork concept. The concept was called *One Winning Team*, and it would be through teamwork that the company would realize its business objectives under a program termed Vision and Strategy 2002.

The Concept of One Winning Team

The ethos and culture of the Sulzer Corporation have been developed around a three-word motto, *One Winning Team*, which aims at adding value at the level of every coworker's internal and external contributions. This motto is fleshed out by a set of declarative principles termed *Our vision—Our contribution*:

Chapter 2: Our Vision
Is to continuously improve the working and living environment of people in buildings through innovative infrastructure solutions.

Chapter 3: Our Contribution
Is to provide and manage infrastructure solutions.
We enhance the competitiveness of our customers by

- Our passion to continuously learn and teach, and to anticipate future needs
- Our expertise across infrastructure life cycles and
- Our ability to serve specific customers on a truly global basis

We endeavor to achieve

- Quality
- Integrity
- Accountability

in all dealings with our business partners, our co-workers, the Sulzer Corporation, and the public. Our success is based on the belief in *One Winning Team*. (Sulzer Infra, Company Documents)

The following company documents were used in the preparation of the case study. These documents range from articles in the company newspaper and annual reports as well as materials generated by the Sulzer Infra Academy:

A charter for *One Winning Team*
Infra Mail: 100 winning teams—Facilitators trained (D. Bright)
P-Team kick-off workshop schedule and other documentation on
    P-Teams
Sulzer Infra: Our leadership principles
Sulzer Infra: International Management Career Program

Sulzer Infra Jahresbericht (Annual report), 1999
Sulzer Infra: Vision and Strategy 2002
Sulzer Infra: The Infra Academy, 2000
Sulzer Geschäftsbericht (Annual Report), 1999
Sulzer Infra CBX Briefing. E-commerce—here comes the future,
March 1999
Sulzer Infra CBX brochure.
Interview with Karl Bochsler, President of Sulzer Infra, reprinted
from *Premises and Facilities Management*, November 1999
The source of *Our vision—Our Contribution* is *A Charter for One
Winning Team* (undated)

The Sulzer Infra Academy is the facility within the company responsible for the task of communicating the *One Winning Team* concept through the company. It is an in-house teaching organization with the aim of establishing the company in the long term as a knowledge-based organization through the promotion of companywide exchange of experience and ideas for continuous renewal. The Academy is a catalyst for personal and organizational development geared to maintaining long-term competitive advantage. Exhibit 7.1 outlines the terms of reference of the Sulzer Infra Academy.

Exhibit 7.1

Terms of Reference of the Sulzer Infra Academy

The Sulzer Infra Academy embodies the principle of Sulzer Infra as a teaching organization. The Infra Academy has 2 completely interrelated parts:

1. As a Center for regeneration and for driving Infra
    *   By challenging, provoking, and questioning, it will operate as a change catalyst promoting Entrepreneurial Excellence.
    *   As a Center where leadership development can take place in a stimulation and challenging environment where external experiences can also be brought into the company and where management can work on topics crucial to the success of Infra Group.
    *   As a regeneration center where management teams can come together to work on team and business development issues and where they can avail themselves of other members of management and experts as facilitators.
    *   It will be through the leaders trained and developed by the Academy that Infra will be driven in the future.
2. The real learning impact will involve all 5,000 employees of Infra.
    *   The leadership culture developed, trained, and generated by the Academy will determine the personality of our company through learning from and teaching each other and through the consequent living according to our beliefs and values.

- All employees will be in daily contact with renewal through P-Teams, management meetings, etc., with the Academy operating as a highway for bringing operational excellence and best practice to all employees.

It is envisaged that the Infra Academy will therefore contain four major elements:

1. Cultural

Through the challenging and stretching of existing and future managers the Academy will promote our values and culture throughout the organization. *"The medium will be the message"* in that *how* we experience the learning and teaching process will be as important as the content itself. The process will therefore by highly interactive, stimulating, and informative. It will be based on operational case studies and on learning from our own experiences and from the experiences of others in an environment of "each one learning from the other."

2. Management Development

Building up gradually as required, the programs will consist of professional, living modules sourced internally, or from corporate, or from external facilitators.

The majority of the modules will be based specifically on our business requirements and while the traditional learning and teaching of technical managerial skills (Finance, HR, Mktg., IT, etc.) will be included, the programs will concentrate on management competencies, interpersonal skills, and how we *use* our managerial skills in practice. The training will again be team based using personal experiences, practical case studies, observation, feedback and assessment from self, peers, and senior management.

3. Management Briefings/Management Challenge

The objective here is to keep the management up-to-date and informed on best practice and new developments and to provide management with stimulation and to challenge to think outside of their usual mindsets.

The briefings/challenges could include corporate programs, external or internal workshops condensing from the essence of the management development modules outlined above. The workshops would be concise, ranging from 2 hours to one day and could be provided to entire management teams on site in the subsidiary.

4. Knowledge Management

Given the methods we will be using within the Academy it is likely that we will build up over a period of time a data bank of knowledge and experience from various sources such as case studies, individual experiences, course materials, reference books, etc., which is essential to remain active within the company. In co-ordination with the Know-how rings and best practices we need to consider how this information will be managed and made available (e.g., intranet).

The Sulzer Infra Academy runs a range of programs, called seminars, for staff at all levels that are concerned with the future-oriented development of competencies and attitudes. The seminars bring together 100 people at one time from all the European companies and usually last three working days. The Academy runs approximately three seminars a year. Here is the company's own description of the present and developing role of the Academy:

The Seminar on Vision and Strategy 2002

In May 2000 the Sulzer Infra Academy ran a three-day seminar for 120 managers from all the European companies with the key aim of focusing their attention of achieving the ambitions and aspirations of Vision and Strategy 2002. This seminar, as we shall see, was a remarkably choreographed event, but it never lost sight of its key aims, which are held together by the company value system and enshrined in the four key points: Simplicity, Speed, Customer Orientation, Enthusiasm. The seminar involved musical interludes; the formation of work groups who discussed, wrote, drew, and even painted their experiences; and a presentation by the company president who explained how his personal values were aligned with those of the firm. Within their various groups participants were encouraged to do the same: for some a difficult, chastening experience.

They discussed with colleagues how they saw the company now, where they thought it might be in the year 2002, what would ensure that the company realized its aspirations, and what might inhibit that. They learned about teamwork and in particular the key role of so-called P-Teams, the new multifunctional, interdivisional, and increasingly multicultural task forces, which were being developed as the critical mechanism for knowledge and experience change. At certain points in the proceedings participants wrote questions and comments on cards for senior managers forming a panel. There were two contrasting presentations contrasting individualism and teamwork. One keynote address was made by the director of the Zürich Chamber Orchestra, who had already been invited to select recorded music that would be played at various times in the seminar and which was produced on a CD for all participants. The other address was given by a famous round-the-world yachtsman.

Consideration and attention was paid to the venue and its appointments. It was a hotel in Martigny in Switzerland, which had all the necessary facilities, including a huge auditorium and spacious anterooms where everybody could see everybody else. The hotel was outstanding in lighting and sound systems. For each day there was a set of objectives, as follows:

Objectives of Day 1:

- Explain "Turnaround" and develop a common understanding of the seminar
- Create an understanding for the "One Winning Team"
- Offer an opportunity to openly communicate with the (top) management

Objectives of Day 2:

- Using the Vision and Strategy for operational excellence
- Dealing with the company mission and Charter
- Raise topics that accelerate the transformation process

Objectives of Day 3:

- Discuss/define participants' role and contribution
- Agree on common responsibility for realizing "One Winning Team"
- Identify possible topics for P-Team projects

(Sulzer Infra, Company Documents)

Although the company language is English, it was known in advance that mastery was by no means uniform for all the participants. Many Swiss participants were more comfortable speaking their native Swiss German. The company paid for professional interpreters to be on hand, who facilitated exchanges using a medley of English, German, French, and Spanish. The interpreters were briefed beforehand, as they would not be static interlocutors but were required to move from group to group, discussion to discussion. On Day 1, groups were mainly formed by people from the same company, but part of the plan was to ensure that by Day 3 participants were involved with colleagues they did not know previously and who were preferably from other countries.

A striking feature of the seminar is that it continually involved energy and movement. Every single person had the opportunity to contribute. At one point participants were asked *as a team* to produce a painting that characterized their attitude to the seminar, to the company, and their future in it. One group trod in the paints and left their footprints on the paper provided—all pointing in the same direction. This was a great joy to Flooris van der Walt, the head of Sulzer Infra Academy, who devised the entire seminar concept. While the painting was being done, music was being played. The idea was that the paintings, which would eventually be displayed for all to see, would become a visual stimulus of the groups' discussion. There was further auditory reinforcement of the experience because each person was given a

CD with the music to be associated with the painting session and other significant occasions of group activity.

The questions that will concern us in due course are: How do the participants take to the seminar as a way of imbibing the concept of *One Winning Team*? Did the seminar help them to meet one of van der Walt's key aims—"to unblock communication across the European companies"? Did it stimulate networking, promote organizational learning and knowledge exchange? And what role, if any, was played by differences in language, national culture, and professional affiliation? Answers to these questions, given below, are based on interviews with Flooris van der Walt, the head of the Sulzer Infra Academy (July 2000) and with three U.K. and two Dutch managers, who had participated in the seminars (September 2000).

A Cross-Cultural Perspective

Nationality became a side issue once there is active cooperation linked to a specific project, but in the context of the seminars differences in language were a slight problem for the U.K. managers, who spoke no other European languages. This was the case despite the fact that the weaving of music and the painting games into the fabric of the seminars was done explicitly to engage people's minds and hearts into a collective experience, which might (and often did) transcend cultural and linguistic factors.

The U.K. managers recognized that their lack of foreign language capability was not just a general disadvantage but a professional shortfall. They encountered hundreds, possibly thousands, of colleagues who were all able to operate in at least two languages, but they could only manage one. Then, as one of them realized, speaking only English was not so much a big advantage in some international meetings, if you did not know how to modify your spoken English by slowing down the speed of delivery or avoiding obscure words. In this connection it was noteworthy how one of the U.K. managers was aware of missing out on the emotional side of personal interactions because he did not have to struggle with attempts to express himself in a foreign language.

In the scenario in question, the communication experience engages the emotions with a sense of professional deficiency. The U.K. manager whose experiences I am describing felt personally limited through his encounter with two colleagues, each with a different mother tongue. The situation suggests that there is more to cross-cultural communication than passing information unambiguously across language and cultural barriers, and that there is more to foreign language capability than the standard communicative competence in that language. The British man was losing out on interanimation, a communion of minds with his colleagues because he was not able to extend emotional solidarity to them. They were doing something in a communicative situation in which he could not act. He was the man who interestingly observed that it was occasionally necessary to "speak louder" in English—a plea of failure as much as a psychological ploy to break into and perhaps dominate a conversation. The two Dutch managers spoke English and German, which gave them specific advantages: English was the language for general Europe-wide, team-based activity; German was used for communicating with counterparts at corporate headquarters in Switzerland.

Concerning the seminar as a forum for networking, reactions from the five informants was mixed, but generally positive. On balance the tasks that aimed to mix up national groups worked, but there was a general feeling that more time was needed to consolidate the contacts before the seminar came to a close. Although there was a difference of opinion about the question-and-answer session with the directors, there was agreement that the presentation by Karl Bochsler, the company president, who spoke about how his personal development was linked to his life with and for Sulzer Infra, had been a success. The fact that his speech was delivered in German and had to be translated did not detract from the importance of the performance.

With that we now turn to a commentary on the recorded experiences of the three companies from a knowledge management perspective.

Knowledge Management Issue 1: General Motors and Japan

The critical point about the disastrous GM experience is that when the carmaker introduced the Japanese practices of just-in-time and *kanban*, it had merely taken over the systems pertaining to technical processes. The company did not take into account the fact that these systems only work in Japan not just because the Japanese worker is "extremely loyal" to the company, but because in Japan worker participation is encouraged and welcomed. Hence it might be said that worker participation is tacitly built into JIT and *kanban*. The fact that GM only took over the explicit aspects of the systems set the scene for tensions in the United States, with repercussions for the carmaker in four other countries.

What on the surface might be taken as a complex U.S.-Japanese cross-cultural misunderstanding is not really that. GM failed to understand the human embeddedness of the systems in the society in which they evolved. There is nothing to be blamed here on the mysteries of Japanese enterprise culture. All major carmakers in the United States and Europe had studied every aspect of the Japanese car industry since the end of the 1970s. The mystery in this case is as follows: How on earth could GM not know about or discount the human element in these systems? Scores of books and articles have been written on the topic. GM had no excuse for ignoring what might be said to have been common knowledge for years.

Knowledge Management Issue 2: Novo Nordisk

One of the rationales behind the facilitator concept was the perceived need to disseminate better practice throughout the company on a worldwide basis. Although the company had installed a sophisticated and expensive intranet communication system, it was found—not for the first time—that individuals prefer human interaction to electronically mediated exchanges with colleagues, even when they know each other well. Thus a calculation behind the facilitator concept was that it met the need for interfaces with direct human contact. The Facilitators appear to have proven themselves to be highly adept at identifying valuable knowledge and examples of good practice. It would not be a misnomer to call them cross-cultural knowledge brokers.

My own in-company research has found that the quality of exchanges can be constrained if (1) unit representatives do not have a very good command of English; (2) interpreters are used who may be unfamiliar with the concepts and terminology associated with, and rationale behind, facilitation; and (3) the language of the unit lacks conceptual or lexical resources for discussing facilitation. The Facilitators experienced some problems of communication in non-Western countries (for example, Eastern European countries, Russia, South Korea, and China), where concepts of management are pragmatic and where people are mystified as to the peculiarly Western (especially American) tendency to oversystematize and "jargonize" the language of merely running a business.

Writers on knowledge management view organizational learning as an intimately related activity. In the case of Novo Nordisk we have every reason to believe that better practices have been successfully transplanted from unit to unit around the world as a result of facilitation. This suggests that the Facilitators have taken tacit knowledge from one location and transferred it as explicit knowledge to other locations, where it may again become tacit knowledge with local inflections, as it were. But there can be little doubt that the most significant group of learners within Novo Nordisk is that of the Facilitators themselves. Through becoming Facilitators they have extended their professional knowledge base by:

- Absorbing and documenting "new" knowledge about the company from the point of view of units, each differently embedded in three interacting levels of culture: national, corporate, and professional
- Adapting personal behavior and communication styles to suit local conditions
- Sharing "facilitation know-how" with other Facilitators
- Prioritizing acquired knowledge
- Converting knowledge into suitable formats for transfer to potential beneficiaries in the company
- Combining their existing professional knowledge with that of other Facilitators in duos or on a group basis
- Doing all these things cross-culturally through the application of intelligence and tact

The personal and organizational achievement behind the latter point cannot be emphasized enough.

Knowledge Management Issue 3: Sulzer Infra

The concept of the Sulzer Infra Academy and the experiences of the interviewed U.K. managers reinforce the more or less accepted conviction that knowledge as the possession of individuals tends to be more easily leveraged in scenarios that encourage not just personal interaction but occasionally intense interaction. What the Sulzer Infra case makes clear, and the Novo Nordisk experience bears out this point, is that it is very difficult to separate the act of transferring knowledge from the cross-cultural know-how needed to effect that. This tends to support the plea of one of the U.K. managers that participants in the seminar need special preparation.

The Sulzer Infra Academy is a relatively new institution, and if training, in the broadest sense of the word, has been neglected in the company for a number of years, the educational concepts may be too advanced at the moment. One U.K. manager said that several people were "going to university without the proper qualifications." It should not be overlooked that many seminar participants are engineers who may have different needs within a group learning activity than, say, marketing people.

One of the most important findings of this case study related to the experience of the U.K. manager, who missed on being able to struggle in a foreign language. This emotional rather than intellectual reaction suggests that interpersonal knowledge transfer, and perhaps especially in cross-cultural scenarios such as these seminars, needs a conducive atmosphere. As I have suggested elsewhere, atmosphere is an elusive yet palpable quality of relationships that is "derived from experience, which serves in turn as a determinant of expectations about future cooperation" (Holden and Burgess, 1994). Managers may not always have the cross-cultural savoir-faire for all situations involving interactions with multiple cultures, but there is always one thing they can do. They help create and sustain a conducive, collaborative atmosphere. They can do this by displaying social adroitness, professional competence, and by applying intelligence and tact to interactions, but, cross-culturally, there is no fixed formula (Holden, 2002).

It should, however, not be overlooked that until recently Sulzer Infra placed comparatively little emphasis on in-company education. Training was, by all accounts, routine and pedestrian. The establishment of the Sulzer Infra Academy places in-company education as a central issue in the company renewal strategy, and it has a lot of lost ground to recover. So far, the experiment appears to be succeeding. No informant suggested that the idea behind the seminar was ill-founded; no one thought the event a waste of time and money, though there were suggestions on how to improve it. The way ahead is surely for the Sulzer Infra Academy to listen to these voices and build them into new in-company education formats. In this way the company can help the Academy to create its own environment for learning, networking, and knowledge sharing.

Conclusion

The experiences of General Motors, Novo Nordisk, and Sulzer Infra provide us with interesting contrasts. In the case of the giant U.S. carmaker we were concerned with the leveraging of Japanese production practices into plants in the United States and other countries. In so far as we can extract a general as opposed to Japan-specific managerial implication, what stands out are major managerial implications:

- The danger of precodified views about the nature of the practices to be obtained.
- The failure to understand those practices in their social setting.
- The lack of provision (it would seem) in the parent company for smooth integration of the externally acquired practices.

As for Novo Nordisk and Sulzer Infra, both companies are, very broadly speaking, attempting to do the same thing—to create a solid and flexible system of knowledge transfer on an international basis, but from opposite approaches. Novo Nordisk disperses its chosen change agents, the 14 Facilitators, throughout its company locations worldwide. This is consistent with the company philosophy of localization and empowerment and its belief in the human factor. Sulzer Infra, like Novo Nordisk, knows it can only secure its future by becoming knowledge-based: it must actively promote what Bartholomew and Adler call "cross-cultural collaborative learning," whilst facilitating productive networking among its European affiliates (1996, p. 27). The Swiss company has invested in its in-house educational facility: its Academy. Through its seminars it brings employees together from all over Europe for concentrated sessions of socialization and interaction. Both the European companies have opted for the meeting-of-minds approach to the matter of transferring knowledge and best practices. Of special relevance is the fact that both companies are consciously engaged in the management of cultural and linguistic diversity. The Novo Nordisk method operates on the principle of allowing local affiliates to have their own voice. The Sulzer Infra approach is integrative.

It is impossible to say whether the Novo Nordisk method is superior to the Sulzer Infra approach. Both companies are developing policies and procedures that best suit their own circumstances, their business sector, and their overall managerial capabilities. What we can say is that the different approaches of Novo Nordisk and Sulzer Infra are *experiments* in how to transfer best practices. At the time of this writing, the Sulzer Infra Academy appears to have had a significant impact, but in the case of Novo Nordisk we can be even more con-

Sustainable Entrepreneurship in a Changing Europe: Pedagogy of Ethics for Corporate Organizations in Transformation

8

Arjen Bos

A Dutch national newspaper published two articles on January 5 and 9, 2000, wherein two authors debated the necessity for corporate enterprises to develop a "code of conduct" based on ethical principles. Of the two opposing views, the first holds that "as long as corporate enterprises do not violate the law, they are free to act—making profit—as they like . . . I cannot identify any unethical behavior that does not break the law in some sort of way" (Plasterk, 2001, in Dutch). The second viewpoint maintains, "There are great examples that prove that corporate enterprises restrain from certain activities and behavior, other than those which are already forbidden by law, for ethical reasons" (De Haan, 2001, in Dutch).

One of the sample cases that De Haan uses to illustrate his argument is the ABN Amro Bank. This Dutch global bank had had a longstanding financial relationship with the state of Carinthia, Austria, until Jörg Haider was elected governor of this state. The ABN Amro Bank concluded that if it were to continue to its financing relationship with Carinthia, indirectly or directly, it would be financing the extreme right wing and xenophobic policies of Haider. The final conclusion of the bank's management was to withhold any investments because they would not be in alignment with their *corporate values*, even though this would cause the loss of a great partnership and source of income for the bank. The bank recognized that refraining from these investments would satisfy other consumers in Europe and local pressure groups, therefore balancing out their initial loss of profit with this ethical recognition.

De Haan, a professor of Corporate Ethics at the University of Amsterdam, continues the debate by indicating that there are two main reasons for corporate organizations to consider the ethical aspects of their behavior. The first is bad publicity; if a corporate enterprise is considered by the general public to behave unethically, this will damage its *corporate identity*. Thus, a loss of income, *profit*, or a consumers' boycott can result. Secondly, there is idealism; more and more in Europe, organizations are considered to be more than solely profit-making institutions. They are also a place where *people* work and where *people* want to feel comfortable and at ease with their employer, the environment, and their colleagues. Corporate enterprises can and will develop a more positive corporate identity when they show respect for *people* and *planet*, instead of only for *profit* (De Haan, 2001). But, as De Haan also stresses, this cannot be achieved in a one-day, simple revision of corporate strategies and policies. It requires a different way of thinking, a shift of paradigm; it requires the organization to transform.

Speaking of people, however, thrusts us immediately into the question of cultural diversity. Diversity can be a source of inspiration, an historically inescapable condition, and a continuous threat to Europe today: "Ethnic, religious, social, and aesthetic multiplicity is an inescapable condition, within nations as well as in Europe at large" (quoted from Arne Ruth in Merry, 2000, p. 3). But within this spider's web of multiculturalism, diversity, and differences, people and organizations desperately seek to enhance their own individual identity in order to "survive." Both try to protect themselves from contrapuntal forces that promote cultural uniformity and the development of strong (sub)cultural groups on the one hand, and uncertainty and fear of differences on the other. In general, this can be the reason for nationalism, racism, discrimination, or a strong need for individualism, as argues Peter Merry in his essay on new ways of learning in a multicultural Europe:

> The spread of cultural uniformity, and a loss of control over one's economic life, perceived by many as coming from the U.S., and

often called "globalization," has been identified as one of the reasons for people feeling less secure about their own identity, and hence latching onto what is often narrow nationalism and racism in the search for some kind of hook to hang their identity on. (Merry, 2000, p. 3)

Focusing more specifically on corporate enterprises in Europe, the impact of the above mentioned diversity factors on organizational behavior and identity have been excellently described and analyzed by Roosevelt Thomas, Jr., in his contribution to *Diversity in Organisations* (1995). Thomas cited an essay written by William Johnston and Arnold Packer called *Workforce 2000* (1987). In this essay Johnston and Packer pointed out the changing demographic composition of the U.S. workforce. These projected shifts of more minorities, women, and immigrants in the European workforce moved many corporate executives to initiate "diversity" efforts (cited by Thomas, 1995, p. 247). Thomas agrees with their analysis to a large extent, but he stresses another driving force behind the reality of diversity and the increasingly urgent managerial need to address its challenges and opportunities.

This even more fundamental cause is *a changing attitude toward being different*. Thomas distinguishes eight different responses to difference: *exclude, deny, suppress, segregate, assimilate, tolerate, build relationships,* and *foster mutual adaptation*. This last response focuses on the following: "The parties involved accept and understand differences and diversity, recognizing full well that those realities may call for adaptation on the part of all components of" the corporation as a whole (p. 247). He goes on to say that "a corporation's managers must explore possibilities of system and culture changes to assure that an environment works for everyone" (p. 251). In this case, "everyone" refers to *all* stakeholders of the corporation.

Thomas, therefore, refers to a similar sort of organizational transformation as does De Haan. Thomas stresses the need that growing diversity has created to shift the corporate paradigm for ethical and sustainability reasons, so that it matches people's changed perception of corporations and their identity. In short, these developments indicate a strong and developing need in Europe for an appropriate response from corporations to growing diversity in order to foster sustainable entrepreneurship as a "new corporate identity" wherein *people* and *planet* are considered stakeholders of the corporation on an equal footing with *profit* for the financially dependent stakeholders.

The Dutch Social-Economic Board (Sociaal-Economische Raad or SER), a socioeconomic advisory board of the Dutch government recently released a document that advises the government what steps to take in order to establish a better notion of *sustainable entrepreneurship* with corporations. The SER stresses that in addition to satisfying the financially dependent stakeholder, corporate managers

> should behave like a good citizen in business. The law does not (and cannot) contain or prescribe the whole duty of a citizen. A good citizen takes account of the interests of others beside himself, and tries to exercise an informed and imaginative ethical judgment in deciding what he should and should not do. This, it is suggested, is how companies should seek to behave. (Dutch Social-Economic Board, 2000, in Dutch, p. 10)

Therefore, if *corporate citizenship* is the desired corporate response to diversity, as sought by De Haan and Thomas, then the big remaining question is how can this kind of citizenship be established? The focus of this chapter will be to uncover and explore the process wherein sustainable entrepreneurship in Europe can result from shifting organizational paradigms that are themselves a result of corporate executives becoming engaged with a pedagogy of ethics. In other words, how can they become social entrepreneurs with newly acquired competencies that help them to start a process of organizational transformation, thus creating a new corporate identity?

The only term I have not yet undefined in this discussion is *pedagogy of ethics*. I have borrowed it from Paolo Freire's book *Pedagogy of Freedom: Ethics, Democracy, and Civic Courage* (1998). Freire outlines five basic assumptions for changing people's behavior through the educational practice for ethics:

1. Human historical unfinishedness—people should be continuously working on educating themselves according to changing societies and human values.
2. "Teaching" ethics is not to transfer knowledge, but to create opportunities for the production or construction of knowledge.
3. Ethical formation should go side by side with an aesthetic appreciation.
4. There exists a strong need to reflect critically on organizational practice.
5. The historical, political, social, and cultural experience of the diversity of men and women can never be acquired outside of the context in which it occurs. Learning ethics in order to build a less ugly and less intolerant but human corporation requires executives to see themselves as "subjects" within this diversity instead of players "on the sidelines." (Freire, 1998, p. 29–48)

In concluding this introduction, we could do no better than to quote Freire's interpretation of the ethical imperative for a process of organizational transformation. We should concern ourselves with this because:

> our being in the world is far more than just "being." It is a "presence," a presence that is relational to the world and to others . . . A presence that can reflect upon itself, that knows itself as presence, that can intervene, can transform, can speak of what it does, but that can also take stock of, compare, evaluate, give value to, decide, break with, and dream. It is in the area of decision, evaluation, freedom, breaking with, option, that the ethical necessity imposes itself. (Freire, 1998, p. 26)

In the rest of this chapter we will examine and describe this "presence" of the key players and how they can contribute to these current developments within corporate Europe as it grows in diversity. Secondly, we will more precisely describe the impact of a *pedagogy of ethics* on corporate practice and how this affects the construction of *corporate identity*. Finally, we will look at real cases that illustrate sustainable entrepreneurship in Europe.

The Three Musketeers: People, Planet, Profit ("One for All and All for One!")

> Business managers should be well aware of what is going on in society, what aims and aspirations exist in other circles, and what forces are at work in industry and society. Instead of just clinging to old positions, half expecting the demolition squad, managers should take initiative and be among the architects of tomorrow's economic and social order. This increase in social awareness and participation may not have a great appeal to some businessmen, who would prefer to stay purely in the realm of production and trade, but it is a duty imperative for all managers who in the world of tomorrow want to be heard and respected as stewards of the growing wealth of nations.
>
> —*R. Kuin (1966)*

The above quote, taken from the SER advisory report (p. 24) to the Dutch government, illustrates that halfway through the twentieth century there was already a certain awareness growing about the social responsibilities of entrepreneurs. The American economist and Nobel

Prize–winner Milton Friedman did not believe in this responsibility, nor does Plasterk, who was mentioned earlier.

Friedman found himself strongly opposing Kuin's way of thinking. In his 1970 *New York Times Magazine* essay, "The Social Responsibility of Business Is to Increase Its Profits," Friedman clearly states that by generating profit a corporate organization can live up to the need of paying salaries to its employees and guaranteeing the continuity of the corporation (cited in Groesbeek, 2001, in Dutch, p. 16). Friedman's reasoning, despite the influence it has had, is waning. Many other organizations, corporate, nonprofit, and governmental institutions have taken a lead in creating new paths for change.

The continuous development of the European Union has caused borders to fade and has enhanced the exchange of information between corporations and their CEOs. The countereffect has been internationalization and globalization. The numbers of financial stakeholders who have a powerful influence on practice their powers on the behavior of corporations have grown to an amazing degree, and they are asking for greater and greater profits. A tight network of codependency has emerged, and many CEOs fear the powerful effects that their decisions and actions have on the stakeholders who benefit financially from the success of their corporations. They simply cannot afford to "lose face" in front of an international audience by making investments in *people* or *planet*, elements that do not have an immediate payback in the form of higher *profits*.

As a result, the influence of governments on these corporations in their international and globalizing networks has strongly decreased. In response to this situation there have arisen strong and repeated appeals from governments and nongovernmental organizations (NGOs) to corporations to care for the *planet* that "hosts" them, to care for marginalized and oppressed people who are being excluded from the benefits of the globalization process, and to care for socially and economically weaker areas and communities. Governments are severely handicapped in pursuing this matter by their own rules, regulations, and policies. National governments are limited to the power they exercise within their own national borders. In multilateral and supranational institutions, such as the European Union, governments fear to commit themselves because of their need to preserve local and national autonomy and because of their fear of giving up power and control. It is this stunning paradox that clearly defines a gap of responsibility that NGOs intensively try to fill (Janssen, 2001, p. 16–17).

Since the early 1960s, NGOs have been, in different ways, attempting to point out to corporations that growing in size, profits, and power should also mean growing in social responsibility for a growingly interdependent world of people and natural resources. This effort is sometimes successful and at other times not. On the other hand, NGOs also have been trying to make people wonder why the public complains and appeals to Presidents and Prime Ministers of national governments about the state of the world, but never to presidents of large corporations. Sometimes this too is successful and sometimes not.

One major recent success has been the development of the Global Reporting Initiative (GRI) in 1997, which resulted from intense cooperation between the Coalition for Environmentally Responsible Economies (CERES) and the United Nations Environmental Program (UNEP). The main aim of the GRI is to set a standard for corporations on how to report their developments regarding policies and outcomes in the areas of *people, planet,* and *profit.* As of this writing, 24 corporations have committed themselves to becoming actors in the pilot phase; among them are Shell, Procter & Gamble, Henkel, and General Motors (Janssen, 2001, p. 31–32).

Another success story resulting from the collaboration of multilateral institutions and NGOs has been the design and implementation of Social Accountability 8000 (SA 8000). This system exhibits a structural similarity with the long-existing ISO (International Organization for Standardization) standards, but it focuses on improving the working conditions in industrial corporations and their factories. The standards that are laid out in SA 8000 have been mainly derived from different conventions agreed upon by the International Labor Organization (ILO), but also include elements of the U.N. Universal Declaration of Human Rights and the U.N. Declaration on the Rights of the Child. SA 8000 has been developed and is being protected by the Council for Economic Priorities (Janssen, 2001, p. 269).

Finally, a major recent achievement in the field of promoting sustainable entrepreneurship has been the recent adoption of the revised *Guidelines for Multinational Corporations* by the members of the Organization for Economic Cooperation and Development (OECD).

> Enterprises should take fully into account established polities in the countries in which they operate, and consider the views of other stakeholders. In this regard, enterprises should contribute to economic, social and environmental progress with a view to achieving sustainable development. (SER, 2000, p. 5)

This is the opening paragraph of the *Guidelines*. The rest of the document spells out the principles and guidelines that have been defined by national governments and are suggested to large corporations for adoption. The guidelines and principles address issues of child labor, forced labor, environmental protection, overtime work, and wages.

In all the work done by NGOs and national governments, it is made clear that no one expects corporations to depart from their profit orientation. In fact, *profit* is considered a primary objective if corporations are to care for their *people*, by providing reasonable salaries and benefits, and to care for the *planet*, for example, by installing environmental protection systems. But, NGOs also point out that corporations need both employees who feel respected and protected and an environment that can deliver natural resources, albeit in limited ways, if they are to generate the profit they need. Therefore they often speak about the cycle of sustainable systems that is needed for their survival. No one element can exclude the others, hence echoing the cry of the Three Musketeers—"All for one, one for all!"

The dynamic of sustainability is also clearly expressed and described in the SER advisory report: "Economic wealth, social acceptability, and a sustainable environment are in constant causal relation to each other. They influence each other, they are complementary, and they can't exist without one another" (SER, 2000, p. 13). The three Ps of *people, planet,* and *profit* are also referred to as the "Triple Bottom Line."

It is clear that NGOs and other multilateral institutions are the key players in trying to effect and influence corporate behavior. Because of the growing diversity in Europe and the increasing globalization process, it is considered both essential and critical to make corporate executives aware that *profit* can only increase if the sustainability of *people* and *planet*, as primary resources in the production process, is protected. On the other hand, *people* and *planet* can only "be protected" if corporations generate enough *profit* to make the necessary investments.

Though many guidelines, conventions, principles, and regulations have been articulated in documents and promulgated to encourage this awareness, we must ask if they really make a difference. Do they really change behavior? Do paradigms shift and organizations transform themselves solely because of rules and declarations on paper?

Pedagogy of Ethics: How to Practice "Corporate Citizenship" in Europe

In my introduction to this chapter I argued that a profit-making corporation must shift its organizational paradigms in order to see itself differently if it wants to exercise sustainable entrepreneurship. It is clearly necessary for such a corporation to transform its *corporate identity* to make clear to *all* the stakeholders the meaning of its "corporate citizenship." In this section we will explore how a well-considered *pedagogy of ethics* can be more effective for setting into motion the needed transformation of identity and practices than documented guidelines and principles are able to do.

To explore *pedagogy* and *transformation* as correlated activities, we must consider the following four sets of questions:

1. Who are the learners and what are their needs? How will these needs be addressed?
2. Who are the educators and what do they need? What methods and approaches shall they apply?
3. What competencies must be created? How can this be done?
4. How does establishing new levels of competence lead to establishing a new corporate citizenship identity?

Let us try to answer these questions one at a time.

1. Who Are the Learners and What Are Their Needs?

The learners in our *pedagogy of ethics* are first and foremost the corporate manager, the executive, and the CEO, or the most powerful people in charge, but also the corporation as a whole, as an entity. It is unreal to assume that one person can change a whole organization or make a whole organization think differently. Taking into account the emphasis we placed earlier on the diversity of organizations, it is of the utmost importance that a corporate manager or management team involve the organization as a whole, crossing all hierarchical levels and all functional subsystems diagonally. A strong organizational dialogue is critical if the organization is to enter a successful learning process that benefits everyone:

> Together we need to be able to recognize and identify problems and opportunities. We need to be able to organize ourselves and other people to do something about them, and we need to be able to sit back and reflect on what has happened in order that we can do it all better the next time around . . . conceptualizing, coordinating and consolidating as a team. (Handy, 1994, p. 204)

Early on in this chapter I outlined Paolo Freire's five basic assumptions about how behavior can be changed by learning ethics. These same assumptions could just as well be used as the list of criteria by which corporations determine whether or not they are prepared to learn about sustainable entrepreneurship. Thus I would suggest changing the language of the list so that its items may lead to a profile that indicates the level of potential that corporations have for practicing *sustainable entrepreneurship*. The ready corporation should:

1. Be dynamic, open-minded, and in an open relation to its context, external markets, and environments.
2. Have internal systems in place in order to internalize values, make choices, and externalize its identity.
3. Have a moral awareness and a shared concern for the world and its people.
4. Allow for critical employees to voice their opinions and express their concerns.
5. Embrace the concept of "power with" management, instead of "power over" management, making enabling leadership the normal practice, rather than being authoritarian or coercive.

Does this imply that certain corporations cannot become sustainable entrepreneurs? In principle, no. What it does suggest is that some corporations have a longer way to go than others. One traditional theory of organizational change identifies three phases in any change process: *unfreezing, moving,* and *refreezing.* For corporations that do not have all the above criteria in place, the road of *unfreezing* will be longer than for those that do, but it does not and should not exclude them from taking action for this kind of change.

The way in which industrial corporations in the early 1980s responded to new European legislation on pollution provides a good illustration of what can be involved in the slow process of change and transformation. At that time, following E.U. guidelines and regulations, more and more national governments adopted legislation on the promotion of a clean and sustainable production process. Industrial corporations had very little time to adjust their processes. Consequently, they tended to choose a quick so-called "end-of-pipe technique." This largely consisted in installing filters and instruments to limit the emission of CO_2 gases. They did not make any radical changes in their production process in order to manage the real sources of the problem.

As Jannsen notes, about halfway through the 1980s, European governments and industries came to realize that a more dramatic transformation was needed to handle these problems more effectively for long-range success. Instead of strict governmental and legislative guidelines, a system of self-regulation was introduced, which allowed the industry to identify strategic, tactical, and operational solutions to the emissions themselves. Combined with external pressure from environmental NGOs and consumers, corporations started to explore new measures and means of disposal that would contribute to a cleaner environment. More and more corporate managers started to realize that an initial investment in new and clean production processes would trigger a more positive response from both society and potential customers. As a result, profit has increased and the return-on-investment has been higher than ever before (Janssen, 2001, p. 67–68).

2. Who Are the Educators and What Do They Need?

As I stated at the outset, NGOs have been among the main *educators and engines* of corporate change in Europe. The Council of Europe (CoE) formed on May 5, 1949 when ten countries signed the treaty constituting the Statute of the Council of Europe. That number has now increased to 41 Member States, from Albania and Andorra to the Ukraine and United Kingdom. The CoE plays an important role in strengthening democracy, human rights, the rule of law, and Europe's cultural heritage in its Member States. In its first three decades, the CoE was primarily an international organization comprised of western European members and concerned with western European issues, but the 1980s and 1990s saw the CoE assume a new role in the democratization of central and eastern Europe. With the accession of the Russian Federation in 1996, the CoE's important role in an enlarged Europe became even more evident. It is made up of

- Committee of Ministers (ministers of foreign affairs from each member state)
- Parliamentary Assembly (appointed or elected members)
- European Court of Human Rights
- European Commission of Human Rights
- The Congress of Local and Regional Authorities

together with a large representation of NGOs, has, with varying degrees of success, appealed to corporations' awareness of the need for sustainable entrepreneurship. The involvement of the Council of Europe is mainly related to the *people* part of the Triple Bottom Line. Although a majority of the NGOs focuses its efforts on the environmental element, the Council of Europe has provoked a long and intense debate on the issue of human rights. The European Convention of Human Rights, as it has been ratified by all members of the Council of Europe, and the juridical protection of these rights by the European Court in Strasbourg, has not only caused governments to adapt their attitudes, but also has had a strong impact on the human behavior of many corporations throughout Europe (Taylor, 1999).

But again, in addition to legislative pressure, the SER advisory report has also identified other forms of *education for corporate citizenship* in Europe by NGOs that have proven themselves successful:

1. Consumer boycotts of products and organizations.
2. Publicizing the contribution to ecological and social sustainability of certain products and production processes.
3. Starting a more ethical competition in business by contributing to the development of more sustainable products. A good example of this occurred at the beginning of the 1990s when Greenpeace challenged a German producer to develop a refrigerator without chlorofluorocarbon (CFC) gasses. Within a couple of years all large producers of refrigerators imitated this line of production.
4. Developing grading systems for the level of sustainability of products and producers.
5. Influencing consumers' buying behavior. (SER, 2000, p. 45)

NGOs and the Council of Europe have been the main "value creating entities" of sustainable entrepreneurship in Europe. They initiated numerous dialogues between consumers, corporations, and governments on setting new values for industrial production, banking, construction, and energy providers (gas, water, electricity, etc.). The major advantage of NGOs in the battle for sustainable entrepreneurship is that they have a single-issue target, whereas the Council of Europe and the European Union have multiple targets. This single-issue target allows for in-depth research and designated investments for developments to be made.

Merry and Freire both list the same criteria for educators for change. In his essay "Open Source Learning: A Key to Multiculturalism, Citizenship, and the Knowledge Society." Online document of Engage! InterAct, October 2000, at http://www.engage.nu/interact/Open_Source_Learning.doc.

Merry distinguishes strongly between the role of experts and the role of educators:

> Experts should simply be seen as people who have some interesting experience in the field you are exploring, people with whom it would be stimulating to listen to and dialogue with.
>
> . . . Rather than being a "sage on the stage," the educator should be a "guide on the side." It is the educator's role to help

people to discover answers for themselves, through a process of stimulation and dialogue, and to help them develop to the maximum of their human potential. (Merry, 2000, p. 17)

Freire states:

in the context of true learning for ethics, the learners will be engaged in a continuous transformation through which they become authentic subjects of the construction and reconstruction of what is being taught, side by side with the educator, who is equally subject to the same process. (Freire, 1998, p. 33)

So NGOs should also see themselves as educators, as "guides on the side," in the process of learning for sustainable entrepreneurship by corporations, because only then can the transformation to corporate citizenship be authentic and truly sustainable. If their interference is too strong or too imposing, the true transformation can and will not take place and the results will not be long-lasting.

In addition, Ivan Illich points out a few concrete arrangements that can be provided by educators (NGOs in the case of sustainable entrepreneurship) in order to help learners, in this case corporations, to decide on their next steps and to share their experiences:

- Reference services to educational tools and spaces;
- An exchange of skills for people willing to do so, and to provide the required conditions for these exchanges to take place;
- Peer matching—establishing a communication network that enables learners to find a partner in their learning;
- Reference services to "educators-at-large"—a database of people, skills, conditions, etc. (Illich, 1971, p. 74)

The following sample cases illustrate the truth and accuracy of the arguments of Merry, Freire, and Illich; they are the success stories of a large number of European NGOs. Here is an abridged list of the work done by some of the established European networks that deal with the promotion of and education for sustainable entrepreneurship.

Center for Innovation in Corporate Responsibility (CICR)

The mission of this organization is to support corporations in redefining and realizing their responsible and international business practice. One of the tools that they provide to corporations is a set of strategies called the CSER (corporate social and environmental responsibility), which is targeted at the integration of environmental, social, and ethical management within overall general management.

Coalition for Environmentally Responsible Economies (CERES)

This is a nonprofit cooperation of investment bankers, environmental organizations, retirement foundations, and employment organizations that, in cooperation with commercial corporations, aims for international shared environmental responsibility.

Corporate Social Responsibility Europe (CSR Europe)

This European network is one of the outcomes of the European Manifesto of Corporations against Exclusion (1995). It helps corporations to share their knowledge and experiences in the field of sustainable entrepreneurship. Together with the European Commission, CSR Europe aims to be a bridge between corporations, national governments, and European policy-makers.

Council for Ethics in Economics

This is a worldwide network of leading corporations, educational institutes, and NGOs who cooperate in the field of business ethics.

Council on Economic Priorities

One of the first and largest research organizations that provides information on the policies of large corporations regarding their behavior toward environmental caution, production of arms and weapons, vivisection, and equal treatment of employees. They are also the initiators of SA 8000.

European Business Ethics Network (EBEN)

EBEN was founded in 1987 and is a nonprofit foundation supported by some large European enterprises. EBEN aims at the promotion of a way of management driven by values and ethical principles.

Social Venture Network (SVN)

SVN is a foundation of corporations and individual corporate managers. It provides the possibility for personal contacts between CEOs who aim to make a significant contribution to solving social and environmental problems on local, European, and global levels and who seek equal-minded colleagues. SVN has developed the Standards of Corporate Responsibility.

Our conclusion from the above list is that (European) NGOs who aim to promote and educate for sustainable entrepreneurship truly fit the profile and principles as described above. None of them attempts to behave as an expert that imposes rules and regulations as a "sage on the stage." All of them profile themselves as "guides on the side" who provide networks, partnerships, sources of information, knowledge, and skills and reference services in order to enable CEOs to draw their own authentic conclusions and develop strategies for sustainable entrepreneurship according to their own needs and contexts.

3. What Competencies Need to Be Created and How Will This Be Done?

Naturally, the topic of "education for corporate citizenship" and our *pedagogy of ethics* is about how and to what extent corporations can apply the Triple Bottom Line of *people, planet,* and *profit to* their own practice and context in order to practice sustainable entrepreneurship. But this does not answer the question regarding what organizational competencies need to be or can be created in order to achieve this.

One of the documents that has been developed by the Council of Europe describes "competencies for active citizenship" as a balance of skills, knowledge, attitudes, and values (Council of Europe, 1999). But since this chapter describes corporate citizenship, this short definition needs to be expanded to include elements of corporate management. Therefore I would like to refer to what Richard Pascale calls the "Seven S Framework," which was originally developed by McKinsey & Company in 1979 as a consulting tool for managers (Pascale, 1990). In fact, the Seven S Framework is nothing more than seven important categories that managers should pay attention to when assessing their corporation. They are Strategy, Systems, Style, Staff, Shared Values, Structure, and Skills (Pascale, 1990, p. 40).

It is of utmost importance that corporations foster their sustainable efforts in an integrated way. It does not make sense for an enterprise to adopt a mission statement wherein they state that the ecological environment has to be taken care of and be used with great care and responsibility, and then to let their unchanged production systems continue to pollute. It is irresponsible to modify the policies in order to hire more diverse human resources, but not to prepare managers for dealing with this new kind of diversity on the work floor.

Pascale also insists that an integrated transformation process needs to be in place for a corporation to be or become successful. Simply modifying individual elements of the Seven S Framework may improve performance in the short term, but will not bring effectiveness in the long run. Pascale stresses that a shift of paradigm or mindset must be at the root of corporate transformation processes, affecting all levels and elements of the corporation as a whole. In order to establish this, Pascale lists three requirements for change initiatives that are to influence the competencies of the organization as a whole. In short, one could say that Pascale favors a holistic approach to organizational transformation. New Age theorist Ken Wilber supports him in this thinking process in his book *A Theory of Everything* (2001).

First, Pascale states that transformation requires a multipronged attack involving strategic repositioning and the promotion of a sense of ownership and participation amongst employees. Second, it is important to consider what kind of organizational leadership is required to match the identified, requisite transformation process; different kinds of transformation require different kinds of leaders to initiate these processes. Third, transformation processes need a certain degree of serendipity from the corporate managers who direct the process, meaning that managers need to show a high degree of openness to outcomes or results that are unexpected, but that might be very beneficial to the process as a whole:

> All that is essential is courage, persistence, and top management's openness to learning, both personal and organizational. . . . Each problem the managers [the CEOs] solved created the opportunity to solve the next problem that their previous solution created. They displayed the characteristic of not just "having the answers" but of "living in the question." They asked questions not merely to generate *answers*, but to reveal *what is possible*. (Pascale, 1990, p. 261–262)

It is clear that Freire and Pascale share an identical vision on the learning organization. Corporations and corporate managers need to see themselves and their corporations as "unfinished" if they are to encourage organizational transformation.

One model of best practice embodying this approach to transformation comes again from Janssen's book on sustainable entrepreneurship. Randstad is a large employment agency whose original business was providing organizations with temporary employees, and therefore assisting both the voluntarily and involuntarily unemployed to find temporary work. In one of its first public annual reports, Frits Goldschmeding, the founder of Randstad, writes:

> The interpretation of "sustainable entrepreneurship" has changed over time, mainly because of the dynamics of our society. Other

terminology is less time-bound. By definition one of the main conditions for an enterprise is to make profit. Equally, other conditions for corporate behavior are to make material and immaterial contributions to international, national, and local groups of people and communities who shape our direct and indirect environment. (Janssen, 2001, p. 139)

In 2000 Randstad decided to review the original values on which the organization was built. These were based on Goldschmeding's view of the labor market in the 1960s and 1970s. A growing sense of diversity triggered the need for a revision of shared values as well as systems, strategy, staff, skills, style, and structures. Their first step was to reformulate the corporate mission to read "using a fresh perspective on the labor market and acting as a driving force for bringing people and organizations together."

The next question they asked was, What organizational elements would shape this "driving force"? When employees of Randstad were asked this question, surprisingly they answered that the original values of the 1960s, such as respect, serving customers, learning from experiences, developing self-confidence, and encouraging self-development, could make a comeback as a source of new solutions. Randstad launched a management project called Managing Diversity that involved a total revision of the organization's existing human resource system. Randstad has succeeded in hiring, at all levels, employees that reflect the cultural diversity of society. They in turn attract potential customers, both employers and temp workers, from all cultural groups in society. In this way, Randstad promotes diversity in all their customers' corporations. Currently, 25% of Randstad's workforce is composed of immigrants, long-term unemployed persons, the elderly, and physically disadvantaged people. This has had an immediate impact on the management styles and working and placement procedures used within Randstad (Janssen, 2001, p. 139–143).

4. How Do We Progress from Changing Competencies to Establishing a New Corporate Citizenship Identity?

From what we have discussed so far, it has become evident that a corporation, in order to practice sustainable entrepreneurship, has to make a coordinated and integrated effort to involve the organization as a whole in its transformation process. Naturally, this includes its communication and PR systems. We can now take further steps by reviewing and researching the correlation between the transformation process and its effects on corporate identity.

James Grunig and David Dozier, in their book *Excellence in Public Relations and Communication Management* (1992), describe the importance of a corporation's efforts to adapt to their context, the external environment of the corporation. They recognize growing diversity and complexity in the corporate environments of Europe, brought about by the growing number of NGOs, activists, and pressure groups that try to influence a corporation's behavior. These efforts at influence can be understood, in the light of this chapter, as attempts to educate corporations for sustainable entrepreneurship. Of necessity, corporations must seek to understand how they can respond appropriately to the demand for transparency in their behavior and actions. Changing demographic statistics, dynamic environments, and new means of communication have made it necessary for corporations to send out their messages by a variety of means and through various channels:

> In an increasingly pluralistic society . . . , we can expect a correspondingly growing number of moral disputes. Their congenial resolution rests at least in part on the shoulders of public relations practitioners. Even if satisfactory resolution eludes the organization, the value of participation in deliberating over the common good cannot be overstated. (Grunig, 1992, p. 528)

Van Riel clearly distinguishes between corporate image and corporate identity (Van Riel, 1996, in Dutch). The *identity* of a corporation refers to its coordinated efforts for self-representation through symbolism, communication strategies, and behavior. Van Riel and others understand corporate *image* as how stakeholders and other interested parties in the external environment see the corporation (Van Riel, p. 37). In the end, every corporation is challenged to strike an ultimate balance between its identity and its image.

A good example of misunderstanding and imbalance of this kind comes from a corporation in the south of Europe that intended to show to their potential customers its new policies for creating an environmentally and ecologically healthy production line. Unfortunately, they shared the news by distributing a door-to-door mailing on chemically bleached paper. Understandably, this form of advertising resulted in resistance and rejection by environmental pressure groups and the general public.

A corporation should unconditionally adopt transparent, honest, and culturally sensitive means of communication in their transformation processes if they are to demonstrate that they are sincere in practicing corporate citizenship. This makes credibility a top priority in setting a corporate identity that promotes integrated efforts to manage the Triple Bottom Line of *people, planet,* and *profit* in relation to the seven organizational elements from the Seven S Framework.

This argument becomes even stronger when we take into account Janssen's list of 10 ground rules for promoting sustainable entrepreneurship:

1. A corporation should start reducing the environmental damage it is causing, respecting human rights and treating its environment and employees with great care *(= Systems and Structure).*
2. Sustainable entrepreneurship has to be a self-initiated process and should not simply be a response to external pressure *(= Shared Values and Strategy).*
3. If a corporation wants to practice sustainable entrepreneurship, it should identify clear aims and targets *(= Strategy and Structure).*
4. The aims should be closely related to the corporation's practice and should match the corporate values and its primary activities *(= Shared Values and Strategy).*
5. The aims have to be closely related to consumers' needs *(= Strategy and Systems).*
6. The corporation has to be capable of explaining the relationship between sustainability and its activities and production process *(= Skills and Style).*
7. The corporation should support these aims on a long-term basis *(= Strategy).*
8. The consumers and pressure groups should have a clear picture of the spending and investments by the corporation related to sustainable entrepreneurship *(= Systems and Structure).*
9. Sustainable entrepreneurship practiced by a corporation should not cause an increase of prices for the customers *(= Strategy).*
10. A corporation should not attempt to overemphasize its efforts *(= Skills).* (Janssen, 2001, p. 39)

We could also add one more rule to this list:

11. A corporation should make sure that its practices are shared by the corporation as a whole, and that they are not solely management-level efforts *(= Staff and Style and Shared Values).*

Canon Europe, producer of cameras, photocopiers, laser printers, faxes, and the like, provides an excellent example, illustrating the effectiveness of what we have been discussing. In 1988 Canon worldwide decided that it needed to adopt a new company philosophy

(= Shared Values) called in Japanese *"kyosei."* *Kyo* means sharing and together, and *sei* means existence, giving birth to, growth and dynamics. Canon explained the new philosophy of *kyosei* as a whole as "mutual rewarding coexistence," by which they intend to express their concern with environmental and ecological damage, violation of human rights, and social and economic injustice in the world. The new philosophy aims at not only increasing the organization's *profits,* but also at investing some of the profits for the benefit of *people* and *planet* (Van Riel, 1996, p. 232–233).

First, Canon adopted the *kyosei* philosophy in a Global Corporation Plan *(= Strategy),* and second, it was decided to begin implementing this plan in the Research and Development department *(= Systems).* Canon started by pulling back from military research and ecologically damaging production processes. They started to invest in developing new, healthier production lines and products on a local level and in the original region where the research had been conducted, instead of directing all innovations at the international level. In this way, local branches and their people can become the main beneficiaries of their inventions and contributions *(= Structure).*

Third, Canon implemented new methods of measuring the results, profits, and effectiveness of the corporation *(= Systems and Style).* Instead of solely focusing on profit numbers, Canon introduced procedures to measure their environmental policies qualitatively, including their sensitivity to local and national rules and regulations for production lines abroad, and their social policies dealing with human resources and societal needs *(= Staff and Skills and Structure).*

Finally, Canon launched a marketing campaign that was fully targeted at specific local cultures, taking into account local considerations, needs, and languages *(= Style and Strategy).* For various countries and different regions within Europe, special slogans were developed and appropriate visual images selected. All of these efforts put strong emphasis on the "company behind the brand" and Canon's investments in *people* and *planet* (Van Riel, 1996, p. 232–243).

Conclusion: "Thinking Critically about Past and Present Practice Makes It Possible to Improve Tomorrow's Practice"

At the start of this chapter we noted the current interest of European corporations and societies in sustainable entrepreneurship as a new way of doing business, in part as a result of growing diversity in Europe. Shifting demography and societal demands have caused corporate managers to reconsider their practices and their corporate identity in order to give *people* and *planet* a deservedly equal position with a corporation's *profit* efforts. Corporate managers need to begin practicing "corporate citizenship," valuing *all* stakeholders of the corporation equally.

The ambiguity surrounding the concepts of diversity and globalization has caused a high degree of uncertainty with corporate managers and governments about how to manage this diversity and environmental concerns. NGOs continuously attempt to fill this gap in and lack of competencies through what we shall call *pedagogy of ethics*.

It is deemed essential that, before any shift of paradigm or organizational transformation can be accomplished, corporations begin to recognize that *people, planet,* and *profit* are related to each other—as were the Three Musketeers. They cannot exist or succeed without each other. *Profit* is needed in order to invest in *people* and *planet*. But investments in *people* and *planet* are needed in order to make employees, consumers, and environment feel respected and, therefore, desirous of contributing to corporations' *profit* line.

The *pedagogy of ethics* emphasizes that for corporations to practice "corporate citizenship" and thus contribute to sustainable entrepreneurship, a sense of unfinishedness is needed. Corporations need to perceive themselves as subject to continuous change and allow themselves to reflect critically on their current practices. For this to happen, the transformation process must not only occur by imposed governmental rules and regulations, but also by strong systems of self-regulation, awareness building, and total involvement within the corporation. This allows corporate managers to look for answers and solutions *and* to ask critical questions and involve the corporation as a whole in the transformation process.

NGOs play the role of educators in this pedagogy. They should act as "guides by the side" providing referral services, partnerships, and access to information, and stimulating the exchange of skills, knowledge, and values. Only then can change be sincere and authentic, setting into play basic conditions for a high level of sustainability for the transformation.

In short, the competencies for corporate citizenship that are the focus of the *pedagogy of ethics* are: Strategy, Systems, Style, Staff, Shared Values, Structure, and Skills, all of which are taken from the Seven S Framework. Various approaches to organizational transformation show one similarity, the need for an integrated approach to transformation and a high degree of openness to "living in the question," as well as tolerance for uncertainty and serendipity. After that, corporate managers need to embrace "power with" management, which allows all employees and stakeholders involved to contribute to and to think along on equal terms in order to stimulate a sense of ownership of the transformation process.

The last step for implementing a true transformational process for beginning to practice corporate citizenship and contribute to sustainable entrepreneurship is for corporations to develop a sincere, integrated, and transparent corporate identity that clearly shows that the corporation's intent is aligned with its corporate image.

To do this, the corporate identity needs to address all organizational elements in its activity and self-presentation. This means that the corporate identity has to be a collaborative output of shared values, strategy, systems, structure, style, staff, and skills in order to be understood and successful. In a pluralistic society it is of utmost importance for corporations to make their efforts at sustainable entrepreneurship meet a high sense of credibility and authenticity.

If we assume that the trend of globalization and internationalization will continue in Europe, that new technologies arise, that cultural diversity will grow, and that corporations feel a sense of responsibility for *people* and *planet*, then it will have to be a shared and collaborate effort of *all* stakeholders of the globe to believe in a *pedagogy of ethics* and to contribute to visible sustainability and the future of Europe.

In closing, let us remind ourselves of the words of Paolo Freire: "Though I know that things can get worse, I also know that I am able to intervene to improve them" (Freire, 1998, p. 53).

Equal Opportunities for Women and Men in the European Union: The Case of E-Quality in Belgium

9

Marie-Thérèse Claes

During the 1970s the European Community adopted several principles related to equal treatment for women and men: the principle of equal pay for men and women (1974); the principle of equal treatment for men and women as regards access to employment, vocational training, promotion, and working conditions (1976); and the principle of equal treatment for men and women in matters of social security (1978). The decisions taken by the European Community are in fact directives that have to be implemented by national bodies in all Member States.

In order to speed up progressive implementation of these principles, the European Commission decided in 1982 to set up a network of specialized information at the disposal of these national bodies*

---

* The European Union is managed by common institutions: a democratically elected **Parliament**; a Council that represents the Member State and is composed of government ministers; a European **Council** of Heads of State or Government; a **Commission** that acts as guardian of the Treaties and has the power to initiate and called the Advisory Committee on Equal Opportunities for Women and Men. This Committee's aim was to "assist the Commission in formulating and implementing the Community's activities aimed at promoting equal opportunities for women and men, and foster ongoing exchanges of relevant experience, policies, and practices between the Member States and the various parties involved" (EUR-Lex, 1999). By 1995 it was clear that the Advisory Committee had made a significant contribution to the Community's activities in this field, and a new midrange action program was proposed.

In the 1980s, the specific action programs stimulated further action in the individual Member States. Furthermore, the European Council declared in 1994 that the promotion of equal opportunities for women and men was a key priority of the European Union and the Member States. In 1995, a first annual report on the Equal Opportunities policy was published, with the United Nations World Conference on Women in Beijing, September, 1995, as the selected target.

In the 1990s, equal opportunities had become a policy that was to intersect all other policies—a mainstream policy that was to be applied by all. "Mainstreaming" is defined as "the systematic consideration of the differences between the conditions, situations, and needs of women and men in all Community policies, at the point of planning, implementing, and evaluation, as applied to Europe, the industrialized countries, and the developing countries" (European Commission, Employment and Social Affairs, 1997, p. 8).

Gender Mainstreaming

The 1996 report gives the following example of mainstreaming:

> An application of mainstreaming policy in, for example, transport policy means that it takes into account the fact that women are much more frequent users of public transport and less frequently own or have access to a car, as compared to men. Women also frequently travel with children and use prams and pushchairs

---

implement legislation; a **Court of Justice** that ensures that Community law is observed; and a **Court of Auditors** that monitors the financial management of the Union. In addition, there are a number of advisory bodies that represent economic, social, and regional interests. A **European Investment Bank** was set up to facilitate the financing of projects that contribute to the balanced development of the Union.

(strollers). The development of good, efficient, and qualitative public passenger transport systems which take into account accessibility for passengers with specific needs would contribute to equal opportunities. (European Commission, Employment and Social Affairs, 1997, p. 8)

The strategy of mainstreaming is seen as a complex and long-term process, which requires a variety of approaches. As gender equality is viewed as a central issue for society, partnership with the social partners is a key element in the program, and the social dialogue brings together the social partners in a regular and structured way.

The concept of mainstreaming has evolved from the implementation of specific measures in favor of women for addressing those structural inequalities in the organization of working and family life that constrain the participation of many women in the labor market and in public life. The European Commission's Technical Paper 3, "Mainstreaming Equal Opportunities for Women and Men in Structural Fund Programs and Projects," for the programming period 2000–2006 states:

> Women and men do not have the same roles, resources, needs, and interests. They do not participate equally in decision-making. The values given to "women's work" and "men's work" are also not the same. These differences vary from one society or culture to another. They are termed "gender differences." (2000, p. 4)

Interesting distinctions are made in the glossary of terms that is annexed to this technical paper, in which sharing of power and decision-making positions between men and women is defined as 40% to 60% representation of either sex. Gender differences are qualified in the glossary as "the social and cultural differences between women and men, as well as the different values placed on women's and men's spheres and activities." It continues, "Gender differences vary from one society or culture to another, and change through time" (p. 24).

Gender Imbalance in the Labor Market

The labor market participation of women has been increasing consistently. Reduced fertility rates, an aging population, and different kinds of households influence the way in which women participate in economic life. Women now account for over 40% of the labor force in the European Union, and nearly 70% of the European women of prime working age (20–60), are in the labor force. Activity rates vary with levels of educational attainment: high rates of educational attainment are generally matched with higher rates of economic activity. More than 80% of European women with a university degree are employed, compared to 63% of the women with lower secondary education level. The vast majority (86%) of employed women in the European Union are employees. Just fewer than 10% are self-employed, and around 4% are family workers.

Occupational segregation continues to be very pronounced: women account for at least half of the workers in service occupations (clerical and technical work), whereas production and transport, administrative and managerial work, and agricultural work are strongly male dominated (84%, 77%, and 66%, respectively). Across the Member States, trends vary and sometimes conflict: in a number of countries, the rate of women in industrial employment has grown in the last decade (over 20% in Germany, Ireland, and the Netherlands); in others, such as France and Italy, it has declined.

Atypical employment is evident in the services sector, a sector where women account for a large majority of part-time and casual workers: 83% of part-time workers and 50% of temporary workers in the European Union are women. Women often have part-time and temporary jobs, while men hold more of those that are well paid and secure. Women make up the majority of part-time workers, and a large proportion of women who work do so on a part-time basis (32% of total female employment compared with 5% for men in 1996). Many of them would prefer a full-time job if it were available. Nonetheless, a large proportion chooses to or is obliged to work part-time because of family responsibilities. For women the outcome of this labor market segmentation is lower income, limited access to qualified jobs, and fewer opportunities for career development.

In practice, the implementation of equal opportunity principles by the Member States varies widely. However, all have made efforts.

Women in Political Life in the European Union zone of interest, including the United States and Canada for comparison; as of 1 July 2001.

A. The Chronology of Women's Suffrage

1788 United States of America (to stand for election)

1906 Finland

1907 Norway (to stand for election)*

1913 Norway**

1915 Denmark

1917 Canada (to vote),* Netherlands (to stand for election)

1918 Austria, Estonia, Germany, Hungary, Ireland,* Latvia, Poland, United Kingdom*

1919 Belarus, Belgium (to vote),* Luxembourg, Netherlands (to vote), Sweden*

1920 Czech Republic, Slovakia, United States of America (to vote), Canada (to stand for election)*

1921 Belgium (to stand for election),* Lithuania

1928 United Kingdom**

1929 Romania*

1930 Turkey (to vote)

1931 Portugal,* Spain

1934 Portugal,* Turkey (to stand for election)

1944 Bulgaria, France

1946 Romania,** F.Y.R. of Macedonia, Yugoslavia

1947 Malta

1948 Belgium**

1952 Greece

1959 San Marino (to vote)

1960 Cyprus

1962 Monaco

1970 Andorra (to vote)

1971 Switzerland

1973 Andorra (to stand for election), San Marino (to stand for election)

1976 Portugal**

1984 Liechtenstein

---

* Right subject to conditions or restrictions.
** Restrictions or conditions lifted.
Source: Adapted from http://www.ipu.org/wmn-e/suffrage.htm.

B. Women in Parliaments

Rank	Country	Lower or Single House				Upper House or Senate			
		Elections	Seats	Women	% Women	Elections	Seats	Women	% Women
1	Sweden	09 1998	349	149	42.7	—	—	—	—
2	Denmark	11 2001	179	68	38.0	—	—	—	—
3	Finland	03 1999	200	73	36.5	—	—	—	—
4	Norway	09 2001	165	60	36.4	—	—	—	—
5	Netherlands	05 1998	150	54	36.0	05 1999	75	20	26.7
6	Germany	09 1998	666	211	31.7	N.A.	69	17	24.6
7	Spain	03 2000	350	99	28.3	03 2000	259	63	24.3
8	Austria	10 1999	183	49	26.8	N.A.	64	13	20.3
9	Bulgaria	06 2001	240	63	26.2	—	—	—	—
10	Belgium	06 1999	150	35	23.3	06 1999	71	20	28.2
11	Switzerland	10 1999	200	46	23.0	10 1999	46	9	19.6
12	Monaco	02 1998	18	4	22.2	—	—	—	—
13	Canada	11 2000	301	62	20.6	N.A.	105	34	32.4
14	Croatia	01 2000	151	31	20.5	04 1997	65	4	6.2
15	Poland	09 2001	460	93	20.2	09 2001	100	23	23.0
16	Portugal	03 2002	230	44	19.1	—	—	—	—

17	United Kingdom	06 2001	659	118	17.9	N.A.	713	117	16.4
18	Estonia	03 1999	101	18	17.8	—	—	—	—
"	Latvia	10 1998	100	17	17.0	—	—	—	—
20	Luxembourg	06 1999	60	10	16.7	—	—	—	—
"	Czech Republic	06 1998	200	30	15.0	11 2000	81	10	12.3
22	Andorra	03 2001	28	4	14.3	—	—	—	—
23	Slovakia	09 1998	150	21	14.0	—	—	—	—
"	United States of America	11 2000	435	61	14.0	11 2000	100	13	13.0
25	Republic of Moldova	02 2001	101	13	12.9	—	—	—	—
"	Slovenia	10 2000	90	11	12.2	—	—	—	—
"	Ireland	06 1997	166	20	12.0	08 1997	60	11	18.3
"	Liechtenstein	02 2001	25	3	12.0	—	—	—	—
29	France	05 1997	577	63	10.9	09 2001	321	35	10.9
"	Cyprus	05 2001	56	6	10.7	—	—	—	—
"	Romania	11 2000	345	37	10.7	11 2000	140	8	5.7
32	Lithuania	10 2000	141	15	10.6	—	—	—	—

B. Women in Parliaments *(cont.)*

Rank	Country	Lower or Single House				Upper House or Senate			
		Elections	Seats	Women	% Women	Elections	Seats	Women	% Women
33	Belarus	10 2000	97	10	10.3	12 2000	61	19	31.1
34	Italy	05 2001	630	62	9.8	05 2001	321	25	7.8
"	Malta	09 1998	65	6	9.2	—	—	—	—
36	Greece	04 2000	300	26	8.7	—	—	—	—
"	Russian Federation	12 1999	449	34	7.6	N.A.	178	6	3.4
"	Yugoslavia	09 2000	138	10	7.2	09 2000	40	1	2.5
39	Bosnia and Herzegovina	11 2000	42	3	7.1	11 2000	15	0	0.0
40	The F.Y.R. of Macedonia	10 1998	120	8	6.7	—	—	—	—
41	Albania	06 2001	140	8	5.7	—	—	—	—
42	Turkey	04 1999	550	23	4.2	—	—	—	—
?	Hungary	04 2002	386	?	?	—	—	—	—
?	Ukraine	03 2002	450	?	?	—	—	—	—

Source: Adapted from http://www.ipu.org/wmn-e/classif.htm.

Gender Balance in Decision-Making

In March 1995, the Council of Ministers stated "the objective of balanced participation of women and men in the sharing of responsibilities between women and men in decision-making in every sphere of life constitutes an important condition for equality between women and men" (European Commission, 1997, p. 85). The necessity of establishing equality by promoting balanced participation in decision-making was established as a principle of democracy. On the one hand, women's underrepresentation in political decision-making positions calls into question the legitimacy of any given democratic system. On the other hand, if women's values and life circumstances are not taken into consideration by the decision-makers, women will tend not to identify with the political system.

So far, only two European countries, Sweden and Denmark, have achieved 40% female representation in their national government, although Finland and Germany are very close:

Exhibit 9.1

Women in the National Governments of the E.U. Member States, 2001

Country	Members	Women	% Women
Sweden	20	10	50.0
Denmark	21	9	42.9
Finland	18	7	38.9
Germany	44	17	38.6
Netherlands	25	9	36.0
UK	85	28	32.9
Austria	16	5	31.3
France	34	10	29.4
Luxembourg	14	4	28.6
Belgium	18	4	28.6
Ireland	32	7	21.9
Spain	17	3	17.6
Italy	78	11	14.1
Greece	88	11	12.5
Portugal	61	6	9.8
Total	**571**	**141**	**24.7**

Source: European Database.

Even within the European institutions, balance in the decision-making bodies has not been achieved, and occupational segregation is apparent: in the European Parliament as well as in the European Commission, women are a minority in senior positions, and an overwhelming majority are in secretarial jobs:

Exhibit 9.2

Employees by Sex and Grade within the Administration of the European Parliament, 1998

Category	Total	Men	Women	% Women
A—Senior management	386	306	80	20.7
LA—Junior management	773	358	415	53.7
B—Assistance	458	198	260	56.8
C—Secretaries	1,422	421	1,001	70.4
D—Qualified Workers	275	227	48	17.5
Total	**3,314**	**1,510**	**1,804**	**54.4**

Source: European Database.

Exhibit 9.3

Employees by Sex and Grade within the Administration of the European Commission, 2000

Category	Total	Men	Women	% Women
A—Senior management	5,183	4,171	1,012	19.5
LA—Junior management	1,782	779	1,003	56.3
B—Assistance	3,260	1,972	1,288	39.5
C—Secretaries	5,234	982	4,252	81.2
D—Qualified Workers	820	636	184	22.4
Total	**16,279**	**8,540**	**7,739**	**47.5**

Source: European Database.

The Council of the European Union is the central decision-making body of the European Union. It is composed of the heads of state, heads of government, foreign affairs ministers, the President of the Commission, and one further member of the Commission. Representatives at the ministerial level from each Member State participate in the Council, and the presidency of the Council is held by each Member State for six months: during the first half of 2001, Sweden was the president, followed by Belgium during the second half. Some Member States send both head of state and head of government to the Council, whereas others may be represented either by their head of state or their head of government. As of 2001, two heads of state in the European Union are women: President Tarja Halonen in Finland, and President Mary McAleese in Ireland. The heads of state of Denmark, the Netherlands, and the United Kingdom are women, but their position is legitimized by birth and not by political elections. Women head the ministries of the Exterior of Luxembourg, Sweden, and Austria.

Women also constitute a minority in financial decisions: they are usually well represented at lower levels, but the higher the decision-making level, the fewer the women:

Exhibit 9.4

Women in the Central Banks in the E.U. Member States, 1998

Country	Female Employees	Women in the Executive Committees (women/total)	Female Heads of Departments (women/total)
Belgium	37%	(1/6) 17%	(2/11) 18%
Denmark	50%	(1/3) 33%	(1/31) 3%
Finland	—	(0/4) 0%	(1/13) 8%
France	52%	(1/10) 10%	(0/9) 0%
Germany	40%	(0/7) 0%	(0/41) 0%
Italy	26%	(0/4) 0%	(0/9) 0%
Sweden	57%	(4/12) 33%	(5/15) 33%
UK	44%	(2/16) 12%	(2/25) 8%

Source: European Database.

Women in Management

As far as women in management are concerned, the 1997 ILO (International Labour Organization) report was revealing. Linda Wirth, Senior Gender Specialist at the ILO, in 1997 reported the International Labor Organization's study on the "glass ceiling." She concluded, "almost universally, women have failed to reach leading positions in major corporations and private sector organizations, irrespective of their abilities" (ILO, 1997). The ILO report says that although women have made substantial progress in closing the gender gap in managerial and professional jobs, most female managers world-wide are still barred from the top levels of organizations, whether in the private or public sector or in political life. They hold a mere 2% to 3% of top jobs in corporations:

Exhibit 9.5

Women in Management

Country	% of All Managers	% in Senior Management	% at Executive Level
USA	43	2.4	1.9
UK	33	3	2
Japan	9	2	—
Germany	17	6	2
France	25	6	13
Netherlands	17	18	—
Finland	25	11	—
Belgium	30	8	6

Source: International Labour Office.

Women in management tend to be clustered in certain activities, to the point where certain company functions are almost feminized. Gender inequality in education and training, reinforced by social attitudes, has largely contributed to occupational segregation, whereby men and women are streamed into different trades, professions, and jobs. This is often referred to as *horizontal segregation*. A lot of women will be found in two occupations: nursing and teaching. On the other hand, in the organizational structures of corporations, career paths in staff functions such as human resource management and administration are less likely to lead directly to the top than strategic functions, or line functions, such as product development or corporate finance. And it is in the staff functions that women will mostly be found.

Exhibit 9.6

Percentage of Women Found in Different Functions

Country	Function	1970s–1980s	1990's Share
USA	Personnel, labor relations	21	58
France	Personnel	25	38
Finland	Personnel	17	70

Source: *International Labour Organisation Report*, 1996.

Even in countries with strong track records of government support for gender equality, the pattern of occupational segregation prevails. In Finland, for example, only 20% of women work in occupations that

show a balanced male/female employment ratio (i.e
of employees are of the same sex) and these jobs
all occupations. There are also differences in th␣
are represented in the hierarchy of positions. Ev␣
dominated by women, men usually occupy the more sk␣
ble, and better-paid positions. This is referred to as *vertical* ␣
regation. In a Belgian survey in 1998 of 43 women, including 1␣
positions, top women agree that it is harder for women to get to ␣
top than for men (Gilsoul, 1998):

Exhibit 9.7

Opinions of Women

	% of Women Who Agree
Women have to work more than men in order to demonstrate their competencies and to succeed	82.5
Women make slower progress than men in the company's hierarchy	78.5
Some levels of responsibility are not easily given to women	79.5

Source: Gilsoul, 1998.

When managers are asked to rank in order of importance three factors that had held them back, men and women seem to have the same problems, but there are additional problems for women (Holton, Rabbetts, and Stone, 1998):

Exhibit 9.8

Factors against Career

Men	Women
1. Lack of sponsor/mentor	1. Stereotypes and assumptions about what I will and won't do
2. Being a specialist	
3. Lack of feedback on my career	2. Lack of sponsor/mentor
	3. Lack of feedback on my career*
	3. Making compromises for my partner's career*

* These two items are tied for third ranking.
Source: Holton, Rabbetts, and Stone, 1998.

Balancing professional and family responsibilities seems to be one of the priorities for women, but also for men. Looking at the advantages

...isadvantages of an appointment at senior level, Holton and her ...eagues found that men and women rank "difficulties of balancing ...me and work life" number one in their list of disadvantages, but the ...eeling is stronger for women (79% of women, compared to 67% of men). In a questionnaire to female senior managers in Belgium, a comparison between an ideal job and the present job reveals that present working conditions are not as good as women wish them to be (Gilsoul, 1998). These are the responses of top-level women who work between 50 and 60 hours per week:

Exhibit 9.9

The Ideal Job Compared to the Present Job

	In an Ideal Job	In Present Job
Flexibility (possibility to work part-time or to take leave for a certain time)	64.3	39.3
Possibility to balance professional and family life	86.1	50.0

Source: Gilsoul, 1998.

The Wage Gap

Generally speaking, women have lower incomes, lower wages, and less advantageous terms of employment than men. Women in the E.U. labor market, on average, are paid 74% of men's wages (European Labor Force Survey, 1999).

Gender pay differentials exist to different degrees in every Member State, reflecting the unequal position of women and men in the labor market. A concentration of women in low-paid jobs and the occupational segregation on the labor market contribute to the persistence of the gender gap across the European Union: among manual workers, women earn between 65% and 90% of men's average pay. In those Members States where strong statutory protections such as a minimum wage exist (e.g., Sweden, France, and Italy), the gap between women and men tends to be narrower. In countries without such protections, the pay gap tends to be wider (e.g., the United Kingdom and Ireland).

Even when women manage to rise to the top, female executives nearly always earn less than men:

Exhibit 9.10

Top Women's Earnings in Percentage of Male Earnings

Country	% Earnings/Male
UK	71
USA	68
Finland	65
Brazil	50

Source: ILO Report, 1996.

Wage discrimination is a complex problem. The Swedish report, "Highlighting Pay Differentials Between Women and Men" (Swedish Ministry for Gender Affairs, 2001) states that the questions we have to ask ourselves are:

1. Why are gender-related pay differentials not disappearing?
2. Why do so few men choose to work in the service sector?
3. Why do men choose to work full-time even when they have young children, and why do they choose to give their careers priority?
4. What is the cause and what is the effect of these pay differentials on the labor market today?
5. Why do women not make the same career choices? (Fransson, Johansson, and Svenaeus, 2000)

Methods have been proposed to make the unseen scale of values visible at the workplace level, such as a "qualifications model" that includes job evaluation and evaluation of qualifications. Job evaluation measures and compares the demands made by jobs, and evaluation of qualifications measures and compares how individuals meet those demands. This qualifications model is a domain where the input of the social partners is much needed.

Europe is faced with the paradoxical situation that a further increase in labor force participation by women is needed to cope with the shrinking number of births and the increasing number of elderly population over the next 10 to 20 years (Olsson, 2000). If, as is commonly recognized, economic and social growth must go hand in hand, "a well functioning social structure seems to be a necessary condition for European men and women in general, and for those women and men who want to combine a life as parents with participation in the paid labor force in particular" (Löfström, 2001, p. 11).

Putting the "E" into Quality

One of the main focuses of the European equal opportunities policy is a better integration of women into socioeconomic life, particularly in the labor market. One of the tools used in this respect is the policy of positive actions in the private as well as in the public sector. Positive actions aim at overcoming the barriers that women find in their professional life, and promoting their more uniform integration in all fields of work.

In the private sector, voluntary equal opportunity plans can be established within a branch of activity or within an enterprise. In 1993, networks of private enterprises were created in which the latest innovations in human resource management were combined with the contributions of positive actions. The objectives of these networks' meetings have been to examine the concrete progress made within the enterprises, to be informed of new initiatives, and to exchange know-how and practices. The networks also offer possibilities for equal opportunity training.

In order to reduce persistent discrimination, such as pay gaps and the absence of women in top positions, equal opportunity services have worked out several methods, such as consulting, training, and the E-Quality Award.

The policy of "E-quality" is based on the principle that quality can only be obtained if it includes equality between men and women. It aims at including equal opportunities in an economic model, the European Foundation for Quality Management (EFQM) Excellence Model. With the integration of this model in its overall functioning, the enterprise can offer its female members numerous advantages, such as the possibility of developing their competencies and holding top positions. However, presenting oneself as an "Equal Opportunity" employer may above all profit the company: a personnel policy seen as an economic instrument to extend opportunities for women enhances productivity. The organization has everything to gain: commitment and loyalty from their workers, higher flexibility, a positive public image, and so on.

The EFQM was founded in 1988 by the presidents of 14 major European companies (including Renault, Nestlé, Philips Electronics, Volkswagen, Dassault Aviation, and Bull SA, among others), with the endorsement of the European Commission. These companies wanted to create an initiative around Quality Management in Europe, following examples in other continents. In Japan, the Japanese Union of Scientists and Engineers (JUSE) has granted the "Deming Prize" to organizations that have made an effort in the field of statistical quality control since 1951. In the United States, the National Institute of Standard and Technology has granted the "Malcolm Baldridge Quality Award" since 1987.

The principal idea behind the discussion of qualitatively different management systems is "the expectation that a paradigmatic shift in personnel policy and personnel management will mean that existing or potential personnel resources may be used in a better way and therefore that they will remain more competitive. As a result, more attention is being focused on corporate planning and actions on human resource management" (Engelbrech, 1997, p. 106). Total Quality Management (TQM) has put a greater emphasis on customers, work patterns, process flows, and above all, employees.

EFQM's mission is available

1. To stimulate and assist organizations throughout Europe to participate in improved activities leading ultimately to excellence in customer satisfaction, employee satisfaction, impact on society, and business results.
2. To support the managers of European organizations in accelerating the process of making Total Quality Management a decisive factor for achieving global competitive advantage.

The EFQM Excellence Model is a practical tool for self-evaluation to help organizations be successful by measuring where they are on the path of excellence, helping them understand the gaps, and stimulating solutions. It is a nonprescriptive framework that recognizes there are many approaches to achieving sustainable excellence. The concept is that customer satisfaction and employee satisfaction, as well as integration into community life, can be achieved through the function of leadership, policy and strategy, human resources management, resources, and processes, all leading to better business results.

The idea that diversity, integrated into the quality discourse, enhances the quality of products and services, ensures creativity in the teams, and improves contacts with customers and the external environment, has been gaining ground. The integration of equal opportunities as a criterion for quality, on the other hand, is quite new. According to G. Shapiro and S. Austin, if the success of Total Quality Management is also considered as enabling all employees in the company, at all levels and to the same extent, to use their knowledge and abilities to the full and to contribute this knowledge and these abilities to the company, then the conditions for an E-quality management strategy (equality and quality) have been created (Shapiro and Austin, 1994).

Truly, the concept of equal opportunities has changed immensely. One used to speak in terms of discrimination, injustice, and inequality between men and women; now the notion is moving toward empowerment of people and good business sense. In order to be competitive, tomorrow's enterprise will have to turn the potential represented by its workforce to advantage. Indeed, equipment, techniques, and computers make up for part of the economic resources only. The structure of human resources has diversified, and system theory tells us that an organization (a system) can only work successfully if the complexity of the external environment is reflected in the internal complexity of the organization. This means that an equal opportunity policy within enterprises is an essentially integral part of the implementation of TQM strategies.

The concept of EFQM is entirely based on this reality. The nine fundamental concepts of the EFQM model are:

1. Results orientation.
2. Customer focus.
3. Leadership and constancy of purpose.
4. Management by processes and facts.
5. People development and involvement.
6. Continuous learning.
7. Innovation and improvement.
8. Partnership development.
9. Public responsibility.

E-quality or equal opportunities is an essential dimension in these concepts, and has been fully integrated into the EFQM model.

In order to integrate equal opportunities into the EFQM model, there were two possibilities. One was to integrate them in Human Resources, with the danger of confining them to personnel management. The other was to integrate them totally into the whole EFQM model. The latter solution was chosen, meaning that equal opportunities permeated each fundamental concept of the model.

The E-quality strategy aims at granting equal opportunities to all employees, at all levels, in order to make the most of their knowledge and capacities on the one hand, and to maximize their contribution to the organization on the other hand. In Human Resources Management, this implies stressing not just the qualifications and competencies of each employee, but also the variety of their interests and potentialities.

This often means profound changes in personnel management in the organization:

1. An awareness in management of the concept of equal opportunities and the identification of this concept as a corporate objective.
2. A conscious corporate reaction to sociocultural changes and a shift in social values in the organization and its philosophy.
3. Training and staff development plans.
4. A recruitment and selection policy that does not discriminate by gender.
5. New work patterns and work flows, with the participation of women in the different projects of the organization.
6. Reconciling family life and work life, with flexible working schedules, parental leave arrangements, childcare services, family support programs, and the like.
7. Encouraging cooperative behavior at the workplace.
8. Institutionalizing activities regarding equal opportunities by establishing a staff unit with responsibility, discussion circles, and codes of practice.

Though the EFQM model can be found in many companies, E-quality remains little known and used in Europe. In order to arouse interest for the model, the Equal Opportunities Service organized an "award," rewarding organizations that have paid attention to equal opportunities and consequently allowing them to publicize their commitment to ethical values.

The E-Quality Award

After a conference of the "Positive Action" network in Como, Italy, in 1994, organized by the European Commission, the Total E-Quality Association was created. Its founders came both from private companies and from public institutions of trade, industry, and education.

The Total E-Quality Association gives an award to those companies who pursue an equal opportunities policy. The award is evidence of the fact that equality of opportunities leads to a more efficient use of human resources that in turn boosts the quality of the company's input and output and guarantees competitiveness. The title is awarded to companies pursuing a personnel policy that is oriented toward equal opportunities, focuses on company employees, and aims to encourage them to achieve their potential. When a company is awarded the title it receives a certificate and a logo that can be used for marketing and public relations activities.

The evaluation process is divided into three phases: the E-quality checklist, the E-quality audit, and the Equal Opportunities jury.

The starting point is the E-quality checklist, a questionnaire of 40 items referring to equal opportunities related to the EFQM quality model. The checklist for Total E-Quality investigates seven areas of activity, developed into possible measures to be taken by the company in human resources management. The investigation covers most issues related to the implementation of an equal opportunities policy for men and women in enterprises, and it leaves the possibility for the company to add other measures in this respect:

1. The first area of activities explores whether the company has a clear vision of the employment situation of its staff and therefore a database in relation to functions, qualifications, family situation, career development, and all other professional aspects that can be collected and analyzed in terms of the percentage of women.

2. The second area of investigation is about staff recruitment and selection: whether a gender-neutral methodology is applied in all phases from recruitment advertisements to evaluation of qualifications and experience.

3. The third area concerns further training and personnel development in conformity with employees' needs and functions, for part-time employees, staff participation in shared responsibilities, use of instruments for goal-oriented personnel development, specific promotion of female employees, surveys, and evaluation data.

4. The fourth area is about ensuring the compatibility of career and family, investigating flexible hours regulations, the support for childcare, contact offers during the career break (meetings, training during and after the break, social benefits), granting leave, if necessary, for family problems, and working from home.

5. The fifth area concerns promoting male/female cooperation in the workplace by means of behavioral training, events, publications, advice units for conflicts, and other programs.

6. The sixth area concerns institutionalizing activities that promote equal opportunity by the establishment of a unit responsible for carrying it out, discussion groups run by female specialists, inclusion of equal opportunity issues in company agreements, and job instructions.

7. The seventh and last area investigated concerns a declaration of equal opportunity as a corporate and sociopolitical objective, public relations work, raising awareness by means of statements

and marketing and advertising strategies (published guidelines, circulars, brochures, etc.), involvement of decision-makers, and steps taken to build awareness among female employees.

This questionnaire has to be filled out by the human resources managers of the candidate organizations and examines the seven areas described above. It is then evaluated according to the EFQM assessment system. The companies scoring over 500 points (out of a total of 1,000 points) are selected for the E-quality audit.

The second phase of the E-Quality Award process, the E-quality audit, checks to see if the organizations are really putting into practice the equality principles reported in the questionnaire. A first interview with the human resources manager aims at getting a clear picture of the company's strategy for equal opportunity. In order to complete this audit, a meeting is also organized with the person in charge of quality and the person in charge of training. After these initial interviews, several meetings are organized with male and female employees at different levels and functions in various departments. The aim of these meetings is to find out to what extent the employees are aware of the equal opportunity policy in the company and can vouch for its actual implementation. These may be group meetings or individual meetings, but they always take place without the management being present. Individual meetings are more detailed, but the choice of method depends on the availability of the employees within the organization. Each visit results in a file that the auditors complete for the members of the jury.

The third and final phase of the evaluation process is the selection by an equal opportunities jury, consisting of decision-makers of the economic, financial, industrial, union, and managerial world, and of equal opportunity specialists and press representatives. The jury gives each company a score, on the basis of which the award is granted.

All the organizations that participate in the E-Quality Award receive a feedback report, released by the auditors, with their conclusions organized according to the E-quality checklist, the firm's statistics, and above all the E-quality audit. This report represents for each of the criteria the strong and weak points of the company regarding equal opportunity. With this detailed report in hand, the companies can identify priorities and opportunities, and establish an action plan for the future. During a feedback conversation with the human resources manager, the report is discussed and analyzed in order to identify possible areas of improvement.

The evolution toward equal opportunity remains a dynamic learning process, and even the progress of the highest achievers in this area, is but a step toward an ideal. The benefits of the award for the companies are both internal and external.

Internally, the E-Quality Award gives visibility to the company's commitment to equal opportunities in their human resources policy, reflects the way the company reacts to changes in values and the new perception of men and women, and contributes to improving the internal image of the company. These are prerequisites if a company wants to stimulate work commitment, encourage identification with corporate objectives, and achieve a higher degree of integration of male and female employees. The E-Quality Award is the expression of a personnel management system that takes into consideration the needs and requirements of women, and fosters motivation, commitment, training opportunities, and achievement potential for female employees.

Externally, the E-Quality Award contributes to enhancing the corporate image, as being a company that takes into account women as employees and as consumers. Hence the company gains reputation and social esteem. This has a positive influence on recruitment and retention of qualified staff, which will improve the company's sales prospects to potential female customers and open new markets.

As we shall see, the E-quality award is not yet very well known by European organizations. In order to meet success, it has to be implemented by the national governments in Europe. If the award is well known in Germany, its implementation in Belgium started later, and the first awards were published in 1997. In what follows, we will examine the Belgian case more closely.

The Case of Belgium

In order to understand the case of E-quality in Belgium, we need to create the context in which it originated. We will first brush the political and feminist background in which the E-quality approach was launched, and we will then examine the cases of several organizations that applied, with or without success, for the award.

Political Context

On January 1, 2000, the total population of Belgium was 10,239,085, of which about 10% were foreign residents without Belgian citizenship. Of these foreigners 57% are other E.U.-citizens (with Italians and French being the largest groups), and another 25% come from Morocco or Turkey. In Brussels, nearly 1 resident out of 3 is non-Belgian, against 1 out of 10 in Wallonia, and 1 out of 20 in Flanders. (Sources: National Institute for Statistics, Center for Equal Opportunities and Opposition to Racism, European Database.)

In 1830, Belgium became an independent state and created a constitution of its own in 1831. From 1970 on, this Constitution has been reformed in several steps. Consequently, the political, legislative, and administrative structures of the originally unitary and centralized Belgian State developed into a federal system. In this federal system, there are three policy levels, each with their own legislative and executive bodies: the federal state, the Communities, and the Regions. There is no hierarchy between these three policy levels; each have their own responsibilities. The federal state has a federal parliament (Chamber of Representatives and Senate) and a federal government.

Three Communities exist in Belgium: the Flemish Community, the French Community, and the German-speaking Community. They are responsible for the cultural and personal affairs within a certain linguistic area. The four linguistic areas are the Dutch-speaking area, the French-speaking area, the German-speaking area, and the bilingual area (the capital of Brussels). The Flemish Community is fully responsible for the Dutch-speaking area and partly for the metropolitan area of Brussels.

There are three Regions: the Flemish Region, the Walloon Region, and the Capital Region of Brussels. They are responsible for matters partly or fully linked up with a well-determined territory. Each Community and Region has its own parliament and government. Normally, Belgium would have seven governments and seven parliaments with its three Communities, three Regions, and the federal state. However, there are only six of each as the Flemings opted to merge the parliament and government of the Flemish Region and the Flemish Community.

Belgium has a system of proportional representation with multi-member constituencies that vary in size depending on the level at which elections take place. For the federal Upper House and the European Parliament the country is divided into two constituencies, one for each of the major linguistic communities. For all the other elections the constituencies are more numerous and based on geographical entities. It is the position on the list that mainly influences whether a candidate gets elected. Belgium has a multiparty system, the main actors being the Flemish and Francophone Christian-Democrats (CVP, PSC), Socialists (SP, PS), Liberals (VLD, PRL), Greens (Agalev, Ecolo), and Regionalists (VU, FDF). On the Flemish side there is also the Vlaams Blok on the extreme right.

From Women's Suffrage to Equal Opportunity

At the establishment of the Belgian State in 1830, the question of women's suffrage was not an issue, and the women's organizations that became active before the end of the nineteenth century considered women's suffrage of secondary importance to fighting economic and social inequality. At the end of the nineteenth century, women's suffrage was included in the fight for universal voting. The outbreak of World War I stopped the discussion, but in 1919 universal suffrage was introduced, with women enjoying passive suffrage (the possibility to be elected) at all levels and active suffrage (the possibility to vote) locally. Although women were not entitled to vote at the national and provincial level, they could, and did get elected and co-opted (chosen by the elected representatives). After World War II the issue came back on the agenda, and in 1948 women obtained the same active and passive suffrage as men.

The law Smet-Tobback of May 24, 1994, stipulates that electoral lists may contain a maximum of two-thirds of candidates of the same sex. If a party does not manage to fill up at least one-third of the places with candidates of the underrepresented sex, these slots must be left open. The law actually became effective at the beginning of 1996. It is very controversial, given the fact that it guarantees no result at all. The question of reviewing mechanisms to increase the participation of women in political decision-making was put on the agenda in 1999 but so far without a concrete result.

In 1974 Belgium set up its first Commission on women and work, but it has considered equal opportunities a separate policy area and competence only since 1985. The women's movement and political women's organizations had demanded the creation of a Minister for Equal Opportunity for quite a while. Miet Smet became Secretary of State for Environmental Affairs in 1985 and negotiated for the added responsibility for equal opportunity. The State Secretary for Social Emancipation was created. In 1991 Smet became Minister of Labor and Employment and took the responsibility for equal opportunity with her. From that point on the position has been formally called Equal Opportunity. The responsibility for equal opportunity has since then been linked to the Minister of Labor and Employment.

The Royal Decree of 1985 that set up the State Secretary for Social Emancipation defined two objectives and tasks. The first involved the promotion of activities focusing on equal opportunity for men and women. The second gave the Secretary of State the responsibility to point out the impact and consequences of the other government members', within Belgium, policies on equal opportunity and to question them about their actions and conduct in this area. As a result, the Belgian national and later federal women's policy machinery contained a mainstreaming element from the very start.

Smet mainly focused on three policy areas during her 14 years as State Secretary and later Minister:

1. The improvement of women's participation in and position on the labor market: improving both young and adult women's education to increase their chances in the labor market; positive actions in both private and public sectors, regarding work and family, equal pay for equal work, night work, the protection of motherhood, independent, and collaborating spouses.

2. Fighting violence against women. This involved overcoming the taboo on speaking about sexual violence, improving the legal position of and developing emergency measures for victims, addressing sexual harassment at work as well as trafficking in women.

3. Improving women's participation in political decision-making. This government objective requires further definition. The most important measures taken so far are the development of a form of positive action, based on the belief that democratic structures can only be democratic if they integrate and include women, partly because women have their own interests and needs.

The E-Quality Award

In 1997, the Belgian Equal Opportunities group within the ministry of Employment and Labor collaborated actively in the European project New Opportunities for Women, which was called "Putting the E into Quality." The project aimed at integrating equal opportunity into an economic model.

In order to strengthen the move toward equal opportunity, Minister Miet Smet initiated the organization of the E-Quality Award in Belgium. The Cell, or department, for Positive Actions was charged with promoting and organizing the activity, as well as selecting the candidates and evaluating the E-quality checklist and audit. The experts of that Cell followed a senior assessor course on the EFQM model, organized by the European Foundation for Quality management. The first companies to be granted the Belgian E-Quality Award in 1997 were IBM Belgium, a French-speaking company, and Dow Corning Belgium, a Dutch-speaking company. Three other categories have since replaced these linguistic ones: large organizations (250 or more employees), small- and medium-size enterprises (under 250 employees), and nonprofit organizations.

Belgian Case Studies

In this section I will report on the case studies of several Belgian companies that sought to obtain the E-Quality Award. These companies include several small- and medium-size enterprises (SMEs), a nonprofit institution, two large private-sector organizations, and a public-sector organization.

Equal opportunities policies may become an advantage for small- and medium-size enterprises, as they offer work close to home, in contrast to employment in large, centralized enterprises. In Belgium, SMEs often come off second best in recruiting and retaining skilled workers, because large organizations generally offer more financial and extra legal advantages.

The first telephone survey in 2000 I conducted, involving eight SMEs, aimed at getting an overall response to questions about whether they had, or had a need for:

1. A database covering the family and professional situation of staff.
2. A gender-neutral methodology for staff recruitment and selection.
3. Further training and personnel development strategies.
4. Plans to ensure compatibility of career and family care.
5. Strategies for promoting cooperation between men and women at the workplace.
6. Internal formal bodies to promote equal opportunities.
7. Actions to promote the enterprise's objective of developing equal opportunities.

The eight SMEs had between 6 and 320 employees each, and two of them, being temporary work agencies, worked with temporary or freelance employees as well. Except for the smallest of them, all SMEs had a human resources manager, but three of them did not have a complete database about their employees (see Exhibit 9.9). The question of gender-neutral recruitment procedures seems to be linked to the sector in which they were active. Here are some examples. A bank employing 160 people answered no to the second question, saying that a gender-neutral recruitment methodology was unnecessary because 50% to 55% of its employees were women already. A bakery answered yes, but said they found it difficult to recruit women because there were few women in bakery schools, and because the work is hard and often done at night. Similarly, a foundry employing 148 people had only 8 women, all in administration.

The three enterprises that did not offer training or personnel development strategies did offer comment. As for the fourth question, on plans to ensure work and family compatibility, only two SMEs said that these did not exist in their enterprise. The others mentioned having policies such as flexible work time, part-time work, career breaks, and use of a temporary workforce. Strategies fostering cooperation between men and women at the workplace did not exist in any of the enterprises surveyed, nor did they have formal internal bodies to promote equal opportunity. Steps to promote equal opportunity existed in the smallest SME, a temporary work agency that employed only women: they promoted equal opportunities by urging customers to employ workers from migrant minorities, such as those from Arab countries.

Exhibit 9.11

Equal Opportunities in SMEs

Data-base		Recruiting		Training		Career/Family		Cooperation		EO Body		EO Actions	
yes	no	yes	no	yes	no	yes	no	yes	no	yes	no	yes	no
5	3	7	1	5	3	6	2	0	8	0	8	1	7

For the case studies, the questions that we asked at the start were the following:

1. Do the Belgian companies know the E-Quality Award?
2. What is their attitude toward the award?
3. Do they practice equal opportunity?
4. If they do, why and how?

Of the 35 companies contacted, 25 responded, usually through the human resources department. Fifteen companies replied that they did not know about the E-quality approach. Among them were some very large companies such as Electrabel, a power company, and Fortis in banking and finance. Three companies, including Dexia Bank and Volkswagen, replied that they were aware of it but did not use it. Only seven companies, among them, coffee maker Douwe-Egberts and Artesia Bank, said that they had effectively applied this strategy. Though a large majority of companies showed interest in equal opportunity, few knew the E-quality method, but those that did know of it were inclined to use it.

A reaction to a question on E-quality in a Belgian bank illustrates this lack of knowledge:

> I don't know the term E-quality, and I think it was not well chosen, because everything with e-something makes one think spontaneously of electronic something! Equality is not an issue at our bank. The number of women grows more than the number of men, at all hierarchical levels, and the same scale of salaries applies. Things happen naturally, so E-quality is not a particular preoccupation.

At Volkswagen Belgium, the answer was:

> Sorry, but we do not apply the E-quality method. By the way, I have just read that we have 300 women amongst our 5,700 workers, which is not many. And at the management level (around 50 people), I count 2 women.

At the other extreme, Caterpillar Belgium has been one of the first industrial enterprises to recruit women for the production floor, in occupations that were traditionally male, such as welders and machine operators. There are also many women in top positions. Four out of seven supervisors are women.

We selected five organizations for our case studies: an SME (Baobab Catering), a noncommercial institution (University Clinics Saint-Luc), two large private sector organizations (Mobistar and Promedia), and a public sector organization (RTBF, Belgian Francophone Radio).

1. Baobab Catering

Baobab Catering is a Flemish enterprise that specializes in multicultural cuisine and employs political refugees. Equal opportunity is a key part of the company's culture and philosophy. This approach devolves from the strong personal commitment of the company's founder, Peter De Roo, who worked in refugee camps in Cambodia before starting his own business in 1998. For De Roo, human capital is primary, and he believes it is essential to take advantage of individual talents and to work democratically. Baobab does not want to be seen as a social service company, so it bases its marketing on quality products and on the unique service it provides.

The company claims that its most important selection criteria for job candidates are their real capacities, be they male or female. For promotion, seniority is taken into consideration, rather than gender. Once a week, all employees meet to discuss planning, but the meeting is also used check the level of job satisfaction and to settle possible conflicts. Remuneration does not discriminate between men and women and is high for this sector of activity. The company offers its employees opportunities for training in the *horeca* (hotel, restaurant, and café business), as well as Dutch language classes. The company is open to flextime for men as well as for women. Overtime can be accumulated and used when needed. As the company is small, there is direct communication between workers and management and a familial atmosphere.

Baobab Catering received the E-Quality Award in May 2000.

2. University Clinics Saint-Luc

Saint-Luc is a hospital center of the Catholic University of Louvain, which is Francophone, that offers hospital care, research, and teaching.

The question of equal opportunities in the noncommercial or nonprofit sector in general is complex, as it is essentially a female sector: 75% of Saint-Luc's personnel are female. The human resources manager, Christine Franckx, became interested in women's working conditions in 1994 after participating in quality groups organized by the Ministry of Labor and Employment as well as in seminars organized by the Equal Opportunities Committee.

Saint-Luc is demanding as an organization: it is a hospital that works 365 days per year, 24 hours a day, and has to insure continuity in care, whatever the family of professional circumstances of the personnel. The management is aware of the fact that it is not always easy to work in this environment: if it wants to keep its employees, it has to listen to them. The clinic endeavors to give women the opportunity to work in comfortable and pleasant conditions.

As far as wages are concerned, inequalities are impossible, as the system works as in the public sector (civil servants, education, etc.) where personnel are paid according to task and grade, whatever their gender. For internal recruitment, a description of the post is made public, and anyone can apply, independently of gender. It appears, however, that more men tend to apply for jobs with greater responsibility, resulting in overrepresentation of men on the management level. This can be explained by the fact that, given the demands of the profession, women tend to make choices in favor of family life. There are childcare facilities, open from 6:30 A.M. until 9:00 P.M., for 72 children. Working time can be full time (100%, which means 38 hours a week), or 20%, 40%, 60%, or 99% and career breaks are accepted. Working "99%" of the time means one is allowed to organize one's time in such a way that half a day per week is free, without financial loss. Sports facilities have been made available for hospital personnel, taking into account their flexible working hours. Saint-Luc pays particular attention to protecting motherhood. When a pregnant woman is exposed to risks in her professional activities, the clinic suggests a change to a different activity or a different service, or a leave. This means that a woman keeps her income, thanks to the intervention of the mutual insurance company and the fund for professional incapacity.

In 1998, the Clinics Saint-Luc were rewarded for their efforts in equal opportunity, and received the E-Quality Award for the nonprofit sector. The auditors concluded that the organization did a lot for equal opportunity, but indicated a lack of communication and visibility of its actions.

3. Mobistar

Mobistar is a Belgian telephone service provider. In 1999, the company counted 14 different nationalities with 38% of its employees being women. The human resource management's strategy at Mobistar is based on equal opportunity and includes both qualitative and quantitative objectives. The E-quality concept is an integral part of the management system of Mobistar, a system that allows the company to implement action for continuous improvement of women's conditions and to attain operational excellence. It is not so much a specific action plan as a permanent process. The company considers equal opportunity to be a key factor of success and a definite competitive advantage. The concept is strongly supported at all hierarchical levels.

Human resource management at Mobistar is based on six fundamental values:

1. Leadership through customer focus.
2. Open communication.
3. Integrity and equal opportunity.
4. Empowered individuals.
5. Employability and continuous improvement.
6. Participation.

The company's mission and values clearly refer to equal opportunity. The company does not want to work with fixed quotas, but prefers to develop a policy that accentuates individuals' competencies and skills. The basic principle is "equality for all." Managers are personally committed, both by word and actions, to lift the barriers to equal opportunity and to solve problems related to it.

Mobistar honors the principle of "equal pay for equal work," accepts flexible working hours for men and for women, has a teleworking project, gives women a greater role in decision-making, and supports parental leave for mothers and fathers. Mobistar is also the telephone service provider with the most female consumers. Its marketing strategy is particularly attentive to women, considering their needs and expectations as customers. It is developing new products specifically addressing women.

In May 2000, Mobistar received the E-Quality Award in the category of large enterprises.

4. Promedia

Promedia is a company that compiles and distributes telephone directories. Of its 702 employees, 450 are women and 252 are men. However, of 79 managers only 28 are women managers but 51 are men.

The equal opportunity policy of Promedia is part of a general policy based on an American concept of "diversity" that consists of not discriminating against anyone on any grounds and valuing the variety of human potential. The company has always paid strong attention to equal opportunity. From the start, it has recruited many women, giving them access to all functions, including those that are viewed as traditionally male, such as management and decision-making positions. Promedia wants above all to optimize the potential of its employees. In order to achieve this, the company has made great visible efforts. By integrating equal opportunities into its external image, it has managed to be and remain an attractive employer.

Recruitment procedures are systematically neutral. All employees are informed of openings and anyone can apply for the function that interests him or her. The company favors internal candidates. Women are increasingly present in management and decision-making posts in the different departments. All employees are free to express their professional ambitions, and initiative is encouraged. Two wage systems coexist: ordinary employees' wages are linked to their function and job category, and increase with seniority and achievement. In the sales department, part of the wage is fixed, and part is based on achievement. The company offers all its members many extra benefits, such as meal tickets and underwriting health expenses for employees' children. Information about flexible working plans is widely publicized, and all employees can use them on request. Promedia considers equal opportunity to be a competitive advantage; hence, the attention it pays to equal opportunity and the effort made to turn those efforts to commercial advantage.

Promedia was one of the candidates for the E-Quality Award in 2000; it was nominated but not elected. The points that needed to be remedied were:

1. The objectives of the equal opportunities policy were not integrated into the objectives of the organization.
2. In spite of the efforts to promote more women to decision-making positions, their numbers were, in fact, much smaller than those of men.
3. Promedia does not draft an annual report on equal opportunity.
4. Procedures for prevention of and combating sexual harassment and are not well known by the employees. More information and wider dissemination is desirable.

5. RTBF (Radio et Télévision Belge Francophone)

RTBF is an autonomous public company, culturally aligned with the French Community in Belgium. Its social objective is to run the radio and television services by producing and broadcasting radio and television programs. The organization employs twice as many men as women (1,527 to 629), and one man out of 7 is a manager, compared with one woman out of 16.

The equal opportunity policy of RTBF is part of its corporate culture and philosophy, and is integrated into everyday behavior in the organization. As RTBF is a public service, it feels it must both lead and provide an example; it hold that it has a moral obligation to stand out as an "Equal Opportunity" employer. The organization includes this in its general objectives and tries to make this policy a way of life for all its members. The enterprise sees to it that individual choices are respected, and it encourages its employees to make finding fulfillment in their private lives a priority.

For several years now, RTBF has publicized its commitment to equal opportunity. It became a member of the European Committee for Equal Opportunities in Radiotelevision in 1986. Following a seminar on the image and the employment of women in television, organized by the University of Brussels, and after pressure by some female members of its management team, the Women's Commission of the RTBF was created. This commission was the basis for the development of an equal opportunities policy and positive actions for female workers at RTBF.

In May 1998, the organization participated in the New Opportunities for Women program of the European Social Fund. In November of the same year, the CEO of RTBF, Christian Druitte, created an Equal Opportunities Service under his direct supervision, with a mediator for questions of equal opportunities between men and women in the organization. One year later, the mediator handed in a Pluri-annual General Plan for Equal Opportunities, with a twofold objective. First, the plan aims to align the RTBF with the evolution of society. Secondly, by encouraging everyone's talents to emerge, it becomes more efficient as an enterprise exposed to competition, and integrates them into the evolution of its management.

The RTBF plan has three main axes. The first axis is career: the plan provides a series of measures with training as a priority. The second axis is the working conditions: the plan provides training for employees and raises the awareness of management to the issue of equal opportunity, establishing it as a priority of the human resources department. The third axis is a change of mentality: the plan is a long-term project, and its success depends on eliminating obsolete ways of thinking that do not take into account the inevitable growth in the female workforce and its increasing level of qualification.

Recruitment processes at RTB are gender-neutral. Job advertising is never by gender, even if the job is traditionally perceived as male or female. By organizational statute, the recruitment procedure is similar to state recruitment exams. If the selection includes an examination with a jury, attention is paid to the composition of the jury so that it contains a sufficient number of women. The RTBF assigns responsibility to women for programs with large audiences and hence those that have strong public impact. The organization offers many benefits such as childcare and holiday programs for children. It intends to extend these facilities geographically to regional centers, and to expand them by adding children's activities on Wednesday afternoons (when there is no school) and on bank holidays.

The RTBF was a candidate for the E-Quality Award in 2000. According to its mediator for equal opportunity, Yves Vandergheynst, the main purpose for competing for the award was to evaluate existing programs and to demonstrate RTBF's political will to be a leader, by making it clear that the organization has integrated equal opportunity into its management practice and operations. To its own surprise, the organization was nominated. It did not, of course, win the award, as it was only starting to set the mediator's plan in motion.

Conclusion

If the balanced participation of women and men in social and professional life is a universal and undeniable value, equality is far from being achieved. In order to reduce persistent discrimination, such as wage inequities and the shortage of women in decision-making positions, the European Commission has launched several programs and elaborated several systems or methods, varying from positive steps to be taken to the comprehensive E-quality initiative.

E-quality is based on Total Quality Management, aims at making better use of existing staff resources, and promotes the principle that quality cannot be achieved without equality between men and women. E-quality is thus embedded in an economic model, the EFQM quality model.

In integrating equality in its overall management, the organization offers its female members several benefits, such as the opportunity to develop their competencies and skills and to rise to high positions in management. However, presenting oneself as an equal opportunities employer is above all a benefit for the organization. Personnel management systems aimed at promoting equality of opportunity contribute to enterprises having at their disposal skilled staff that may be employed in a flexible way, which means that enterprises can raise their internal productivity. Greater attractiveness and higher social esteem have a positive effect on recruiting and retaining skilled employees, and open up new markets.

However, although the EFQM model is generally well known in many organizations, the E-quality concept is still rather little known and used. For this reason, the E-Quality Award was created, to be conferred on enterprises with a personnel policy aimed at promoting equality of opportunity. The granting of the award is based on quality systems such as Total Quality Management, where the focus is on both male and female employees, and whose objective is to use equal opportunity to foster the potential of both male and female employees.

In Belgium, as in other European countries, the government adopted the E-quality project, and awards have been granted every year since 1997. The selection procedure and the questionnaire are useful tools for companies, large or small, commercial or nonprofit, to examine their own policies, to discover what the criteria are, and to plan future actions.

The award needs, however, to be more publicized with the public as well as with companies, as it appears that too many organizations and too many employees, current and potential, are not familiar with the concept and its implications.

Who Is the European? Prognosis and Recommendations

10

George F. Simons

Who is the European? was at best a peripheral question at the time of the agreement that created the European Economic Community (EEC). The focus was peace and economic survival and success in the wake of World War II's devastation of the continent. This cooperation succeeded and prompted more common initiatives. After the Treaty of Maastricht (1992), there began an ongoing negotiation about, "Who shall be included in Europe?" as expansion of the E.U. to the east and to the south became an agenda item.

In May 2000, French president Jacques Chirac and Prime Minister Lionel Jospin, along with German chancellor Gerhard Schröder and Minister of Foreign Affairs Joschka Fischer, met at a closed-door seminar at Rambouillet near Paris. Fischer proposed a federal government for Europe, with a bicameral parliament and a federal president directly elected by the citizens. Reaction was swift. The outcry surfaced fears of loss of power and identity particularly, but not exclusively on the part of the smaller states of the E.U., highlighting the long road—or perhaps endless process—involved in developing Europe politically, as well as determining what is Europe and who is the European. Should Europe be a nation, a federation or a commonly executed set of policies and economic functions?

This is not an academic debate. Under discussion is whether "the position of a widespread feeling of identity of the union is a desirable asset, believed to improve the odds of survival of a multinational and multicultural union" (Delgado-Moreira, 1997, online document). Despite growing legislation, policy-making, and the creation of

European institutions, individual E.U. Member States and their peoples still strongly tie their interests to their cultural identity. They continue to exercise a wide range of freedom in how they interpret for themselves what the European Union says and does.

So, instead of asking who the European is, it might be more instructive to phrase the question as, Who Is Proud to Be European? What are people's feelings about this? Shortly we ill take a brief look at what the soundings tell us about the mixed attitudes of younger Europeans toward the E.U., generally speaking, a certain cautious optimism. Looking at the larger picture though, what do we see? Although the French support the European Union and bring to it their sense of social solidarity, they think of themselves first as French, then possibly as Europeans. Many Germans, on the other hand, are happy to be seen as just Europeans, for this frees them from the burden of the recent past. It is, however, the Belgians who are unreservedly proud of their place in the European Union. Loss of sovereignty and adoption of the euro means success to them. Belgium, with its two cultures and extensive and decentralized government, as discussed in Chapter 9, is a European Union in microcosm already. And it helps, of course, to think of Brussels as the capital of the European Union, as it hosts so many of the E.U. governmental institutions and is home to vast numbers of non-Belgians. Like other small E.U. countries, Belgium sees the European Commission as a bulwark and defender against the bigger countries ("Guy Verhofstadt, Belgium's Suitable Prime Minister," 2000).

Perhaps even more interesting is a look at how Europeans are "voting with their feet" when it comes to lifestyle and livelihood in Europe. With the automatic right of E.U. citizens to live and work where they please, European cosmopolitanism seems to follow opportunity. As of 1999 Britain has enjoyed economic growth at twice the average of Europe and half the unemployment. As a result, more non-British E.U. nationals live and work in London than in any other European city, including Brussels. Foreign companies based in Britain are responsible for 40% of British exports. Although it has been slow to accept the euro, London reflects a pan-European culture more than any continental capital (Sullivan, 1999).

Despite, or perhaps because of their cultural centralism and strong sense of identity at home, the French seem to travel well abroad and succeed as expatriates. They have become the sixth largest immigrant group in Britain, for example. French immigration to the United Kingdom has been rising at a steady 10% a year:

> Individual French workers as well as well over 150 French organizations have taken advantage of the easy transportation and

lower taxes and social charges in the United Kingdom to resettle there, mostly in the London area. The concentration of French in South Kensington has become such that Brits have started to call it "Froggy Valley." ("Les Français sont arrivés," 1999)

Within Europe one finds places where a critical mass of people not only work but also live in a global culture. The high-tech area surrounding Sophia Antipolis on the Côte d'Azur of France is one of those places:

> A quarter of the 22,000 employees of this technopolis are expats and represent close to 66 different nationalities, making them into a parallel economy with its own doctors, insurers, lawyers, organizations and clubs. (Untitled sidebar, 1999, p. 34)

Longer-term residents of this area can testify to the changes wrought by the combination of leisure tourists and technology workers. Friendly and easy-going Mediterranean attitudes toward taking one's time and enjoying social contact have combined with up-to-date technology and the expectations of a diverse population to produce impeccable customer service that reaches broadly across retail and service sectors, affecting the performance of government offices as well—a very good example of the value-added to be found in diversity.

This mobility in the European Union, in addition to outright immigrants and their children, is now bringing into the European workforce countless multicultural young people—men and women whose parents each came from another country and culture—who have had the experience of living in several countries in the course of their formative years. They often enjoy a repertoire of identities and cultural behaviors to choose from, while sensing again and again that, perhaps, they "don't belong" in any one place. They embody Europe's uncertain identity and its desire to build something new.

What does Europe look like through the eyes of the future? To answer this question, Eurobarometer (Europe's public equivalent to Gallup) carried out an opinion poll between April 20 and June 7, 1997, on the attitudes of young people between the ages of 15 and 29 at the request of Directorate-General XXII (Education, Training, and Youth) of the European Commission. These Eurobarometer findings highlight both diversity concerns and how business must relate to the culture of the younger generation in days to come:

- When asked to choose a set of features that best characterize Europe, young people listed the following topics: "go wherever I like" (34.8%), "a better economic situation" (34%), "provide more employment opportunities" (29.9%), "higher unemployment" (14.6%), "lots of bureaucracy" (14.4%), and "loss of cultural identity" (12%).

- 43.4% use a computer or PC regularly.

- 57% of young Europeans had visited another European Union country in the two years preceding the survey.

- When asked about their perception of "European citizenship," the three proposals gaining most support were: "Being able to work anywhere in the Union" (62.4%); "Being able to establish oneself permanently anywhere in the Union" (51.5%); "Being able to study in any country in the Union" (45.7%).

- The answers to the question, What skills are most useful for finding employment? were as follows: "Good general training" (42.8%); "Language ability" (40.4%); and "Familiarity with information technologies" (32.3%).

- Only 6.6% of young people were using the Internet. Values change in different countries: in Sweden there were 31.8%, in Finland 28.3%, and in Denmark 15.4%.

- Between 2000 and 2015, there will be more people between the ages of 55 and 64 than between 15 and 24.

- 71.3% of young Europeans stated that they could converse in a second language. In Sweden there are 97.4%, in Finland 96%, in Austria 68.1%. The most often spoken languages are English (53.7%), French (19.9%), German (11%), and Spanish (8.7%).

- 62.3% of young people regularly watch television in their free time.

- Young people feel most ill at ease with drug addicts (28.1%), alcoholics (20.1%), homosexuals (13.3%), the homeless (12.8%), and even people of another nationality living in their country (3.2%).

- 27.5% of young Europeans think that there are "too many foreigners" in their country; 14.7% are "pleased to have foreigners living in their country"; 10.4% say that "the presence of foreigners adds to their country's strength."

- 41% of young Belgians think there are too many foreigners in their country. (European Commission, Directorate-General XXII, 1997. Eurobarometer is a very useful source of information about public opinion in the European Union.)

Who is the new European? Young Irish, who two decades ago saw emigration as their only hope for success, now view and advertise themselves as the "new Europeans." Ireland's economy got a fresh start with the rise of information technology, and Ireland's best and brightest started seeing the world with open eyes. In addition, the diaspora started coming home and bringing with it the language skills and intercultural experience they had gained. They have learned well. The lilt of an Irish accent is often hard to detect behind the French, German, Dutch, and Spanish spoken by the friendly customer service representatives at airline and high-tech call centers in Ireland.

E.U. Abstainers: Switzerland and Norway— The Rich and the Nouveau Riche

There are two European nations with deep ambivalence about being Europeans in the sense of belonging to the E.U.—Switzerland and Norway.

Switzerland has long played the role of Europe's go-between and "neutral banker." The Swiss have prided themselves on their unique role as a kind of "clearing house" for the diplomacy and finances of nations, and as a safe host for international humanitarian services, the best known of these being the Red Cross, all of which have played an often essential role in the last century. Despite this humanitarian concern, Switzerland is very conservative. Full and universal suffrage for women, for example, occurred only in 1971.

An excellent though not perfect example of successful pluralism, Switzerland has been struggling to reconcile its traditional diversity and independence (verging on isolationism) with a new Europe, in the form of the European Union, and with the rights, needs, and desires of the new diversity found in the many foreign and international workers who make their home within its borders. But what of Switzerland in the new millennium? Recently a shadow side of the country's past has come to haunt the Swiss. Their self-respect and world image have been tarnished by evidence of collaborating with and benefiting from Nazi atrocities, their financial freedom challenged as a result of money laundering and other unseemly transactions. These have resulted in reparations and reluctant but greater openness and collaboration in financial affairs, but the challenge to Swiss identity remains.

Perhaps even more unsettling for business and public confidence was the bankruptcy of the country's flagship carrier whose crash dragged Sabena and several other airlines to disaster along with it.

Such events say to other Europeans and to the Swiss themselves that Switzerland is a place very much like any other, even financially, even if the Swiss themselves do not think so.

Switzerland's separate diplomatic role is becoming redundant or even an anachronism in the face of powerful institutions such as the European Union, the United Nations, and NATO, in which it also does not hold membership. Indications are that slowly, and with extreme caution, the Swiss are trying both to retain their traditional strengths and their sense of freedom and, at the same time, to find better ways to be a part of Europe. In a referendum on May 21, 2000, 67% of Swiss voters agreed to measures that would begin opening Switzerland to the European Union. A wide range of steps were envisioned, including opening freight routes through the country to E.U. carriers and putting an end to restrictive job quotas that limit the free flow of labor from surrounding countries. It also provides for a gradual opening of the borders in both directions for Swiss and E.U. travelers.

Will this movement toward openness accelerate? Younger Swiss seem unhappy with the feelings of aloofness and apartness that their nationality confers on them in the eyes of other Europeans. Only time will tell if this is a harbinger of further culture change, or whether conservatism will set in at a later stage in their lives ("Less-Suspicious Switzerland," 2000).

Unlike Switzerland, the history and social fabric of Norway is much more entwined with its Scandinavian neighbors, despite its seeming remoteness. The recent boom in North Sea oil has made Norway, once an economically struggling country, into one of wealth, high prices, and incoming foreign workers. European, yes, but Norwegians ask at what price, culturally speaking. Home-grown Norwegian values and institutions are being challenged to accept diverse newcomers and to find accommodations for them and their values as they participate in the military and enjoy freedom of worship, despite a governmentally supported Lutheran Church.

Norway in its post oil boom affluence is still finding itself. KIM, the Contact Committee for Immigrants and the Authorities (Kontaktutvalget mellom innvandrere og myndighetene) is a government-appointed advisory board made up of representatives from immigrant organizations, political parties, and relevant governmental agencies and ministries. It is a forum for contact and dialogue and has the responsibility to review immigration and questions and policies affecting minorities. KIM addresses a broad range of issues that affect the condition of asylum seekers, immigrants, and refugees. In recent years it has been looking at the relation between the native Norwegians and the growing minority groups in Norway. Norway shares with Finland, Sweden, and Russia, the Saami, northern Scandinavia's indigenous people, who are organized in semiautonomous social and political entities.

Popular sentiment continued to reject E.U. membership as too much, too fast, but the introduction of the euro and the planned eastward expansion of the Union have Norwegians rethinking their isolation. Polls starting in March 2001 show for the first time a slim majority of Norwegians in favor of E.U. membership.

Cultural Boundaries: Do Good Fences Make Good Neighbors?

This variety of views about being European makes it much more possible, but does not make it easy for the organization or the individual businessperson crossing cultural boundaries. The cultural "unity in diversity," which ended with the birth of nation states and is now espoused as the motto and vision for the European Union, will be worked out in the cultural considerations lurking beneath interpersonal exchanges, business transactions, and E.U. policy decisions. So, it becomes essential to talk about boundaries, how they have been created, how they are maintained, and how one crosses over them. Meanwhile, current, and no doubt future crises, will continue to press Member States toward common, cross-boundary endeavors and regulatory action, while the desire to penetrate and control markets will pose the cultural challenges of globalization and localization to organizations.

Whether we talk about the European Union and its future, or discuss a European enterprise, organization, or team, the task at hand is empowering diverse members of a group to decide who they are in common and agree on the cultural context in which they will live and work together. Corporate citizens and global organizations are, in Europe, and elsewhere involved in the same struggle to create an identity crisis for themselves and their brands in an increasingly global environment.

Every group has a culture or soon develops one, a framework for "how we will do things around here." When a group comes together and experiences its environment and comes to grips with what it must do in order to survive and succeed in it, a culture emerges, usually patched together from cultural bits that people bring with them or innovate on the spot (see Simons, Vazquez, and Harris, 1993). Creating a culture produces a connection between people but also a boundary separating them from others. Despite the many external manifestations that both express and reinforce culture, culture lives essentially inside of us. Our external boundaries are set by our internal ones. We hear culture speaking to us again and again as we interpret our everyday reality and attempt to make decisions that work for us on a moment-to-moment basis.

People inevitably come together unconsciously carrying with them their culture and its boundaries. When diverse groups of people meet, they inner question is always, "Can we talk to each other and do business, or not?" This is true whether we meet with potential clients, vendors, or partners, or whether as citizens of one culture we explore how to live in security and peace side by side with one another. Diversity means that our discourse and behavior are rarely based on identical beliefs, values, and attitudes. It means that we are obliged to bring our inner processes to the surface, and talk to each other about them, to identify or establish some level of compatibility and mutual interest out of which to create a larger agenda. We agree on protocols and enter into social contracts with one another. We bridge boundaries.

We have to be constantly aware that breakdowns in communication are opportunities to go deeper into the process of sharing values, attitudes and beliefs, and we need to provide safe places for these discussions. Historically, human groups developed culture and "civilization" in specific niches and, when necessary, defended these niches (and the discourse that went along with them) from other groups. Boundaries and borders—natural and constructed, mental and physical—are used to protect or at least insulate uncommon cultures from each other. And, as best as we can ascertain, throughout human history defending and breaching these frontiers by invasions, migrations, and trade wars has brought about one bloody mess after another. This process sadly continues unabated today with untold violence in much of the world. It has taken a fresh turn as terrorism becomes the new face of warfare, illustrating the fact that the internal boundaries are indeed more important than physical and geographical ones. In this light, fighting terrorism by attacking territories, nations or communities, is essentially off the mark, at most a stop-gap and partial strategy that needs replacing by a new paradigm of human interanimation.

It is in response to the human dynamics of cultures and boundaries, contemporary diversity management attempts to introduce the principle and practice of *inclusivity*, identifying and bringing all stakeholders into a common context. There is a strong conviction that what we value and learn about working with each other and *mainstreaming* all participants in multicultural workplaces and marketplaces can be important in diminishing conflict on a larger scale.

Progress, however, is not inevitable. Despite unprecedented peace and prosperity in the E.U. at the start of a new millennium, it continues to discover its own complicity in social inequity, poverty, environmental depredation and violence both within its own societies and beyond its borders, as do other "developed" nations. The dream that many of us shared of a peaceful and prosperous new millennium was shattered in the September 11, 2001 terrorist attack on the U.S.A. If anything, the reversal of environmental policies of the Bush administration in the United States has made Europeans feel more positive about their commitments to ecology. Unfortunately it has become fashionable for Europeans to smugly blame the United States' lower standards of environmental and social protection for the sorry state of the world, without realizing that Europe is still cut out of much the same cloth.

Their very success makes societies and organizations inward-looking and grudging in their response to outsiders, as well as to their own problems of sustainability. Reflecting on Jean-Jacques Rousseau's notion of the social contract, Edmund Burke observed that a social contract was necessary for living together, but added that it must be a contract between the living, the dead, and those who have not yet been born. Responsibility to the rest of the world and to the future have never been greater, and the decisions that need to be made about diversity across time as well as about diversity in contemporary culture have never been more critical (Coleman, 2000).

Why We Must Learn to Construct Culture

The concept of the social contract was developed in the "Age of Reason" when it was thought that clarity, "reasonable behavior," and common sense would suffice to create society and promote harmony among states. We now know, however, that what is seen as "reasonable" is strongly determined by culture of the people doing the reasoning. We need to go beyond reason in an age of increasingly porous national boundaries and in a borderless virtual world.

To live and work together, people must become shapers and owners of common, reliable, and inclusive cultural contexts. When we must do things in common to achieve a result, whether it be managing traffic or writing software, we need to be in agreement about how to do it. This does not mean forced assimilation, but it does mean negotiating and agreeing about operative principles, definitions, and processes, and, above all, nurturing at least a minimum of trust and reliability to make it begin to work. We also need requisite diversity, enough differing perspectives to see the whole or at least a bigger picture both of our diverse selves and of what lies beyond our cultural constructs, if we are to identify both our problems and our resources on a global scale.

Finally, we need a process that helps us create viable cultural contexts in which social contracts and business agreements can be starting points, but are only a small part of the whole process. Successful cultural constructions allow us to act without having to examine every assumption each and every time that we want to do something. Yet we create such a context in a multicultural environment or activity only by examining everyone's assumptions and needs well enough, and revisiting them often enough, not to have to examine them each and every time we want to act. Managing diversity means becoming experts at creating and maintaining these habitable and sustainable social contexts both within and between our existing cultures and embracing what we create. It means, as a Chinese colleague put it, "much tea," lots of sitting and talking to each other. In times of accelerated change, it also means creating and sustaining one or more "hypercontexts"—secure ambiances that allow us to going in and out of other contexts willingly and safely. Managing the delicate boundary between sameness and difference, between what we have in common and what separates us—walking this tightrope, and making sure we have a safety net is the challenge of managing diversity.

While "much tea" is certainly necessary, action also creates cultural contexts. Common projects can provide hypercontexts and create culture and identity over time as they succeed and serve the Member States of the European Union. Much of what Europe enjoys in economic prosperity has been the result of E.U. initiatives from the Treaty of Rome to the agreements in Nice. Nonetheless, each new project is fragile, fraught with the potential to damage or destroy the Union as well as create greater unity, functionality, and identity. Each incertitude raises cultural ghosts. At this writing, the euro is not strong, but it seems stable and the transition to the new currency can be seen as one more well-managed success at creating a cultural hypercontext among the majority of E.U. nations.

Each project and each breakdown along the way reveal something about Europe's cultures and its people. With the euro transition mostly behind us, discussions and reactions to the prospect of a united and centrally directed European defense force may next show how strongly critical levels of autonomy are understood and valued by the peoples of the Member States.

E.U. Member States today are torn between interdependence and independence, between protecting and setting aside their differences at the same time that they are driven to making the E.U. an even greater hypercontext. Difference of culture delights. Difference of culture without a larger supporting framework, without understanding and trust, threatens. Difference of culture invites creativity. Difference of culture without an embracing context creates resistance. No boundary challenge looms greater on the European horizon than that of the expansion of E.U. membership and it raises the question of who is the European in yet another way.

Can Only Europeans Be Europeans?

The Turkish economy may be the current and obvious practical hurdle to admitting Turkey to the European Union, but there is little doubt that differences of culture and values and a great deal of history lurk behind E.U. fears of inviting Turkey to join. Equally, Turks, too, must ask themselves who they are, especially when their Islamic neighbors cynically view Turkey's secularity and turning westward as, "Choosing to be the rump of Europe instead of the head of Islam" as it once was.

Many Europeans see the free flow of labor across borders from Turkey, North Africa, and Central and Eastern Europe as a serious threat to the stability of the Union. This economic concern masks as well a fear of cultural disintegration. Although this book is not primarily concerned with the growth of the E.U.'s membership, watching the struggles that surround migration and expansion highlights how crossing cultures requires the ongoing attention of its business people.

Vast numbers of Turks and other Muslim peoples now live permanently in Europe. Even in Catholic Italy some Europeans are becoming Muslims, and Islam is Europe's fastest growing religious group. Yet acknowledgment and affirmation of this diversity has been slow in coming, first hampered by unemployment and ensuing criminality in immigrant communities, and now further stalled now by the view of Muslims as potential terrorists.

It is important to remember, that despite Islamic nationalism and fundamentalism and the expulsion of many European commercial colonies in the Levant and the Maghreb (the formally colonized parts of the Middle East and North Africa), there is still "a wider Europe" that can be found on all coasts of the Mediterranean. Tunisia, for example, considers itself a Francophone nation and is an associate member of the European Federation for Intercultural Learning (EFIL). There is another wider Europe that historically embraced Central and Eastern European countries, that is also easily forgotten in the popular understanding of European identity as a result of the 50-year reign of the Soviet Union. It is this forgetfulness that Alain Finkielkraut describes as "*Ingratitude,*" in the title of his insightful book (Finkielkraut, 1999). Once again, but slowly, western European peoples are beginning to think of Prague and Budapest as being as European as Paris and Barcelona.

Fictitious Bloodlines and Faith—Healing the Hurts of History

Is or can "Europe" become a large enough metaphor to hold the directions in which it will grow? Old stories are powerfully at work at the same time as a new definition and culture are being sought. Such a truth is hard to face. Cultural commentator Stuart Miller described European boundaries in the title of in his 1987 book: *Painted in Blood: Understanding Europeans.* Interestingly, in the book's second edition (1996) the all too frank "blood" of the original was drained from the title. It is simply called *Understanding Europeans.* Diversity work and cultural competence require learning how to heal the hurts of history. As U.S. writer John Steinbeck, once noted, "The past is not dead, it's not even past." A good part of healing our humanity is facing denials of the past.

Historically cultures were often established and maintained by bloodlines. More recently these have been fictitious bloodlines. Never mind that Turks and Greeks are genetically identical. Never mind that, as one Croatian doctor remarked during the war with Serbia, "When two soldiers kill each other, the same grandmother weeps at both funerals." Forget that researchers analyzing the Y chromosome taken from 1,007 men from 25 locations in Europe found a pattern suggesting that 4 out of 5 of the men shared a single male ancestor about 40,000 years ago, with the remaining 20% descended from a few other individuals in the Middle East (Recer, 2000). These diverse peoples of Europe are virtually *all* related to each other by blood. Never mind that genocide is fratricide. Today as I write the television is showing the trial of Slobodan Milosevic droning on in The Hague. It is clear that fictitious bloodlines are still important enough for people to kill and die for.

Over a century ago the French writer and historian Ernest Renan saw that, "Truth to tell, there is no pure race." This truth resists being believed in Europe as elsewhere (see Allen and Eade, 1999). It is not surprising then that Jean Monnet, who fathered the European Community, was heard to say, "If I were again facing the challenge of integrating Europe, I would probably start with culture." In short, we are who we believe we are, and it is in changing or not changing this belief more than in the development of portable phone technology or citing genetic evidence that the future unity in diversity of Europe lies.

One of these denials concerns the religious subtext of European diversity. As over a decade of violence in Southeastern Europe has shown, there are still real boundaries between Western Christianity and Eastern Orthodox Christianity, as well as separating Christianity from Islam. No one needs to attend church, temple, or mosque for these cultural contexts to be distinct from each other and to continue to cause tension that can turn into violence.

Today's boundaries of east and west, in terms of affinities and alliances, are roughly drawn along the same lines that divided the eastern and western Roman Empires in the fourth and fifth centuries (Exhibit 10.1). These boundaries became the fault line for the split between Latin Catholicism and Eastern Orthodoxy. Trying to keep the peace in southeastern Europe can be about these boundaries. While politicians and peacekeepers aim to facilitate a modicum of political

Exhibit 10.1

Crossing Boundaries: The Bayeux Tapestry Showing the Death of Harold the Saxon King at the Battle of Hastings in the Norman Conquest of England

Source: Centre Guillaume le Conquerant, Bayeux, France.

stability and economic normalcy, they do it from a western perspective, and this western vision of things is not inevitable beyond the pale of Latin influence, as Samuel Huntington has maintained (Huntington, 1996).

Blood, real and fictitious (in the form of family and clan ties), has persistently proven itself thicker than water (shared faith via baptism) in European behavior, despite attempts to define Europe against non-Christian outsiders throughout much of the last two millennia.

European religious and cultural boundaries include, as we are even more likely to forget, the subdivision in the West between Catholicism and Protestantism and the marginalization of the Jews, the Roma and Sinti (popularly still referred to as Gypsies in most European languages) whose "problem" of not having their own land and boundaries kept begging a "solution" historically. The solutions of ghettoization, persecutions, expulsion, exploitation, and extermination have been the favored European approaches and, in the case of the Roma and Sinti, continue today particularly in Central Europe. The Balfour Declaration was another culturally unsavvy "solution" whose consequences imperil world stability more each day:

> His Majesty's Government view with favour the establishment in Palestine of a national home for the Jewish people, and will use their best endeavours to facilitate the achievement of this object, it being clearly understood that nothing shall be done which may prejudice the civil and religious rights of existing non-Jewish communities in Palestine, or the rights and political status enjoyed by Jews in any other country. (Letter of Arthur James Lord Balfour to Lord Rothschild, November 2, 1917)

Most Europeans avoid discussing religion, but when they do, it is not uncommon for deeply held prejudices and a surprising level of antisemitism to surface with unexpected vehemence. At some levels many Europeans have not forgiven each other for massacres, witch hunts, genocides, pogroms, and inquisitions. Religion division still smolders in Ulster, but generations of religion-based propaganda still poison the memory. *La Leyenda Negra*, the so-called "Black Legend" of the misdeeds of the Catholic Spaniards, became solidly knit into the teaching of history in the Protestant North and in North America (Exhibit 10.2). This historical propaganda is still a subconscious pull that separates the North of Europe from Southern attitudes, values, and behavior, and sustains the distrust the people of these regions harbor for each other. The way much history is still taught in schools has a way of telling us very clearly who the "good guys" and who the "bad guys" are. Political correctness is not a new weapon. It simply shifts targets over time.

Exhibit 10.2

La Leyenda Negra

Source: Foro Hispanoamericano, Centro Universitario Francisco De Vitoria.

Although religion may underlie European conflicts and their resolution, the discussion of religion and religious values is distinctly absent —one might even say "taboo"—from the literature and practice of interculturalists, and religious bias in the business world goes undetected and denied. It is a suppressed discussion, probably because we fear how it so easily bursts out of the bounds of "rational" discourse. It is commonplace to blame religion for its shortcomings in order to appear enlightened. This is a loss, for religions contain, as well, important visions of humanity along with values of compassion, love, honesty, and trust that today often consciously or unconsciously motivate individuals and groups to address cultural issues and conflicts. Religion often challenges "business as usual" to better and more humane global performance by providing alternative perspectives and values.

Religion can be a diversity resource. The Jesuit Robert de Nobili who declared himself a Sannjasi and lived as a Brahmin in India (1606) could be considered as one of the first European interculturalists of modern times. Though the Jesuits were attacked and destroyed by jealous competing religious orders and by political powers, religious groups still make similar efforts to understand the nature of and adapt to the cultures to which they go on missions today. The cultural information gathered by religious groups is an important part of the knowledge base of cultural competence.

The Catholic Church, which solidified resistance to Communism, grouses about its dramatically decreased influence now that its enemy to the left has disappeared. But it continues to watchdog right leaning "materialism" and the widening disparities between rich and poor in market economies. One must remember that Catholic resistance was to "godless" communism, not to social solidarity.

While Christian divisions and Judaism are *sotto voce* topics for most Europeans, the growth of Islam and other religions not indigenous to "Christian" Europe are not. Consciousness of Islam exploded with two incidents in the 1980s. First came the "Salman Rushdie affair." In response to the publication of Rushdie's novel *The Satanic Verses* in 1988, the Ayatollah Khomeini issued a *fatwa* (religious decree) urging that Rushdie, though a British citizen, be killed for having insulted the Prophet and Islam. The second incident involved three young women who persisted in wearing head scarves in compliance with Muslim law while attending a secondary school. This defied a ban on religious garb in French public schools:

> Whereas the head scarves affair showed the refusal of a substantial proportion of Muslim immigrants and their children to adhere to the model assigned to them, namely that of confining religion to the private sphere, the "Rushdie affair" demonstrated that many Muslim communities wanted their religion to be granted the same public status as that of the Christian religion. Both events placed the subject of Muslims in Western Europe on the academic and political agendas, with the realization that there was a growing "Islamic factor" in the social and political processes associated with immigration and ethnic minorities. (Furseth, 2000)

Given the historical relationship of church and state in most European nations, these issues are likely to continue as matter for public debate. The absolute separation of church and state in the United States seems to some Europeans hostile to all religion, compared to the harder-to-manage benevolence that exists in some European constitutions. Only time will tell if religion will become explicit in the diversity debate as well. Wise accommodation on the part of organizations is already taking place. Management Center Europe in Brussels, for example, like many institutions and employers, and hospitality services provides a place of prayer for its Islamic customers and employees.

It is almost impossible to count the cost of these ideological divides and the conflicts that arise from them to Europe's economy and to individual businesses. The mixture of religion and economic strife discourages inward investment in Northern Ireland and in other conflicted areas. Yet here as usual with diversity, there is the potential for value-added as well as conflict. Islamic immigrants to Europe often bring a different sense of solidarity and fresh views on the investment and use of money.

Preserving and Accommodating European Regional Culture

Since World War II, Western Europe has managed rather well; it has largely achieved peaceful coexistence between cultures and great prosperity has followed. Its challenges now will be to manage the turbulence that still exists in these differences as it expands its boundaries and replenishes its aging peoples with immigrants holding different beliefs and attitudes. These two challenges are not unrelated in that they require similar vision, tolerance, energetic attention, and, above all, continued courage to accept rather than suppress difference.

Europe's historical attempts to suppress ethnic and religious cultures in the effort to establish powerful, united nation states—whether led by Napoleon, Bismarck, Mussolini, the Soviet occupation, or simply the fear of difference and social fragmentation—has left it nonetheless with regional and linguistic movements for recognition and, in some cases, independence. At worst it has also left Europe with animosities, lust for revenge, hatred, and distrust. The words "managing diversity" may have been created in the United States, but the truth for Europe, as well as for many other regions around the globe, is that managing diversity is not just a solution to conflict, economic stability, and sustainability. *It is the only ethically acceptable and ultimately practical solution.*

The same energies that encourage hard-pressed regional cultures to reassert themselves may be paralleled in the behavior of national groups in the face of the growth of the European Union and its functions. France, though by far not the only power for cultural preservation in Europe, provides the outstanding example of this. Currently I am living about half the time in France. Here I enjoy the social cohesion found in French culture and the illusion of stability that the French seem able to maintain in the face of constant change. Jack Lang, former French minister of culture, defended this French preoccupation with culture by describing culture as, "something fragile. It needs attention and tenderness. The market system cannot assure it." France sees itself as different and wants to stay that way. Here issues of culture are a matter of high policy and endless debate. Extraordinary efforts to preserve its language and culture include, for example:

- An ever-growing government list of over 120,000 English terms that may not be used in official French documents.
- A 40% minimum of TV programming and popular music broadcasting that must be of French origin. (Henley, 1999)

Simply put, France is unique in Europe in the energy it invests in promoting, protecting, and developing its identity and its cultural patrimony. Such centralized effort is not a recent phenomenon, either, as the *Economist* recently noted:

> Back in 1794, during Robespierre's reign of terror, the revolutionary Abbot Grégoire preached "the need to erase dialects and make French universal." The Académie Française has spent the past 366 years guarding the purity of the French language from foreign and regional contamination. With the underlying assumption that France is both unique and united, politicians across the board talk of the "French exception." Even its shape, the hexagon, commonly defines the coherence of the country. ("How Multilingual Is France?" 2000, p. 26)

And despite, or perhaps because of, France's conscious defense of language, media, food, and art, many French people feel that they are losing the battle to privatization, global marketing, and what many believe is a conscious conspiracy on the part of the United States—symbolized by *MacDo* (McDonald's)—and they are not bashful about expressing this, while at the same time beginning to make space for their previously suppressed regional cultures.

"Le pouvoir aux citoyens, pas au marché"—Power to the people and not to the market!—was the cry of the 20,000 anti–World Trade Organization (WTO) demonstrators in Paris and the groups that protested in Lyon and Strasbourg at subsequent meetings. Although demonstrations against the WTO, World Bank, and the like are far from exclusively French, those taking place in France were flavored by the presence of numerous French organizations, trade unions, and political groups demanding that these supranational bodies be subject to the United Nations Declaration on Human Rights and answerable to the public. Much like the anti–Vietnam War demonstrations of the

last century, the root complaint was the lack of "civilian" control over these bodies and the commercialization of the world that they are seen to favor over sustainable co-development.

Whatever one's judgment on the issues, the cultural fact is the insistence on social cohesion that the French bring to such expressions of disagreement. As international management consultant Grant Levitan observes, "in the best of times and the worst of times, French history has been filled with mass strikes and other forms of civil disobedience, and the French seem to come out of these events all the stronger for them" ("Tales from Loire Valley," 2000). Much of the love-hate relationship that France has with the United States stems from the French perception that U.S. democracy possesses ample freedom (*liberté*), and a great measure of fairness (*égalité*), but lacks a necessary sense of social cohesion (*fraternité*) to make it all work properly. This may be one more indication of the subliminal difference between the Protestant versus Catholic view of society, as described earlier.

The right to strike and demonstrate is probably nowhere exercised with such frequency as in France, where such attention is paid to sociocultural issues, whether they be bus drivers demanding greater protection from thieves or farmers in the *terroirs* seeking redress from the cultural depredations of *MacDo*. Strikes and demonstrations can turn nasty in France, but they are paid attention to. The fact that they are such a fundamental right is probably part of the social cohesion we mentioned above. There is a safe tradition of disagreement in France, and even though violence may at times occur it is rare, because people remain connected with each other even in disagreement.

Such a system is also slow. Large decisions are often made after much debate. Though women were given suffrage in 1944, some 25 years later than elsewhere (see Chapter 9), French women are rather poorly represented in politics today. A recent *Economist* report highlighted this:

> They occupy 10.9% of the seats in the lower house of the parliament, a smaller share than in any European Union country except Greece, and only 5.9% of those in the Senate. Barely 8% of mayors are female. Women won a mere 7.8% of the seats in the 1998 regional elections. And only one of the country's 22 regional governments is presided over by a woman. ("Liberty, Equality, Sorority," 2000, p. 31)

Redress was in order, and on May 3, 2000, the decision was taken to enforce equal quotas for women and men at all French elections by requiring parties to field an equal number of male and female candidates.

This same social cohesion has another side, namely the challenge it raises to admitting and assimilating foreign minority groups in France. Minorities tend to be made or are asked to make themselves French or keep themselves invisible.

But the new law of equal quotas does pose some awkward questions. No sooner was it passed than a fresh row broke out over a separate proposal, made by the co-ruling Greens, to give non-E.U. foreigners the right to vote in French elections—an idea promptly branded "dangerous" and a threat to national independence by the right. Integrating female citizens is one thing, it seems, even if they have been considered such for less than half a century, but long-time resident "foreigners" is quite another ("Liberty, Equality, Sorority," 2000, p. 31). Again, it seems that what is at stake is identity.

The history of immigration in France is long and complex. Immediately following World War II, France was the only country in Europe to encourage permanent immigration. Yet economic downturns and political struggles between right and left endowed the country with a heritage of contradictory laws and feelings. More than any other European country, France has debated the questions of immigration and migrants' rights. In the 1990s Jean-Marie Le Pen's extreme-right and xenophobic National Front party seemed to be on its way to a significant power-brokering role as it continued to gain in local elections. The immigration law of 1998 gave wide naturalization rights to children born in France of foreign parents and to foreigners who marry French citizens, creating functional standoff between the political extremes. Now France continues, in line with E.U. standards, to receive new immigrants and struggle with the challenge posed by refugees and asylum-seekers.

Reluctant inclusion is a fact of life that is perhaps typified by the advertising industry. Unlike the United States, France and other European nations have paid scant attention to the challenges of marketing to domestic ethnic groups. Protests against *"la télé monochrome"* (single-color TV programming) and *"l'apartheid culturel"* (cultural exclusion) of blacks have been raising consciousness and encouraging greater inclusion of minorities in television, Internet, and print products and advertisements. These mediums tend to ignore the existence of blacks along with that of North Africans ("Le pub française fait l'impasse sur les minorités ethniques," 2000).

Diversity Strategies at the Demographic Crossroads

Although Europe both resists and emulates globalization (a.k.a. Americanization), there is a second crossroad lying squarely in the path of Europe's future for which the North American experience may provide some useful models as well as cautions. Given what we have already said about the aging of Europe and the demographic crisis described earlier in Chapter 3, large-scale immigration and naturalization may be the only road to economic stability for Europe's working populations. How governments and businesses meet this demographic crisis will most certainly and profoundly affect both culture and social structure, and it will bring both European identity and its influence in the world even more into discussion.

Europe needs not only semiskilled or unskilled workers, but workers at every level of expertise. About 135 million immigrant workers are needed in the next 25 years to maintain the ratio of active to retired workers (Crossette, 2000). The United States, Canada, and Australia have been using a model of open citizenship in this regard and consequently are applying diversity initiatives based on this assumption.

Europe is not, and it may ultimately choose another route. More likely is that this decision will be made or make itself over time, with continued emphasis on providing acculturation programs for immigrants both publicly and at work. In these programs, language and cultural skills are taught to newcomers to integrate them into the society and find them productive work as quickly and thoroughly as possible. These programs are actually spreading in Europe and becoming normative for less skilled immigrants.

Acculturation does not happen as quickly and thoroughly as many Europeans might expect or desire, and the numbers of the hardcore "indigestible" immigrants, asylum seekers, and itinerant labor will probably make inevitable more investment and perhaps more borrowing of U.S. and Canadian corporate diversity practices. North American diversity models are appearing now in both global and national corporations in the European Union. The need, not the fad, is upon them, and adaptation is more likely than reinvention.

Identity in Europe has been traditionally dependent on language and in the history and customs of where one is from, and it is into this context that newcomers are absorbed. Although Europe would prefer to avoid the massive rich-versus-poor discrepancy that is the heritage of free market capitalism in the United States and elsewhere in the world, its present policies are not decisive enough to prevent growing numbers of marginalized people in its cities. As London financial executive Fields Wicker-Miurin reported on the World Economic Forum, "We do not have to go to distant countries to see the poor and needy, just to parts of south London and the banlieus [suburbs] of Marseilles." An important objective of diversity initiatives both public and private ought to be this blending of European social priorities with useful practices coming from North America or elsewhere. We will be looking for this blend as we proceed into the future.

De facto, as we have discussed earlier in this chapter Europe is extensively mixed in terms of ethnicity, both historically and in the present. It is language and history that creates and maintains its cultural boundaries. Germany's traditional sense of identity and admission to citizenship were based on bloodlines, and though its laws are changing, the mentality of many Germans is firmly fixed in that traditional definition. In France, on the other hand, language is critical. Anyone, in theory, can become a citizen, but they must truly make the effort to become French to do so successfully.

Capitalism and Democracy: The Unbridled Team

As Fareed Zakaria, editor of Newsweek International has pointed out, "Capitalism and democracy are the two dominant forces of modern history; they unleash human creativity and energy like nothing else, but they are also forces of destruction" (2000, p. 8). From the fall of the Soviet system until the arrival of organized terrorism, capitalist countries and businesses have had no serious predators except each other. One senses the inevitable though slow shift of China toward a market economy and greater freedom. This leaves only the voices raised in parts of the Islamic world, and the criticism of demonstrators nourished within the capitalist system to decry its excesses. The twin forces of capitalism and democracy, Zakaria continues, "destroy old orders, hierarchy, tradition, communities, careers, stability, and peace of mind itself. Unsentimental about the world as it exists, they surge forward, changing everything they encounter. The challenge of the West in the next century will be to find ways to channel the sweeping power of these two—the last surviving big ideas—as they reorganize all human activity. Otherwise, for much of the world, it may be too fast a ride" (2000, p. 8). Twinned with the new power of the media in an online world, they seem more unstoppable than ever.

That ride, a market-based, bottom-line approach to economy and diversity, may be too fast for Westerners themselves, to say nothing of the chaos it has brought to Eastern Europe and the reactions it has generated in the Islamic world. "Americans," Zakaria adds, "accept the chaos that comes from an ever-changing economy and a chaotic political system. They believe that in the end, it all works out for the best. . . . Indeed, one could argue that the American way is so successful because both capitalism and democracy are tightly regulated by the rule of law" (p. 10)—and, we might add, an insuppressible optimism about frontiers.

Certain financial extravagances may be possible and tolerated in the United States because, among other reasons, it has the longest-standing stable constitutional government in the world. U.S. citizens have reason to believe that the system will not fall, although most European governments within living memory have fallen or undergone significant constitutional change. Honoring this stability may be the reason that U.S. dollars are rarely redesigned and are likely to remain black on the front and green on the back for quite a while, despite there being absolutely no practical or aesthetic reason for keeping them so.

U.S. self-confidence and faith in its system relies on more than hype or naïveté, as many Europeans would like to believe. During the U.S. election crisis of November 2000, visiting and expatriate Americans were constantly beset by questioning Europeans who were concerned that the United States was undergoing a constitutional crisis, an unraveling of government and social stability. When I tired of these conversations, I created a strategy of asking a question in return: "Do you think that the Joint Chiefs of Staff at the Pentagon will seize power and declare martial law?" The obvious answer was "no," but usually the question was left hanging in the air and the discussion turned to another topic.

Yes, the United States is here to stay for a while yet and so is Europe. Their responsibilities toward managing diversity, each in its own way are heavy ones. Europe and North America have opened the doors to a global economy and must respond well to both its opportunities and consequences as the Stratfor organization, a global intelligence provider points out,

> Europe has been the international system's center of gravity for about 500 years. Atlantic Europe—Portugal, Spain, England, France, and the Netherlands—conquered most of the world, creating the first single system of international relations. Until the

European conquest, the world had consisted of sequestered, frag-
mented systems. Aztecs had nothing to do with the Chinese, who
had nothing to do with Mali. The European conquest of the world
not only created a single international system, but made Europe
both the crossroads and arbiter of that system. (Stratfor, "Europe
Comes to a Crossroads," 1999)

Many of the challenges of diversity are shaped as they are today due
to the choices and behaviors of Europeans toward each other and
toward the rest of the world for over half a millennium. "In the next
decade, Europe will face burning questions over the extent to which it
can integrate, over whether one power will be forced into a leadership
role, and over whether the European experiment in integration will
begin to fragment" (Stratfor, 1999). Both government and businesses
will answer the questions of diversity with whatever intercultural competence and leadership they can or cannot muster. At the very least, the
management of diversity will be the bellwether or the scapegoat of
Europe's future. Given the European Union's short history, we have
both high hopes and frightening challenges in front of us. Acting out
this responsibility will depend on governments and popular support,
however business will continue to be the stage on which much of the
drama is acted out.

How and where globalization and localization meet will provide a
great deal of the agenda for this new century. The leadership of both
newly merged global corporations and those of long standing has been
challenged by how to organize and use the diverse knowledge that
resides in their human resources. We discussed some dimensions of this
in Chapter 7. Unilever is another outstanding example of this challenge. With an annual turnover of close to 40 billion U.S. dollars, the
Anglo-Dutch conglomerate faces as uncertain a future as any other
organization when it comes to accommodating the diverse requirements of its workforce and taking advantage of the knowledge resid-
ing in it. Chairman Niall FitzGerald described the challenge:

> The management of diversity and the richness that one gets from
> diversity is going to be hugely important for business in the future.
> If you pressed me and said, what is the one unique thinking that
> Unilever has?—and don't tell me about brands and people, be-
> cause everybody has those—I would say, our knowledge. It has
> accumulated over 70 years; it's encapsulated in 265,000 people
> across 100 countries . . .
>
> If I were to predict the sorts of organization which will succeed
> in 10 or 20 years time, it will be those which are extremely good
> at managing informal networks of alliances . . . good at managing

knowledge; and extremely good at managing diversity. (Quoted in Ashworth, online document, 1999)

This short treatment of EuroDiversity does not pretend to do much more than open to discussion the issues of diversity from a European perspective. It is far from touching on all of the countries of the European Union to say nothing of its many regional cultures and the challenges they offer. The authors hope, however, that it will provoke both appreciation of the unique history and qualities of European diversity as well as ongoing and productive exchange among those who work and do business here.

Resources

Chapter References

Prologue

Grove, Cornelius, and Willa Hallowell. "Can We Export Our Diversity Approach?" *Cultural Diversity at Work* (Newsletter), January 1994.

Chapter 1

Becht, Marco, and Ailsa Roëll. "Blockholdings in Europe: An International Comparison." *European Economic Review* (1999). Available at: http://www.ecgi.org/research/Control_Europe/documents/becht_roell_eea98.pdf.

Berry, M. "Communicating Cultural Dimensions of Gender-Related Identity in Female Austrian and Finnish Business Students' Responses to Joanna Kramer (and to each other)." *Studies in Cultures, Organizations, and Societies*, 2002 (in press).

Black, Charles H. "Culture's Effects on Organizations: The Cross-Cultural Challenge of Globalization." Ph.D. diss., California State University, Hayward, 2001.

Bryson, Bill. *Notes from a Small Island.* New York: Avon Books, 1997.

Bryson, Bill, and William Morrow. *Neither Here nor There: Travels in Europe.* New York: Hearst Books, 1993.

Cannon, Margaret. *The Invisible Empire: Racism in Canada.* Toronto: Random House Canada, 1995.

Centre for Diversity and Business. Available at: http://www.diversityandbusiness. com, 2000.

"Cross about Holdings." *The Economist*, 29 April 2000, 14–18.

"Culture 2000 Programme." The European Commission, 2000. Available at: http://europa.eu.int/comm/culture/c2000-index_en.html.

Dechert, Dominique. "French Views of Religious Freedom." *U.S.-France Analysis*. Available at The Brookings Institute website: http://www. brook.edu/dybdocroot/fp/cusf/analysis/relfreedom.htm.

Delgado-Moreira, Juan. "Cultural Citizenship and the Creation of European Identity." *Electronic Journal of Sociology*, 1997. Available at: http://www. sociology.org/content/vol002.003/delgado.html.

"The Helpers." Available at: http://freepages.folklore.rootsweb.com/~kaelin/ helpers.html.

Hill, Richard. *Sharks and Custard: The Things that Make Europeans Laugh.* Bruxelles, Belgium: EuroPublic, 2001.

"How Multilingual Is France?" *The Economist*, 29 April 2000:26.

Jarvis, J. "Training Global Managers for Cultural Dexterity." *Cultural Diversity at Work* (Newsletter), March 1997;9(4).

"Lean, Mean European." *The Economist*, 29 April 2000:3–9.

Lorbiecki, A., and E. Hutchings. "A Snapshot" of Diversity Management with Britishness in the Foreground. Paper delivered at the Relocating Britishness Conference, sponsored by the Department of Management Learning, Lancaster University, 22–24 June 2000.

"Mariage à la Mode. " *The Economist*, 29 April 2000:10–14.

Mayle, Peter. *French Lessons: Adventures with Knife, Fork, and Corkscrew.* New York: Alfred A. Knopf, 2001.

Mayle, Peter. *A Year in Provence.* New York: Random House, 1991.

McGrath, P. "You Are a Data Subject." *Newsweek*, 6 December 1999:90.

Mole, John. *Mind Your Manners: Managing Business Cultures in Europe.* London: Brealey, Nicholas Publishing, 1996.

Pirie, Barbara. Intercultural Insights Discussion Group. 25 June 2001.

Rankin, Aidan. *The Politics of the Forked Tongue: Authoritarian Liberalism.* London: New European Publications, 2001.

Shaw, Graham. "Diversity in Europe." *Profiles in Diversity Journal*, Spring 2000, Centre for Diversity and Business. Available at: http://www. diversityandbusiness.com.

Simons, George, Baudoin Knaapen, and Guurt Kok. "A Comprehensive Model for Addressing Diversity." In *The Cultural Diversity Sourcebook*, edited by George Simons and Bob Abramms. Amherst, MA: ODT, 1996.

Simons, George, and Ineke de Raaff. "The Clinton Affair—*Vive la difference*: A Cultural Retrospective." *Managing Diversity Newsletter*, November 1998.

University of Central Lancashire, June 2000. Available at: http://www.uclan. ac.uk/business_services/conf/brit/brit.htm.

"You Are a Data Subject." *Newsweek Special Edition*, December 1999– February 2000:90.

Chapter 2

"Britain: Of Secrecy and Madness." *The Economist*, 28 October 2000:43.

"Britain: Plague Island." *The Economist*, 3 March 2001:35–36.

"The BSE Inquiry: Wait for It." *The Economist*, 7 October 2000:52–54.

Coleman, John. "Editorial." *European Business Review*, 2000:2.

Europe's Agenda 2000: Strengthening and Widening the European Union. Luxembourg: Office for Official Publications of the European Communities, 1999.

Finkielkraut, Alain. *Ingratitude: Conversation sur notre temps.* Paris: Gallimard, 1999.

"Foot-and-Mouth Disease: The Costs and the Cures." *The Economist*, 31 March 2001:81–83.

"France's Mad Cows Go Political." *The Economist*, 11 November 2000:53.

Garcea, E.A.A. "How Europeans Perceive Europe: A Case Study from Italy." *European Business Review*, 2001.

"German Unification: Togetherness: A Balance Sheet." *The Economist*, 30 September 2000:27–32.

Mehl, R. "Research on Intercultural Conflict Solution: Emerging Conflicts in Merging Societies, Given with the Example of the Unified Germany." Paper presented at the Young SIETAR Congress, Brussels, 29–31 October 1999.

"The Nice Summit: So That's All Agreed, Then." *The Economist*, 16 December 2000, 23–26.

"Le pacte civil de solidarité" (PACS). LOI no. 99-944 du 15 novembre 1999 relative au pacte civil de solidarité Available at: http://www. legifrance.gouv.fr/citoyen/jorf_nor.ow?numjo=JUSX9803236L.

Rösgen, Anne. *ProInnovation* (Newsletter), Saarbrücken, Germany, March 2001.

"Scottish Finance: Raising the Standard." *The Economist*, 24 June 2000, 104–105.

Simons, George, "The Future of 'Diversity' in Europe." *European Business Review*, 2000;12(2).

"Time to Save the Sacrificial Lambs." *Financial Times Weekend*, April 2001; XXIV:21–22.

Zuckerman, A.J., and G.F. Simons. *Sexual Orientation in the Workplace: Gay Men, Lesbians, Bisexuals, and Heterosexuals Working Together.* Santa Cruz: International Partners Press, 1994.

Chapter 3

Bloendal, S., and Scarpetta, S. *The Retirement Decision in OECD Countries.* Paris: Organisation de Cooperation et De Developpement Economiques (OECD), 1998.

"Bridging Europe's Skills Gap." *The Economist*, 31 March 2001:67–68.

"Displaced People: When Is a Refugee Not a Refugee?" *The Economist*, 3 March 2001:21–23.

Eures. Employment Agency of the European Union. Available at: http://europa.eu.int/comm/employment_social/elm/eures/index.htm.

"Europe: Unwelcome to Iberia." *The Economist*, 10 February 2001:31–32.

"The European Union: Bigger When?" *The Economist*, 11 November 2000: 53.

Europe's Agenda 2000: Strengthening and Widening the European Union. Luxembourg: Office for Official Publications of the European Communities, 1999.

"Europe's Gypsies: Are They a Nation?" *The Economist*, 25 November 2000:47–48.

"Europe's Immigrants: A Continent on the Move." *The Economist*, 6 May 2000:21–25.

"Europe's Migrants: Riding the Tide." *The Economist*, 5 August 2000:31–32.

"France: Strike to Retire." *The Economist*, 3 February 2001:33–38.

"France's Economy: Now for the Hard Bit." *The Economist*, 8 July 2000:32–33.

Garcea, E.A.A. "How Europeans Perceive Europe: A Case Study from Italy." *European Business Review* 2001;13(5):263–268.

"German Business: Zeissmic Shift." *The Economist*, 11 November 2000: 97–98.

"Germany: A Row about a Bigger E.U." *The Economist*, 9 September 2000:40–41.

"Germany: Fighting Racism." *The Economist*, 5 August 2000:32.

"Germany: Radical Pensions." *The Economist*, 18 November 2000:44–45.

"Go for It." *The Economist*, 6 May 2000:15–16.

Hall, C.-H. "EU's Smarteste Medlesland." *Jullands-Posten*, July 1995:20.

Hviding, K., and M. Mérette. *Macroeconomic Effects of Pension Reforms in the Context of Aging Populations: Overlapping Generations Model Simulations for Seven OECD Countries.* Paris: OECD, 1998.

"Ireland: Come Back!" *The Economist*, 28 October 2000:38.

"Italy: A Few Bad Apples." *The Economist*, 13 January 2000:30–31.

Kohl, R., and P. O'Brien. *The Macroeconomics of Aging, Pensions Ad Savings: A Survey.* Paris: OECD, 1998.

"The Nice Summit: So That's All Agreed, Then." *The Economist*, 16 December 2000:23–26.

"A Not-So-Popular Nordic Bridge." *The Economist*, 7 October 2000:45.

"Pension Funds: Old Hopes Stirring." *The Economist*, 14 October 2000: 110.

Rea, A. "Social Citizenship and Ethnic Minorities in the European Union." In *Migration, Citizenship, and Ethno-National Identities in the European Union*, edited by M. Martiniello. Proceedings of the International Sociological Association, 13th World Congress, Bielefeld. Aldershot, UK: Avebury, 1994.

Shaw, Graham. "Diversity in Europe." *Profiles in Diversity Journal*, Spring 2000, Centre for Diversity and Business, 2000. Available at: http://www.diversityandbusiness.com.

"Switzerland: Foreign Relief." *The Economist*, 30 September 2000:42–45.

Vitorino, A. "Direzione generale Istruzione e cultura." *L'Europa senza frontiere* (Newsletter), 9 October 2000:1.

"Waiting for Lord Rogers's Urban Renaissance." *The Economist*, 5 August 2000:35–36.

Chapter 4

"Advertising to Children: Kid Gloves." *The Economist*, 6 January 2001:58.

"Beer Makers: The Big Pitcher." *The Economist*, 20 January 2001:65–66.

"Britain: Sunshine, with a Chance of Showers." *The Economist*, 8 July 2000:41–43.

Castells, Manuel. "La cuestión europea." *El Pais*, 26 April 1996.

"Catch up If You Can." *The Economist*, 23 September 2000:34–38.

"A Constitution for the European Union." *The Economist*, 28 October 2000:22–28.

"The DaimlerChrysler Emulsion." *The Economist*, 29 July 2000:69–70.

Directorate General Education and Culture. *Europe and Its Budget: What Your Money Are Used For?* Brussels: Author, 2000.

Ernsberger, R., Jr. "Meet the New Boss." *Newsweek*, 30 March 1998.

"Europe: From Bad to Worse, Down on the Farm." *The Economist*, 3 March 2001:27–28.

Europe's Agenda 2000: Strengthening and Widening the European Union. Luxembourg: Office for Official Publications of the European Communities, 1999.

"Europe's dot.bombs." *The Economist*, 5 August 2000:18.

"Europe's Economies: Stumbling Yet Again?" *The Economist*, 16 September 2000:91–94.

"Europe's Internet Drought." *The Economist*, 5 August 2000:59–60.

"Europe's Stock Exchanges: Beating a Retreat." *The Economist*, 16 September 2000:102–104.

"The European Central Bank: The Terrible Twos Begin." *The Economist*, 6 January 2001:61–64.

"European Economies: Working Wonders." *The Economist*, 25 November 2000:121.

"The Euro's Chronic Weakness." *Financial Times*, 9 September 2000:8.

"Ford in Europe: In the Slow Lane." *The Economist*, 7 October 2000:94.

"France: Strike to Retire." *The Economist*, 3 February 2001:33–38.

Frankel, Barbara. "New Head of BBC Ties Compensation to Diversity Goals." *Hemisphere Inc.*, 11 April 2000. Available at: http://www.diversityinc.com.

"French Corporate Governance: Ambivalent." *The Economist*, 7 October 2000:93–94.

"German Retailing: Cheap and Cheerless." *The Economist*, 2 September 2000:65–66.

"Germany: The Church Victorious." *The Economist*, 2 September 2000:26–27.

"The Global Gambles of General Motors." *The Economist*, 24 June 2000:81–82.

"The Internet and the Law: Stop Signs on the Web." *The Economist*, 13 January 2001:19–23.

"The Internet: Vive la Liberté." *The Economist*, 25 November 2000:101–102.

Hall, C.-H. "E.U.'s smarteste Medlesland." *Jullands-Posten*, 20 July 1995.

"Hot and Sticky in Ireland." *The Economist*, 29 July 2000:25–26.

Naughton, K., and K. Lowrey-Miller. "A Mess of a Merger." *Newsweek*, 11 December 2000:60–64.

"A Not-So-Popular Nordic Bridge." *The Economist*, 7 October 2000:45.

"Old World, New Economy." *The Economist*, 2 September 2000:17.

"Opel Loses a Packet, and Another Boss." *The Economist*, 20 January 2001:64.

Rea, A. "Social Citizenship and Ethnic Minorities in the European Union." In *Citizenship and Ethno-National Identities in the European Union*, edited by M. Martinello. Aldershot, UK: International Sociological Association World Congress, Bielefeld, 1994.

"Shocking Times in Throgmorton Street." *The Economist*, 2 September 2000:69–70.

"Six Days Shalt Thou Shop." *The Economist*, 2 September 2000:66.

"A Suit and Case for Treatment." *The Economist*, 16 December 2000:97.

"Sweden: Taxcuts? Why?" *The Economist*, 5 August 2000:30–31.

"Telecoms in Trouble: When Big Is No Longer Beautiful." *The Economist*, 16 December 2000:91–93.

"What? Sell the Exchange?" *The Economist*, 2 September 2000:13–14.

Chapter 5

Coquel, Herman. Personal e-mail correspondence, 13 September 2001.

Davis, Stanley M., and C. Meyer. *Blur: The Speed of Change in the Connected Economy*. New York: Warner Books, 1999.

Dipollina, A. "Europa divisa al supermarket." *Il Venerdì di Repubblica*, 9 June 2000:75–78.

European Commission. "An Information Society for All of Europe." *eEurope 2002*. Available at: http://europa.eu.int/information_society/eeurope/index_en.htm.

European Commission. "eLearning: Designing Tomorrow's Education." Available at: http://www.europa.eu.int/comm/education/elearning/index.html. This site is the online home of the *e*Learning initiative of the European Commission. Its purpose is "to mobilize the educational and cultural communities, as well as the economic and social players in Europe, in order to speed up changes in the education and training systems for Europe's move to a knowledge-based society."

Heilemann, John. "All Europeans Are Not Alike." *New Yorker*, 28 April–5 May 1997:174–181.

Hsieh, T., J. Lavoie, and R. Samek. "Are you taking your expatriate talent seriously?" *McKinsey Quarterly*, 1999;3:71–82.

Marr, Andrew. "Perils of Ethnic Purity." *The Observer*, 4 July 1999.

Masie, Elliot. "TechLearn TRENDS #169." 1 June 2000. Available at: http://www.masie.com.

Minister of Public Works and Government Services. *Plain Language, Pure and Simple*. Ottawa: Canada Communication Group Publishing, 1993.

Minister of Public Works and Government Services. *Pour Un Style Clair Et Simple*. Ottawa: Canada Communication Group Publishing, 2000.

"New Economy, Old Problems." *The Economist*, 29 April 2000:23–25.

Norman, Tony. Unpublished paper in preparation for 4 Kongress für Wirtschaftspsychologie, "Global denken—vor Ort handeln" (4th Congress of Business Psychology, "Think Globally—Act Locally"), 6–8 May 2002.

PC Webopaedia. Available at: http://www.pcwebopaedia.com is an online lexicon of computer terminology, a good example of just-in-time-learning.

Sullivan, John. *Personnel Today*, 17 July 2001.

"Western Europe's Job-Seekers Limber Up." *The Economist*, 3 June 2000:35–36.

Online or CD-ROM tools for cultural profiling:

The Belbin Team Roles Inventory. Available at: http://www.belbin.com.
The Cross-Cultural Assessor. Available at: http://www.promentor.fi/cca/
The Cross-Cultural Adaptability Inventory. Available at:
  http://www.reidlondonhouse.com/reidlondonhouse/tests/ccai.htm.
The Cultural Orientation Inventory (COI). Available at: http://www.
  tmcorp.com/.
The Culture Compass. Available at: http://www.7d-culture.nl/index62.
  htm.
The Meyers-Briggs Type Inventory (MBTI). Available at: http://www.
  cpp-db.com.

Chapter 6

Johnston, William B., and Arnold E. Packer. *Workforce 2000: Work and Workers in the Twenty-First Century*. Indianapolis: Hudson Institute, 1987.

Chapter 7

Bartholomew, S., and N. Adler. "Building Networks and Crossing Borders: The Dynamics of Knowledge Generation in a Transnational World." In *Managing Across Cultures*, edited by P. Joynt and M. Warner. London: International Thompson Business Press, 1996:7–32.

Bresman, H., J. Birkinshaw, and R. Nobel. "Knowledge Transfer in International Acquisitions." *Journal of International Business Studies* 1999;30(3):439–462.

Burton-Jones, A. *Knowledge Capitalism: Business, Work, and Learning in the New Economy*. Oxford: Oxford University Press, 2000.

Coles, M. "Sharing Knowledge Boosts Efficiency." *Sunday London Times*, 30 April 2000:16.

Davenport, T.H., and L. Prusak. *Working Knowledge: How Organizations Manage What They Know*. Boston: Harvard Business School Press, 1998.

Dixon, N.M. *Common Knowledge: How Companies Thrive by Sharing What They Know*. Boston: Harvard Business School Press, 2000.

Holden, N.J. *Cross-Cultural Management: A Knowledge Management Perspective*. London: Financial Times/Prentice Hall, 2002.

Holden, N.J., and M. Burgess. *Japanese-Led Companies: Understanding How to Make Them Your Customers*. Maidenhead, U.K.: McGraw-Hill, 1994.

Joynt, P., and M. Warner. *Managing across Cultures: Issues and Perspectives*. London: International Thomson, 1996.

KPMG. *Knowledge Management Research Report 2000*. London: KPMG, 1999.

Nonaka, I., and H. Takeuchi. *The Knowledge-Creating Company*. New York: Oxford University Press, 1995.

Novo Nordisk. Various company documents.

Rosen, R. "Build an Expert Culture on Shared Values: Mads Øvlisen and Novo Nordisk A/S (Denmark)." *Global Literacies: Lessons on Business Leadership and National Values*. New York: Simon & Schuster, 2000.

Rosenzweig, Philip. "Strategies for Managing Diversity." In *Mastering Global Business: The Complete MBA Companion to Global Business*, edited by G. Bickerstaffe. London: Pitman, 1999.

Sulzer Infra. Various company documents. (The following company documents were used in the preparation of the case study. These documents range from articles in the company newspaper and annual reports as well as materials generated by the Sulzer Infra Academy):

> *A Charter for One Winning Team*
> Infra Mail: 100 Winning Teams—Facilitators Trained (D. Bright)
> P-Team Kick-off Workshop Schedule and Other Documentation on P-Teams
> Sulzer Infra: Our Leadership Principles
> Sulzer Infra: International Management Career Program
> Sulzer Infra Jahresbericht (Annual Report), 1999
> Sulzer Infra: Vision and Strategy 2002
> Sulzer Infra: The Infra Academy, 2000
> Sulzer Geschäftsbericht (Annual Report), 1999
> Sulzer Infra CBX Briefing. E-commerce—Here Comes the Future, March 1999
> Sulzer Infra CBX brochure
> Interview with Karl Bochsler, President of Sulzer Infra, reprinted from *Premises and Facilities Management*, 1999 November.
> The source of *Our Vision—Our Contribution* is: *A Charter for One Winning Team* (undated)

Tackney, C. "Organizational Forms of the Modern Enterprise: A Comparison of U.S., German, and Japanese Employment (or Legal) Ecologies." Paper presented at seminar at Copenhagen Business School, 12 April 2000.

Chapter 8

Berger, P., and T. Luckmann. *The Social Construction of Reality*. Middlesex, England: Penguin Books, 1991.

Bowie, N.E., and R.F. Dusha. *Business Ethics*. London: Prentice Hall, 1998.

Catlette B., and R. Hadden. *Contented Cows Give Better Milk*. Germantown, TN: Saltillo Press, 1998.

Chemers, M.M., ed. *Diversity in Organizations*. Thousand Oaks, CA: Sage Publications, 1995.

Council for Economic Priorities. *SA 8000*. New York: CEP Accreditation Agency, 1998.

Council of Europe. *Sites of Citizenship*. Strasbourg, France: Council of Europe, 1999.

Crijns, G., and G. Oonk. "Enterprises Are Not That Sensitive." *Volkskrant*, 2001 (in Dutch).

De Haan, J. "The Benefit of Codes of Conduct for Enterprises." *Volkskrant*, 2001 (in Dutch).

Dutch Social-Economic Board (SER). *The Profit of Values: Advisory Report on Sustainable Entrepreneurship*. Dutch Social-Economic Board (SER), 2000 (in Dutch).

Elkington, J. *Cannibals with Forks*. London: Capstone, 1999.

European Business Network for Social Cohesion. *CSR* [Corporate Social Responsibility] *Magazine: Equality and Diversity—A Competitive Advantage*. Bruxelles, Belgium: 2000.

Freire, Paolo. *Pedagogy of Freedom: Ethics, Democracy, and Civic Courage*. Oxford: Rowman & Littlefield, 1998.

Freire, Paolo. *Pedagogy of the Oppressed*. London: Penguin Books, 1972.

Friedman, Milton. "The Social Responsibility of Business Is to Increase Its Profits." In *Sustainable Entrepreneurship: Theory, Practice, Instruments*, edited by M. Janssen Groesbeek. Amsterdam: Uitgeverij Business Contact, 2001 (in Dutch).

Grunig, J.E., and D. Dozier. *Excellence in Public Relations and Communication Management*. Hillsdale, NJ: Lawrence Erlbaum Associates, 1992.

Handy, C. *The Empty Raincoat*. London: Arrow Books, 1994.

Illich, I. *Deschooling Society*. Middlesex, England: Penguin Books, 1971.

Janssen Groesbeek, M. *Sustainable Entrepreneurship: Theory, Practice, Instruments*. Amsterdam: Uitgeverij Business Contact, 2001 (in Dutch).

Johnston, William B., and Arnold H. Packer. *Workforce 2000: Work and Workers for the Twenty-First Century*. Indianapolis: Hudson Institute, 1987.

Kaptein, M. *Ethics Management*. Dordrecht, the Netherlands: Kluwer Academic Publishers: 1998.

Martin, J. *Cultures in Organizations: Three Perspectives*. New York: Oxford University Press, 1992.

McIntosh, M., ed. *Corporate Citizenship*. London: Financial Times Management, 1998.

Merry, P.D. *Open Source Learning*. Utrecht: Engage! InterAct, 2000.

Morgan, G. *Images of Organization*. Thousand Oaks, CA: Sage Publications, 1997.

Pascale, R. *Managing on the Edge*. Middlesex, England: Penguin Books, 1990.

Plasterk, R. "Ethical Behavior for Enterprises." *Volkskrant*, 2001 (in Dutch).

Taylor, M. *Europe Is More Than You Think*. Strasbourg, France: Council of Europe, 1999.

Thomas, Roosevelt, Jr. "A diversity framework." In *Diversity in Organisations*, edited by M.M Chemers. Thousand Oaks, CA: Sage Publications, 1995.

Van Riel, C.B.M. *Identity and Image: Basics for Corporate Communication*. Schoonhoven, the Netherlands: Academic Service, 1996 (in Dutch).

Wilber, K. *A Theory of Everything*. Dublin: Gateway, 2001.

Additional Online Sources

Business and Human Rights in Europe. Available at: http://www.business-humanrights.org/europe.htm

Center for Living Democracy. Available at: http://www.livingdemocracy.org.

Change and Transformation Strategies. Available at: http://www.cats3000.org.

Corporate Social Responsibility Europe (CSR). Available at: http://www.csreurope.org.

Council of Europe. Available at: http://www.coe.fr.

Duurzaam Ondernemen [Sustainable Enterprises]. Available at: http://www.duurzaam-ondernemen.nl (in Dutch).

Engage! InterAct. Available at: http://www.engage.nu/interact.

European Institute for Business Ethics. Available at: http://www.nyenrode.nl/research_faculty/eibe/.

European Union. Available at: http://europa.eu.int.

Financial Institute for Global Sustainability. Available at: http://www.figsnet.org.

Greenpeace. Available at: http://www.greenpeace.org.

Human Rights Education Associates. Available at: http://www.hrea.org.

International Business Ethics Institute. Available at: http://www.business-ethics.org.

KPMG Consultants. Available at: http://www.KPMG.com.

Social Venture Network. Available at: http://www.svn.org.

Chapter 9

ABC of Women Workers' Rights and Gender Equality. Geneva: International Labour Organization, 2000.

Anker, Richard. *Gender and Jobs: Sex Segregation of Occupations in the World*. Geneva: International Labour Office, 1997.

Center for Equal Opportunities and Opposition to Racism. Available at: http://www.antiracisme.be.

Engelbrech, Gerhard. "Total E-Quality Management: Paradigmatic Shift in Personnel Management." *Women in Management Review*, 1997;12(3): 105–115.

EUR-Lex, the portal to European Union law. Available at: http://www.europa.eu.int/eur-lex/en/news/20010601_01.html.

European Commission. *Technical Paper 3. Mainstreaming Equal Opportunities for Women and Men in Structural Fund Programs and Projects.* Luxembourg: Office for Official Publications of the European Communities, 2000.

European Commission, Employment and Social Affairs, Equal Opportunities. *Equal Opportunities for Women and Men in the European Union. Annual Report 1996.* Luxembourg: Office for Official Publications of the European Communities, 1997.

European Database. "Women in Decision-Making." Available at: http://www.db-decision.de.

European Foundation for Quality Management (EFQM). Available at: http://www.efqm.org.

European Labor Force Survey 1999, Eurostat, Statistical Office of the European Commission, Bruxelles, Belgium.

Federal Ministry for Education and Science Research and Technology, and Commission of the European Communities. *Total E-Quality: Chancenglichheit im Unternehmen, Paradigmenwechsel in der Personalpolitik.* Köln: Verlag Deutscher Wirschaftsdienst, January 1997.

Fetherolf Loutfi, Martha, ed. *Women, Gender, and Work: What Is Equality and How Do We Get There?* Geneva: International Labour Office, 2000.

Fransson, S., L. Johansson, and L. Svenaeus. *Highlighting Pay Differentials Between Women and Men.* Stockholm, Sweden: Government Offices, 2000.

Gilsoul, Anne. "Cadres supérieurs . . . Cadres supérieures?" Université Catholique de Louvain-la-Neuve, 1998.

Holton, Viki, J. Rabbetts, and R. Stone. *Women Managers: Reflecting on the Glass Ceiling.* Ashridge, UK: Ashridge Centre for Business and Society (ACBAS), 1998.

International Labour Organization, Sectoral Activities Program. *Breaking through the Glass Ceiling: Women in Management.* Geneva: International Labor Organization, 1997.

Löfström, Åsa. *A Report on Gender Equality and Economic Growth.* Stockholm, Sweden: Regierngskansliet, 2001.

Melkas, Helinä, and Richard Anker. *Gender Equality and Occupational Segregation in Nordic Labour Markets.* Geneva: International Labor Organization, 1997.

National Institute for Statistics. *Population in Belgium*. Available at: http://www.statbel.fgov.be/.

Olsson, Hans. *Social Security, Gender Equality, and Economic Growth*, 2000. Available at: http://social.regeringen.se/ansvar/ordf/pdf/socialforsakringar_en.pdf.

Reinhart, Ariane. *Sexual Harassment: An ILO Survey of Company Practice*. Geneva: International Labour Organization, 1999.

Shapiro, G., and S. Austin. *Equality-Driven Total Quality*. Brighton, England: University of Brighton Business School, 1994.

Swedish Ministry for Gender Affairs. "Highlighting Pay Differentials Between Women and Men," 2001. Available at http://www.scb.se/eng/omscb/eu/Highlighting_pay_diff.pdf.

Wirth, Linda. *Breaking Through the Glass Ceiling: Women in Management*. Geneva: International Labour Organization, 2001.

Chapter 10

Allen, Tim, and J. Eade, eds. *Divided Europeans: Understanding Ethnicities in Conflict*. Den Haag, The Netherlands: Kluwer Law International, 1999.

Ashworth, John. "Time Is Running out for the Clocking-in Mentality." *The Times (London)*, 18 September 1999.

Coleman, John. "Review: Christie, Ian. Sustaining Europe: A Common Cause for the European Union in the New Century." *The European Review of Business* 12, no. 2(2000):xiv.

Crossette, Barbara. "Europe Stares at a Future Built by Immigrants." *The New York Times*, 2 February 2000.

Delgado-Moreira, Juan. "Cultural Citizenship and the Creation of European Identity." *Electronic Journal of Sociology*, 1997.

European Commission, Directorate-General XXII. "Young People on the Threshold of the Year 2000: A Eurobarometer Survey." Luxembourg: Education, Training, and Youth, 1997. Available at: http://europa.eu.int/comm/dg22/youth/youth.hml.

Finkielkraut, Alain. *L'ingratitude. Conversation Sur Notre Temps*. Paris: Editions Gallimard, 1999.

"Les Français sont arrivés." *The Economist*, 23 October 1999.

Furseth, Inger. "Religious Diversity in Prisons and in the Military: The Rights of Muslim Immigrants in Norwegian State Institutions." Oslo: KIFO Centre for Church Research, 2000.

"Guy Verhofstadt, Belgium's Suitable Prime Minister." *The Economist*, 27 May 2000:34.

Henley, Jon. "Mon Dieu! Those Americans Are Ruining Everything French!" *San Diego Union-Tribune*, 13 November 1999.

"How Multilingual Is France?" *The Economist*, 29 April 2000:26.

Huntington, Samuel. *The Clash of Civilizations and the Remaking of World Order*. New York: Simon & Schuster, 1996.

"Le pub française fait l'impasse sur les minorités ethniques." *Le Monde*, 23 May 2000:5.

"Less-Suspicious Switzerland." *The Economist*, 27 May 2000:15–16.

"Liberty, Equality, Sorority." *The Economist*, 13 May 2000:31.

Miller, Stuart. *Painted in Blood: Understanding Europeans*. New York: Atheneum/Macmillan, 1987.

Nice Matin, 27 October 1999:34.

Recer, Paul. "4 in 5 European Men Share Ancestor from 40,000 Years Ago." *Washington Post*, 10 November 2000.

Simons, George, C. Vazquez, and P. Harris. *Transcultural Leadership*. Houston, TX: Gulf Publishing, 1993.

Stratfor. "Europe Comes to a Crossroads." Global Intelligence Update, 24 December 1999. Available at: http://www.stratfor.com.

Sullivan, Andrew. "There Will Always Be an England." *The New York Times Magazine*, 21 February 1999.

"Tales from Loire Valley." Available at: http://www.workforce.com/, 24 November 2000.

Zakaria, Fareed. "Across the Great Divide." *Newsweek Special Edition*, December 1999–February 2000:8.

Bibliography

Books

Abramms, Bob, and George Simons (eds). *The Cultural Diversity Sourcebook*. Amherst, MA: ODT Inc., 1996.

Elashmawi, Farid. *Competing Globally: Mastering Multicultural Management and Negotiations*. Boston: Butterworth–Heinemann, 2001.

Elashmawi, Farid, and Phillip R. Harris. *Multicultural Management 2000: Essential Cultural Insights for Global Business Success*. Boston: Butterworth–Heinemann, 1998.

Fraser, Nicholas. *The Voice of Modern Hatred: Encounters with Europe's New Right*. New York: Overlook Press, 2000.

Gopnik, Adam. *Paris to the Moon*. New York: Random House, 2001.

Hainsworth, Paul, ed. *Politics of the Extreme Right: From the Margins to the Mainstream*. New York: Continuum, 2000.

Harris, Phillip R., and Robert T. Moran. *Managing Cultural Differences, Fifth Edition*. Boston: Butterworth–Heinemann, 2000.

Katsioloudes, Marios. *Global Strategic Planning: Cultural Perspectives for Profit and Non-Profit Organizations*. Boston: Butterworth–Heinemann, 2001.

Kirton, Gill, and Anne-Marie Green. *The Dynamics of Managing Diversity: A Critical Approach*. Oxford: Butterworth–Heinemann, 2000.

Kopper, Enid, and Ralf Kiechl, eds., *Globalisierung: von der vision zur praxis*. Zurich: Versus Verlag, 1997.

Moran, Robert T., and David O. Braaten. *International Directory of Multicultural Resources*. Boston: Butterworth–Heinemann, 1996.

Moran, Robert T., David O. Braaten, and John E. Walsh. *International Business Case Studies for the Multicultural Marketplace*. Boston: Butterworth–Heinemann, 1994.

Moran, Robert T., Philip R. Harris, and William G. Stripp. *Developing the Global Organization: Strategies for Human Resource Professionals*. Boston: Butterworth–Heinemann, 1993.

Sears, Woodrow H., and Audrone Tamulionyte-Lentz. *Succeeding in Business in Central and Eastern Europe: A Guide to Cultures, Markets, and Practices*. Boston: Butterworth–Heinemann, 2001.

Simons, George, and Amy Zuckerman. *Working Together: How to Succeed in a Multicultural Workplace, Third Edition*. Menlo Park, CA: Crisp Publications, 2002.

Simons, George F., Carmen Vazquez, and Philip R. Harris. *Transcultural Leadership: Empowering the Diverse Workforce*. Boston: Butterworth–Heinemann, 1993.

Stripp, William G., and Robert T. Moran. *Dynamics of Successful International Business Negotiations*. Boston: Butterworth–Heinemann, 1991.

Wederspahn, Gary. *Intercultural Services: A Worldwide Buyer's Guide and Sourcebook*. Boston: Butterworth–Heinemann, 2000.

Titles from the Council of Europe Publishing Series

(All titles are available in French as well as English.)

Competences and Practices in European Local and Regional Cultural Policy (Studies and Texts No. 69) (2000).

Cultural Policies in Europe: Regions and Cultural Decentralisation (2000).

Diversity and Cohesion: New Challenges for the Integration of Immigrants and Minorities (2000).

The Emergence of Human Rights in Europe: An Anthology (2001).

Framework of Integration Policies (2000).

Linguistic Diversity for Democratic Citizenship in Europe: Proceedings, May 1999 (2000).

The Margin of Appreciation: Interpretation and Discretion under the European Convention on Human Rights (Human Rights Files No. 17) (2000).

Social Identity and the European Dimension: Intercultural Competence through Foreign Language Learning (2000).

Social Protection in the European Social Charter (Social Charter Monographs No. 7) (2000).

Teaching Twentieth-Century Women's History: A Classroom Approach (2000).

Articles

Coward, Ros, and Stuart Hall. "A Question of Identity." *The Observer*, 15 Oct 2000.

Finn, Peter. "German-Born Foreigners Wonder What It Takes to Be a True German." *International Herald Tribune*, 27 November 2000.

Fischer, Matthias. "The Uneasy Road to Successful Cross-Border Co-operations and Mergers." *SIETAR Europa Newsletter*, 2000:1.

Kohl, Karl Heinz. "Die andere Seite der Globalisierung: Über die fruchtbaren Spannungen zwischen den Kulturen." *Frankfurter algemeine Zeitung*, 14 November 2000.

Shaw, Graham. "Diversity in Europe," *Profiles in Diversity Journal*, Spring 2000:12. Centre for Diversity and Business, 2000. Available at: http://www.diversityandbusiness.com.

Zappi, Sylvia. "La société française semble moins crispée face a l'immigration." *Le Monde*, 10 August 2000.

Assessment and Training Materials

Simons George and Bob Abramms, eds. *The Questions of Diversity, Seventh Edition*. Assessment Tools for Individuals and Organizations. Amherst, MA: HRD Press, 1996.

Simons George, Selma Myers, and Jonamay Lambert, eds. *Global Competence: 50 Exercises for Succeeding in International Business*. Amherst, MA: HRD Press, 2000.

Internet Resources

Discussion Groups

Intercultural Insights discussion group at
http://www.groups.yahoo.com/group/interculturalinsights
The Delta Intercultural Academy at http://www.dialogin.com

Information Services and Online Newsletters

Arbeitsstelle Friedensforschung Bonn (AFB)
http://www.bonn.iz-soz.de/afb

Also known as the Peace Research Information Unit Bonn (PRIUB). Provides information and research on Peace issues and initiatives worldwide.

Crocobill
http://www.crocobill.com
Crocobill is a children's site focusing on learning about others.

David Michael
http://www.dmichael.co.uk/case.html
David Michael is a 30-year veteran of the London Metropolitan Police Service who has documented case studies of racism in the city.

Directorate General for Education and Culture
europa.eu.int/comm/dg10/publications
The website of the Directorate General for Education and Culture gives information on their publications.

Diversity at Work
http://www.diversityatwork.com/
This site is dedicated to helping managers and diversity practitioners find the information, support, and guidance they need to effectively implement diversity in the workplace.

Eures
http://www.europa.eu.int/comm/employment_social/elm/eures
European Employment Services aim to facilitate the free movement of workers within the 17 countries of the European Economic Area. Partners in the network include Public Employment Services, Trade Unions and Employer Organizations.

European Data Bank for Sustainable Development
http://www.sd-eudb.net
This website aims at providing lists and links of institutions and individuals involved in sustainable development between society and nature, North and South, and present and future generations.

KnowEurope.com
http://www.knoweurope.net
This is a commercial documentation service that presents articles in the original language or variant languages as well as in English translation.

Organization for Economic Cooperation and Development (OECD)
http://www.oecd.org
Helps governments tackle the economic, social, and governance challenges of a globalized economy.

Organization for Economic Cooperation and Development (OECD)
http://www.oecd.org/subject/ageing
The ageing of OECD societies over coming decades will require comprehensive reform addressing the fiscal, financial and labor market implications of ageing, as well as the implications for pension, social benefits and systems of health and long-term care. The OECD analyzes the challenges that ageing implies for Member countries in these policy domains.

The Council of Europe and Related Sites

Agenda 2000
http://www.europa.eu.int/comm/agenda2000
This server describes the enlargement of the European Union. It sets up the detailed strategy for strengthening and widening the Union in the early years of the twenty-first century.

CELEX (Communitatis Europae Lex; European Community Law)
http://www.europa.eu.int/celex/
This is a comprehensive and authoritative information source on European Community Law. This server provides legal acts including the founding treaties, binding and non-binding legislation, opinions and resolutions issued by European Union institutions, and the case law of the European Court of Justice.

Centre for European Economic Politics
http://www.uni-trier.de/infos/ew/home.htm
This site contains, in addition to economic and political data, the addresses of all European documentation centers.

Centre for Europe's Children
http://www.eurochild.gla.ac.uk
A reliable and comprehensive source of information on children's rights in Europe.

Committee of Ministers
http://www.cm.coe.int

This is the website of the Committee of Ministers of the Council of Europe, presenting this organ (role, activities, members, etc.), its calendar of activities, and its composition (Ministers for Foreign Affairs of the Member States of the Council of Europe and Permanent Representatives of the Council of Europe). This site also presents public texts (adopted texts, decisions, and statutory reports).

Committee of the Regions
http://www.cor.eu.int
Brief overview of the committee and its activities, its members, and its press center.

The Congress of the Local and Regional Authorities of Europe
http://www.coe.fr/cplre
The Congress of the Local and Regional Authorities of Europe is the consultative body that aims to preserve democracy and freedom in Member States as well as on the local and regional level. Since 1994, it has been helping new Member States of the organization toward establishing effective local and regional self-government. This site contains the structure, activities, programs, and projects of the Congress. It also provides the Congress yearbook with references to Member States, special guests, political groups or observers, and statutory texts and texts adopted by the Congress.

CORDIS (Community Research and Development Information Service)
http://www.cordis.lu
This is a European Commission information service providing efficient access to complete information on European Union research and exploitation possibilities (participation in E.U.-funded research program). CORDIS has 10 databases.

Council of European Municipalities and Regions (CEMR)
http://www.ccre.org
This site lists programs and activities of the Council of European Municipalities and Regions (CEMR).

Council of the European Union
http://www.ue.eu.int
This Web server of the Council of the European Union provides general information, a newsroom facility, common foreign and security policies, and information on justice and home affairs.

Council of Europe
http://www.coe.int
This is the main site of the Council of Europe. This site is divided into four sections: general presentation, activities, texts, and news. It presents the main websites of organs and Directorates of the Council of Europe. We list those we found most relevant to diversity.

Council of Europe, European Treaties
http://www.coe.fr/eng/legaltxt/treaties.htm
This site presents the European Conventions and Agreements and details the statutes of the Council of Europe with these headings: aims, membership, general, Committee of Ministers, Consultative Assembly, Secretariat, finance, privileges and immunities, amendments, final provisions, texts of a statutory character, partial agreements, and statutory resolution. This site also contains signatures and ratifications of each Member State.

Council of Europe and NGOs
http://www.coe.fr/ong/ngo.htm
A source of information about the relationship of the public sector to nongovernmental organizations.

Council of Europe and Personal Data Protection
http://www.legal.coe.int/dataprotection
Provides information on the legal issues surrounding data protection and privacy.

ECHO, European Commission Host Organisation
http://www.echo.lu
This server, "Information Market Europe WWW," is an interactive service of Directorate General XIII of the European Community whose aim is to provide the general public with information on European markets for multimedia content and electronic information services. This server is very complete because it provides articles and programs referring one to multimedia published throughout year.

Economic and Social Committee (ESC)
http://www.esc.eu.int
This site offers the organization, activities, and documents of the ESC, and allows the user to make a virtual tour of European institutions in Brussels.

Environment Policy
http://www.eea.dk/frlinks.htm
This server presents all possible links of the European Environment Agency.

ERCOMER (European Research Centre on Migration and Ethnic Relations)
http://www.ercomer.org/
This site lists all nongovernmental organizations (NGOs) as well as a list of all documentation centers on human rights.

European Science Foundation (ESF)
http://www.esf.org/
This is the site of a European scientific organization that works to promote the sciences; it contains complete information about this organization and its activities.

EU-Employers' Network
http://www.euen.co.uk./
A site created by 150 European employers who employ more than 2 million persons. This site could be very useful for employees because it contains the list of rights in case of layoff.

EUR-LEX
http://www.europa.eu.int/eur-lex/
This site of the European Community gives free access to important legal resources such as Union Treaties, legislation, the main Community texts, and the last 20 daily publications of the European Official Journal.

EUROPA
http://www.europa.eu.int/
This is a very interesting site on Europe that gives, among other things, a detailed and complete description of all European institutions with plenty of information about the political activities of the European Union.

European Agency for Safety and Health at Work
http://www.eu-osha.es
This agency is based in Bilbao, and its objective is to encourage improvements in the working environment; it gives scientific and economic information about health and safety at work.

European Bibliographic Database
http://www.analysys.com/race/
This site, which is based entirely on computing and new technologies, gives precious information on new databases and new communication channels.

European Centre for the Development of Vocational Training
http://www.cedefop.gr
This center has been involved in promoting and developing the vocational training of young people and the continuing training of adults. The center has published many reports, sponsored research in all Community Member States, and since 1985 has been organizing its programs of "study visits," which bring together vocational training specialists.

The European Centre for Global Interdependence and Solidarity
http://www.nscentre.org
This site is the website of the North South Centre in Lisboa, Portugal. It contains a presentation on the center (creation, objectives, member states, and the quadridialogue), public information and media relations programs, global education and youth programs, dialogue for global partnership program, and cross-dimensional projects.

European Citizens
http://www.citizens.eu.int
This site gives information about European citizens' rights. After the user has selected the country of origin and the country of interest, he or she may choose a subject of interest; the server provides information. Questions may also be sent by e-mail for assistance and resolution of problems.

European Commission Against Racism and Intolerance
http://www.ecri.coe.int
This is a very complete site lauding equality between people and encouraging the fight against racism. This field contains the main activities of the Council of Europe (Vienna Summit, plan of action, relevant speeches), a list of contact details of specialized bodies, research institutes, and intergovernmental organizations or NGOs active in these areas. Also, there is direct access to the legal framework and texts of the main relevant international legal instruments in the field of combating racism and intolerance. Finally, the site proposes examples of good practice and lists Council of Europe publications in the field of human rights.

European Committee for the Prevention of Torture and Inhuman or Degrading Treatment or Punishment
http://www.cpt.coe.int
This site presents, in its "What's new?" section, the latest events linked to CPT (Committee for the Prevention of Torture). It also presents the European Convention for the Prevention of Torture and Inhuman or Degrading Treatment or Punishment, and the program and press releases of visits organized by CPT in Member States since its beginning in 1990. Also, everyone has direct access to the full text of all reports published by the CPT on its visits to the Member States of the Council of Europe, the list of CPT members, and other public documents (reference documents, annual reports).

European Court of Auditors
http://www.eca.eu.int
This site provides a presentation of the European Court of Auditors, information, list of reports and opinions, social reports, and an organization chart.

European Court of Human Rights
http://www.echr.coe.int
This site contains general information about the Court (composition, organization and working of the Court, statistics), the list of pending cases and of scheduled public hearings, the list of judgments and their effects, all basic texts (conventions, protocols, and Rules of the Court), press releases, and, finally, speeches of sessions.

European Court of Justice
http://www.europa.eu.int/cj/
This site presents the Court of Justice and its activities as well as providing recent judgments, information on publications, and press releases.

European Environment Agency
http://www.eea.dk
The server of this agency (based in Denmark) gives information about its mission (protection and improvement of Europe's environment), its documents, and environmental events throughout the world.

European Governments
http://www.gksoft.com/govt/en/europa.html
This site contains the Internet addresses of all European governments. In addition, France's site provides information on French institutions

and the different ministries as well as the complete declaration of Human Rights and the Constitution. Moreover, site visitors can take a virtual tour of the Elysée and the presidential residences.

European Investment Bank (EIB)
http://www.eib.org
This site presents the EIB, describes its structure and role (mission, key data, EIB contacts), provides press releases, lists publications, and defines projects and how they are fulfilling their objectives.

European Monetary Institute (EMI)
http://www.europa.eu.int/emi/emi.html
This site contains information on the role of the EMI in promoting monetary union in Europe, including some full-text information and a list of EMI publications.

European Ombudsman
http://www.euro-ombudsman.eu.int
This site presents the procedure for lodging a complaint: who can complain, how, with whom, what happens to the complaint lodged, and how to make contact.

European Parliament
http://www.europarl.eu.int
The multilingual Web server of the European Parliament contains four groups: ABC: an overview of the European Parliament, useful addresses, etc.; Press: news, news reports, background information, etc.; Activities: sessions, committees, etc.; References: documents, bulletins, official journals, etc.

European Patent Office
http://www.european-patent-office.org/index.htm
This site contains information concerning patents (registration, attribution, etc.). It also gives a list of the best sites for engineers and scientists in search of a job.

European Regional Development Fund and Cohesion Fund
http://www.inforegio.org/wbover/over_fr.htm
The site of the European Regional Development Fund and Cohesion Fund gives national and regional information, and provides a glossary.

European Technology Transfer and Innovation Resources
http://www.argia.fr/evariste/europe

This site contains information about the theme of technology transfer and innovation in the 15 countries of the European Union. It refers to many other organizations such as CORDIS (Community Research and Development Information Service), Information Market, ESPRIT (European Strategic Programme for Research and Development in Information Technology), EUREKA (European Research Coordination Agency, an organization that promotes market-oriented research and development).

European Training Foundation
http://www.etf.it
This site promotes cooperation and coordination of assistance in the field of vocational training. It also provides information on programs for cooperation between the European Union and other countries (the Tempus program).

European Union/Documents and Publishing
http://www.europa.eu.int/comm/opoce
This server is a reference for the European Union's official documents.

European Youth Centre (EYC)
http://www.coe.fr/youth
This site is divided into five parts: the European Youth Centre (activities, annual program, EYC library and how to apply for activities), the European Youth Foundation (how to apply for a grant, mobility fund), intergovernmental program (recommendations of Committee of Ministers), youth research program, and many other links.

The Europe of Cultural Cooperation
http://www.culture.coe.int
This site presents aspects of Europe and cultural cooperation based on the European Cultural Convention. Here 47 Member States of this Convention are coordinating their activities in fields such as education, culture, cultural heritage, higher education, research, sport, and youth. The site gives access to all these fields (texts, events, and activities).

Europinion
http://www.europa.eu.int/en/comm/dg10/infcom/epo/eo/kw.html
Using key words or sentences, this site refers the readers to issues of EUROPINION, which documents results of monthly surveys of European opinion.

EUROTEXT
http://www.eurotext.ulst.ac.uk
A mine of information about the new measures taken by the European Union concerning work, the environment, education, health, etc.

Governmental Server
http://www.europa.eu.int/en/gonline.html
This site presents a list of Web addresses of governments and other official institutions of European Union Members States.

Green Book
http://europa.eu.int/comm/development/index.htm
This site presents the Green Book about relations between the European Union and ACP (African, Caribbean, and Pacific States) countries at the dawn of the twenty-first century.

Human Resources and Work
http://www.emplaw.co.uk/
This is a very useful site containing a wide range of information for employers, employees, and human resources professionals. There are various sections, such as holidays, discrimination, health and safety at work, layoff and short time, and wages.

Human Rights
http://www.humanrights.coe.int
This site contains information about the European Court of Human Rights, the European Commission on Human Rights, and the European Social Charter.

Information and Documentation Centres of the Council of Europe
http://www.coe.fr/eng/present/cid.htm
This site contains addresses of all Information and Documentation Centres of the Council of Europe.

International Law and International Organizations
http://www.gddc.pt/fr/dioifr/indexfr.htm
This site groups together Council of Europe, United Nations, European Cooperation and Safety Organization, humanitarian international law, the conference of the Hague on private international law, the International Institute for Unification of private law, and the Convention and Agreements in force concerning Portuguese juridical procedure.

The Introduction of the Euro
http://www.europa.eu.int/euro/
This server provides information to the European citizen about the introduction of a single currency and gives answers to questions and requests for information.

ISPO (Information Society Project Office)
http://www.ispo.cec.be
This server is a measure conceived to support, promote, and orient private and public actions in the field of the information society. Its interlocutors are entrepreneurs, administrations, universities, and other research bodies. ISPO helps all interested parties who need assistance and orientation and proposes a new marketplace of ideas.

Legal Aid
http://www.open.gov.uk/lab/legal.htm
"Legal aid" is a site for England and Wales that provides information for anyone faced with a legal problem, such as divorce, social security, family and children, claims, job and discrimination, credit and debt, accidents, medical negligence, and the like.

Legal Information in United Kingdom
http://www.pavilion.co.uk/legal/
This site contains many legal links within the United Kingdom: free legal information for individuals, free legal information for companies, and information for barristers and solicitors.

Legal Resources
http://www.argia.fr/lij/resourcesj3.html
This site has all you need to know about law and information and the NITs. Five sections group together information technologies and law in relation to information technologies, such as associations linked to the Internet, electronic legal journal, reports and articles, Europe and information technologies and law.

Legal WWW Site, European Resources
http://www.rabenou.org/web-europe.htm
This site contains a selection of addresses of sites on the European right.

Local Policy
http://www.elgo.co.uk/

European local government database (ELGO) is a unique information source for database marketing to 49,400 decision-makers in local and regional governments. ELGO covers 27 countries, including Central and Eastern Europe. This server presents many interesting links with European institutions and local governments' websites.

Office for Official Publications of the European Communities
http://www.eudor.com
This site gives the products (official journals, documents, etc.) of the Eudor, their tariffs, and procedures for ordering.

Organization for Economic Cooperation and Development (OECD)
http://www.oecd.fr
This site contains information on the OECD, including general background and work, members, news and events, statistics, reports of recent speeches and conferences, free publications, and a book shop and search.

Parliamentary Assembly of the Council of Europe
http://www.stars.coe.int
The statutory aim of the Council of Europe, which started with 10 Member States and now has 41, is to achieve greater unity among its members through debates, agreements, and common action.

Parliamentary Server
http://www.europarl.eu.int/dg4/cerdp/fr/public/assembly/list.htm
This is the site of the European Center for Parliamentary Research and Documentation (ECPRD). It presents the Parliamentary Assembly of the Council of Europe, the International Institute for Democracy, the European Parliament, and the Assembly of the Western European Union.

Prometheus-Europe Association
http://www.prom.org
This is the site of the Prometheus-Europe Association, which intends to help the process of European integration by creating prospective European and regional networks for information.

RAPID (The Press and Communication Service of the European Commission)
http://www.europa.eu.int/en/comm/spp/rapid.html
This server is the Spokesman's service of the European Commission and gives a day-by-day view of the activities of the European Union as

presented by the institutions in their press releases. A user name and a password are necessary to connect to RAPID.

Research Institute for European Affairs
http://www.fgr.wu-wien.ac.at/nentwich/euroint.htm
This site contains, among other things, many scientific texts in their full text version and many addresses of European economic sites.

SCADPlus
http://www.europa.eu.int/comm/sg/scadplus
This is a practical guide to a better understanding of the European Union. This server presents a calendar of European Institution meetings, summaries of European Union policies, information about free movement, social programs, and a glossary on institutional reform of the European Union.

Statistical Office of the European Communities
http://www.europa.eu.int/eurostat.html
This site is the statistical office of the European Communities: presentation of the office, products and databases, online statistical publications and indicators, data shop network, and press releases. The mission of this office is to provide the European Union with high-quality statistical information services.

United Nations High Commission for Refugees (UNHCR)
http://www.unhcr.ch
This site contains basic information about UNHCR and refugees: who are they? where are they? how can they live? Also, there are articles on specific themes, such as refugee children, environment, women, etc. Also available are back issues of *Refugees* magazine, official documentation of the HCR, and photographs of refugees around the world.

Useful Addresses List
http://www.esc.eu.int/fr/org/partners.htm
This site presents many electronic addresses for European Organizations (mainly regarding social issues) classified in five themes: employers, workers, various interests, economic and social Councils, and others. It also documents treaties and studies.

Online Articles

"Race Policy in France." U.S.-France Analysis by Erik Bleich for the Center on the United States and France (May 2001). Available at: http://www.brookings.edu/fp/cusf/analysis/race.htm.

"New forms of work organization and productivity." Business Decisions Limited. Available at: http://www.europe.eu.int/soc-dial/work.org/ewon/surveys/new-workorg-eng.pdf.

Appendix 1

Declaration on Cultural Diversity

Adopted by the Committee of Ministers at the 733rd meeting
On 7 December 2000

Preamble

The Committee of Ministers, Recognising that respect for cultural diversity is an essential condition of human society; Recognising that the development of new information technologies, globalisation, and evolving multilateral trade policies have an impact on cultural diversity; Reaffirming that to sustain, protect, and promote cultural co-operation and democratic norms and structures in European societies is a central task of the Council of Europe; Recalling that cultural diversity has always been a dominant European characteristic and a fundamental political objective in the process of European construction, and that it assumes particular importance in the building of an information- and knowledge-based society in the 21st century; Acknowledging that all democratic societies based on the rule of law have in the past developed measures to sustain and protect cultural diversity within their cultural and media policies; Aware of the tradition of the Council of Europe to protect and foster cultural diversity and recalling, in this context, the instruments already developed by the Organisation on the basis of the European Convention on Human Rights and the European Cultural Convention; Emphasising that, in the context of global market influences on cultures and cultural exchange, modern democratic states have a new challenge: the development of policies for assuring the recognition and expression of forms of cultural diversity coexisting within their jurisdictions; Recalling the commitments of the Member States of the Council of Europe to defend and promote media freedoms and media pluralism as a basic precondition for cultural exchange, and affirming that media pluralism is essential for democracy and cultural diversity; Recalling in this respect the important contribution made by public service broadcasters; Convinced that all Member States and other States Party to the European Cultural Convention must confront this challenge from a culturally distinct perspective, but that the shared global context for development requires the elaboration of a set of principles which will provide a coherent framework for sustaining and enabling cultural diversity at all levels; Affirms that the legitimate objectives of Member States to develop international agreements for cultural co-operation, which promote cultural diversity, must be respected, Declares the following:

1. Cultural Diversity

1.1. Cultural diversity is expressed in the co-existence and exchange of culturally different practices and in the provision and consumption of culturally different services and products;

1.2. Cultural diversity cannot be expressed without the conditions for free creative expression and freedom of information existing in all forms of cultural exchange, notably with respect to audio-visual services;

1.3. Sustainable development, as defined in relation to cultural diversity, assumes that technological and other developments, which occur to meet the needs of the present, will not compromise the ability of future generations to meet their needs with respect to the production, provision, and exchange of culturally diverse services, products, and practices.

2. Cultural and Audio-Visual Policies for Sustainable Cultural Diversity in a Global World

2.1. Cultural and audio-visual policies, which promote and respect cultural diversity, are a necessary complement to trade policies;

2.2. Cultural diversity has an essential economic role to play in the development of the knowledge economy. Strong cultural industries, which encourage linguistic diversity and artistic expression when reflecting genuine diversity, have a positive impact on pluralism, innovation, competitiveness, and employment;

2.3. Culturally diverse forms of production and practices should not be limited but enhanced by technological developments;

2.4. Wide distribution of diverse cultural products and services, and exchange of cultural practices in general, can stimulate creativity, enhance access to, and widen the provision of such products and services;

2.5. Public service broadcasting plays an important role for the safeguarding of cultural diversity;

2.6. Education, training of professionals, and users of new services, and reinforcement of cultural and audio-visual production, are notable factors in the promotion of cultural diversity.

3. Sustaining and Enabling Cultural Diversity

3.1. Member States are called upon to examine ways of sustaining and promoting cultural and linguistic diversity in the new global environment, at all levels;

3.2. Member states are urged to pay particular attention to the need to sustain and promote cultural diversity, in line with the relevant Council of Europe instruments, in other international fora where they might be called on to undertake commitments which might prejudice these instruments;

3.3. The competent organs of the Council of Europe are requested to identify those aspects of cultural policy which are in need of special consideration in the context of the new global economy, and to elaborate a catalogue of measures which may be useful to member states in their quest to sustain and enable cultural diversity;

3.4. The Committee of Ministers agrees to review the situation at regular intervals.

Appendix 2

Commission of the European Communities

Brussels, 14.04.2000
© (2000) 853

COMMUNICATION FROM THE COMMISSION
TO THE MEMBER STATES

establishing the guidelines for the Community Initiative EQUAL concerning transnational cooperation to promote new means of combating all forms of discrimination and inequalities in connection with the labour market

1. On 14 April 2000, the Commission of the European Communities approved these guidelines for the Community Initiative entitled EQUAL.

2. Under EQUAL Community funding, in the form of European Social Fund (ESF), grants will be made available for activities which respect the guidelines laid down in this notice, and which are included in proposals presented by each Member State and approved by the Commission of the European Communities in the form of Community Initiative programmes (CIPs). EQUAL applies to the whole territory of the European Union.

I. AIM

3. The aim of EQUAL is to promote new means of combating all forms of discrimination and inequalities in connection with the

labour market, through transnational cooperation. EQUAL will also take due account of the social and vocational integration of asylum seekers.

II. POLICY CONTEXT

4. The growing interdependence of Member State economies has led to the inclusion of a new Title on employment in the Amsterdam Treaty. This provides for a co-ordinated strategy for employment and the adoption of guidelines which the Member States take into account in their employment policies. The employment guidelines (based on the four pillars of Employability, Entrepreneurship, Adaptability, and Equal Opportunities) and their transformation by the Member States into National Action Plans for employment (NAPs) provide the framework for financial support at EU level, in particular through the Structural Funds.

5. The European Employment Strategy has the goal of achieving a high level of employment for all groups in the labour market. To achieve this, the development of the skills and employability of those currently outside the labour market is essential. The skills of those already in work, especially in exposed or vulnerable sectors, must also be renewed and updated. Furthermore, the capacity for entrepreneurship must be broadened. The equal participation of women and men in the labour market must also be ensured. This requires action to counter inequality and discrimination suffered by both the jobless and the employed.

6. To be fully effective, the European Employment Strategy must be translated into action at the local and regional level, in urban and rural districts—that is to say, at the level of territories able to generate local cooperation. It requires new approaches to shared priorities and the effective dissemination of successful ideas.

7. The European Social Fund (ESF) is one of the Structural Funds, along with those dealing with agriculture and regional development. The ESF is concerned with measures to prevent and combat unemployment and to develop human resources and promote equal opportunities for all in accessing the labour market. In particular, it is intended to contribute to action which supports the European Employment Strategy.

8. At the Community level there is an integrated strategy to combat discrimination (in particular that based on sex, racial or ethnic origin, religion or belief, disability, age, or sexual orientation) and

social exclusion. Focusing on the labour market, EQUAL will form part of that strategy. It will be complementary to other policies, instruments and actions developed in this respect and which go beyond the labour market area and, in particular, the specific legislation and action programmes under Articles 13 and 137 of the Treaty. The Commission and the Member States will ensure coherence between EQUAL and such activities. EQUAL will, therefore, play a key role in linking together the EU supported actions under Articles 13 and 137, the ESF supported programmes, and the political objectives pursued in the framework of the European Employment Strategy.

III. GENERAL PRINCIPLES

Introduction

9. Building on lessons learned under the EMPLOYMENT and ADAPT programmes, EQUAL will act as a testing ground to develop and disseminate new ways of delivering employment policies in order to combat all sorts of discrimination and inequality experienced by those seeking access to the labour market and those already within it. The particular needs of asylum seekers will be addressed, taking into account their specific situation.

10. EQUAL will operate in a number of thematic fields, defined in the context of the four pillars of the employment strategy and following discussion with the Member States. These are the priority fields where groups of Member States consider that transnational cooperation will assist them in improving ways of delivering their national policies. In accordance with Article 1 of Regulation (EC) No. 1260/1999,[1] and the European employment guidelines, Member States will adopt a gender mainstreaming approach in each thematic field.

11. EQUAL will be implemented by partnerships established at geographical or sectoral level and called Development Partnerships (DPs). The partners within the DPs will define and agree on a strategy to be followed, along with the means of bringing it to fruition using innovative approaches. DPs will undertake

---

[1] Council Regulation (EC) No. 1260/1999 of 21 June 1999 laying down general provisions on the Structural Funds.

transnational cooperation and participate in the dissemination and mainstreaming of good practice.

12. The successful innovation developed under EQUAL should be disseminated widely in order to achieve the maximum impact on policy, and, where appropriate, it should be incorporated into the Objective 1, 2, and 3 Structural Fund programmes and the NAPs.

13. EQUAL will be distinguished from the Objective 1, 2, and 3 Structural Fund programmes by its focus on testing new ways of delivery for policy priorities in the framework of the European Employment Strategy and by the emphasis on partnership in a context of transnational cooperation.

Thematic Approach

14. Member States shall formulate their strategy for EQUAL on the basis of thematic fields in the four pillars of the European Employment strategy. Within these fields Member States shall ensure that their proposals principally benefit those subject to the main forms of discrimination (based on sex, racial or ethnic origin, religion or belief, disability, age, or sexual orientation) and inequality. Each thematic field shall be fully accessible to all such groups. Within this horizontal approach, the promotion of equality between women and men will be integral to the thematic fields in all four pillars as well as being targeted through specific actions in the fourth pillar.

15. The thematic fields, which will serve as the basis for the first call for proposals, are set out below. The list of thematic fields may be reviewed, before subsequent calls for proposals, to take account of developments in the labour market and in the employment guidelines. Proposals for revised thematic fields will be put forward by the Commission following the necessary consultations. They will be submitted for agreement to the Committee pursuant to Article 147 of the Treaty, after discussion in the Employment Committee, and presented to the European Parliament.

Thematic Fields for the First Call for Proposals

16. In setting out their strategy, based on these themes, Member States should have in mind the ideal of improving the supply of and demand for quality jobs with a future. They should also encourage

the effective use of existing mechanisms (for example, those that exist for social dialogue) to sensitise those in the labour market to the factors leading to discrimination, inequality, and exclusion for certain groups in connection with the labour market.

Employability

a) Facilitating access and return to the labour market for those who have difficulty in being integrated or re-integrated into a labour market which must be open to all

b) Combating racism and xenophobia in relation to the labour market

Entrepreneurship

c) Opening up the business-creation process to all by providing the tools required for setting up in business and for the identification and exploitation of new possibilities for creating employment in urban and rural areas

d) Strengthening the social economy (the third sector), in particular the services of interest to the community, with a focus on improving the quality of jobs

Adaptability

e) Promoting lifelong learning and inclusive work practices which encourage the recruitment and retention of those suffering discrimination and inequality in connection with the labour market

f) Supporting the adaptability of firms and employees to structural economic change and the use of information technology and other new technologies

Equal Opportunities for Women and Men

g) Reconciling family and professional life, as well as the re-integration of men and women who have left the labour market, by developing more flexible and effective forms of work organisation and support services

h) Reducing gender gaps and supporting job desegregation.

17. Member States will select only the thematic fields in which they want to cooperate. In addition, each Member State must plan at

least a minimum level of action aimed at asylum seekers, in line with the dimensions of the problem in the Member State.

18. Normally Member States will be expected to choose at least one thematic field in each pillar for each call for proposals. Exceptionally, the Commission may agree to a reduction in this requirement in a Member State.

Asylum Seekers

19. The position of asylum seekers within the Union is complex. They may be divided essentially into three categories:[2]

   - those whose application for asylum is under consideration by the Member State concerned;

   - those who have been admitted under a humanitarian resettlement or evacuation programme or who benefit from a temporary protection arrangement;

   - those who have not been granted refugee status, but who benefit from another form of protection (complementary or subsidiary protection) because their individual situation prevents their return to their country of origin.

20. In the majority of Member States, access to the labour market by asylum seekers as such (the first category above) is either forbidden or hedged around with very restrictive conditions. As regards the latter two categories, however, Member States have shown themselves more willing to consider access to the labour market. It could also be noted that in the Joint Action of 26 April 1999, the Council recognised the desirability of helping asylum seekers who face repatriation with education and training, which would give them skills useful in their home country.[3] It is important that this state of affairs be respected in implementing the "asylum seeker" element in EQUAL.

---

[2] Refugees are not included under this heading because, as long-term residents, they are eligible under normal EQUAL Development Partnerships.

[3] JOINT ACTION of 26 April 1999 adopted by the Council on the basis of Article K.3 of the Treaty on European Union, establishing projects and measures to provide practical support in relation to the reception and voluntary repatriation of refugees, displaced persons, and asylum seekers, including emergency assistance to persons who have fled as a result of recent events in Kosovo: OJ L114/2 of 1 May 1999; cf. Article 5 ©.

21. Action in respect of asylum seekers may be programmed either as a sectoral DP (i.e., a national partnership, involving all the appropriate partners to support social and vocational integration for asylum seekers), or as a geographical DP in a territory where there is a high concentration of asylum seekers. The same types of partnership, strategy, and activity should be envisaged as for other EQUAL development partnerships.

Partnership Approach

22. EQUAL will fund activities implemented by strategic partnerships. The EQUAL partnerships will operate within the thematic fields and will be called Development Partnerships (DPs). They will bring together interested actors, with relevant competence, who will cooperate to develop an integrated approach to multi-dimensional problems. The partners shall work together to identify the factors leading to inequality and discrimination in connection with the labour market within their chosen thematic field/s. They shall pool their efforts and resources in pursuit of innovative solutions to jointly defined problems and common goals.

23. DPs should have a core of partners from the outset. They should also ensure that relevant actors, such as public authorities, the public employment service, non-governmental organisations (NGOs), the business sector (in particular SMEs), and the social partners, can become involved during the life of the partnership. Small organisations with innovative ideas must be able to make their contribution by participating fully in DPs. The experience of EMPLOYMENT and ADAPT has shown the importance of involving local and regional authorities to ensure coherence between the planned activities and the development needs of the territory. Their participation will also strengthen the probability of mainstreaming the results.

24. DPs may be geographically based, bringing together relevant actors in a given geographical area. These will be known as *geographical partnerships*. Geographical partnerships may not always be the most effective way to tackle an identified problem, and other forms of partnership are possible within the above guidelines. These could cover particular economic sectors or industries. If justified, they might equally relate mainly to one or more specific group amongst those subject to discrimination or inequality in connection with the labour market. These other partnerships will be known as *sectoral partnerships*.

25. Under EQUAL, the final beneficiaries are the DPs, as already described in § 22–24 above. At the point of application for EQUAL funding, each DP must have arrangements for ensuring that the administrative and financial responsibilities are handled by an organisation which has the capacity to manage and account for public funding.

Empowerment

26. The principle of empowerment will be central to each DP. In practice this will mean that those involved in the implementation of activities should also take part in the decision-making. On the other hand, the active participation of those targeted for assistance should be positively assessed in the selection for Action 1 funding and the confirmation of selection for Action 2.

Transnational Cooperation

27. EQUAL will be based on the principle of transnational cooperation. The experience gained under the Community Initiatives EMPLOYMENT and ADAPT shows that transnationality is a dimension which can bring significant added-value to project operators working with others in similar situations. In addition, it shows that considerable policy innovation can be achieved through transnational cooperation. Transnationality will, therefore, be an essential element of EQUAL.

Innovation

28. EQUAL will test innovative approaches to policy delivery. These may be completely new approaches, or the transfer of elements from elsewhere, which increase the effectiveness of policy delivery.

29. The definition of innovation in EQUAL is based on the typology which emerged from the evaluation of EMPLOYMENT and ADAPT and which differentiated between three types of innovation:

- process-oriented innovations will cover the development of new methods, tools, or approaches as well as the improvement of existing methods;
- goal-oriented innovations will centre around the formulation of new objectives, and innovation could include approaches to

identify new and promising qualifications and the opening up of new areas of employment for the labour market;

- context-oriented innovations relate to political and institutional structures. Context-oriented innovations will be concerned with system development in connection with the labour market.

Mainstreaming

30. EQUAL will fund the development of innovative solutions to the delivery of the policy priorities of Member States as set out in their NAPs. In order to obtain the maximum impact from EQUAL, the results must be analysed, benchmarked, and disseminated both within Member States and across the Union. It is important that policy makers, in particular those in charge of the NAPs, and those involved in the Objective 1, 2, and 3 Structural Fund Programmes, receive input from EQUAL.

IV.   ACTIONS TO BE FUNDED BY EQUAL

31. EQUAL will fund activity under the following four actions:

Action 1: setting up Development Partnerships and transnational cooperation.

Action 2: implementing the work programmes of the Development Partnerships.

Action 3: thematic networking, dissemination of good practice, and making an impact on national policy.

Action 4: Technical Assistance to support actions 1, 2, and 3.

Actions 1 and 2 are sequential. Member States will be expected to be in a position to start Action 3 at the earliest point that results are available to disseminate. Action 4 will provide support from before the commencement of Action 1.

Action 1: Setting Up Development Partnerships and Transnational Cooperation

32. The objective of Action 1 is to facilitate the creation or the consolidation of durable, effective Development Partnerships (DPs)

and to ensure that transnational cooperation will have a real added-value. The time period available for this Action will be decided by the managing authority but would not normally exceed 6 months. Overall, the Commission would not expect Action 1 to represent a significant part of total funds available to the Member State.

33. Selection for Action 1 will be the main stage in selection for funding under EQUAL. It will be based upon an application submitted jointly by a number of organisations (DP initiators). In the context of the thematic field and territory/sector of operation, the application should identify:

    - the partners to be involved in the DP at the outset; the arrangements for ensuring that all relevant partners can become involved during the life of the partnership, including, in particular, appropriate small organisations; and the arrangements for handling the administrative and financial responsibilities;

    - the rationale for the partnership, a diagnosis of the problem to be addressed, and an explanation of how the needs of all the potential beneficiary groups will be taken into account;

    - the objectives of the partnership;

    - a work programme for Action 1;

    - the nature of the activities they intend to implement in Action 2;

    - the expectations for the transnational cooperation.

34. Whilst the procedures for selecting Development Partnerships fall within the competence of the managing authority, in cooperation with the monitoring committee of the CIP, the Commission would expect selection criteria to reflect the general principles of EQUAL, which are explained in Section III. Unsuccessful applicants should be given reasons for their non-selection.

35. At the end of Action 1, the DP should be able to present a common strategy in the form of a *Development Partnership Agreement*. As a minimum this should contain:

    - an assessment of current labour market exclusion, discrimination, and inequality, within the thematic field and territory/sector concerned;

    - objectives and priorities for action, reflecting the learning from previous relevant action in the territory/sector;

- a detailed work programme accompanied by a realistic budget;
- a clear identification of the role of each partner, including the arrangements for steering and managing the partnership and administering the financial support;
- a mechanism for on-going assessment, including the presentation of data and information on the DP and the analysis of results;
- the commitment of the DP to collaborate on Action 3;
- its strategy and mechanisms for implementing a gender mainstreaming approach.

Transnational Cooperation

36. DPs must identify at least one partner from another Member State. As a general rule, cooperation should be established between DPs selected by the Member States under EQUAL, and preferably those working in the same thematic field; such cooperation may also extend to similar projects supported in a non-Member State eligible for funding under the *Phare*, *Tacis*, or *Meda* programmes. The CIP proposal may define parameters for exceptions to the general rule, subject to the condition that the potential value added of cooperation with partners outside EQUAL is clearly identified, and that these partners are able to demonstrate their capacity to cover their own costs incurred by this cooperation.

37. At the end of Action 1, the DP should set out in the form of a *Transnational Cooperation Agreement:*

- a transnational work programme accompanied by a budget;
- the role of each transnational partner, the common methods of decision making, and the organisational arrangements for implementing the common work programme;
- the methodologies for monitoring and assessment of joint activities.

Action 2: Implementation of the Work Programmes of Development Partnerships

38. In order to have selection confirmed and to receive funding to implement its work programme through Action 2 of EQUAL, each Development Partnership must submit two documents, a Development Partnership Agreement and a Transnational

Cooperation Agreement, which meet the criteria set out under Action 1. These documents must also demonstrate that the DP fulfils the following conditions:

- *Transparency:* the DP must demonstrate the availability of the necessary co-financing. The DP must also accept that the results obtained (products, instruments, methods, etc.) will be public property.

- *Representative capacity:* the DP must be able to demonstrate its capacity to mobilise different actors in order that they work together. Particular attention will be given to the arrangements for ensuring that all relevant actors, such as public authorities, the public employment service, NGOs, the business sector (inparticular SMEs), and the social partners, can become involved during the life of the partnership. The DP must show that appropriate small organisations are able to participate fully.

- *Cooperative spirit:* the DP must be able to demonstrate its capacity and its willingness to work in a context of transnational cooperation, and explain the expected value added of transnational cooperation in implementing the different components of the work programme. In addition, the DP must plan to cooperate in networking, dissemination, and mainstreaming activities at both the national and European level.

39. If the conditions in § 38 are fulfilled, the managing authority will confirm the initial selection of the Partnership, and notify it of the multi-annual budget available to implement its work programme.

40. This work programme would normally cover an initial period of 2 to 3 years. However, if the results obtained justify an extension, a further grant could be approved, along with an extension of the period of financing for the DP.

Eligibility of Activities

41. The normal eligibility rules of the ESF apply (cf. Article 3 of the ESF Regulation[4]). However, in order to achieve the maximum effectiveness of activities EQUAL may fund action normally eligible under the ERDF, EAGGF Guidance, or FIFG rules (Article 21(2) of Regulation (EC) No. 1260/1999).

---

[4] Regulation (EC) No. 1784/1999 of the European Parliament and of the Council of 12 July 1999 on the European Social Fund (OJ L 213, 13.8.1999).

42. Member States shall check the activities of the DPs for compatibility with the provisions of the Treaty, in particular with the state aid provisions, and if necessary notify them under Article 88(3).

Action 3: Thematic Networking, Dissemination of Good Practice, and Making an Impact on National Policy

43. There will be a separate action for networking, dissemination, and mainstreaming activities within EQUAL. Participation in this Action shall be mandatory for all DPs in order to ensure the mainstreaming impact that EQUAL seeks. It shall be organised under the responsibility of the Managing Authority in such a way as to facilitate maximum input into labour market and employment policy, and should involve the social partners.

44. Member States shall establish mechanisms which will facilitate mainstreaming at both the horizontal level (the level of organisations active in the same or a similar field) and the vertical level (the level of regional and national policy, including the NAP and the Structural Funds). These mechanisms should aim at:

    • identifying factors leading to inequality and discrimination, and monitoring and analysing the impact or potential impact of the DPs on the policy priorities set out in the NAP and on the different groups subject to discrimination and inequality in connection with the labour market;

    • identifying and assessing the factors leading to good practice and benchmarking their performance;

    • disseminating good practice, from the end of Action 1.

45. These activities will normally involve DPs acting either singly or in groups on the basis of their specific expertise and proven capacity. For this purpose, these DPs would receive additional funding.

Action 4: Technical Assistance

46. Technical assistance will be available to support the implementation of the CIP and will be used particularly:

    • to advise on and facilitate the consolidation of partnerships and the search for suitable transnational cooperation partners (Action 1);

- to collect, edit, and disseminate the experience and results, including annual reports of the DPs (Action 2);

- to support the thematic networking, the horizontal dissemination activities, and the setting up of mechanisms for policy impact (Action 3);

- for cooperation in European networking and to ensure the sharing of all relevant information with the other Member States and the Commission (cf. V. Actions at European Level).

47. Technical assistance will also be available to support the monitoring, audit, and evaluation of actions both within Member States and at the European level.

48. The budget for technical assistance may not exceed 5% of the total ESF contribution to the CIP. The ESF rate of contribution will be subject to the ceilings in Article 29(3) of Regulation (EC) No. 1260/1999.

49. Member States will apply their own procedures to the selection and funding of those who will carry out Technical Assistance activities in a transparent way.

V. DISSEMINATION AND EVALUATION AT EUROPEAN LEVEL

50. If EQUAL is to fully play its role as a testing ground for developing and promoting new ways of delivering employment policies, there will need to be close cooperation between Member States and social partners and the Commission to successfully exploit the potential for impact on the European Employment Strategy of good practice identified all over the Union.

51. Evaluation of the impact of EQUAL is crucial. At the Union level, the Commission will set up an evaluation mechanism, to assess the implications of EQUAL for the European Employment Strategy and other Community programmes.

52. The Commission proposes implementing three types of action to support the process of creating an impact at the Union level:

- thematic review at the Union level;

- a periodic assessment of the value added by EQUAL in relation to the National Action Plans for Employment (NAP);

- the use of discussion fora at the Union level.

Thematic Review

53. In order to disseminate good practice and benchmark the achievements, the Commission will organise a series of "thematic reviews" with clusters of Development Partnerships for each of the EQUAL thematic fields.

54. The results will be summarised and made public, and will be used to enrich the policy peer reviews set up in the context of the European Employment Strategy, the evaluation activities at Union level, and the dissemination and exchange activities planned in the Community Programmes under Articles 13 (fight against discrimination) and 137 (in favour of social inclusion) of the Treaty. Candidate countries will be associated with the discussion and exploitation of the results.

Periodic Assessment—EQUAL and the NAPs

55. On the basis of the activities undertaken in the framework of Action 3 in each of the Member States, and data and information collected from DPs by Member States, the Commission will establish a database of good practice under EQUAL. The information can be used as a basis for periodic assessment of the actual and potential impact on the NAPs. These assessments should be presented for information to the Objective 1, 2, and 3 Structural Fund monitoring committees and be taken into account in the implementation of the European Social Fund.

Discussion Fora

56. EQUAL will be discussed in a number of existing fora:

- the Employment Committee will be kept informed of the results and on the review of the thematic fields;
- the Committee, pursuant to Article 147 of the Treaty, will deliver its opinion on the result of the review of the thematic fields and respond to specific questions referred by the Commission;
- a forum for the discussion of EQUAL will be organised on an annual basis with the existing NGO platform at Union level in order to facilitate discussions and feedback from the organisations concerned.

If required, the Commission will organise meetings focussing on more specific issues under EQUAL, such as the transfer of good practice to policies in candidate countries.

Technical Assistance

57. The successful implementation of EQUAL demands a significant amount of collaboration between Member states and the Commission: collecting and processing information about Development Partnerships, setting up databases, animating the thematic review process, organising seminars, publicising results, etc. A certain number of specific tasks which cannot take place without support at the European level will be assigned to outside service providers, at the initiative and under the supervision of the Commission, on the basis of calls for tender to be published in the Official Journal of the European Communities. The execution of these tasks shall be financed at a rate of 100% of the total cost.

VI. PREPARATION, PRESENTATION, AND APPROVAL OF PROGRAMMES

58. Section III of this Notice sets out the general principles within which EQUAL will operate. This section sets out the elements which the Commission expects to see in the programme proposals to be presented by the designated authorities in Member States in consultation with the appropriate partners. The financial and administrative management of the CIP fall entirely within the competence of the designated managing authority, in cooperation with the Monitoring Committee of the CIP.

59. On the basis of the indicative financial allocations per Member State, adopted by the Commission, Member States should propose their draft Community Initiative Programmes (CIPs) for EQUAL. These proposals should meet the requirements set out in Article 16 of Regulation (EC) No. 1260/1999. The CIPs will take the form of a Single Programming Document, supplemented by a Programme Complement, as provided for in Article 19(3) of Regulation (EC) No. 1260/1999. The priorities in the CIP proposals will be taken from the list of thematic fields set out in § 16 above. The Actions outlined in Section IV should be considered as the measures within those priorities.

60. Member States will be expected to introduce a gender perspective in the programming, implementing, monitoring, and evaluating phases of EQUAL.

CIP Proposals

61. *The proposal for a CIP put forward by the Member States shall contain the following:*

- A description of the current situation as regards discrimination and inequality in the labour market in relation to the chosen themes, and as regards asylum seekers;

- An evaluation of the expected impact, including on the social and economic situation at the local or sectoral level, and on the situation in terms of equality between men and women, in accordance with Article 41(2) of Regulation (EC) No. 1260/1999;

- A description of the strategy for the implementation of EQUAL, based on the selection of priorities, from the list in § 16, plus specific action focused on asylum seekers (cf. § 19–21 above). This should include specific objectives, quantified where they lend themselves to quantification;

- A description of the relationship between the strategy and the prevailing NAP as interpreted in the policy frame of reference referred to in Article 1 of Regulation (EC) No. 1260/1999;

- A synthesis of the lessons learnt from ADAPT and EMPLOYMENT for the selected thematic priorities;

- A summary of arrangements to ensure complementarity between EQUAL and other Community instruments and programmes and the Territorial Employment Pacts;

- A summary description of the measures planned to implement the priorities and the information needed to check the compliance with Article 87 of the Treaty;

- An indication of whether and to what extent the actions proposed under each priority will contain activities normally eligible under the ERDF, EAGGF, or FIFG (Article 21(2) of Regulation (EC) No. 1260/1999), to enable the Commission to make the appropriate provision in its Decision on the CIP proposal;

- A description of the arrangements for technical assistance expected to be required to implement the CIP; both the types of activities and the procedures for selecting those who will carry them out;

- An indicative financing plan specifying for each priority and each year, in accordance with Article 19(3)(c) of Regulation (EC) No. 1260/1999, the financial allocation envisaged for the contribution of the ESF, as well as the total amount of eligible public or equivalent and estimated private funding relating to the ESF contribution;
- A description of the actions and methods planned to implement the gender mainstreaming approach effectively;
- An account of the process of programming, including the arrangements made to consult partners, including those with a specific interest in the main areas of discrimination or inequality, and the social partners, and the results of the consultations;
- Provisions for the implementation, monitoring, and evaluation of the CIPs as described below.

Provisions for the Implementation, Monitoring, and Evaluation of CIPs

62. The provisions for implementing, monitoring, and evaluating the CIP shall be set out, in line with the requirements in Article 19(3)(d) of Regulation (EC) 1260/1999. In addition, the CIP should cover the following:

- a description of the mechanism for at least two calls for proposals (procedures for publicity, guidelines, and procedures for selection, including appeals);
- types of contracts with final beneficiaries;
- national mechanisms to facilitate mainstreaming at both the horizontal and vertical levels, as described in Action 3;
- arrangements to ensure that the Monitoring Committee membership provides for the involvement of the social partners and those people with direct experience of the main forms of discrimination and inequality in connection with the labour market, including relevant representative NGOs;
- the type and amount of data and information that DPs will be required to produce each year for on-going monitoring, and the mechanisms for assessment within the DP;
- the mid-term evaluation, at the level of the CIP, which will be launched, upon adoption, to ensure continuous feedback for any readjustments necessary for successive calls for proposals. The CIP will indicate the specific parameters and quantitative

and qualitative indicators to be taken into account for the mid-term evaluation and the final assessment, in line with common minimum requirements for all Member States.

Presentation and Approval of CIPs

63. These draft CIPs shall be submitted to the Commission by the Member States within four months of the date of publication of this notice in the Official Journal. A five-month period for negotiation with the Commission will follow.

64. In accordance with Article 28 of Regulation (EC) No. 1260/1999, the Commission will approve each CIP by means of a Decision confirming the allocation of ESF funding to each priority it contains.

65. Each CIP shall be supplemented by a programme complement, as defined in Article 9(m) and described in Article 18(3) of Regulation (EC) 1260/1999.

66. The programme complement will be sent to the Commission no later than three months after the Commission Decision approving the CIP. However, in order to simplify the process, Member States are encouraged to send this at the same time as the draft CIP.

VII. FINANCING

67. The EQUAL Initiative will be jointly financed by the Member States and the European Community. The total contribution of the European Social Fund to EQUAL for the 2000–2006 period is 2,847 million euros. In accordance with Article 7(7) of Regulation (EC) 1260/1999, the ESF contribution to EQUAL shall take account of the rate of indexation of 2% a year up to 2003, and shall be decided at 2003 prices for the years 2004 to 2006. By 31 December 2003, the Commission shall determine the rate of indexation applicable for 2004 to 2006.

68. The rates of Community contribution defined in Article 29 of the Regulation (EC) No. 1260/1999 will apply. In view of the innovative nature of the methods used, a systematic application of the ceilings indicated in the Regulations is recommended.

69. An indicative amount of a maximum of 2% of the total ESF contribution will be reserved to finance activities carried out at the initiative of the Commission as set out in Section V. These activities shall be financed at a rate of 100% of the total cost.

VIII. TIMING

70. The Commission invites Member States to present their draft Community Initiative Programme for EQUAL within 4 months of the date of publication of this notice in the Official Journal.

Address for all correspondence concerning this communication:

Mr. A. LARSSON
Director General
Directorate General Employment and Social Affairs
Rue de la Loi, 200
B-1049 Brussels, Belgium

Done at Brussels, 14.04.2000.

Appendix 3

Declaration on a European Policy for New Information Technologies, Budapest, 7 May 1999

(Adopted by the Committee of Ministers on 7 May 1999 at its 104th Session)

The Committee of Ministers, On the occasion of the 50th anniversary of the Council of Europe; In response to the decision of the Council of Europe's Second Summit to develop a European policy for the application of new information technologies with a view to ensuring respect for human rights, promoting cultural diversity, fostering freedom of expression and information, and maximising the educational and cultural potential of these technologies; Taking into consideration all relevant international texts in this field, including those which have come into being since the Second Summit, notably the political texts adopted in Thessalonika by the 5th European Ministerial Conference on Mass Media Policy (December 1997) and Resolution 53/70 adopted by the General Assembly of the United Nations (December 1998); Conscious of the profound changes brought about by the digitalisation, convergence, and continuing globalisation of information networks; Welcoming the opportunities offered by the new information technologies to promote freedom of expression and information, political pluralism, and cultural diversity, and to contribute to a more democratic and sustainable information society; Recognising the potential of new information technologies to improve openness, transparency, and efficiency at all levels—national, regional, and local—of the governance, administration, and judicial systems of Member States and hence to consolidate democratic stability; Aware also of the potential risks involved in the use of these technologies for both individuals and democratic society; Convinced that a clear regulatory framework will help to promote those opportunities and avoid those risks; Acknowledging the important role of the private sector in the creation, development, and use of the new information technologies, and wishing to foster partnership between the public and private sectors to maximise the benefit of these technologies to their societies; Convinced that a genuinely democratic information society based on the core values of the Council of Europe can be achieved through a policy framework encouraging Access and Participation, Competence and Empowerment, Creativity, Diversity, and ensuring Protection; Urges the governments of Member States, acting, where appropriate, with public and private partners,

(i) With respect to Access to and Participation in new information technologies

— to promote the broadest possible access for all to the new information and communication services, for example, through the development of widespread access points in public places;

— to enable all individuals to play a more active role in public life, at national, regional, and local levels, by using the new information technologies to:

• provide easy access to information about and direct links to local, regional, and national administrative and judicial services;

• make available official texts of local, regional, and national laws and regulations, of international agreements, and of the jurisprudence of national and international jurisdictions;

— to encourage the free flow of information, opinions, and ideas through the use of the new information technologies;

— to encourage the development, production, and distribution of cultural and educational material and its widespread dissemination;

— to encourage effective international co-operation to deliver the benefits of improved access and increased transparency;

— to contribute towards equal possibilities in the use of new technologies for all European countries.

(ii) With respect to Competence and Empowerment with regard to new information technologies

— to promote broad understanding in all sectors of society of the new information technologies and their potential;

— to help individuals to develop competence in the use of new information technologies:

  • through training at all levels of the education system, formal and informal, and throughout life;

  • through the definition of new professional profiles and training curricula;

— thereby to enable individuals to make active, critical, and discerning use of these technologies;

— to promote better and wider use of the new information technologies in teaching and learning, paying special attention to gender equality issues;

— to encourage use of information networks in the education field to promote mutual understanding between peoples, both on individual and institutional levels.

(iii) With respect to Creativity of individuals and of cultural industries

— to encourage the use of the new information technologies as a form of artistic and literary expression and as a means of forming creative partnerships, in particular between art, science, and industry;

— to stimulate the innate creativity of each individual through media literacy and the development of educational programmes using new information technologies;

— to work, in the context of the convergence and continuing globalisation of information networks, with the cultural industries to help ensure that their development enhances creativity;

- to encourage the European cultural industries to work together to increase their creativity and so provide a wide variety, while ensuring the quality of products and services in the information networks.

(iv) With respect to Diversity of content and language

- to encourage the development of a wide range of communication and information networks, as well as the diversity of content and language, so as to foster political pluralism, cultural diversity, and sustainable development;

- to promote the full use by all, including minorities, of the opportunities for exchange of opinion and self-expression offered by the new information technologies;

- to acknowledge the usefulness of these technologies in enabling all European countries and regions to express their cultural identities;

- to encourage the provision of cultural, educational, and other products and services in an appropriate variety of languages, and to promote the greatest possible diversity of these products and services;

- to ensure, as far as possible, that information systems, in the administrative and legal fields, offer material which takes account of regional and linguistic criteria, and which meets the specific needs of concerned minorities.

(v) With respect to Protection of rights and freedoms

- to ensure respect for human rights and human dignity, notably freedom of expression, as well as the protection of minors, the protection of privacy and personal data, and the protection of the individual against all forms of racial discrimination in the use and development of new information technologies; through regulation and self-regulation, and through the development of technical standards and systems, codes of conduct, and other measures;

- to adopt national and international measures for the effective investigation and punishment of information technology crimes, and to combat the existence of safe havens for perpetrators of such crimes;

- to ensure the effective protection of the rights holders whose works are disseminated on the new information and communication services;

— to encourage the establishment of international standards and safeguards essential for the guarantee of authenticity of electronically transmitted documents and legally binding agreements;

— to enhance this framework of protection, including the development of codes of conduct embodying ethical principles for the use of the new information technologies.

QUEEN MARY
UNIVERSITY OF LONDON
LIBRARY

Appendix 4

Survey of Diversity Challenges in the E.U. Region

The following survey provided the basis for much of the information found in Chapters 2, 3, and 4. We include it here as a possible tool to be used as a diversity audit within organizations and for benchmarking efforts. The authors would be grateful if readers using this survey would appraise us of the results via e-mail at challenges@diversophy.com.

For our forthcoming project on diversity in the E.U. region, we would like to identify the principal challenges faced by businesses and organizations in the region and examine how these affect their policies and practices.

Please look at our Draft List of Diversity Challenges below. We have tried to identify these challenges and to provide an example or description of each. Once you have completed "My response" in each challenge, we would like to ask you to:

- Comment on how you see each challenge, adding to or challenging its premises
- Add any challenges you identify that are not yet on the list
- Give examples of how the challenge affects your organization
- Describe any initiatives or activities that you or your organization have undertaken that are serving to meet at least partially any of these challenges

Leave blank any items you do not wish to comment on.

You may also go to our website if you would prefer to respond to the survey online. German and Italian versions of the survey are available there.

Please respond, however, in whatever language you find most comfortable.

Draft List of Diversity Challenges

1. **Managing subtle historical biases** that are likely to add heat, consciously or unconsciously, to debates over the policies and practices of E.U. states. The Anglo-French fight over British beef is an example, where more smoke than light seems to have been generated.
   My response:

2. **Creating value-added from the diversity of E.U. member cultures** by managing issues of intercultural communication, cooperation, and synergy. This means getting beyond current crises and conflicts to making things work better because of diversity.
   My response:

3. **Dealing with the ambitions of powerful regional cultures and cultural enclaves within the individual E.U. states.** As the protection of national borders lessens within the European Union, ethnic pride is reemerging in force. Significant in this respect is the return of local parliamentary rule to Scotland and Wales and the lessening of the grip of Westminster on Ulster. Old languages are being taught, updated, and contributing to the cultural patrimony of many European regions.
   My response:

4. **Managing the in-country challenges of diversity** in societies and in workforces that include native residents, expatriates, traditional enclaves, immigrants, asylum seekers, ex-colonials, and economic migrants. We have separated traditional enclaves from regional cultures because their history and dynamics are different. Today, dealing with the future of such enclaves as the Roma is a perplexing situation for a number of European states.
   My response:

5. **Managing shifts in demographics, both within E.U. countries themselves and within the European Union as a whole.** Europe, even within the Union itself, will need to remain aware of the

sudden shifts of demographics caused by economic factors as well as by economic and political asylum-seeking immigrants from outside the Union.
My response:

6. **Managing ethnic-focused civil unrest** as numbers of laborers originating outside the European Union (and their families) become significant and visible, no longer to be either ignored or quickly assimilated. Problems are particularly acute when unemployment remains high. Both the unrest of the new population and the feeling of disenfranchisement on the part of the traditional population will require attention.
My response:

7. **Managing the flow of illegal immigration** at borders in accordance with the Schengen Treaty and in response to political pressures. There is both a legal and policy dimension to this, as well as a humanitarian one. The freedom of movement of peoples is a value that comes into conflict with the need and capability to integrate newcomers in a meaningful way without causing major social disruptions.
My response:

8. **Adjusting to new roles for women** across the spectrum of diversity listed above. This is an issue whether we are discussing native-born women or those belonging to recent waves of immigration and asylum seekers. A study of the French Employment Ministry (DARES) has indicated the evolution of several different models along which women's professional and familial roles have developed.
My response:

9. **The aging of Western Europe and the precarious state of older people from former Soviet economies.** Cultural shifts are being accelerated on two age fronts. The indigenous peoples of western nations with their low birth rates are quickly growing older. The newcomer minorities within their borders are replacing them. In the former East Germany, for example, the over-50s tend to be ill-equipped for the new economies, and further east, the social security system has evaporated for those who reach pensioner age. Diversity along age lines is driving a deep wedge between these people and the under-35s with freedom, mobility, and career flexibility.
My response:

10. **Managing cultural stresses and strains within the development of the European Union itself,** as its complexity increases through new membership and the shifting center of gravity that this implies. Where the French see a European individual and a way of life to be nurtured and protected as essential to the European Union, the British, who sense themselves as least attached to Europe, take a much more pragmatic view of the Union, while the Dutch, equally individualistic in their own way, are inclined to see the European Union as an act of enlightened self-interest. If current applicants to the European Union were to join, it would mean increasing the population of the Union by over 25%. These countries average a farming population of 20% compared to the 4% of the current 15 member states.
My response:

11. **Facing the challenges of globalization, seen in great part as a result of the power of the U.S. economy and media.** More than anyone else, the French have served as Europe's bellwether in respect to the invasiveness of the global mentality into the culture of peoples. Providing alternatives to the cultural and economic forces of the United States may be one of the most compelling reasons for European unity, for an independent military, and for concomitant diplomatic capability.
My response:

Name: _____

Title: _____

Organization: _____

Work Phone: _____

E-mail: _____

URL (website): _____

I am willing to discuss this further *by e-mail* and/or *by telephone.* (Leave or delete one or both responses).

You *may / may not* quote me in the final publication. (Delete either "may" or "may not.")

Please return this survey by mail to:

Dr. George F. Simons
Résidence L'Argentière, Bâtiment A
637 Boulevard de la Tavernière
F-06210 Mandelieu la Napoule
FRANCE

Appendix 5

Benchmarking Initiative

European Diversity Survey

The following is a précis of a significantly larger survey format used to develop the material found in Chapter 6 by Michael Stuber of mi·st [Consulting. For further information contact him at mi.st@NetCologne.de.

1. Aim

Mapping European Diversity initiatives (commercial) in order to identify best practices.

2. Approach

Identify 20+ European organizations (with operations in 5+ E.U. Member States) who have Diversity practices in place or who were working on Diversity during the past three years. Apply standard question roster based on the following content.

3. Contents

Questions will have a multiple-choice format with open spaces in addition.

3.1. Definitions of Diversity

Which **paradigm(s)** does your organization follow regarding "Diversity": phenomenon, mind set, management tool, or program (with explanations).

What is the initiative actually called? (Diversity, Diversity and Inclusion, etc.)

Which **dimensions** are part of the concept (explicitly mentioned— actively addressed):

- core dimensions (gender, race/ethnicity, age, (dis)ability, sexual orientation, religious beliefs)
- external dimensions (languages spoken, education, parental status, work style, etc.)
- organizational dimensions

3.2. The Business Case behind Diversity

Which of the following **challenges** do you address with Diversity (drivers of Diversity):

- Demographic Changes: workforce, market (ethnicity, age, gender mix, etc.)
- Technological Innovation (computerization, e-commerce, increased information flow)
- Cultural Changes (values, attitudes, preferences, lifestyles, life concepts, etc.), and specific cultural issues according to George Simons' questionnaire
- Increased M&A, strategic alliances, cooperation
- International shifts (European integration, globalization, Eastern European changes)
- Ongoing organizational change (restructuring, reengineering, general flexibility, multidimensional matrixes, etc.)
- Pressure on productivity, cost side
- Pressure on market/revenue side
- Strategic necessity (need for differentiation)

Which **benefits** do you expect to reap from Diversity:

External: (consumers/markets, investors, recruitment) <specify>
Internal: (individual, interpersonal, organizational) <specify>

3.3. Diversity Objectives

Do you have set objectives that you are trying to achieve through Diversity directly?

For example, "To have a diverse workforce that reflects our marketplace," or "To have an environment in which everyone feels valued and respected," etc.

3.4. Organization of Diversity

Project Management/Structure of Diversity: Councils/task forces (make up), champions (business/HR), competence centers, European manager (full-time, part-time), European team (staff), learning labs, conferences.

Scope of Diversity initiative: European Union, Europe, EMEA, other.

Which are the **dominating dimensions** for the introduction of Diversity in your organization? <in terms of sponsorship or ownership>

Business sectors, National organizations, specialized functions (OD, HR, etc.)

3.5. Building Blocks to Introduce Diversity

Which of the following **implementation activities** do you pursue:

Top-Down: training (mandatory, voluntary), management accountability, staff meetings, European Diversity statement/ policy/mission, speeches/presentations

Bottom-Up: intranet site, posters, leaflets, stickers, badges, newsletter/magazine, focus groups, surveys

Structural: Diversity office/hotline, employee network groups

Work/Life Balance: flexible scheduling (part-time, flextime, job sharing, telecommuting, phase retirement); childcare (on-site, off-site, emergency/sick, summer camp, daycare, baby-sitting); elder care; paid time off/leave policies; counseling (general employee assistance, stress management, fitness, pre-retirement); convenience programs (banking, shopping, postal, fitness)

Which of the following **integration activities** do you pursue:

HR: review job descriptions; align recruitment processes; review interview training; review performance appraisal; align personnel development; review compensation/benefits policy;

align holiday/food policies; align training content (general); review harassment policy

Corporate Communication: align vision/mission statements; review internal/external language used ensure diverse sponsoring policies; install diversified scholarship programs, awards, etc.; align advertisement and media policies; review target group definitions; etc.

Which of the following (other) **corporate initiatives** do you have in place? Have they been introduced under the roof of Diversity, are they coordinated with Diversity activities, or are these separate issues/programs?

- Language training
- Team building
- International exchange programs
- (Cross-) Mentoring programs
- Fast track career paths
- Social responsibility activities (homeless, environment, fighting diseases, etc.)
- Campaigning for tolerance
- Lifelong learning initiatives

3.6. Monitoring Diversity (Evaluation, Tracking)

Which of the following **success criteria** do you measure:

- Demographics (workforce, customer base, applicants)
- Employee satisfaction (turnover, sick leave, etc.; over gender, age, ethnicity, etc.)
- Customer satisfaction (over gender, age, ethnicity, etc.)
- Market share, penetration by target groups
- Recruitment image (over gender, age, ethnicity, etc.)
- Public image (surveys, media reports)
- Investor ratings
- Specialist perception (invitation to conferences, hearings, etc.; co-op proposals from associations, universities, etc.; nomination for, winning of, awards)

Index

Page references followed by "t" denote tables; "f" denote figures.

QUEEN MARY
UNIVERSITY OF LONDON
LIBRARY